Shojo Beat

Yona of the Dawn

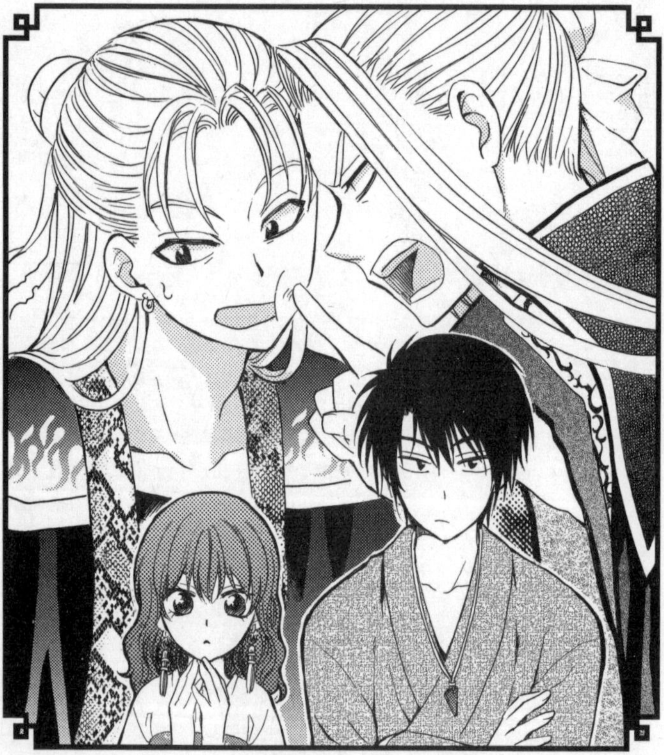

28

Story & Art by

Mizuho Kusanagi

YONA OF THE DAWN

Story Thus Far

Hak

One of the greatest heroes in the nation, known as the "Thunder Beast." He'd obeyed King Il's orders and became bodyguard to his childhood friend, Yona. He walks away from his position as general in order to protect his tribe.

Yona

While on the run, this princess of Kohka comes to the realization that she's spent her life being protected by other people. She sets out to locate the Four Dragons in order to protect herself and the people who are most important to her.

Su-won

A young scion of the royal bloodline and king of Kohka. To keep Kohka safe from invasion by the Kai Empire to the north or the nations of Xing and Sei to the south, he is trying to create a powerful nation by uniting and ruling over the Five Tribes.

Keishuk

Having helped Su-won take the throne, he's now the king's advisor. When he learns that Yona is still alive and that the Four Dragon Warriors really exist, he fears they will threaten Kohka's current status quo.

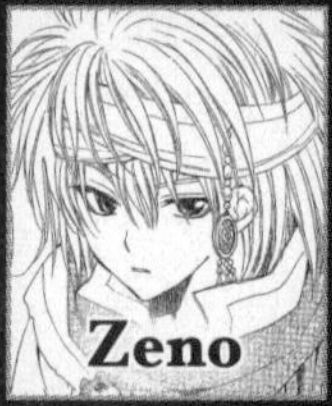
Zeno

The Yellow Dragon of the Four Dragon Warriors. He has the power of a dragon in his body—the power of immortality! He is one of the first Dragons who served the Crimson Dragon King, and he finally met Yona after many years of waiting.

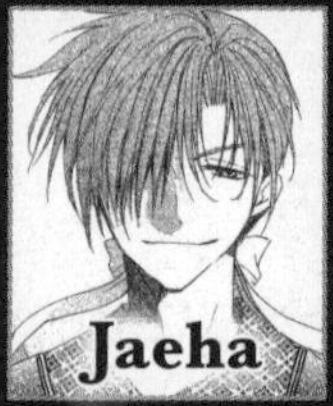
Jaeha

The Green Dragon of the Four Dragon Warriors. With the power of a dragon in his right leg, he can leap to tremendous heights. He loves freedom and hates the idea of being tied down to duty as one of the Four Legendary Dragons.

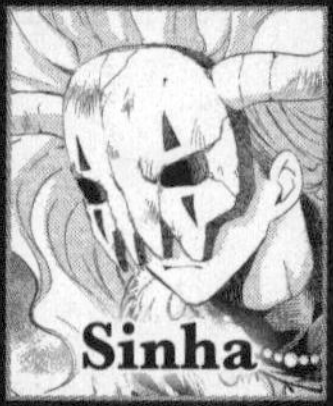
Sinha

The Blue Dragon of the Four Dragon Warriors. With the power of a dragon in his eyes, he can paralyze anyone he looks at. He grew up being hated and feared for his incredible power.

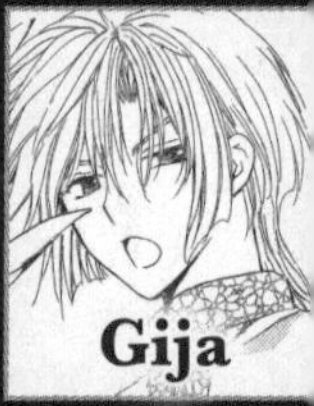
Gija

The White Dragon one of the Four Dragor Warriors. His right hanc contains a dragon's might and is more powerful than ten men He adores Yona anc finds fulfillment in hi role as one of the Fou Legendary Dragons.

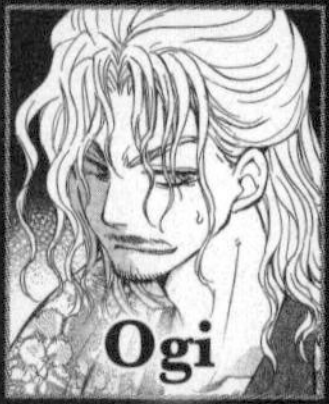
Ogi

An informant from Kohka. He traveled with Yona to confirm the rumors about the Four Dragon Warriors. He also knew Yona and Hak when they were children.

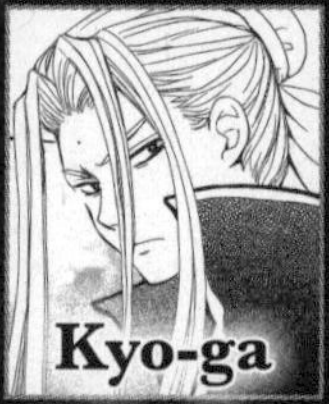
Kyo-ga

The Fire Tribe chief. He was appointed to replace his father, Kang Su-jin, who rebelled against the throne.

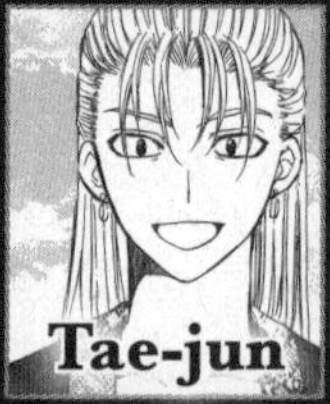
Tae-jun

Kyo-ga's younger brother. He has devoted himself to doing all he can for the Fire Tribe's impoverished towns, and he adores Yona.

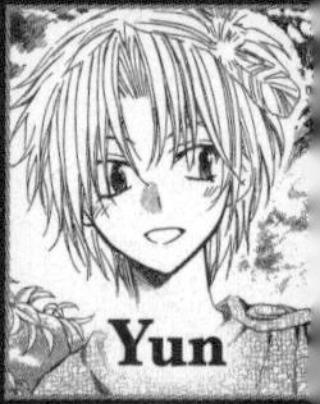
Yun

A mouthy pretty boy he has a lot of practica knowledge and take good care of others. H is like a mother to Yon and her friends.

The Four Dragon Warriors… In the Age of Myths, a dragon god took on human form and founded a nation. As the Crimson Dragon King, he was the first ruler of the Kingdom of Kohka. Four other dragons shared their blood with humans so that they could protect him. Those warriors became known as the Four Legendary Dragons, or the Four Dragon Warriors, and their power has been passed down for generations.

STORY

Yona, the princess of the Kingdom of Kohka, was raised by her kind, loving father, King Il. She has deep feelings for her cousin Su-won, a companion since childhood. On her 16th birthday, she sees her father being stabbed to death—by Su-won!

Driven from the palace, Yona and Hak meet a priest named Ik-su who tells Yona a prophecy that leads her to gather the Four Dragon Warriors together. Yona then decides to take up arms and defend her nation with the Four Dragon Warriors at her side.

War between Xing and Kohka is narrowly averted thanks to Yona and her friends. After this tension lifts, Hak tells Yona the truth about his feelings for her.

Zeno reveals that proximity to Hiryuu Palace can heal the Dragon Warriors, so the group head toward Kuuto to recover from their battle wounds. Along the way, they learn that the Kai Empire has invaded Fire Tribe lands, so they step in to help the outnumbered Fire Tribe troops and drive back the invading Kai Empire forces. The Fire Tribe, devout followers of the Crimson Dragon King, now know about Yona and her Dragon Warriors…and their chief, Kyo-ga, informs King Su-won of the situation.

*The Kingdom of Kohka is a coalition of five tribes: Fire, Water, Wind, Earth and Sky. The throne is held by the tribe with the greatest influence, so the current royal family are of the Sky Tribe. The royal capital is Kuuto. Each tribe's chief also holds the rank of general, and the Meeting of the Five Tribes is the nation's most powerful decision-making body.

yona of the Dawn

Volume 28

CONTENTS

CHAPTER 158: RUMORS

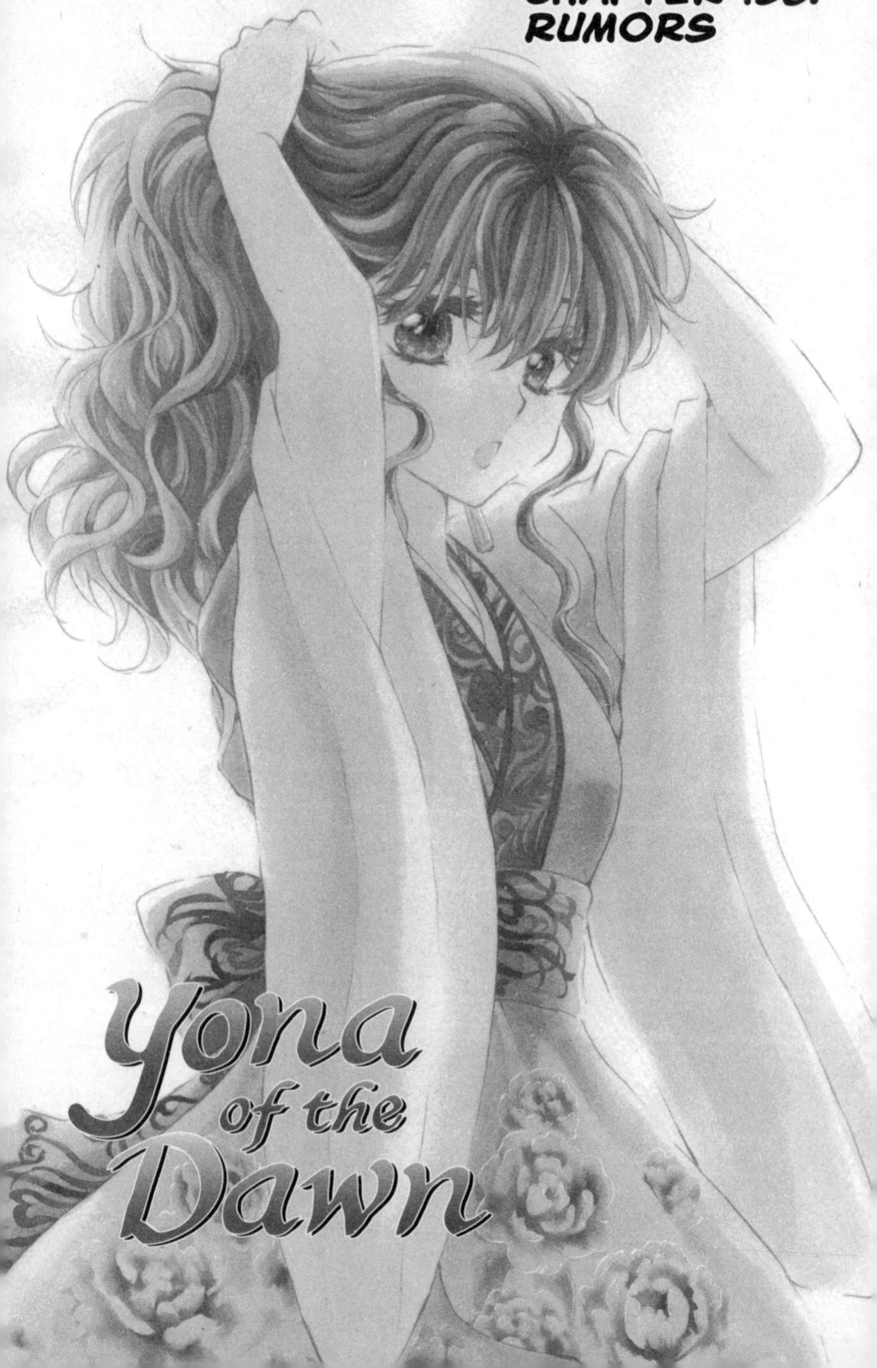
Yona of the Dawn

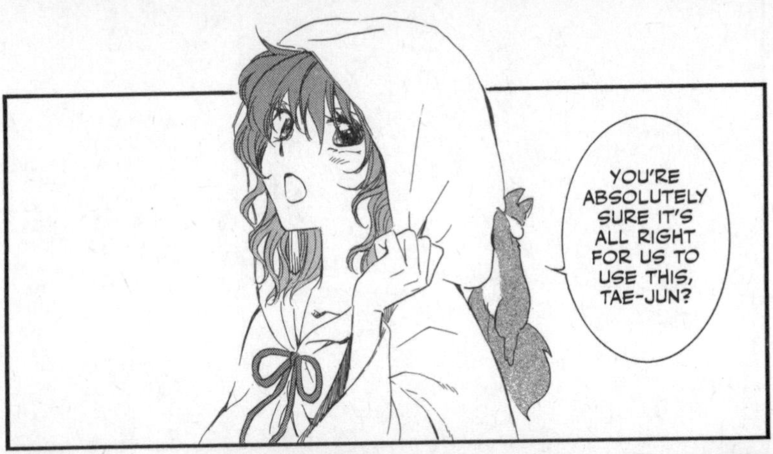
YOU'RE ABSOLUTELY SURE IT'S ALL RIGHT FOR US TO USE THIS, TAE-JUN?

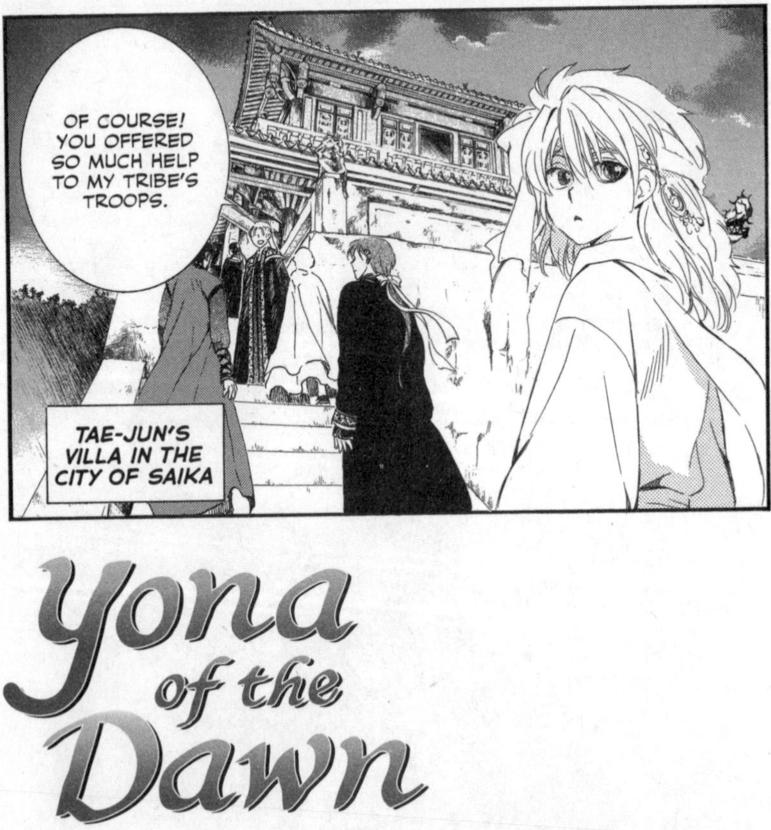
OF COURSE! YOU OFFERED SO MUCH HELP TO MY TRIBE'S TROOPS.
TAE-JUN'S VILLA IN THE CITY OF SAIKA

Yona of the Dawn

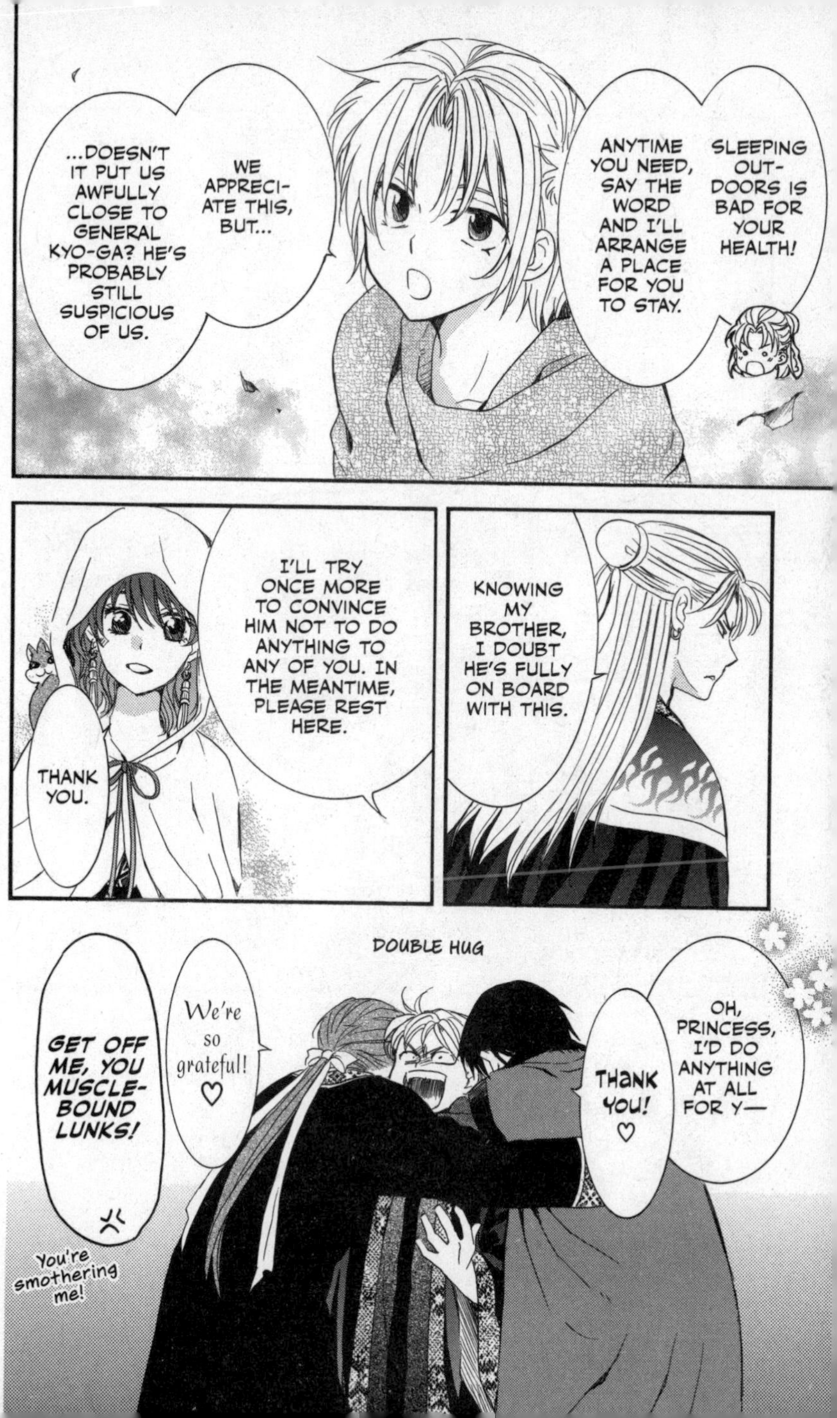
SLEEPING OUT-DOORS IS BAD FOR YOUR HEALTH!
ANYTIME YOU NEED, SAY THE WORD AND I'LL ARRANGE A PLACE FOR YOU TO STAY.
WE APPRECI-ATE THIS, BUT...
...DOESN'T IT PUT US AWFULLY CLOSE TO GENERAL KYO-GA? HE'S PROBABLY STILL SUSPICIOUS OF US.
KNOWING MY BROTHER, I DOUBT HE'S FULLY ON BOARD WITH THIS.
I'LL TRY ONCE MORE TO CONVINCE HIM NOT TO DO ANYTHING TO ANY OF YOU. IN THE MEANTIME, PLEASE REST HERE.
THANK YOU.
DOUBLE HUG
OH, PRINCESS, I'D DO ANYTHING AT ALL FOR Y—
THANK YOU! ♡
We're so grateful! ♡
GET OFF ME, YOU MUSCLE-BOUND LUNKS!
You're smothering me!

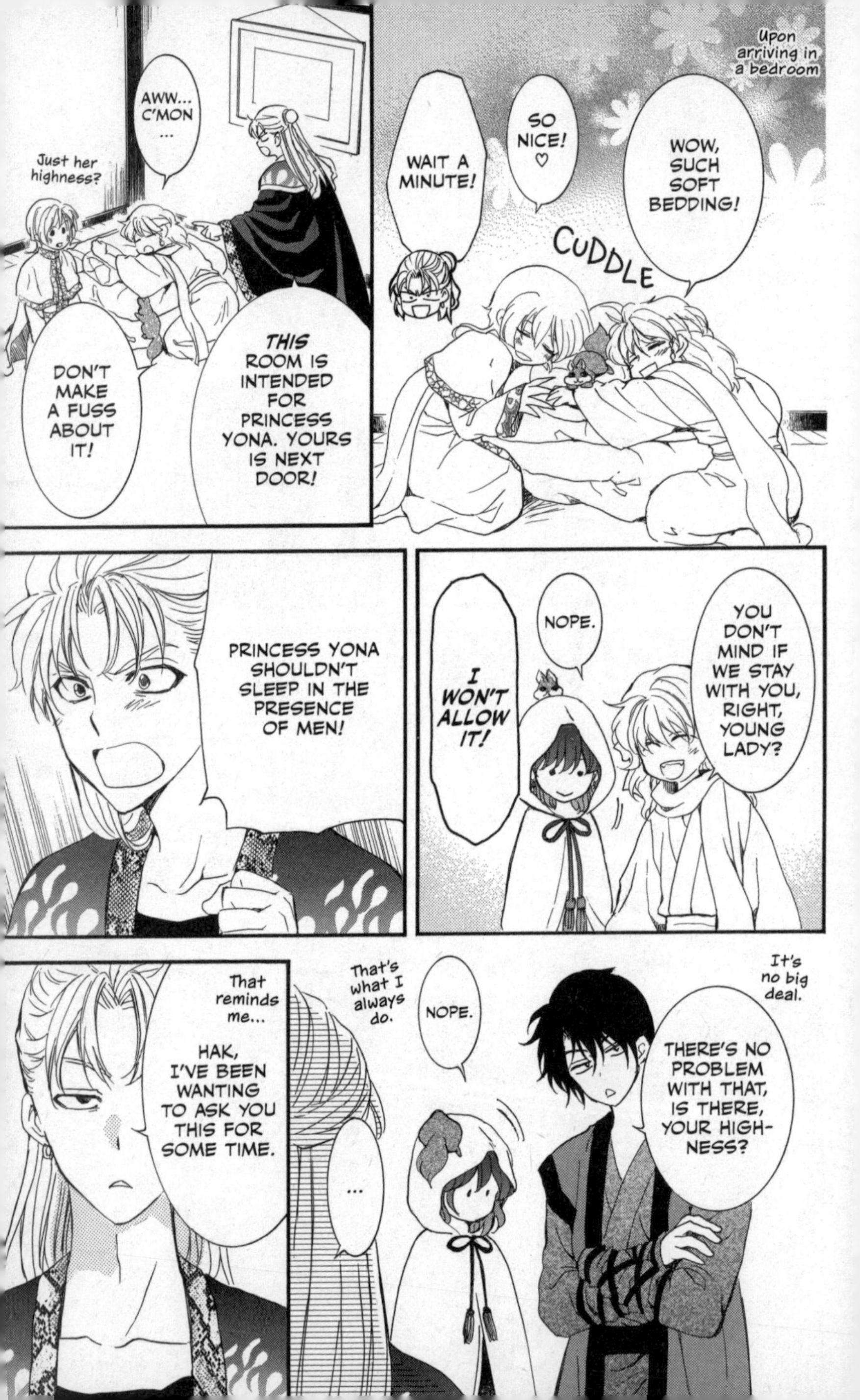

Upon arriving in a bedroom
WOW, SUCH SOFT BEDDING!
CUDDLE
SO NICE! ♡
WAIT A MINUTE!
AWW... C'MON ...
Just her highness?
THIS ROOM IS INTENDED FOR PRINCESS YONA. YOURS IS NEXT DOOR!
DON'T MAKE A FUSS ABOUT IT!
YOU DON'T MIND IF WE STAY WITH YOU, RIGHT, YOUNG LADY?
NOPE.
I WON'T ALLOW IT!
PRINCESS YONA SHOULDN'T SLEEP IN THE PRESENCE OF MEN!
It's no big deal.
THERE'S NO PROBLEM WITH THAT, IS THERE, YOUR HIGH-NESS?
NOPE.
That's what I always do.
...
That reminds me...
HAK, I'VE BEEN WANTING TO ASK YOU THIS FOR SOME TIME.

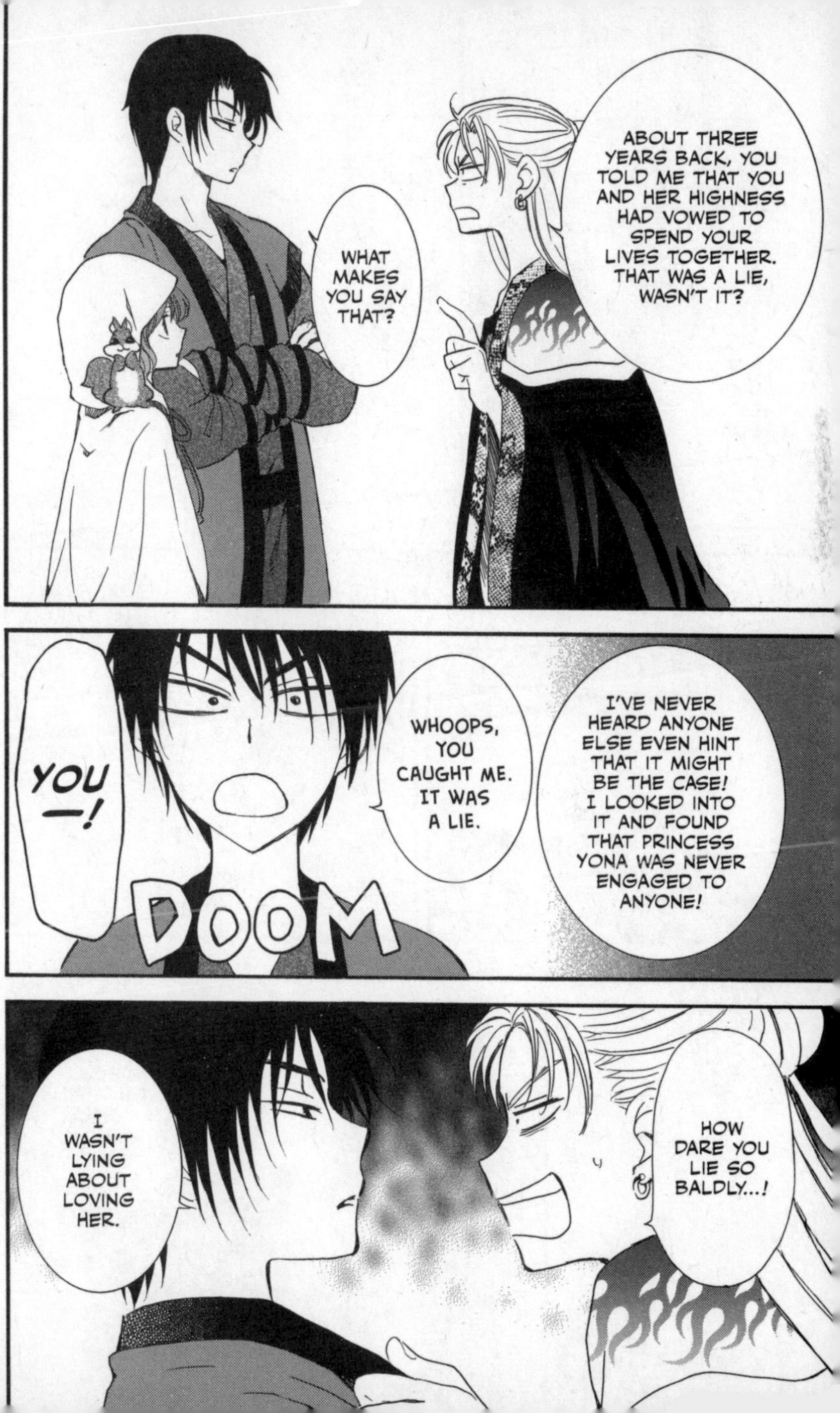
ABOUT THREE YEARS BACK, YOU TOLD ME THAT YOU AND HER HIGHNESS HAD VOWED TO SPEND YOUR LIVES TOGETHER. THAT WAS A LIE, WASN'T IT?
WHAT MAKES YOU SAY THAT?
I'VE NEVER HEARD ANYONE ELSE EVEN HINT THAT IT MIGHT BE THE CASE! I LOOKED INTO IT AND FOUND THAT PRINCESS YONA WAS NEVER ENGAGED TO ANYONE!
WHOOPS, YOU CAUGHT ME. IT WAS A LIE.
YOU—!
DOOM
HOW DARE YOU LIE SO BALDLY...!
I WASN'T LYING ABOUT LOVING HER.

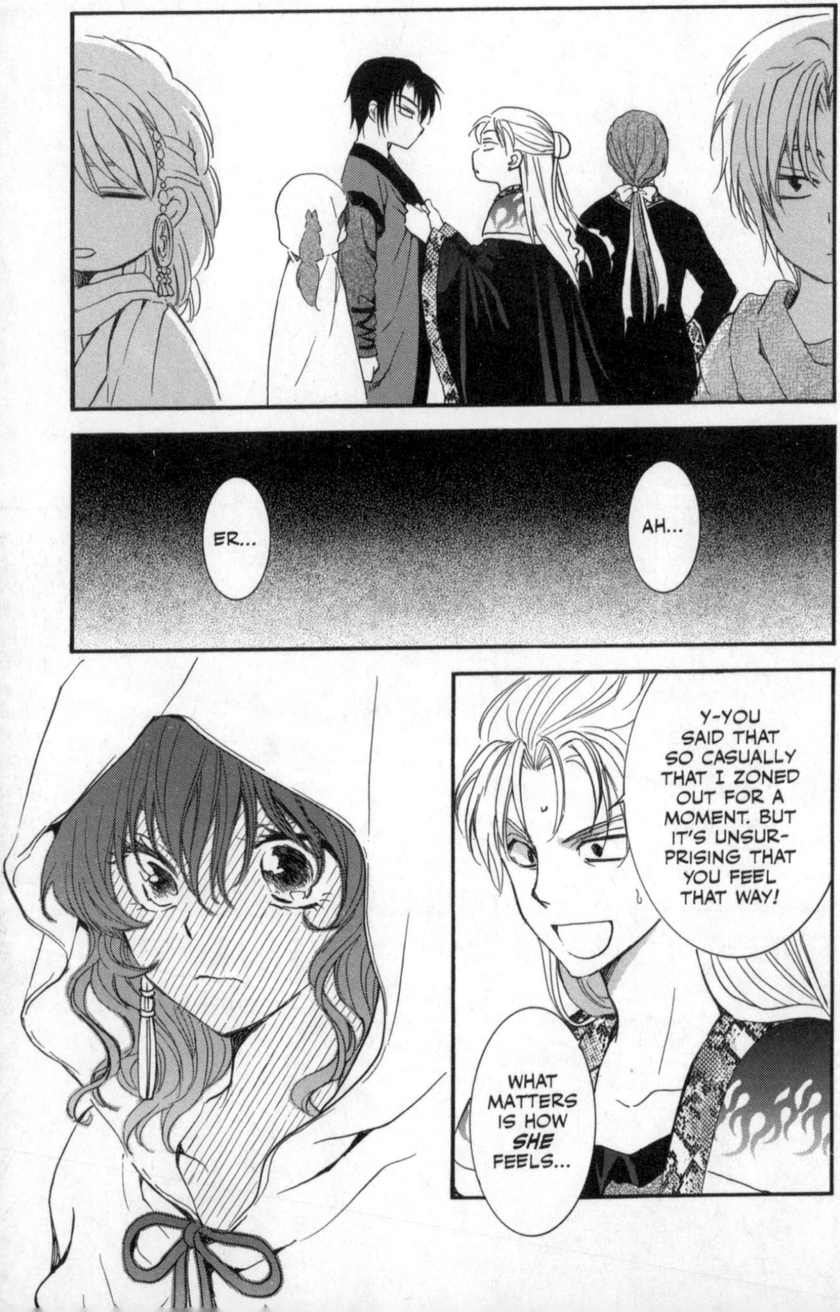
AH...
ER...
Y-YOU SAID THAT SO CASUALLY THAT I ZONED OUT FOR A MOMENT. BUT IT'S UNSURPRISING THAT YOU FEEL THAT WAY!
WHAT MATTERS IS HOW *SHE* FEELS...

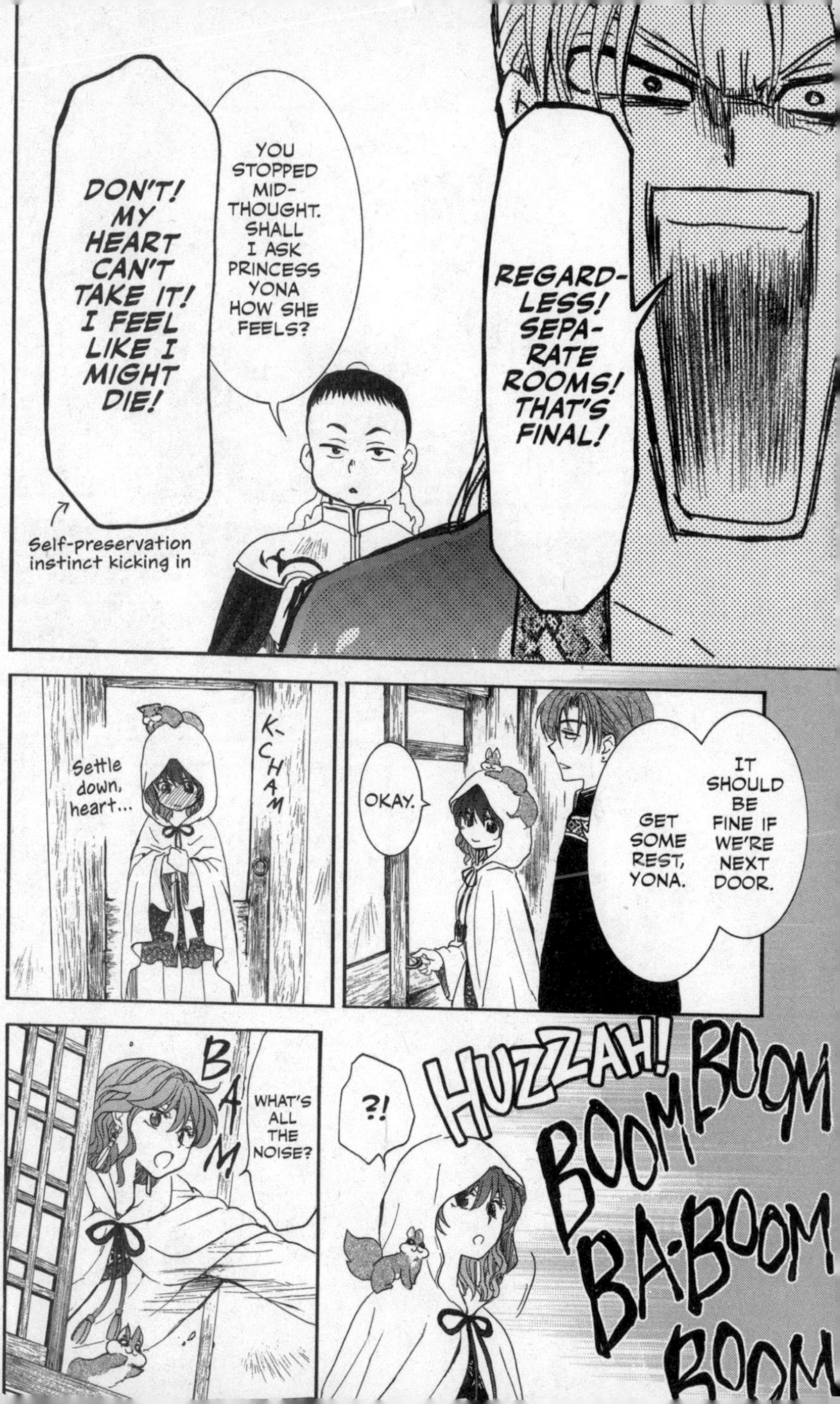
REGARDLESS! SEPARATE ROOMS! THAT'S FINAL!
YOU STOPPED MID-THOUGHT. SHALL I ASK PRINCESS YONA HOW SHE FEELS?
DON'T! MY HEART CAN'T TAKE IT! I FEEL LIKE I MIGHT DIE!
Self-preservation instinct kicking in
IT SHOULD BE FINE IF WE'RE NEXT DOOR.
GET SOME REST, YONA.
OKAY.
K-CHAM
Settle down, heart...
HUZZAH!
BOOM BOOM
BOOM
BA-BOOM
BOOM
?!
BAM
WHAT'S ALL THE NOISE?

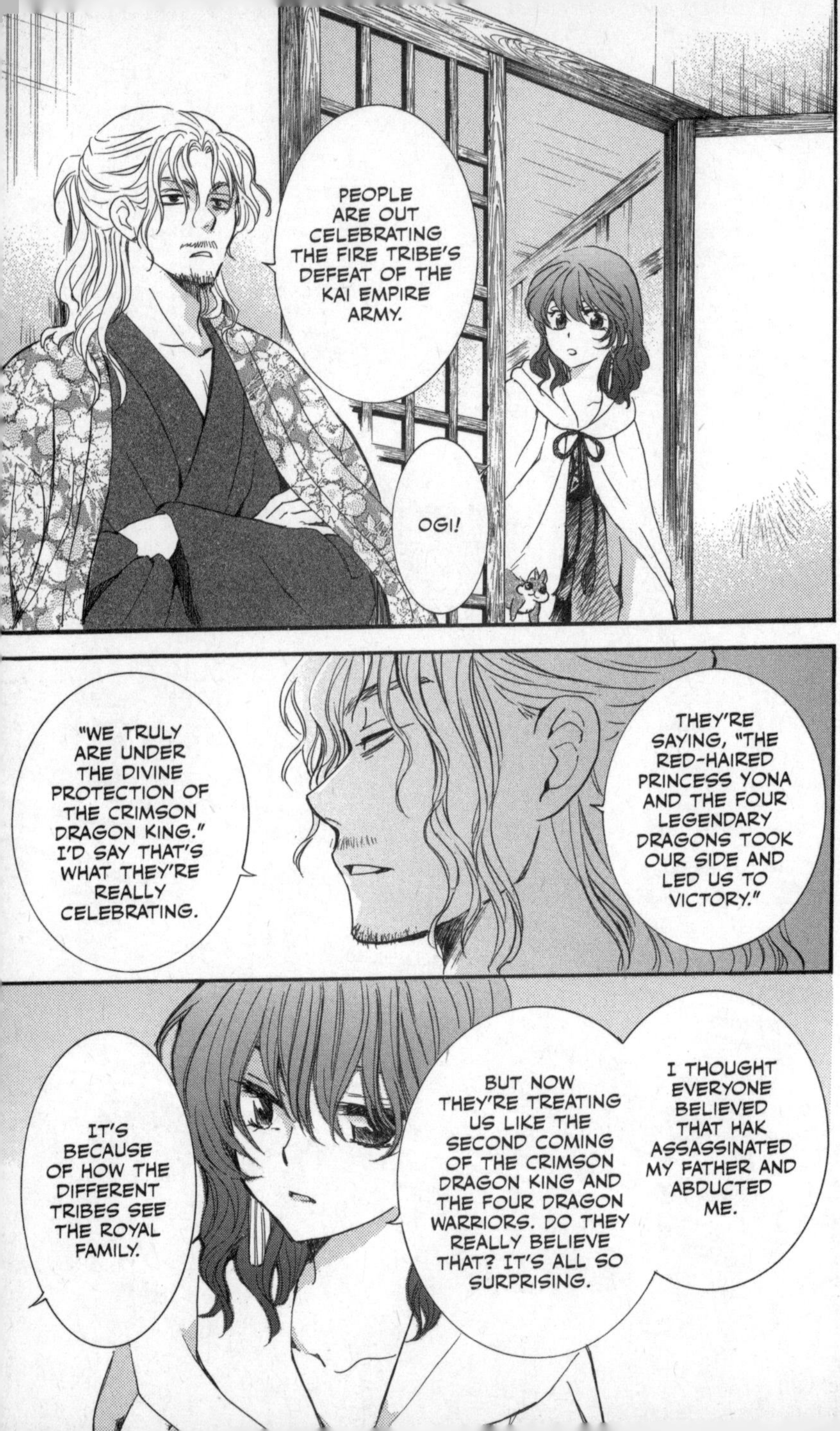
PEOPLE ARE OUT CELEBRATING THE FIRE TRIBE'S DEFEAT OF THE KAI EMPIRE ARMY.
OGI!
THEY'RE SAYING, "THE RED-HAIRED PRINCESS YONA AND THE FOUR LEGENDARY DRAGONS TOOK OUR SIDE AND LED US TO VICTORY."
"WE TRULY ARE UNDER THE DIVINE PROTECTION OF THE CRIMSON DRAGON KING." I'D SAY THAT'S WHAT THEY'RE REALLY CELEBRATING.
I THOUGHT EVERYONE BELIEVED THAT HAK ASSASSINATED MY FATHER AND ABDUCTED ME.
BUT NOW THEY'RE TREATING US LIKE THE SECOND COMING OF THE CRIMSON DRAGON KING AND THE FOUR DRAGON WARRIORS. DO THEY REALLY BELIEVE THAT? IT'S ALL SO SURPRISING.
IT'S BECAUSE OF HOW THE DIFFERENT TRIBES SEE THE ROYAL FAMILY.

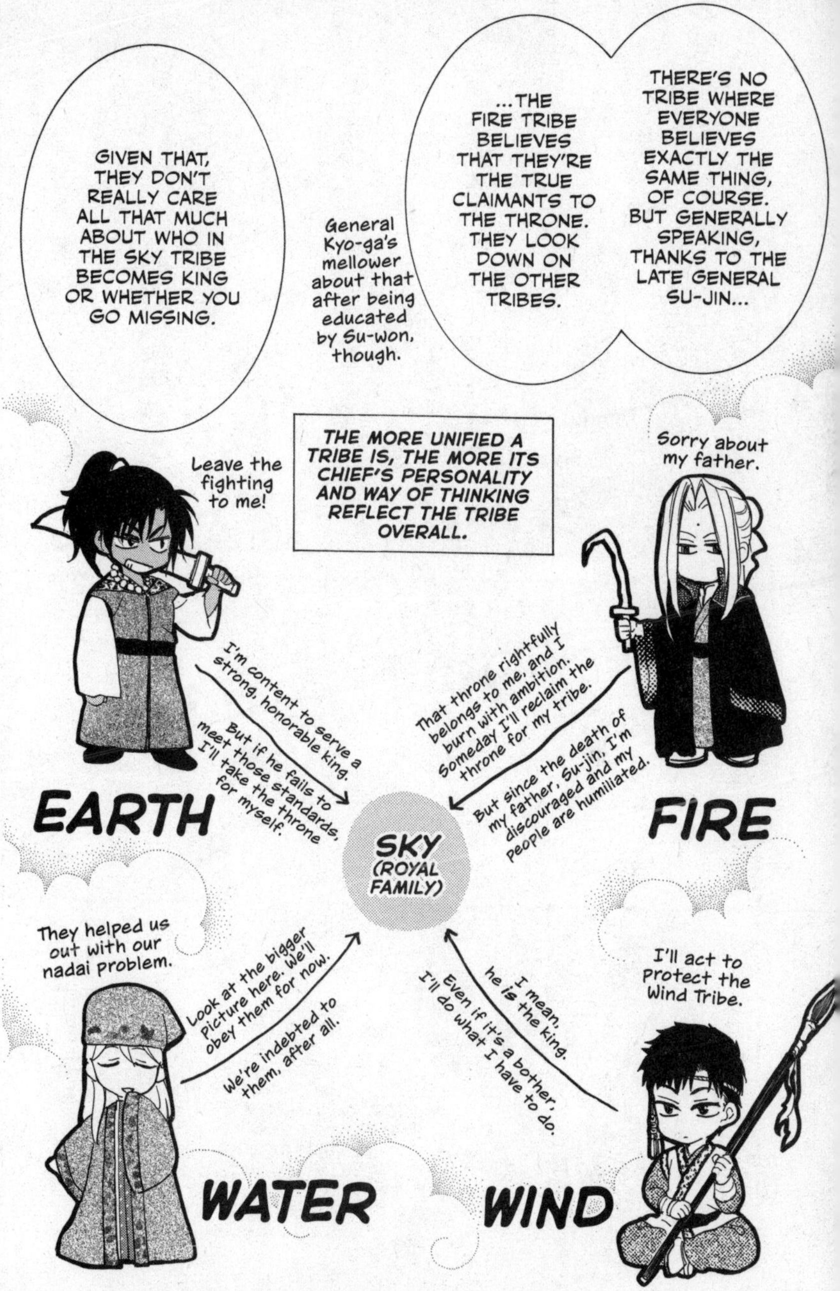

THERE'S NO TRIBE WHERE EVERYONE BELIEVES EXACTLY THE SAME THING, OF COURSE. BUT GENERALLY SPEAKING, THANKS TO THE LATE GENERAL SU-JIN...
...THE FIRE TRIBE BELIEVES THAT THEY'RE THE TRUE CLAIMANTS TO THE THRONE. THEY LOOK DOWN ON THE OTHER TRIBES.
General Kyo-ga's mellower about that after being educated by Su-won, though.
GIVEN THAT, THEY DON'T REALLY CARE ALL THAT MUCH ABOUT WHO IN THE SKY TRIBE BECOMES KING OR WHETHER YOU GO MISSING.
Sorry about my father.
THE MORE UNIFIED A TRIBE IS, THE MORE ITS CHIEF'S PERSONALITY AND WAY OF THINKING REFLECT THE TRIBE OVERALL.
Leave the fighting to me!
That throne rightfully belongs to me, and I burn with ambition. Someday I'll reclaim the throne for my tribe.
But since the death of my father, Su-jin, I'm discouraged and my people are humiliated.
FIRE
I'm content to serve a strong, honorable king.
But if he fails to meet those standards, I'll take the throne for myself.
EARTH
SKY (ROYAL FAMILY)
I'll act to protect the Wind Tribe.
I mean, he is the king.
Even if it's a bother, I'll do what I have to do.
They helped us out with our nadai problem.
Look at the bigger picture here. We'll obey them for now.
We're indebted to them, after all.
WIND
WATER

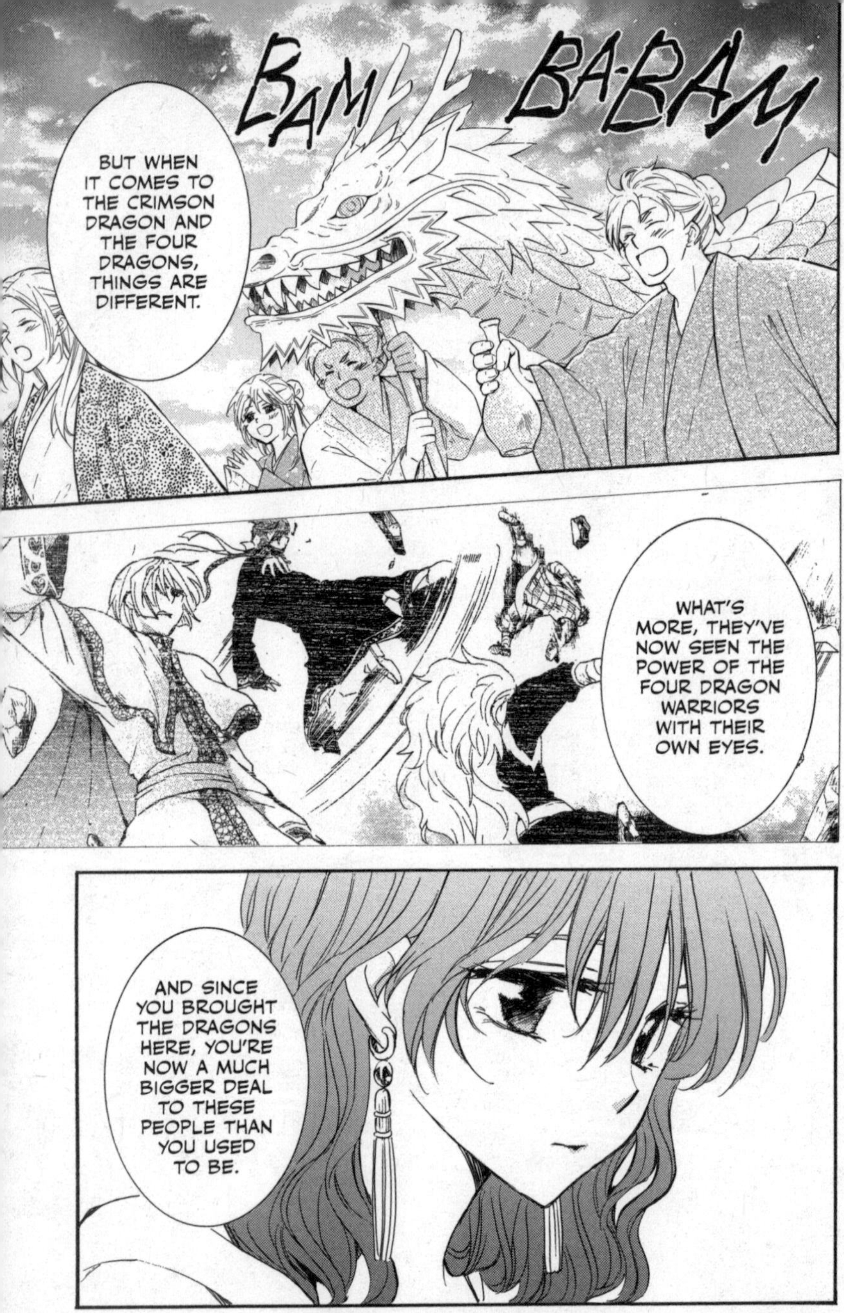
BAM
BA-BAM
BUT WHEN IT COMES TO THE CRIMSON DRAGON AND THE FOUR DRAGONS, THINGS ARE DIFFERENT.
WHAT'S MORE, THEY'VE NOW SEEN THE POWER OF THE FOUR DRAGON WARRIORS WITH THEIR OWN EYES.
AND SINCE YOU BROUGHT THE DRAGONS HERE, YOU'RE NOW A MUCH BIGGER DEAL TO THESE PEOPLE THAN YOU USED TO BE.

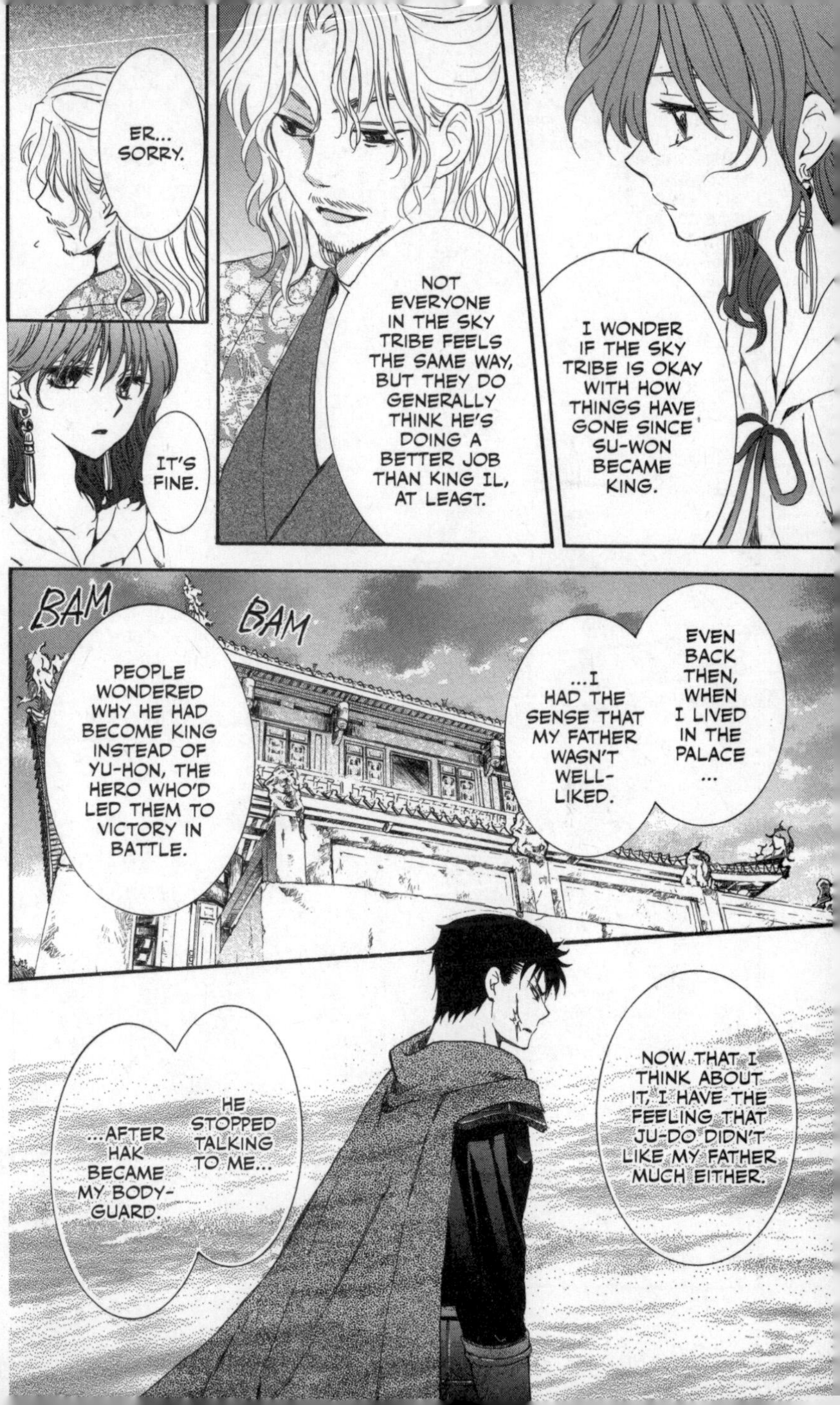
I WONDER IF THE SKY TRIBE IS OKAY WITH HOW THINGS HAVE GONE SINCE SU-WON BECAME KING.
NOT EVERYONE IN THE SKY TRIBE FEELS THE SAME WAY, BUT THEY DO GENERALLY THINK HE'S DOING A BETTER JOB THAN KING IL, AT LEAST.
ER... SORRY.
IT'S FINE.
BAM
BAM
EVEN BACK THEN, WHEN I LIVED IN THE PALACE...
...I HAD THE SENSE THAT MY FATHER WASN'T WELL-LIKED.
PEOPLE WONDERED WHY HE HAD BECOME KING INSTEAD OF YU-HON, THE HERO WHO'D LED THEM TO VICTORY IN BATTLE.
NOW THAT I THINK ABOUT IT, I HAVE THE FEELING THAT JU-DO DIDN'T LIKE MY FATHER MUCH EITHER.
HE STOPPED TALKING TO ME...
...AFTER HAK BECAME MY BODY-GUARD.

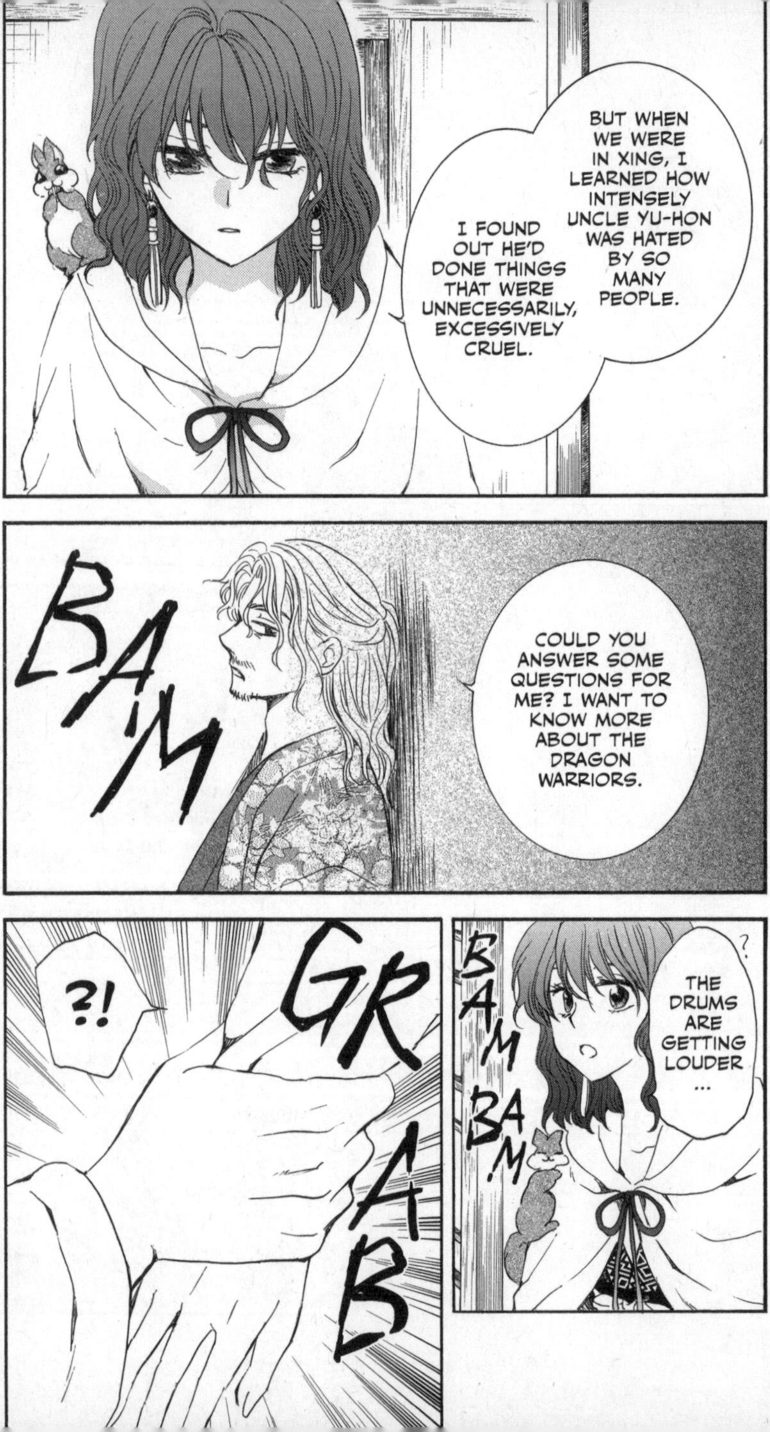
BUT WHEN WE WERE IN XING, I LEARNED HOW INTENSELY UNCLE YU-HON WAS HATED BY SO MANY PEOPLE.
I FOUND OUT HE'D DONE THINGS THAT WERE UNNECESSARILY, EXCESSIVELY CRUEL.
COULD YOU ANSWER SOME QUESTIONS FOR ME? I WANT TO KNOW MORE ABOUT THE DRAGON WARRIORS.
BAM
?
THE DRUMS ARE GETTING LOUDER ...
BAM BAM BAM!
GRAB
?!

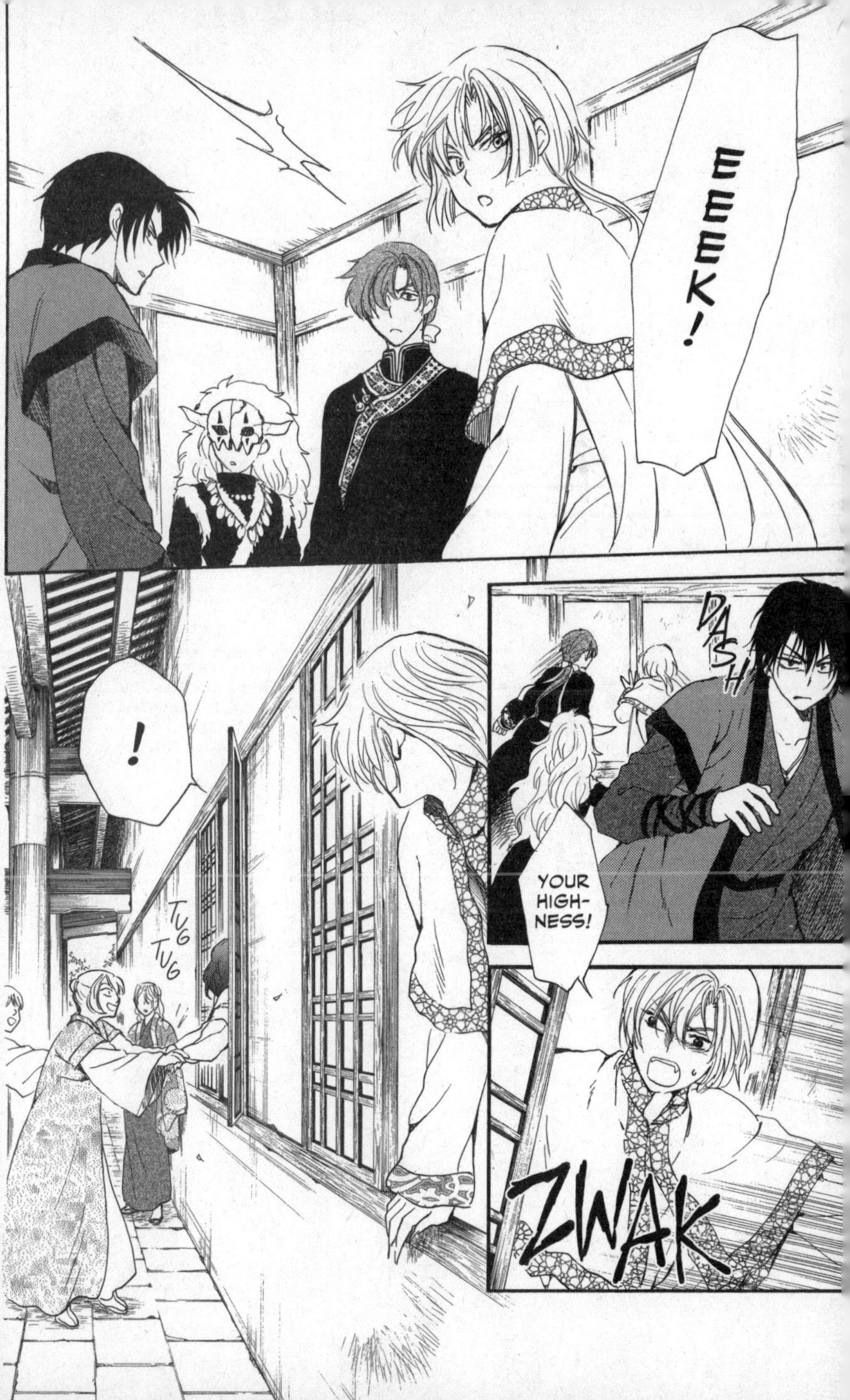
EEEK!
DASH
YOUR HIGH-NESS!
ZWAK
!
TUG TUG

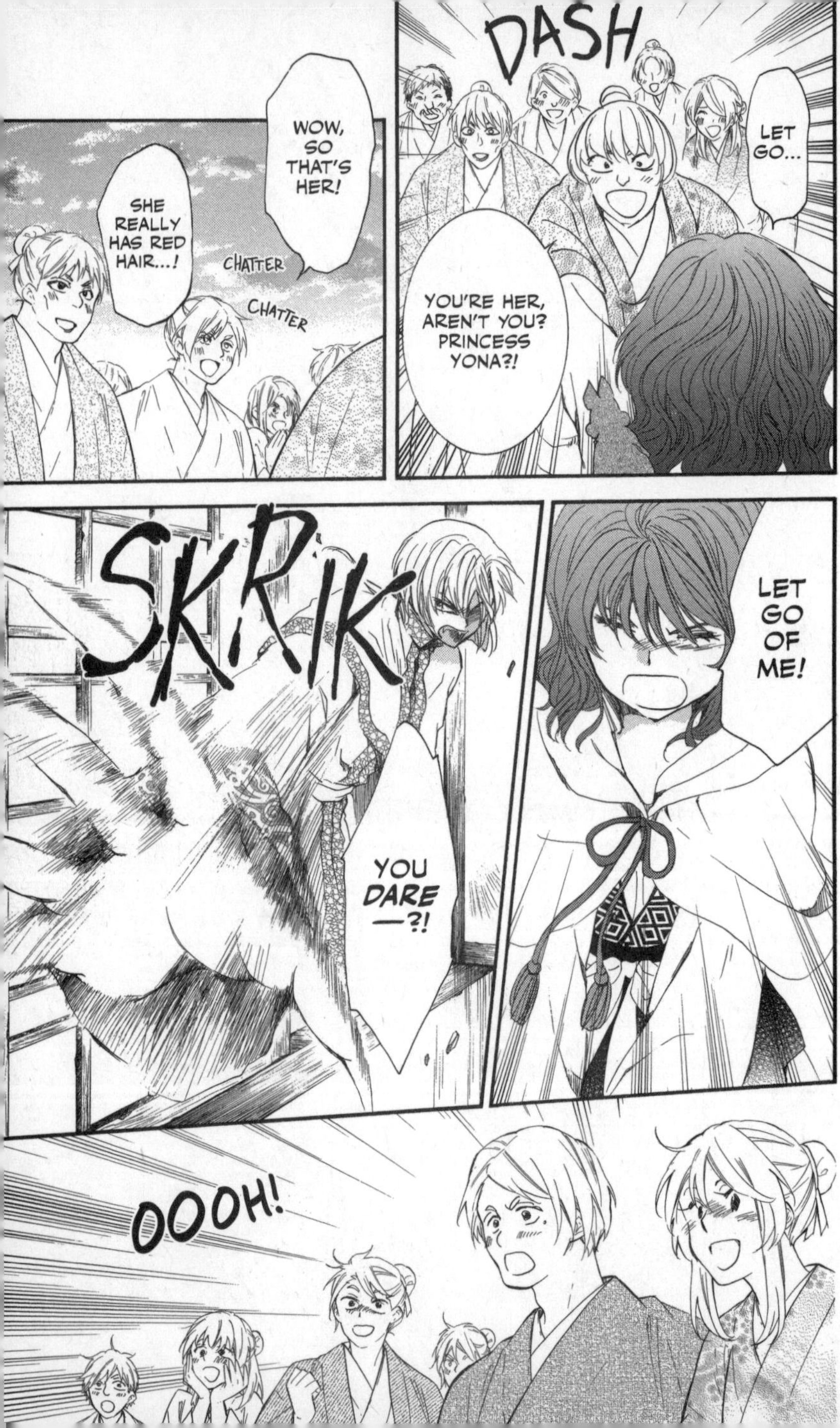
DASH
LET GO...
YOU'RE HER, AREN'T YOU? PRINCESS YONA?!
WOW, SO THAT'S HER!
SHE REALLY HAS RED HAIR...!
CHATTER
CHATTER
LET GO OF ME!
SKRIK
YOU DARE—?!
OOOH!

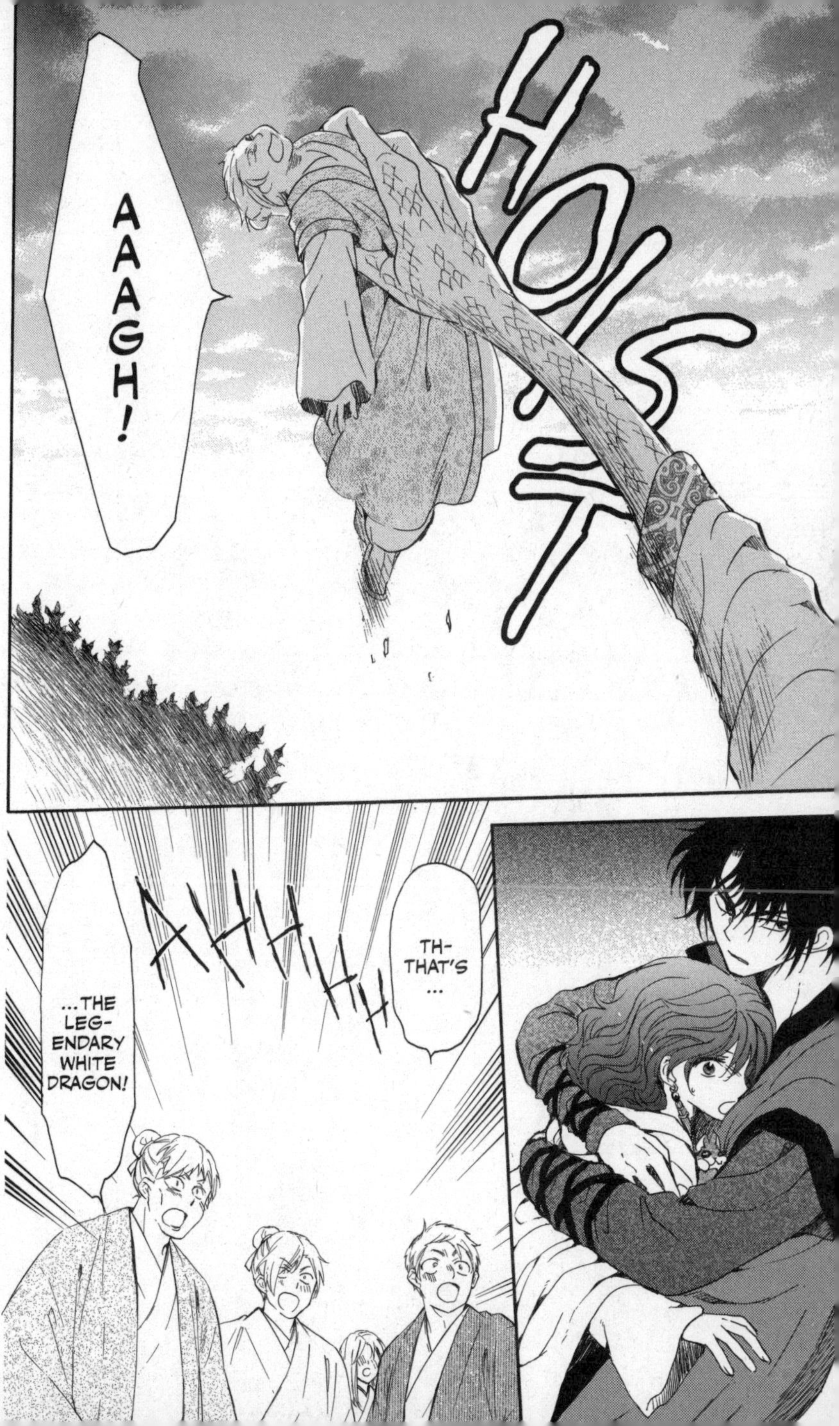
HOIST
AAAGH!
TH-THAT'S ...
AHHHH
...THE LEG-ENDARY WHITE DRAGON!

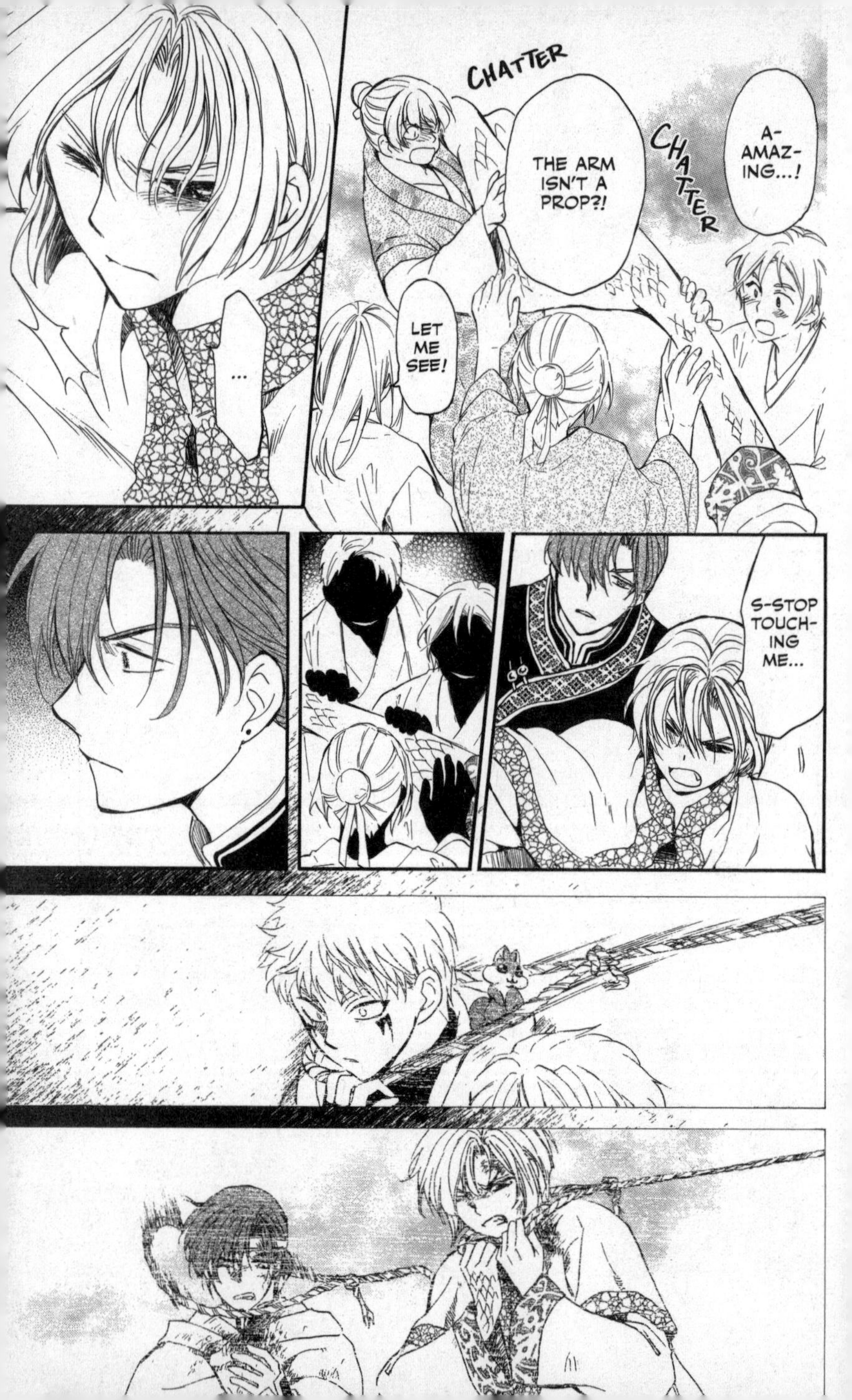
A-AMAZING...!
CHATTER
THE ARM ISN'T A PROP?!
CHATTER
LET ME SEE!
...
S-STOP TOUCHING ME...

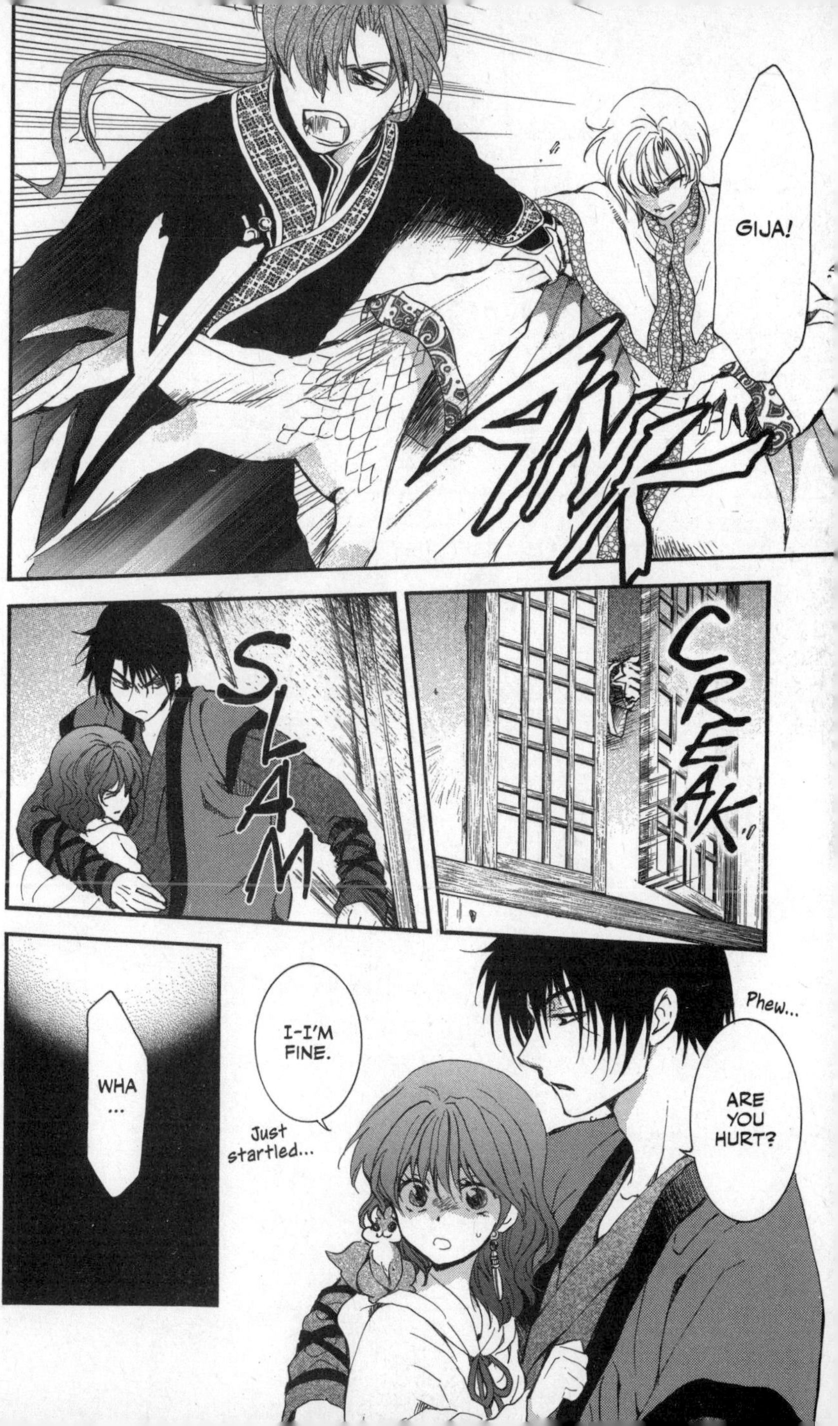
GIJA!
YANK
CREAK..
SLAM
Phew...
ARE YOU HURT?
I-I'M FINE.
Just startled...
WHA...

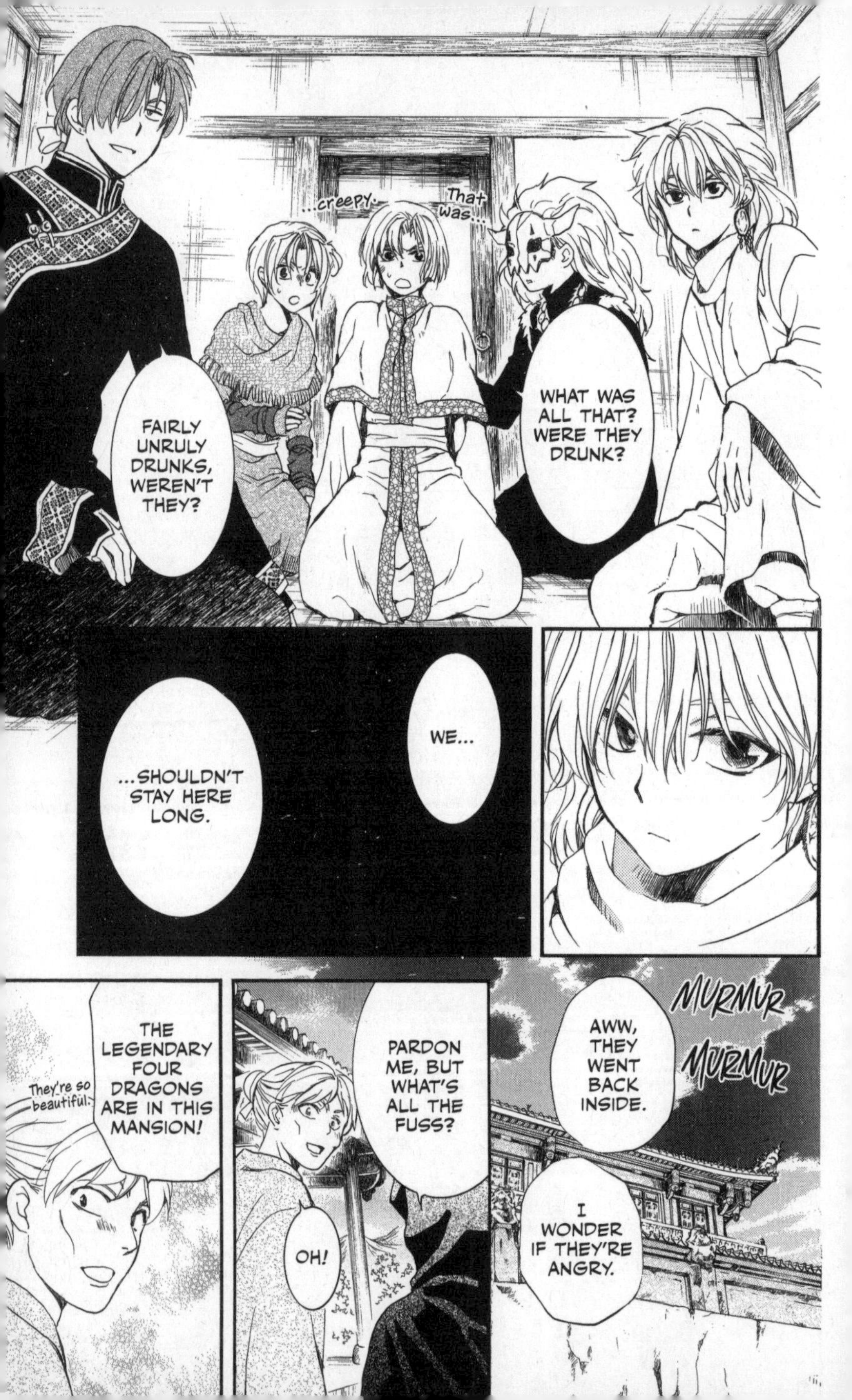
That was...
...creepy.
WHAT WAS ALL THAT? WERE THEY DRUNK?
FAIRLY UNRULY DRUNKS, WEREN'T THEY?
WE...
...SHOULDN'T STAY HERE LONG.
MURMUR
MURMUR
AWW, THEY WENT BACK INSIDE.
I WONDER IF THEY'RE ANGRY.
PARDON ME, BUT WHAT'S ALL THE FUSS?
OH!
THE LEGENDARY FOUR DRAGONS ARE IN THIS MANSION!
They're so beautiful.

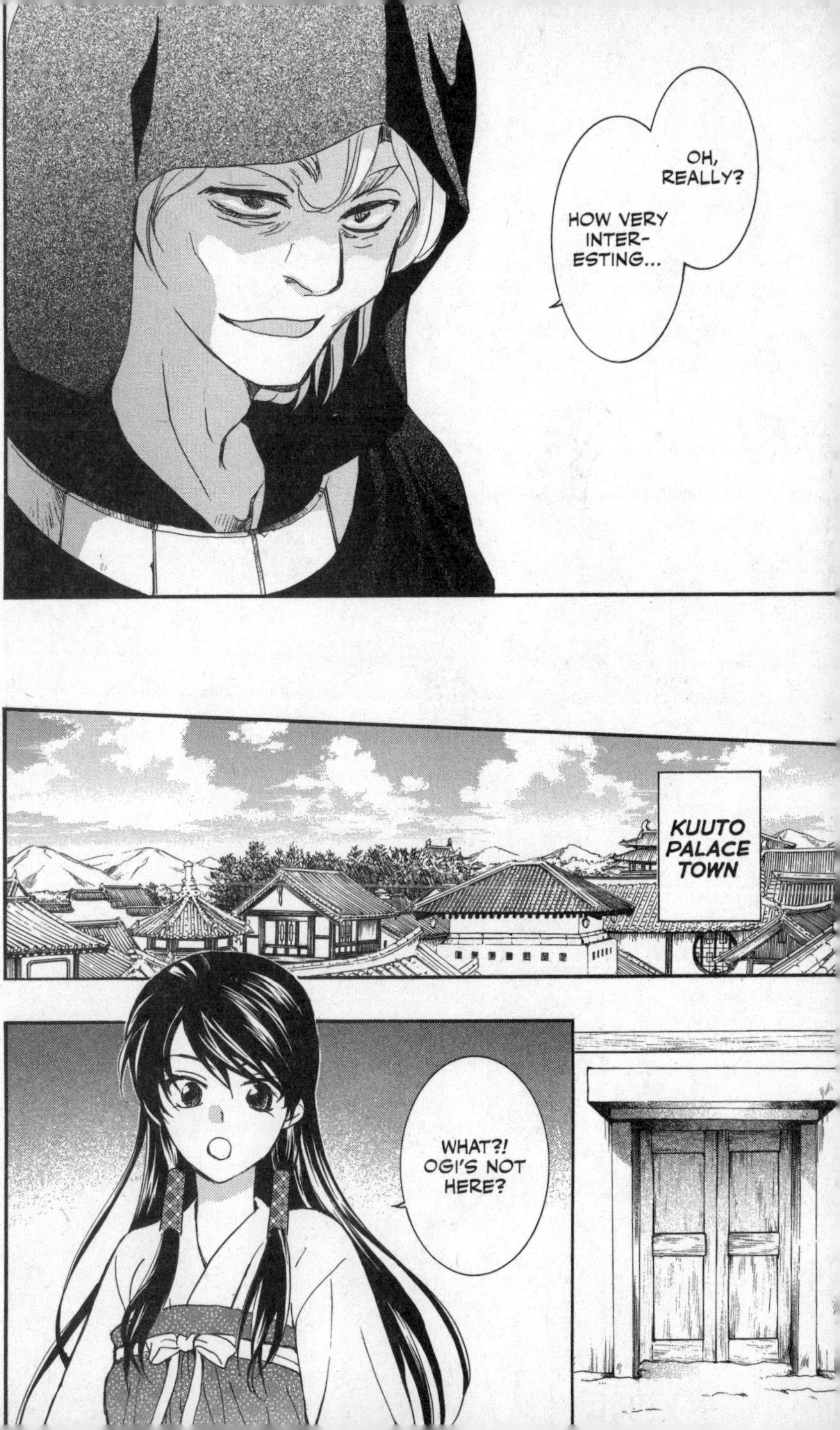
OH, REALLY?
HOW VERY INTER-ESTING...
KUUTO PALACE TOWN
WHAT?! OGI'S NOT HERE?

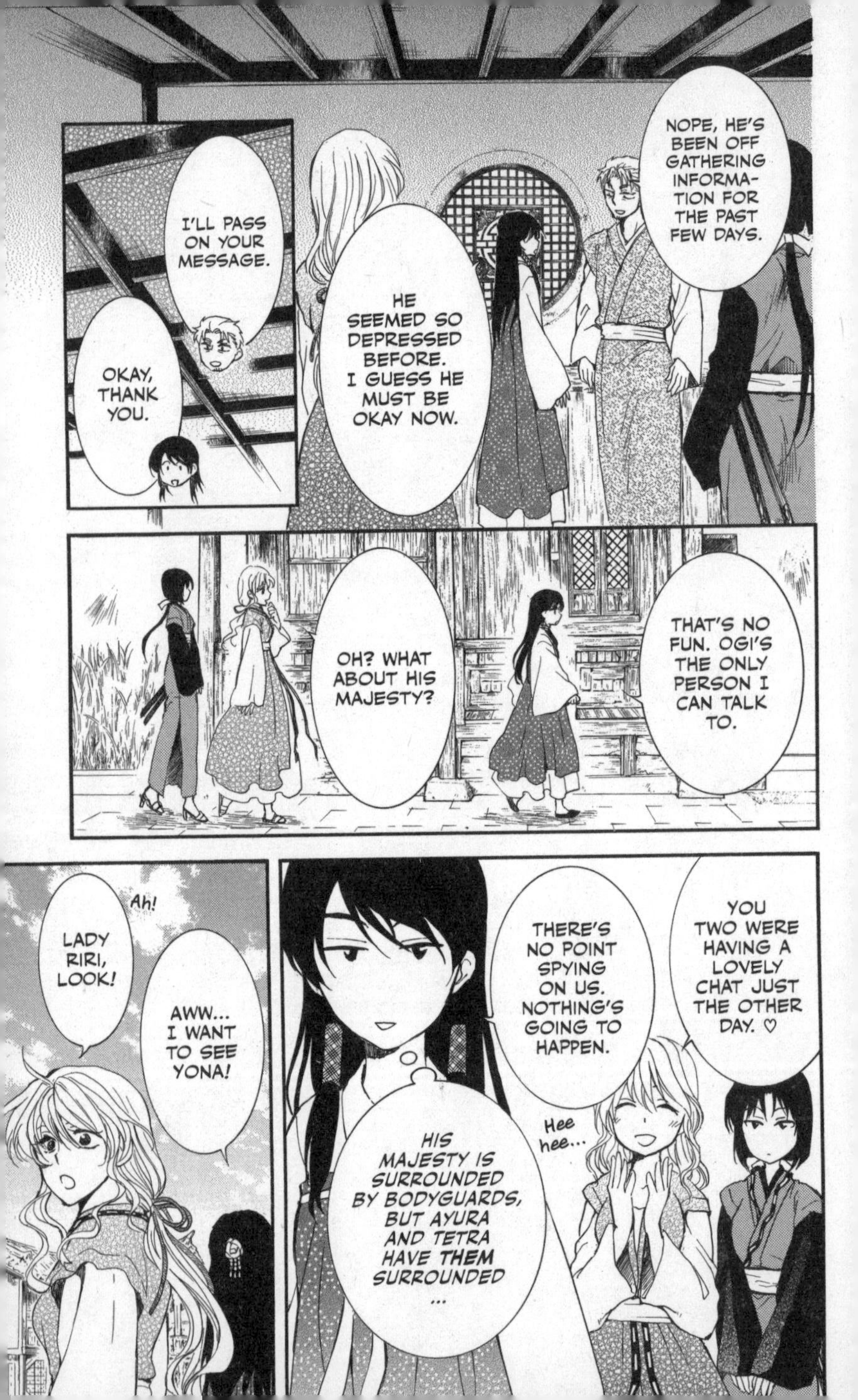
NOPE, HE'S BEEN OFF GATHERING INFORMATION FOR THE PAST FEW DAYS.
HE SEEMED SO DEPRESSED BEFORE. I GUESS HE MUST BE OKAY NOW.
I'LL PASS ON YOUR MESSAGE.
OKAY, THANK YOU.
THAT'S NO FUN. OGI'S THE ONLY PERSON I CAN TALK TO.
OH? WHAT ABOUT HIS MAJESTY?
YOU TWO WERE HAVING A LOVELY CHAT JUST THE OTHER DAY. ♡
THERE'S NO POINT SPYING ON US. NOTHING'S GOING TO HAPPEN.
Hee hee...
HIS MAJESTY IS SURROUNDED BY BODYGUARDS, BUT AYURA AND TETRA HAVE THEM SURROUNDED ...
Ah!
LADY RIRI, LOOK!
AWW... I WANT TO SEE YONA!

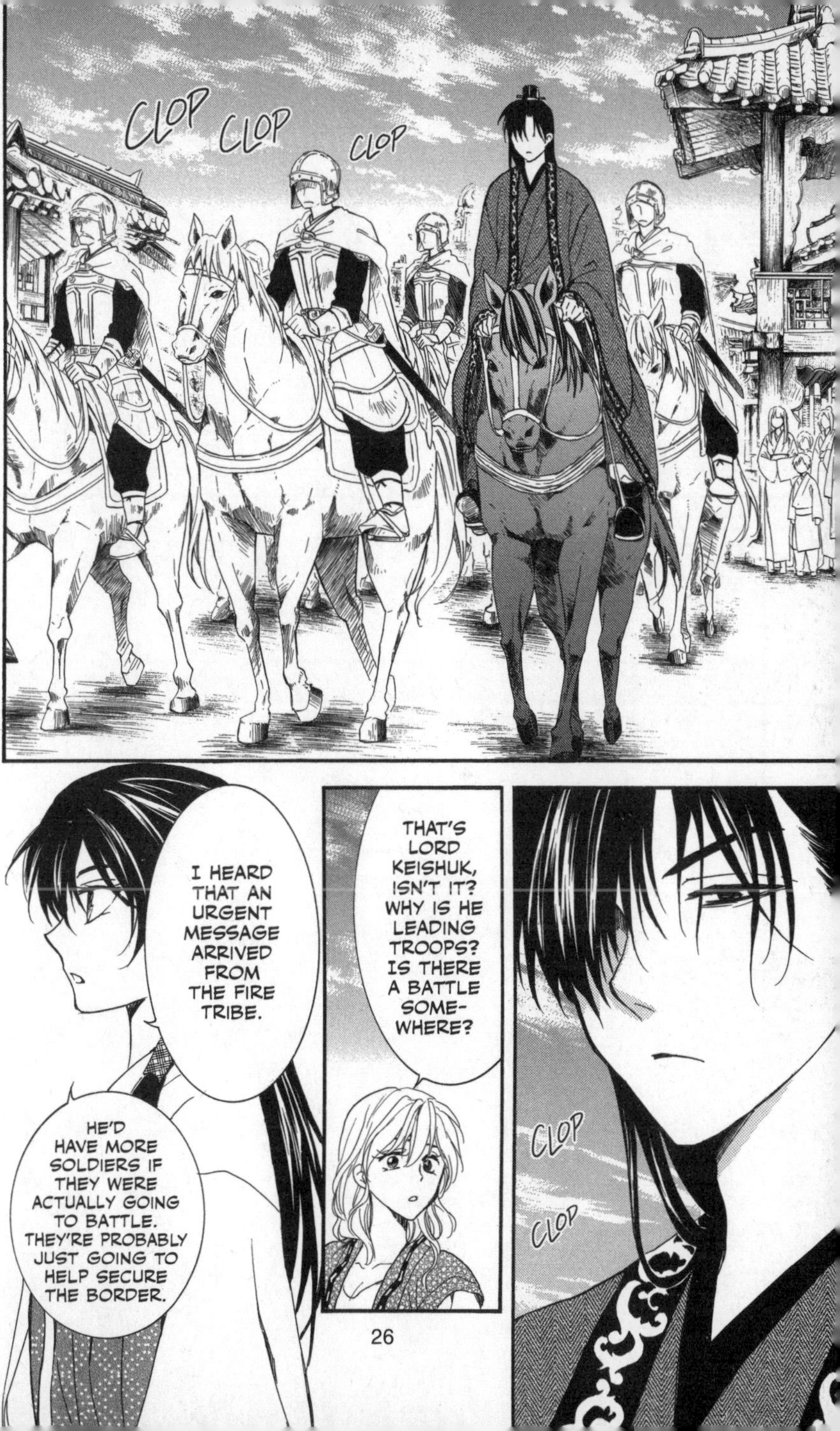
CLOP
CLOP
CLOP
CLOP
CLOP
THAT'S LORD KEISHUK, ISN'T IT? WHY IS HE LEADING TROOPS? IS THERE A BATTLE SOME-WHERE?
I HEARD THAT AN URGENT MESSAGE ARRIVED FROM THE FIRE TRIBE.
HE'D HAVE MORE SOLDIERS IF THEY WERE ACTUALLY GOING TO BATTLE. THEY'RE PROBABLY JUST GOING TO HELP SECURE THE BORDER.

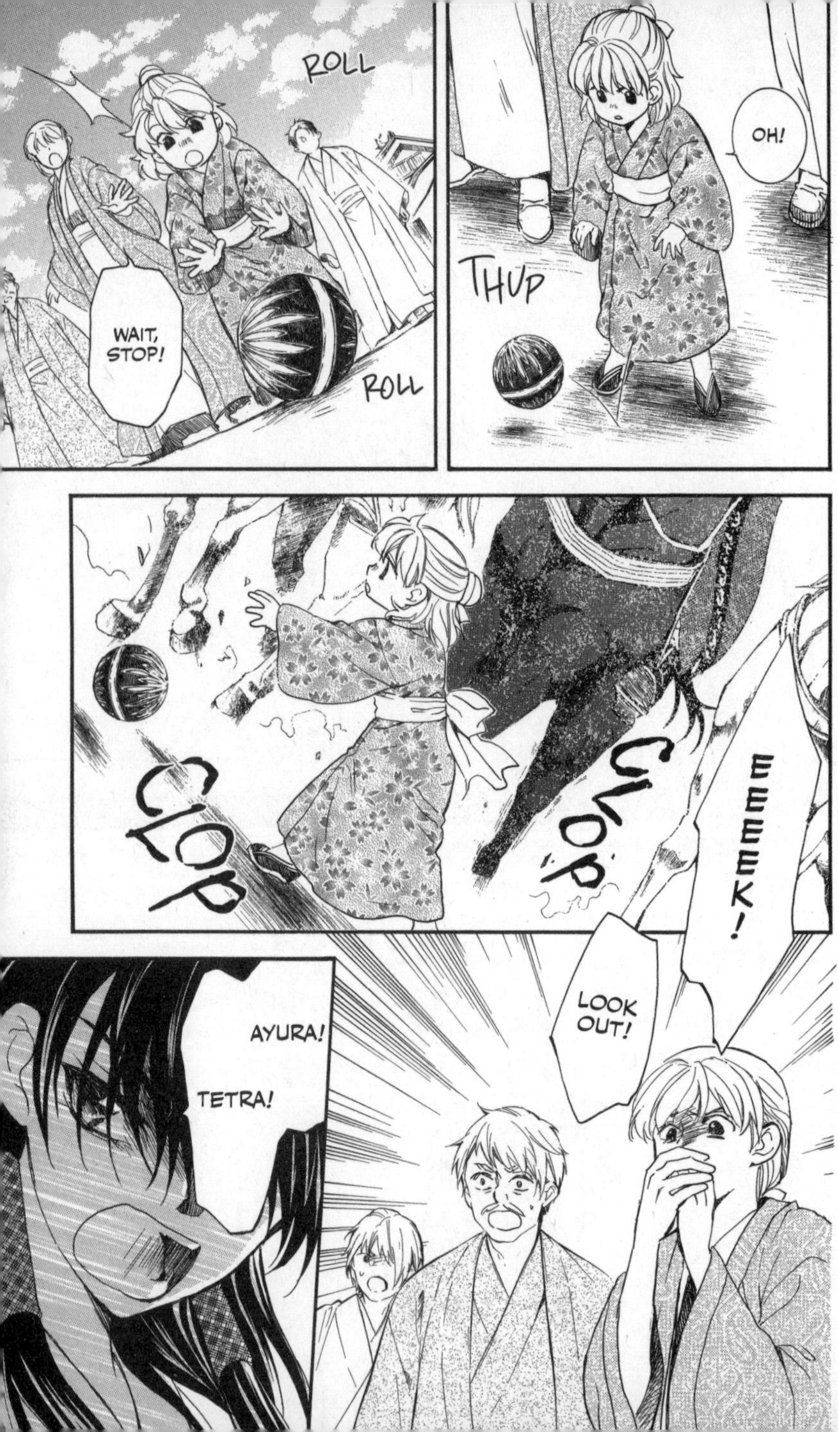
OH!
THUP
ROLL
WAIT, STOP!
ROLL
EEEEK!
CLOP
CLOP
LOOK OUT!
AYURA!
TETRA!

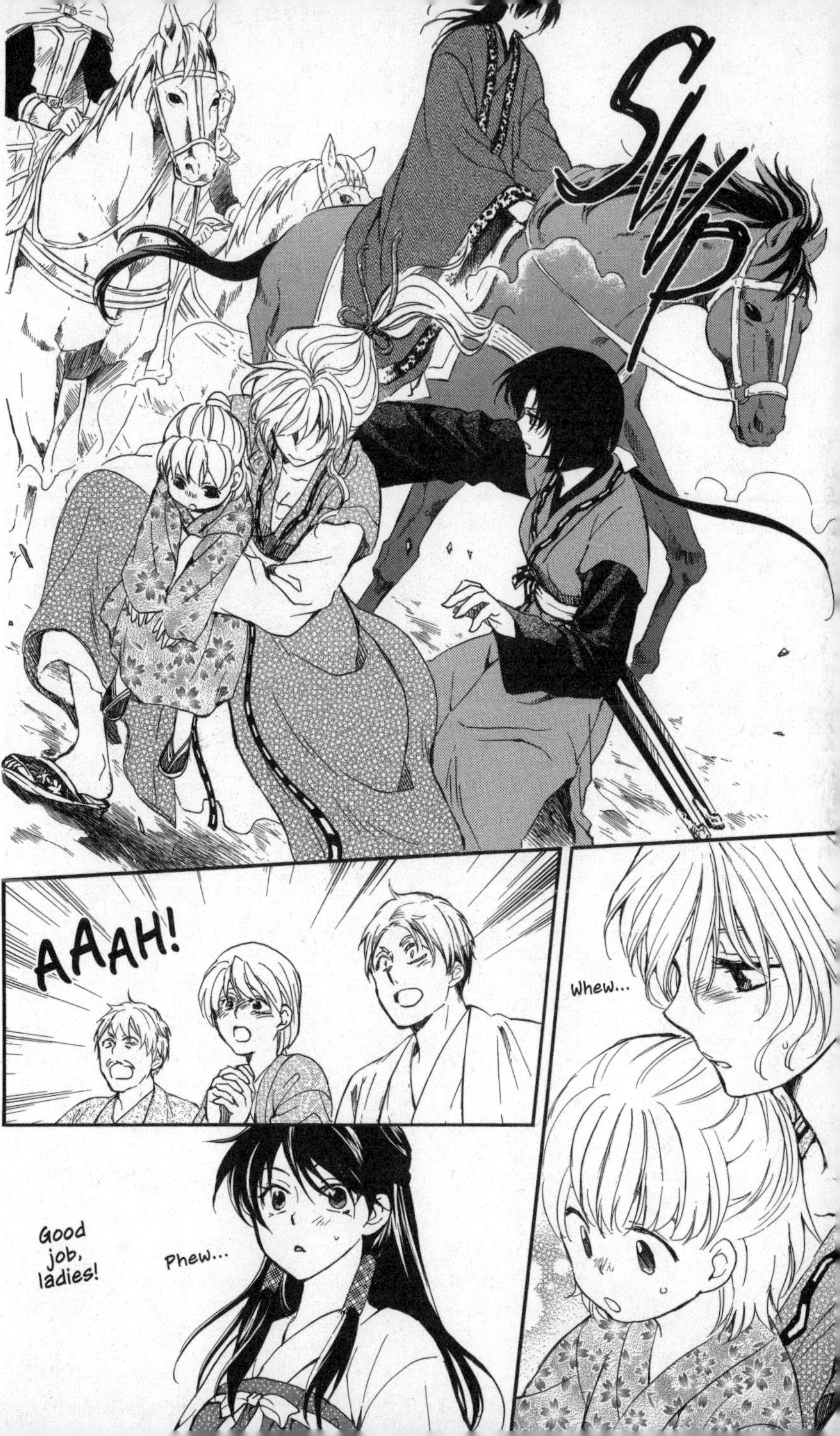
SWP
Whew...
AAAH!
Good job, ladies!
Phew...

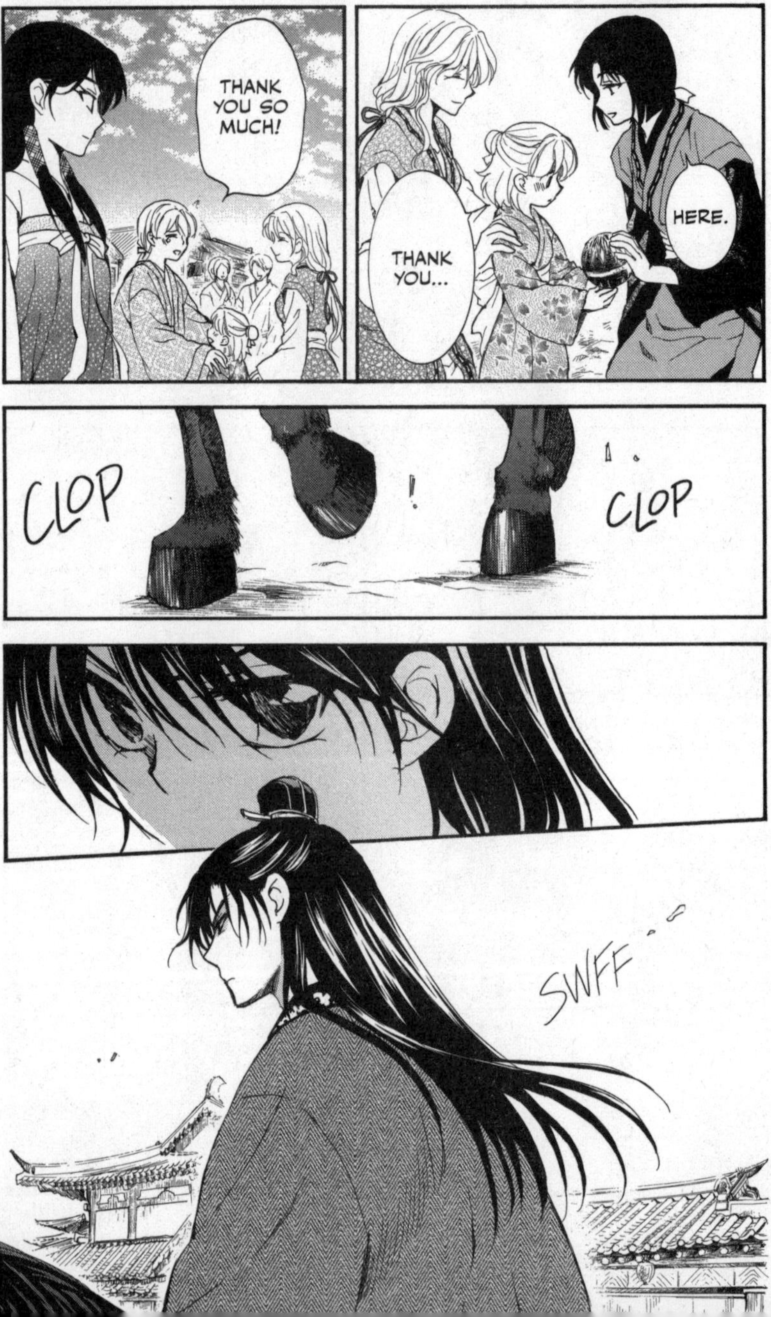
HERE.
THANK YOU...
THANK YOU SO MUCH!
CLOP
CLOP
SWFF

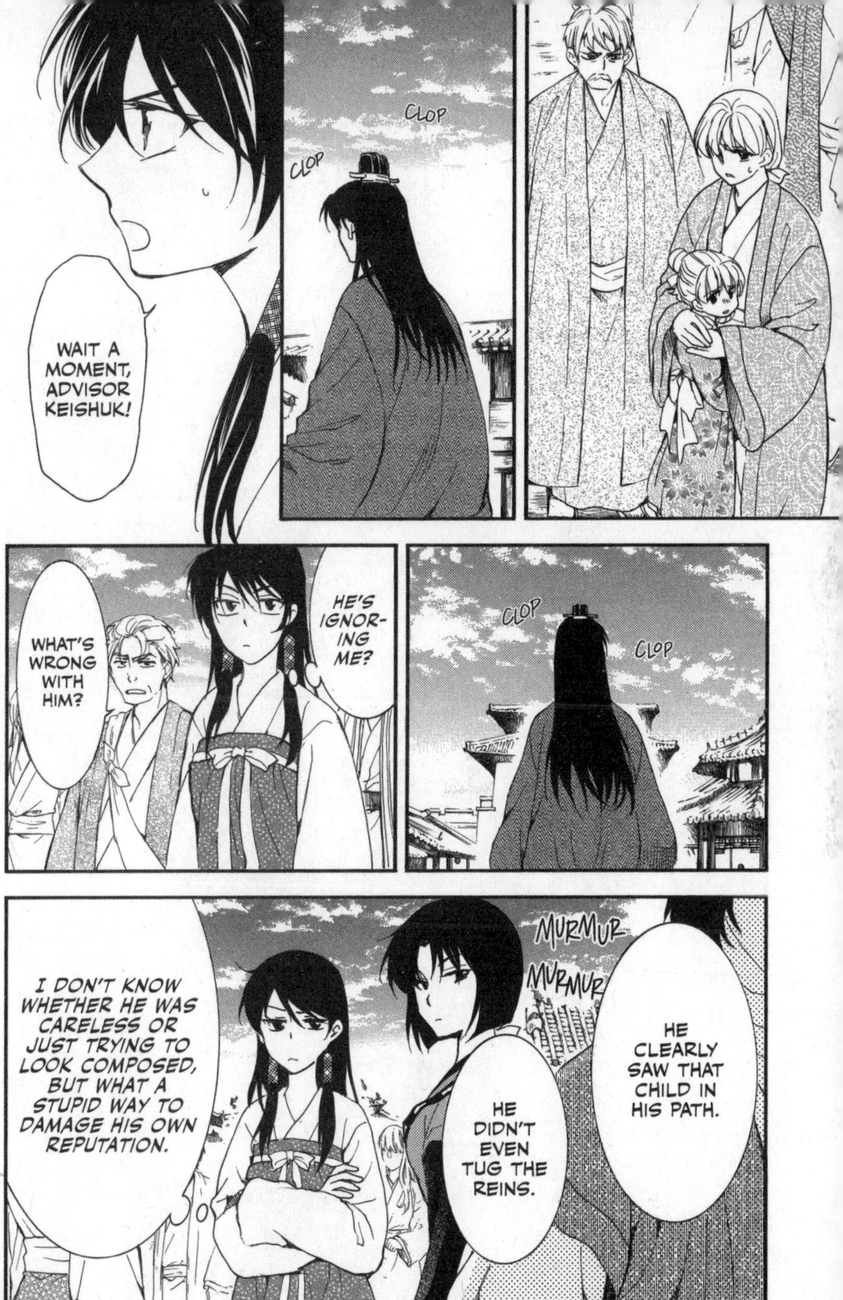
CLOP
CLOP
WAIT A MOMENT, ADVISOR KEISHUK!
CLOP
CLOP
HE'S IGNORING ME?
WHAT'S WRONG WITH HIM?
MURMUR
MURMUR
HE CLEARLY SAW THAT CHILD IN HIS PATH.
HE DIDN'T EVEN TUG THE REINS.
I DON'T KNOW WHETHER HE WAS CARELESS OR JUST TRYING TO LOOK COMPOSED, BUT WHAT A STUPID WAY TO DAMAGE HIS OWN REPUTATION.

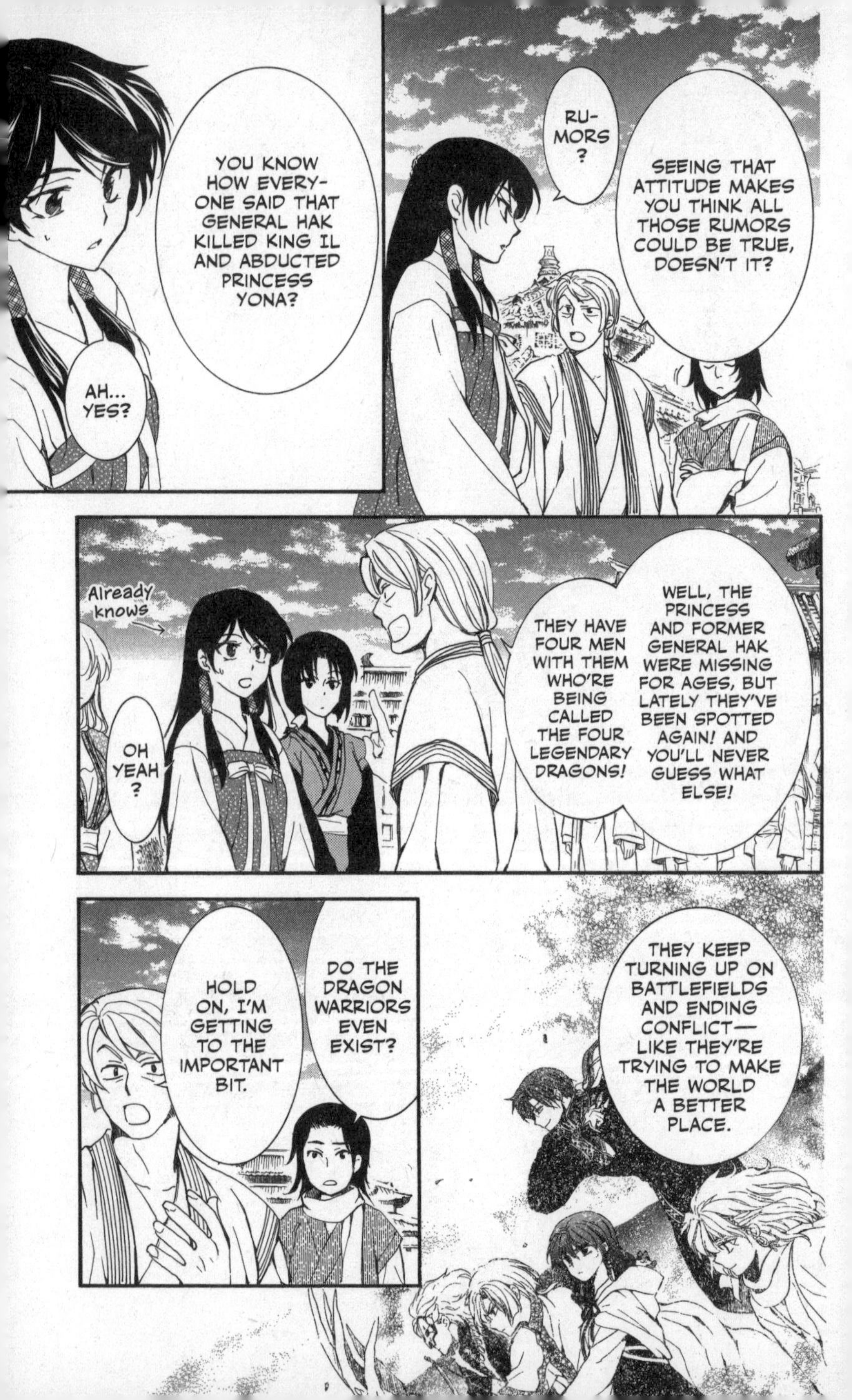
SEEING THAT ATTITUDE MAKES YOU THINK ALL THOSE RUMORS COULD BE TRUE, DOESN'T IT?
RU-MORS?
YOU KNOW HOW EVERY-ONE SAID THAT GENERAL HAK KILLED KING IL AND ABDUCTED PRINCESS YONA?
AH... YES?
WELL, THE PRINCESS AND FORMER GENERAL HAK WERE MISSING FOR AGES, BUT LATELY THEY'VE BEEN SPOTTED AGAIN! AND YOU'LL NEVER GUESS WHAT ELSE!
THEY HAVE FOUR MEN WITH THEM WHO'RE BEING CALLED THE FOUR LEGENDARY DRAGONS!
OH YEAH?
Already knows
THEY KEEP TURNING UP ON BATTLEFIELDS AND ENDING CONFLICT— LIKE THEY'RE TRYING TO MAKE THE WORLD A BETTER PLACE.
DO THE DRAGON WARRIORS EVEN EXIST?
HOLD ON, I'M GETTING TO THE IMPORTANT BIT.

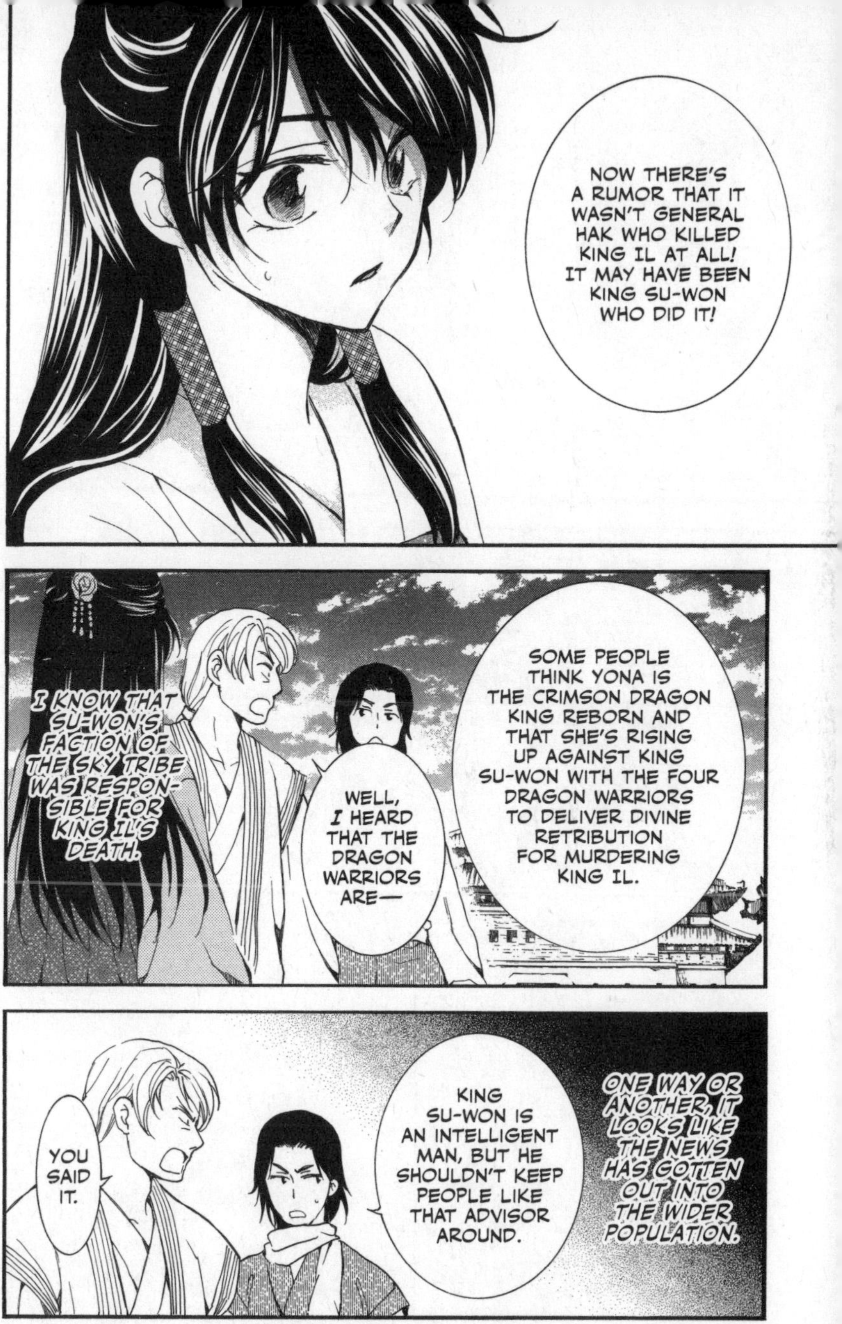
NOW THERE'S A RUMOR THAT IT WASN'T GENERAL HAK WHO KILLED KING IL AT ALL! IT MAY HAVE BEEN KING SU-WON WHO DID IT!
SOME PEOPLE THINK YONA IS THE CRIMSON DRAGON KING REBORN AND THAT SHE'S RISING UP AGAINST KING SU-WON WITH THE FOUR DRAGON WARRIORS TO DELIVER DIVINE RETRIBUTION FOR MURDERING KING IL.
WELL, *I* HEARD THAT THE DRAGON WARRIORS ARE—
I KNOW THAT SU-WON'S FACTION OF THE SKY TRIBE WAS RESPONSIBLE FOR KING IL'S DEATH.
ONE WAY OR ANOTHER, IT LOOKS LIKE THE NEWS HAS GOTTEN OUT INTO THE WIDER POPULATION.
KING SU-WON IS AN INTELLIGENT MAN, BUT HE SHOULDN'T KEEP PEOPLE LIKE THAT ADVISOR AROUND.
YOU SAID IT.

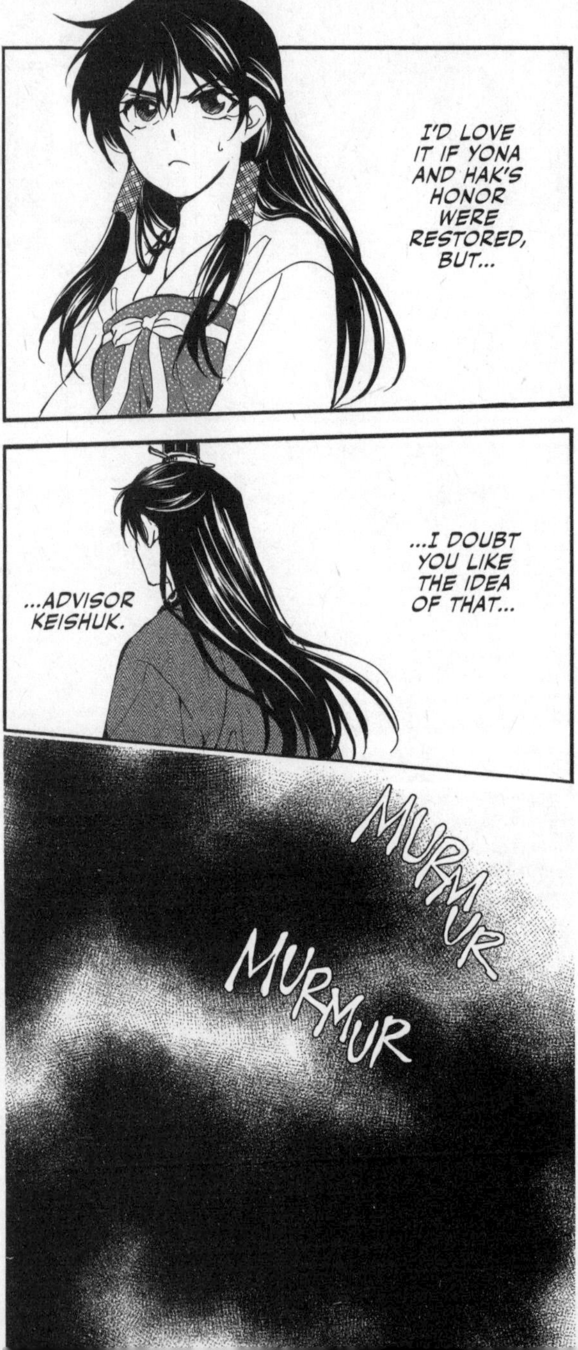
I'D LOVE IT IF YONA AND HAK'S HONOR WERE RESTORED, BUT...
...I DOUBT YOU LIKE THE IDEA OF THAT...
...ADVISOR KEISHUK.
MURMUR
MURMUR

This is Yona of the Dawn volume 28! Thank you so much to my readers who have been following the story for so long.

This time, Yona of the Dawn is coming out with a fan book [in Japan]. I drew about 30 pages of cover illustrations, short comics, four-panel comics, illustrations, etc. I've even included the color art I've uploaded to Twitter. I think this book will help you to learn more about the characters in Yona of the Dawn, so I hope you check it out.
It was hectic working on it alongside my serialized comic.
I still haven't seen the final product, so I hope it turned out well!

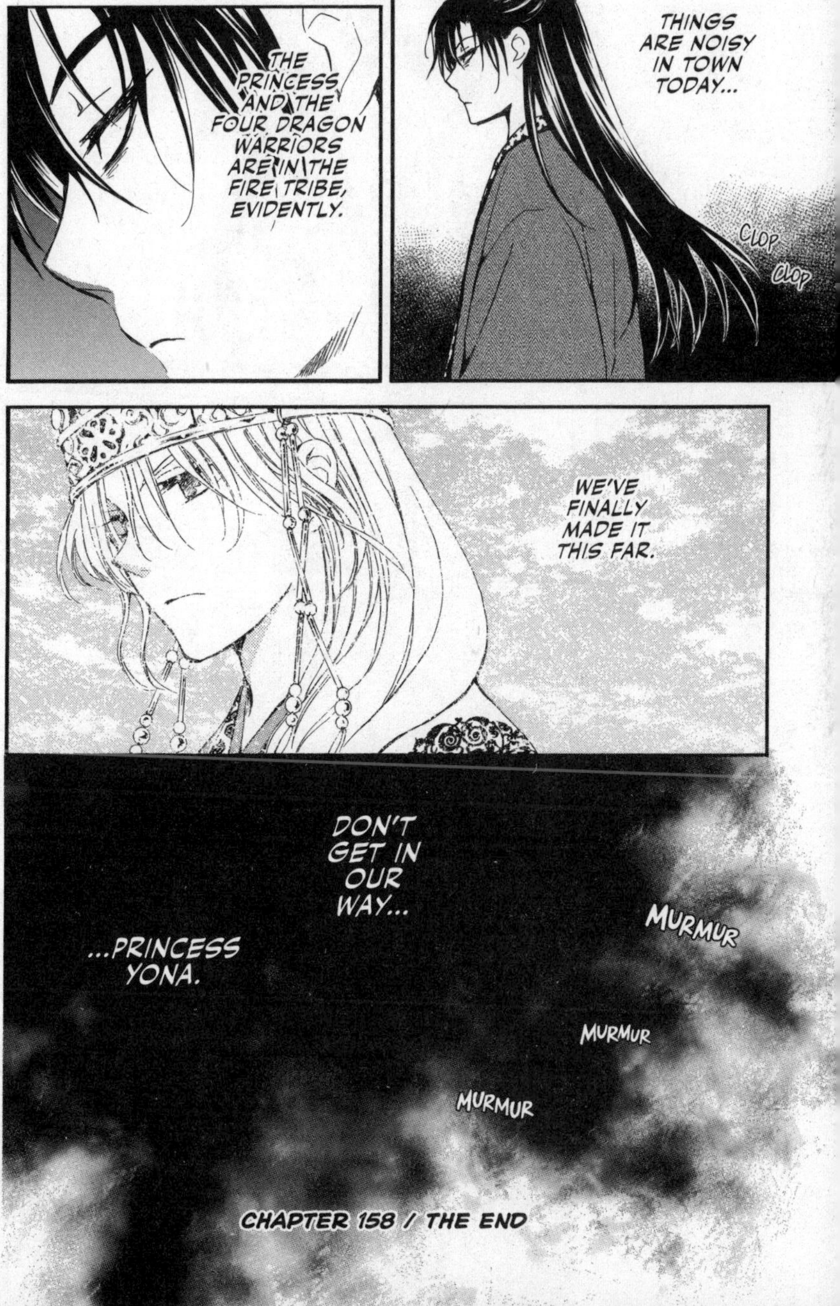
THINGS ARE NOISY IN TOWN TODAY...
CLOP
CLOP
THE PRINCESS AND THE FOUR DRAGON WARRIORS ARE IN THE FIRE TRIBE, EVIDENTLY.
WE'VE FINALLY MADE IT THIS FAR.
DON'T GET IN OUR WAY...
MURMUR
...PRINCESS YONA.
MURMUR
MURMUR
CHAPTER 158 / THE END

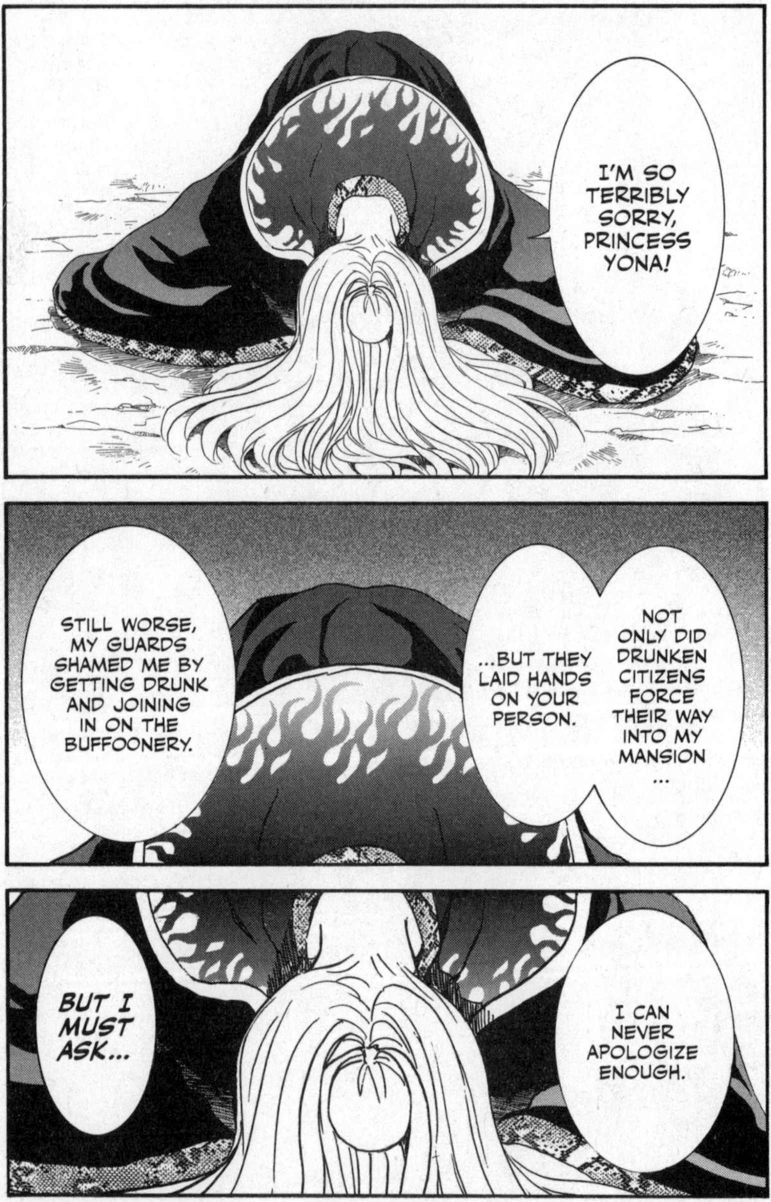
I'M SO TERRIBLY SORRY, PRINCESS YONA!
NOT ONLY DID DRUNKEN CITIZENS FORCE THEIR WAY INTO MY MANSION...
...BUT THEY LAID HANDS ON YOUR PERSON.
STILL WORSE, MY GUARDS SHAMED ME BY GETTING DRUNK AND JOINING IN ON THE BUFFOONERY.
I CAN NEVER APOLOGIZE ENOUGH.
BUT I MUST ASK...

CHAPTER 159: TAE-JUN'S CARELESSNESS

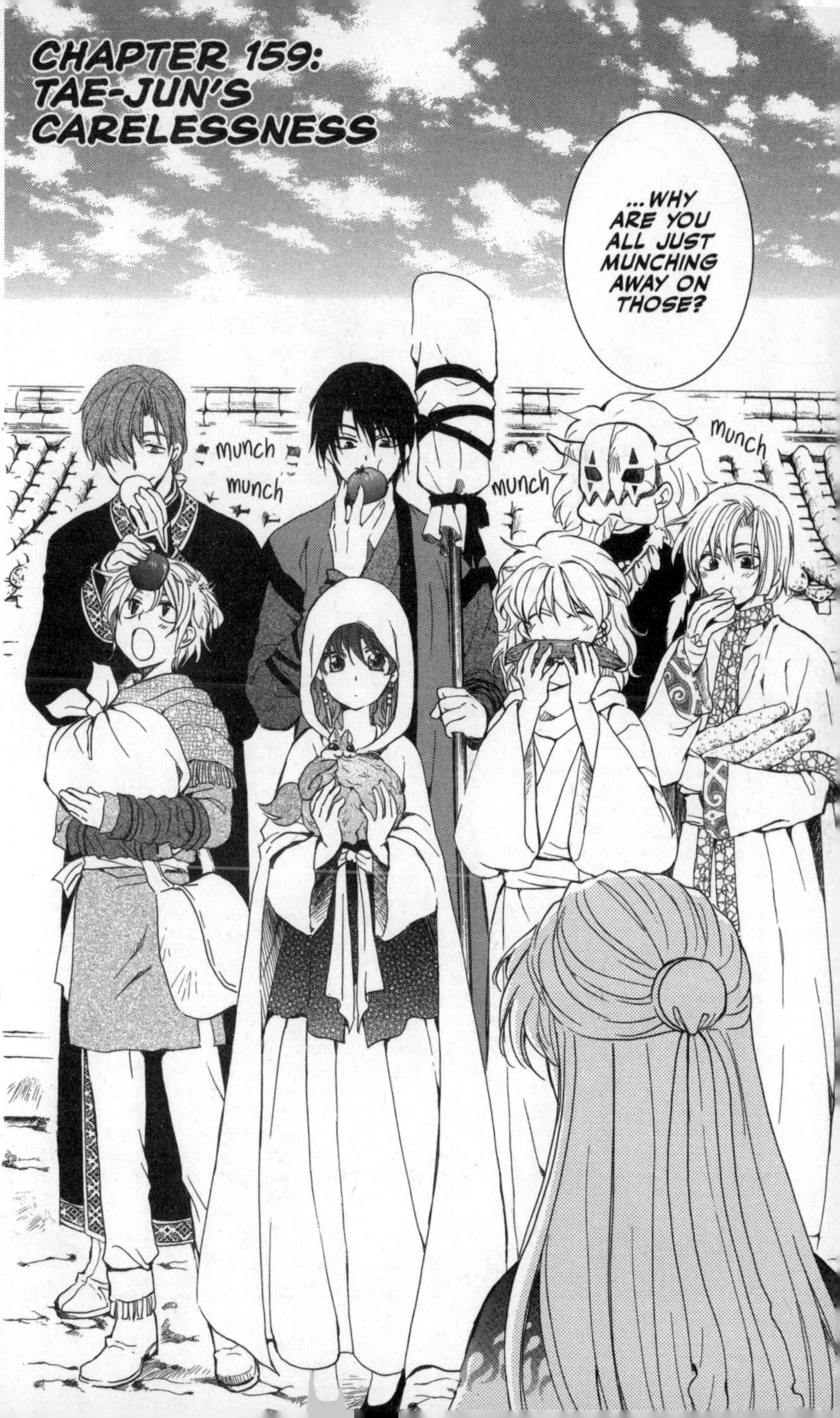
...WHY ARE YOU ALL JUST MUNCHING AWAY ON THOSE?
munch
munch
munch
munch

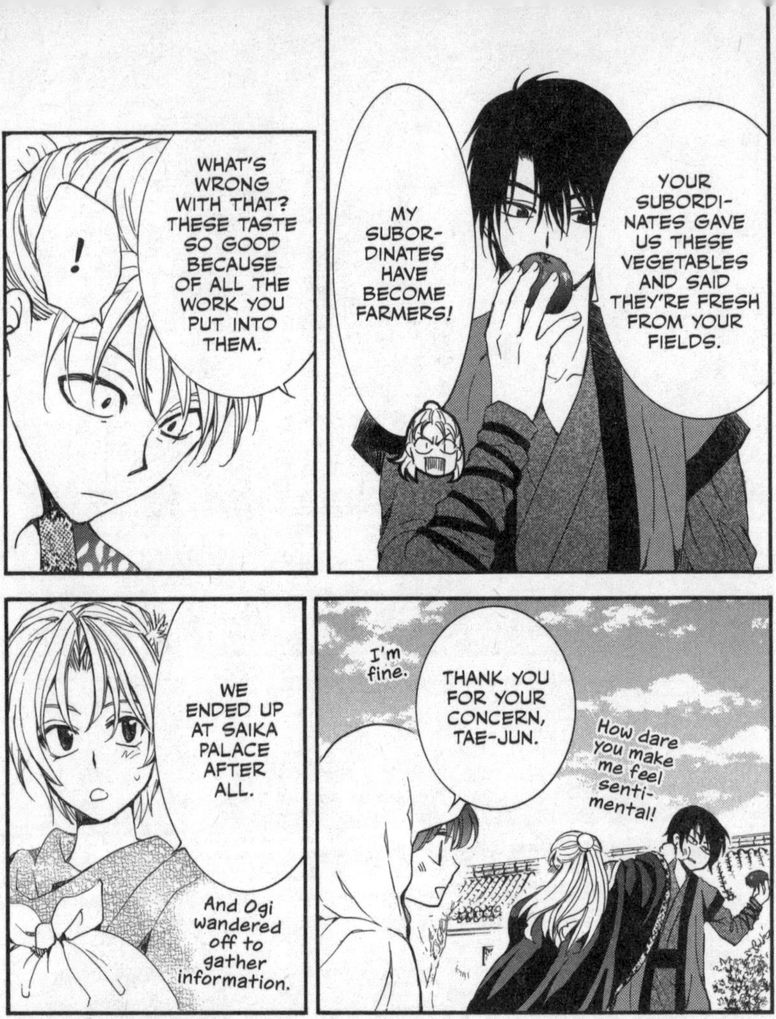
YOUR SUBORDINATES GAVE US THESE VEGETABLES AND SAID THEY'RE FRESH FROM YOUR FIELDS.
MY SUBORDINATES HAVE BECOME FARMERS!
!
WHAT'S WRONG WITH THAT? THESE TASTE SO GOOD BECAUSE OF ALL THE WORK YOU PUT INTO THEM.
THANK YOU FOR YOUR CONCERN, TAE-JUN.
I'm fine.
How dare you make me feel sentimental!
WE ENDED UP AT SAIKA PALACE AFTER ALL.
And Ogi wandered off to gather information.

Yona of the Dawn

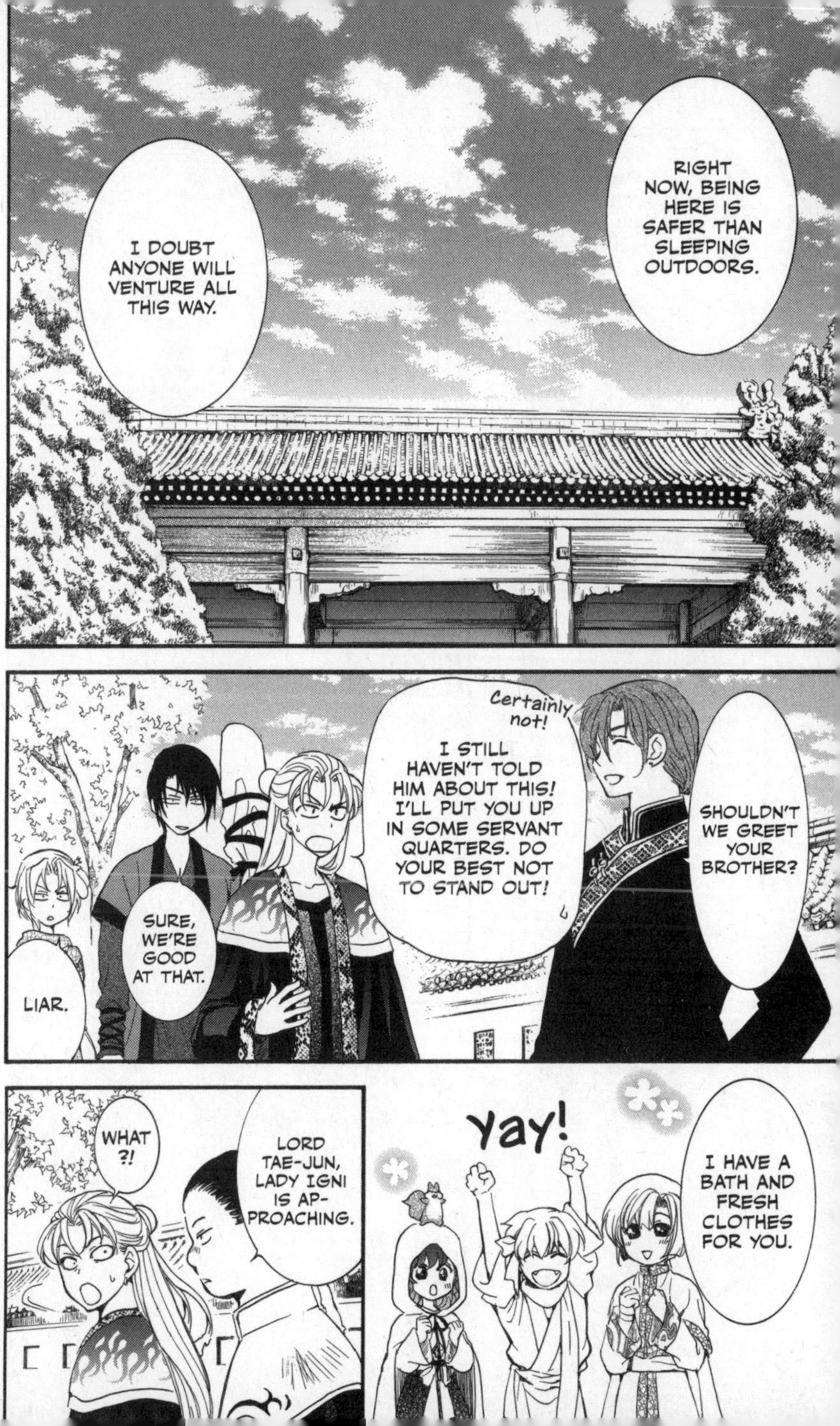
RIGHT NOW, BEING HERE IS SAFER THAN SLEEPING OUTDOORS.
I DOUBT ANYONE WILL VENTURE ALL THIS WAY.
SHOULDN'T WE GREET YOUR BROTHER?
Certainly not!
I STILL HAVEN'T TOLD HIM ABOUT THIS! I'LL PUT YOU UP IN SOME SERVANT QUARTERS. DO YOUR BEST NOT TO STAND OUT!
SURE, WE'RE GOOD AT THAT.
LIAR.
I HAVE A BATH AND FRESH CLOTHES FOR YOU.
Yay!
LORD TAE-JUN, LADY IGNI IS AP-PROACHING.
WHAT ?!

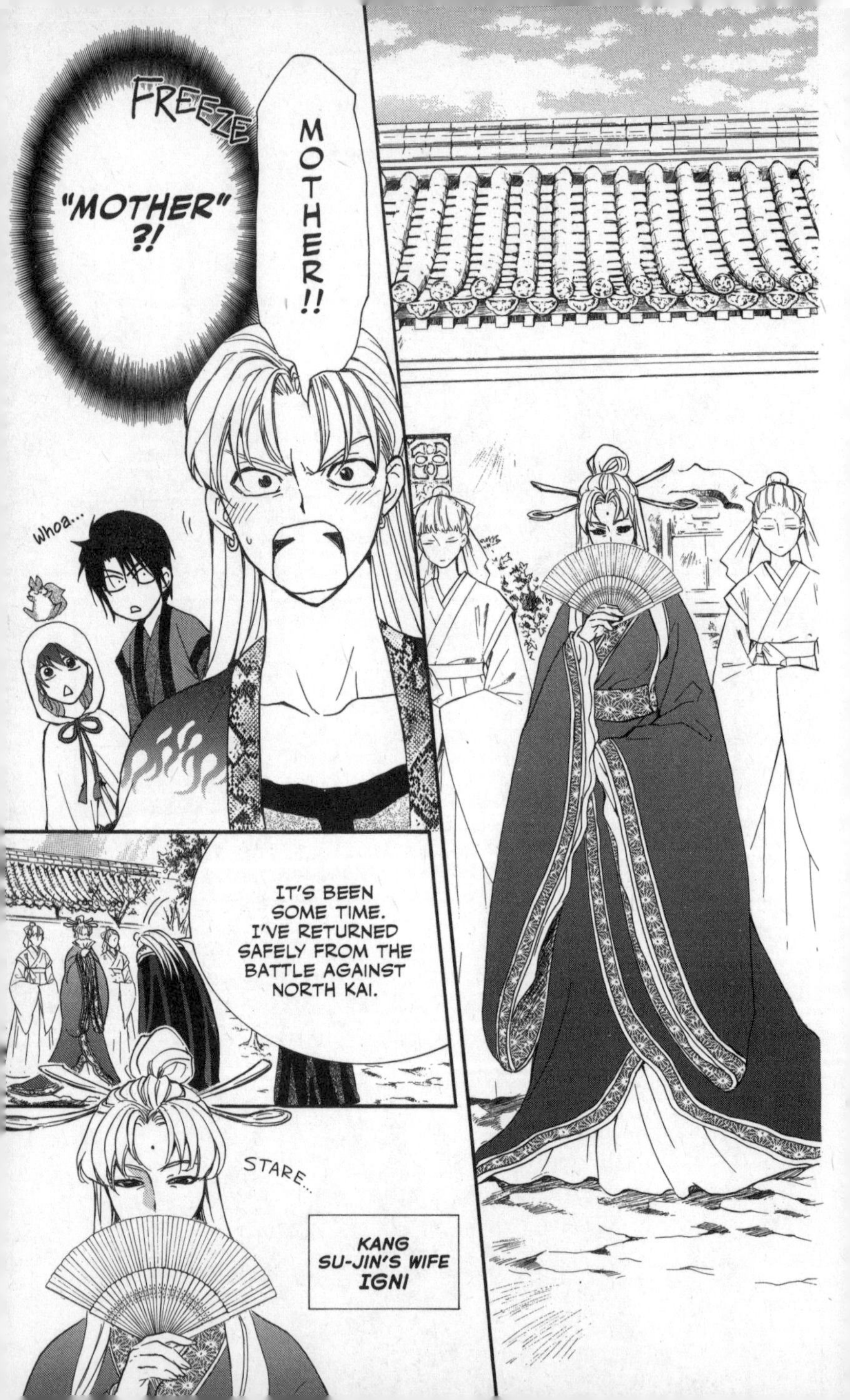
MOTHER!!
"MOTHER" ?!
FREEZE
whoa...
IT'S BEEN SOME TIME. I'VE RETURNED SAFELY FROM THE BATTLE AGAINST NORTH KAI.
STARE...
KANG SU-JIN'S WIFE IGNI

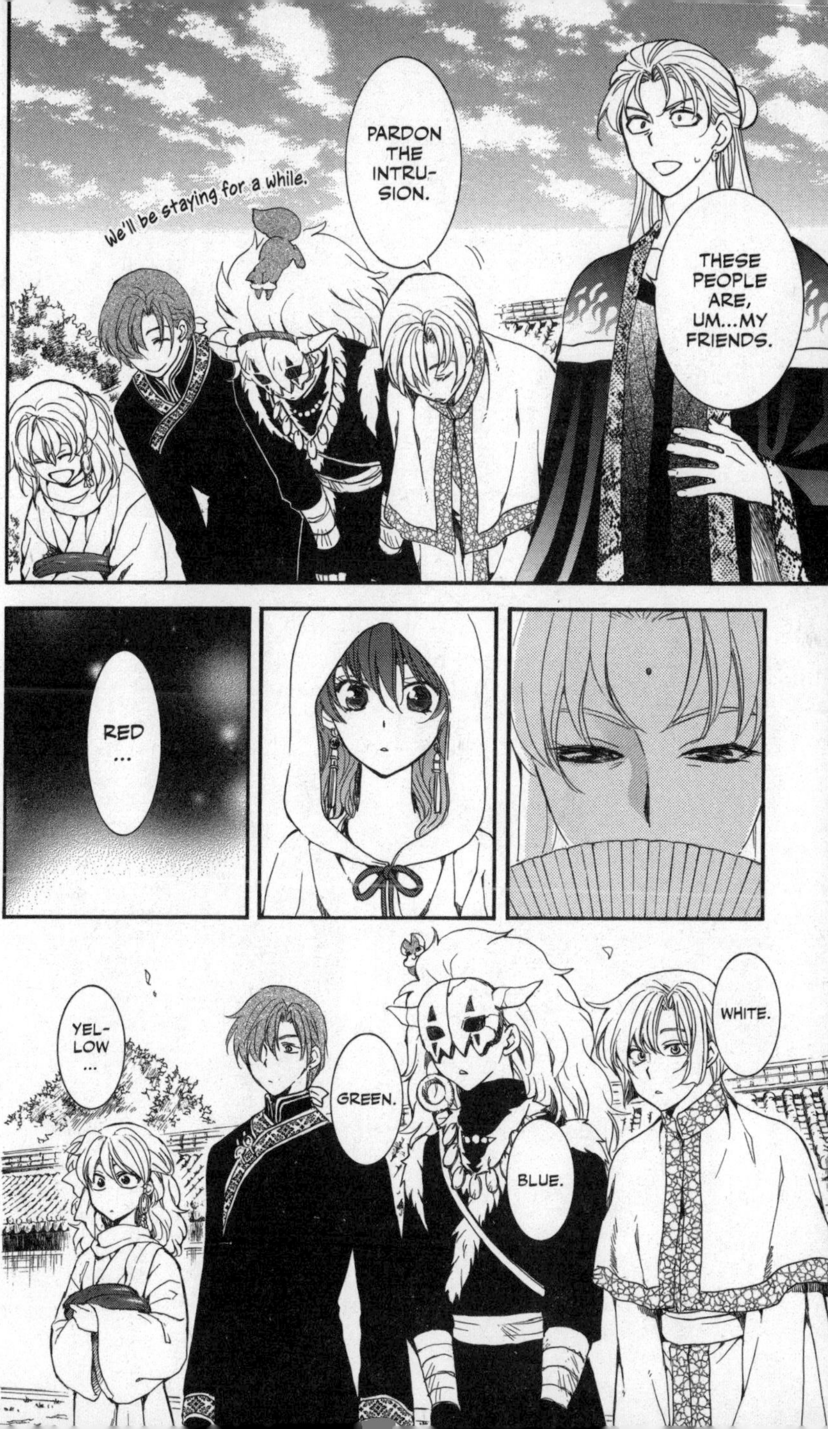
THESE PEOPLE ARE, UM...MY FRIENDS.
PARDON THE INTRU-SION.
We'll be staying for a while.
RED ...
WHITE.
BLUE.
GREEN.
YEL-LOW ...

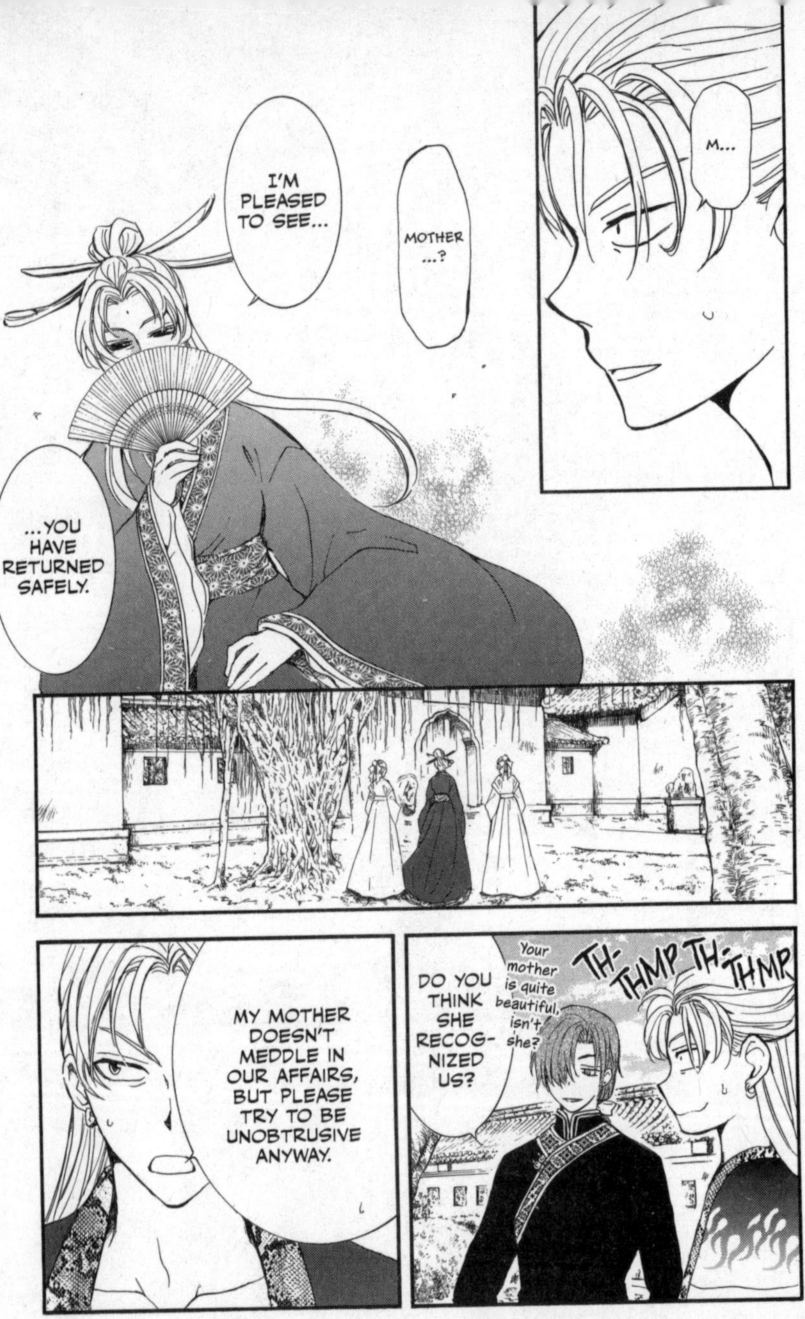
M...
MOTHER ...?
I'M PLEASED TO SEE...
...YOU HAVE RETURNED SAFELY.
TH-THMP TH-THMP
Your mother is quite beautiful, isn't she?
DO YOU THINK SHE RECOG-NIZED US?
MY MOTHER DOESN'T MEDDLE IN OUR AFFAIRS, BUT PLEASE TRY TO BE UNOBTRUSIVE ANYWAY.

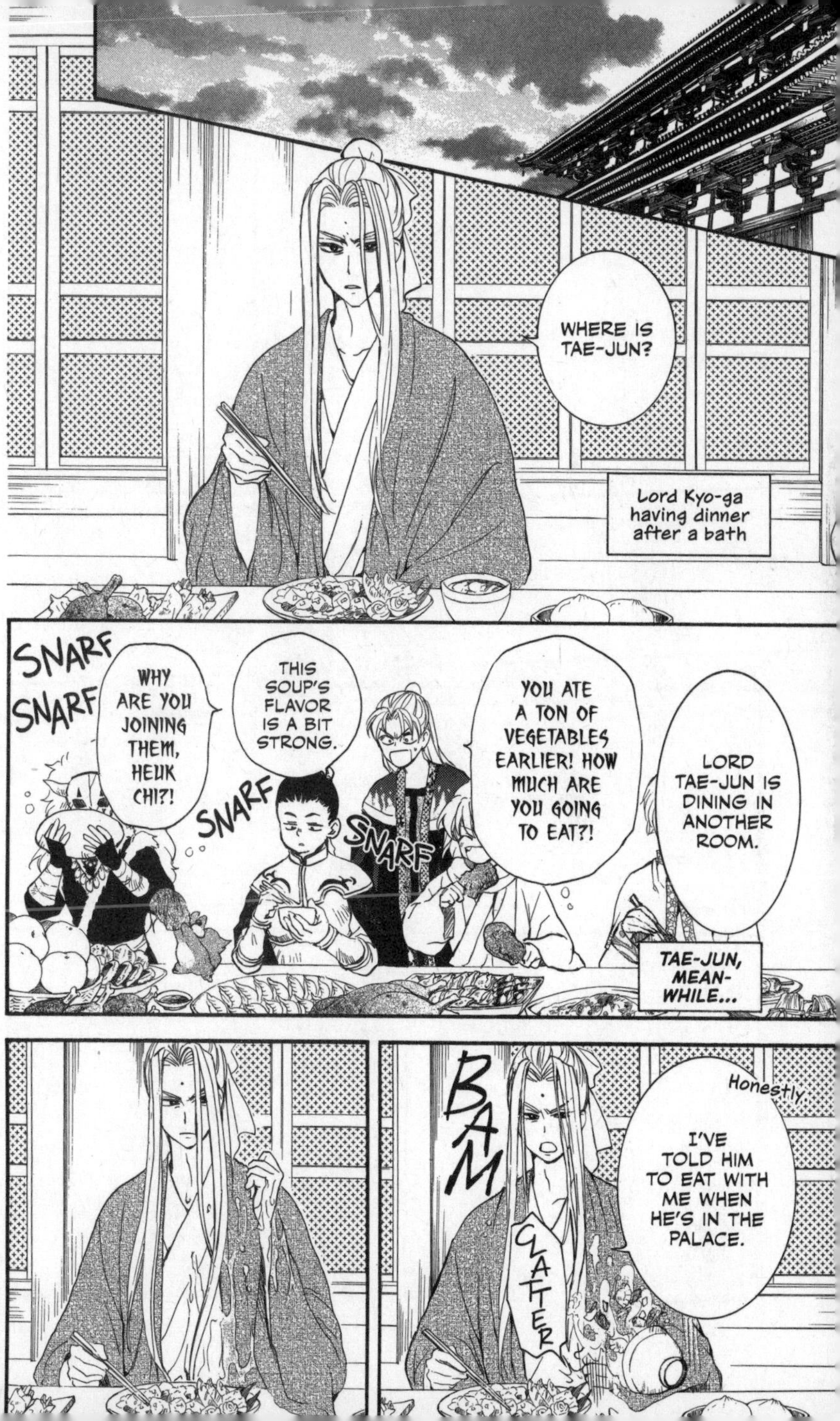
WHERE IS TAE-JUN?
Lord Kyo-ga having dinner after a bath
LORD TAE-JUN IS DINING IN ANOTHER ROOM.
TAE-JUN, MEAN-WHILE...
YOU ATE A TON OF VEGETABLES EARLIER! HOW MUCH ARE YOU GOING TO EAT?!
SNARF
THIS SOUP'S FLAVOR IS A BIT STRONG.
SNARF
WHY ARE YOU JOINING THEM, HEUK CHI?!
SNARF
SNARF
Honestly.
I'VE TOLD HIM TO EAT WITH ME WHEN HE'S IN THE PALACE.
BAM
CLATTER

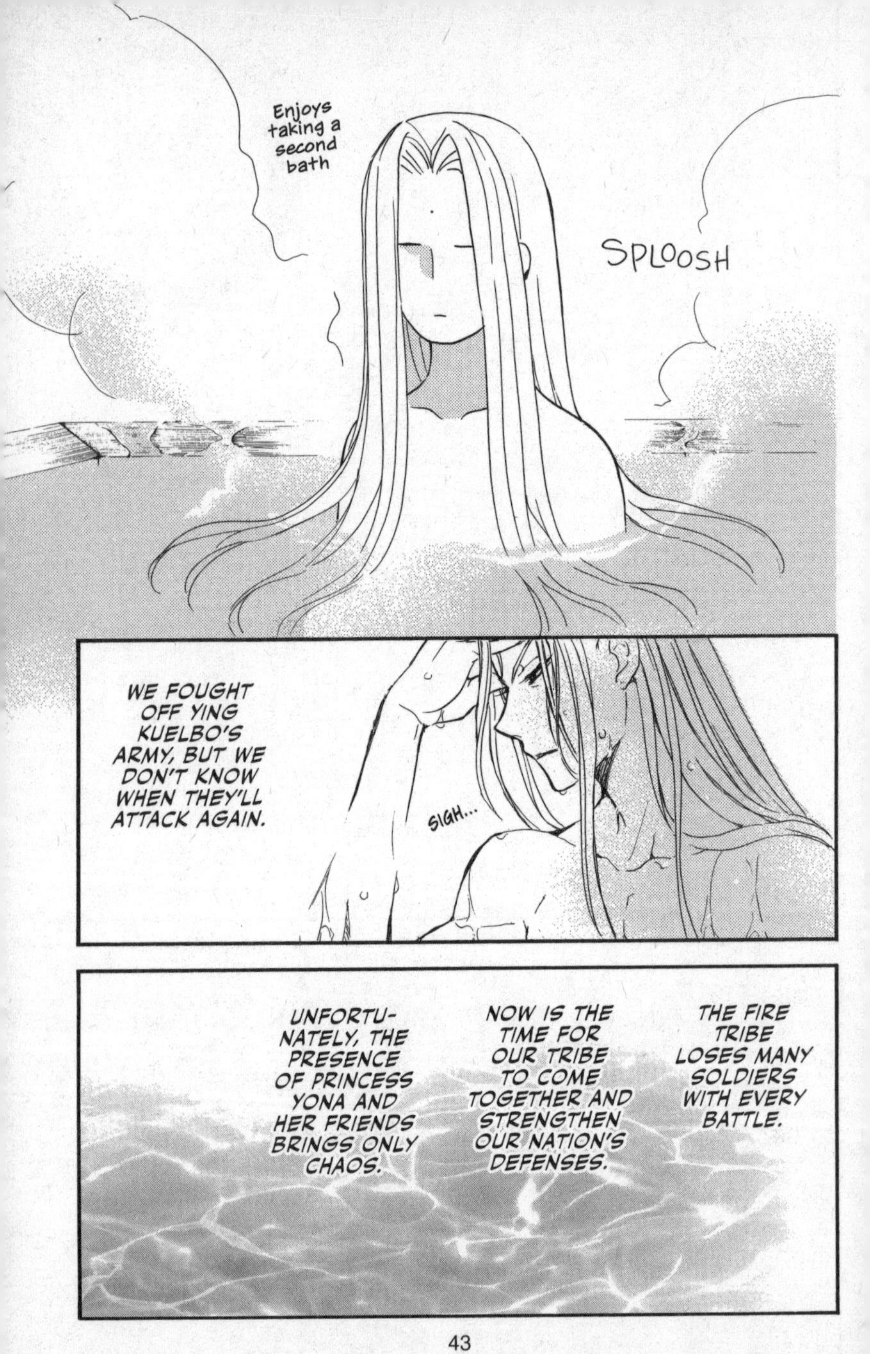
Enjoys taking a second bath
SPLOOSH
WE FOUGHT OFF YING KUELBO'S ARMY, BUT WE DON'T KNOW WHEN THEY'LL ATTACK AGAIN.
SIGH...
THE FIRE TRIBE LOSES MANY SOLDIERS WITH EVERY BATTLE.
NOW IS THE TIME FOR OUR TRIBE TO COME TOGETHER AND STRENGTHEN OUR NATION'S DEFENSES.
UNFORTU-NATELY, THE PRESENCE OF PRINCESS YONA AND HER FRIENDS BRINGS ONLY CHAOS.

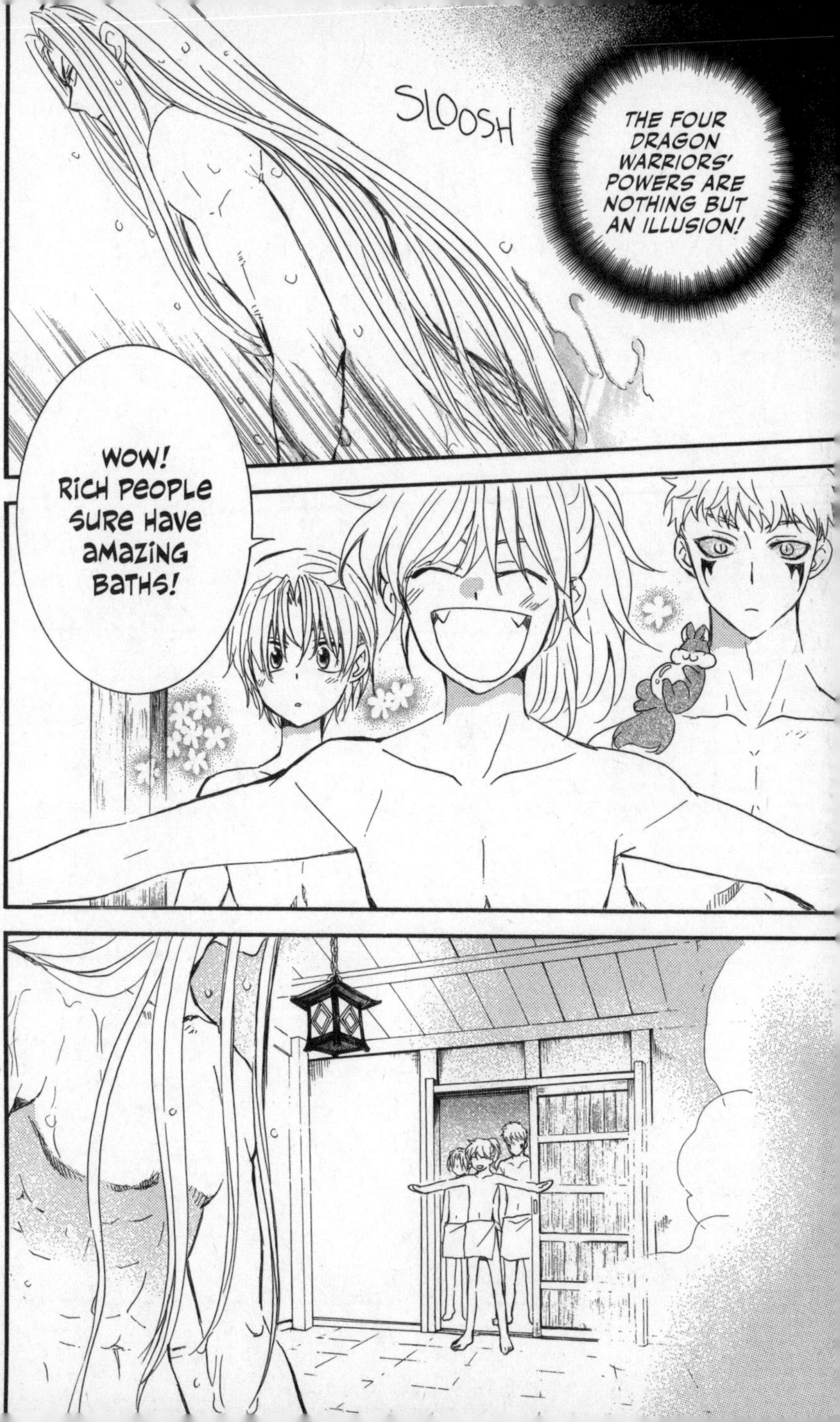
THE FOUR DRAGON WARRIORS' POWERS ARE NOTHING BUT AN ILLUSION!
SLOOSH
WOW! RICH PEOPLE SURE HAVE AMAZING BATHS!

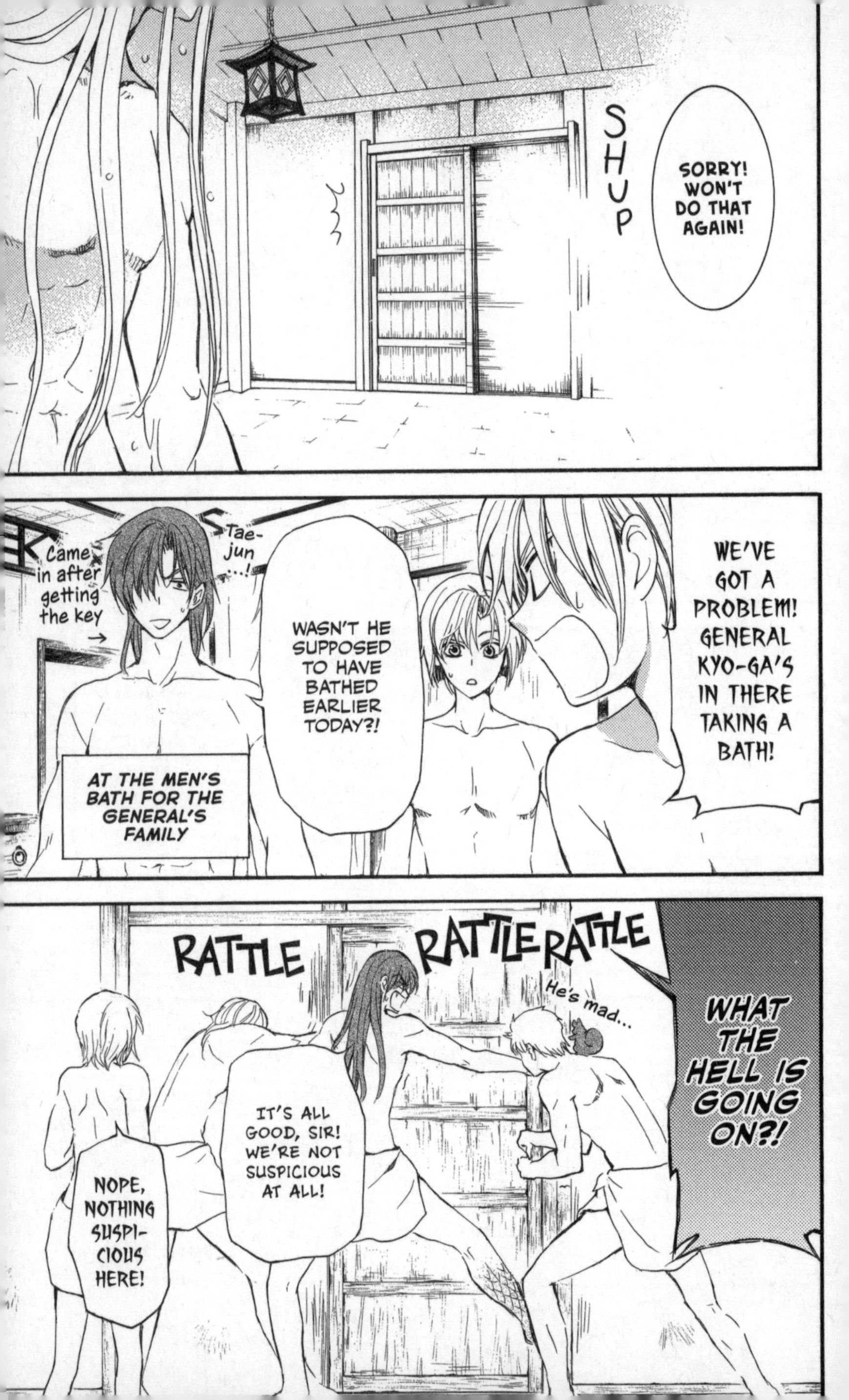
SORRY! WON'T DO THAT AGAIN!
SHUP
WE'VE GOT A PROBLEM! GENERAL KYO-GA'S IN THERE TAKING A BATH!
WASN'T HE SUPPOSED TO HAVE BATHED EARLIER TODAY?!
Tae-jun...!
Came in after getting the key
AT THE MEN'S BATH FOR THE GENERAL'S FAMILY
WHAT THE HELL IS GOING ON?!
RATTLE RATTLE
He's mad...
RATTLE
IT'S ALL GOOD, SIR! WE'RE NOT SUSPICIOUS AT ALL!
NOPE, NOTHING SUSPI-CIOUS HERE!

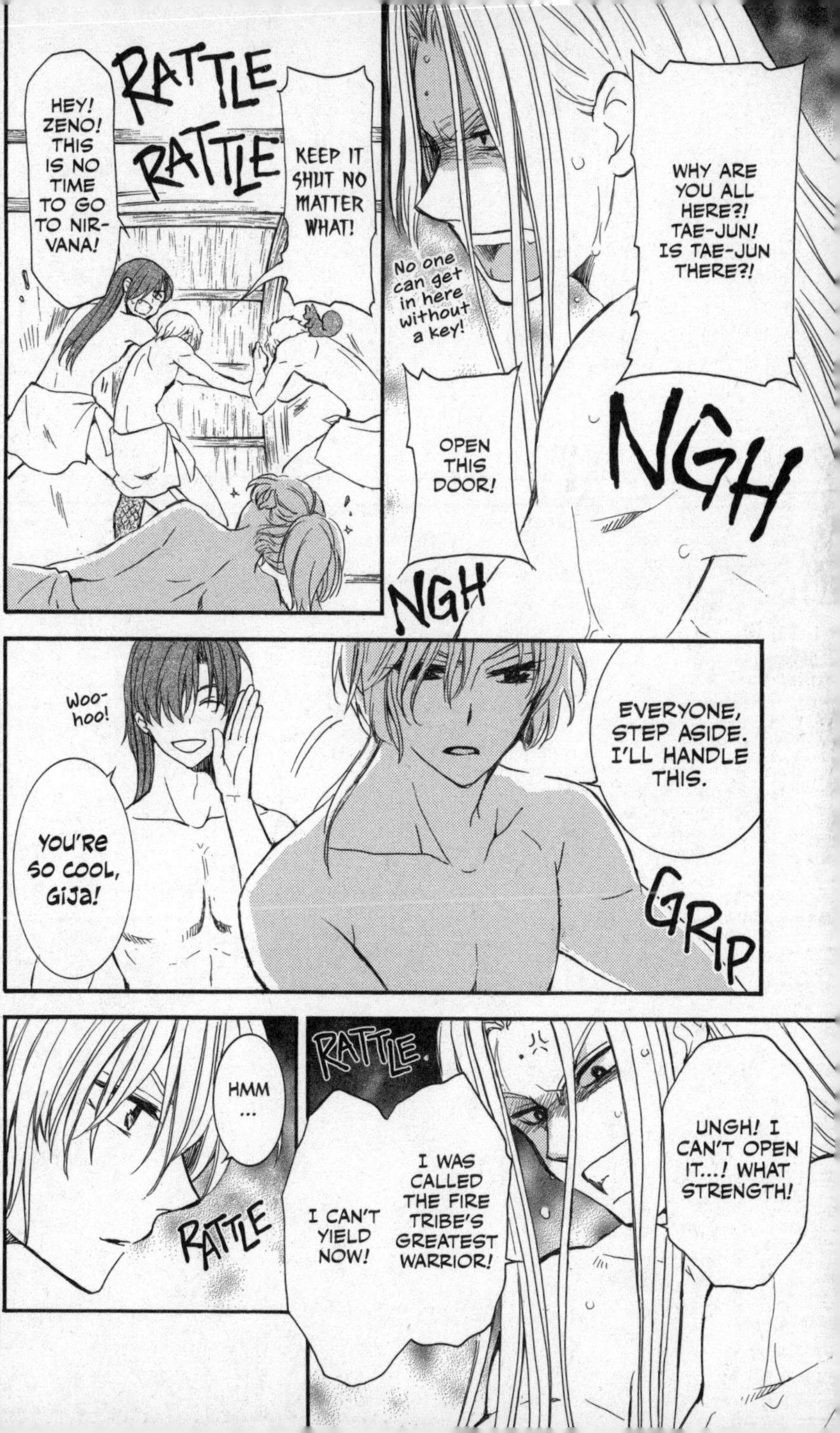
WHY ARE YOU ALL HERE?! TAE-JUN! IS TAE-JUN THERE?!
No one can get in here without a key!
NGH
OPEN THIS DOOR!
NGH
KEEP IT SHUT NO MATTER WHAT!
RATTLE RATTLE
HEY! ZENO! THIS IS NO TIME TO GO TO NIR-VANA!
EVERYONE, STEP ASIDE. I'LL HANDLE THIS.
GRIP
Woo-hoo!
YOU'RE SO COOL, GIJA!
UNGH! I CAN'T OPEN IT...! WHAT STRENGTH!
RATTLE.
I WAS CALLED THE FIRE TRIBE'S GREATEST WARRIOR!
I CAN'T YIELD NOW!
HMM...
RATTLE

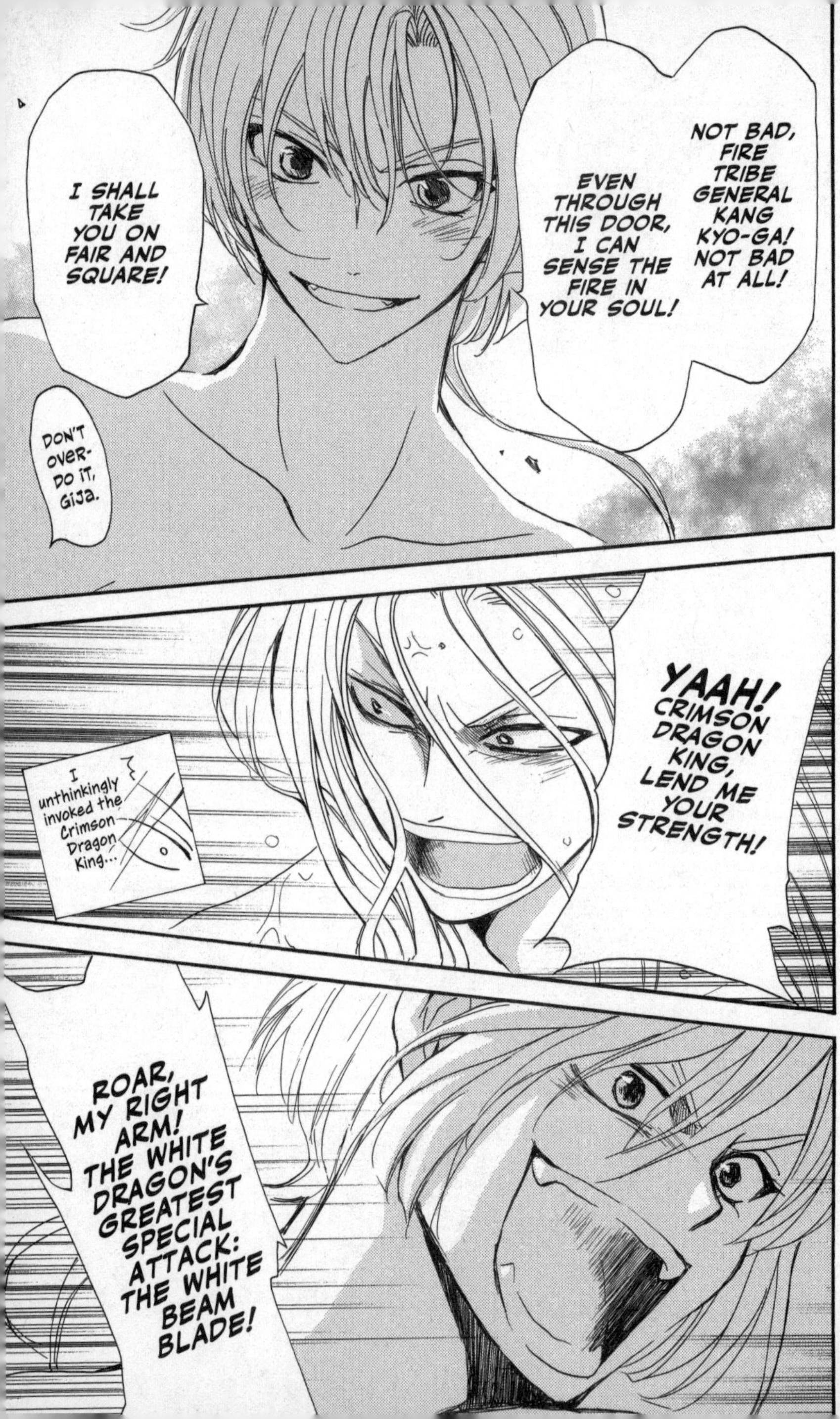
NOT BAD, FIRE TRIBE GENERAL KANG KYO-GA! NOT BAD AT ALL!
EVEN THROUGH THIS DOOR, I CAN SENSE THE FIRE IN YOUR SOUL!
I SHALL TAKE YOU ON FAIR AND SQUARE!
DON'T OVER-DO IT, GIJA.
YAAH! CRIMSON DRAGON KING, LEND ME YOUR STRENGTH!
I unthinkingly invoked the Crimson Dragon King...
ROAR, MY RIGHT ARM! THE WHITE DRAGON'S GREATEST SPECIAL ATTACK: THE WHITE BEAM BLADE!

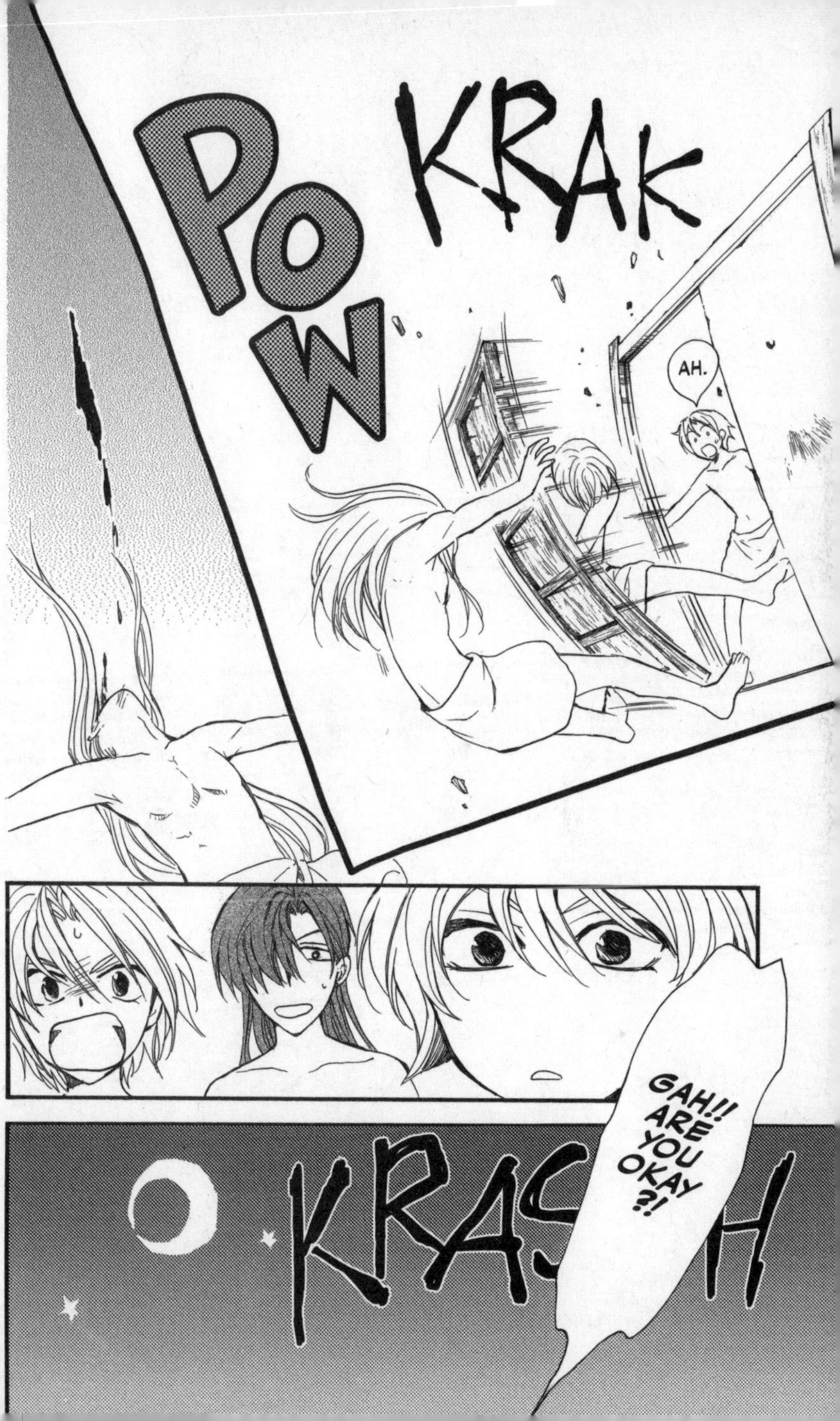
KRAK
POW
AH.
GAH!! ARE YOU OKAY?!
KRASH

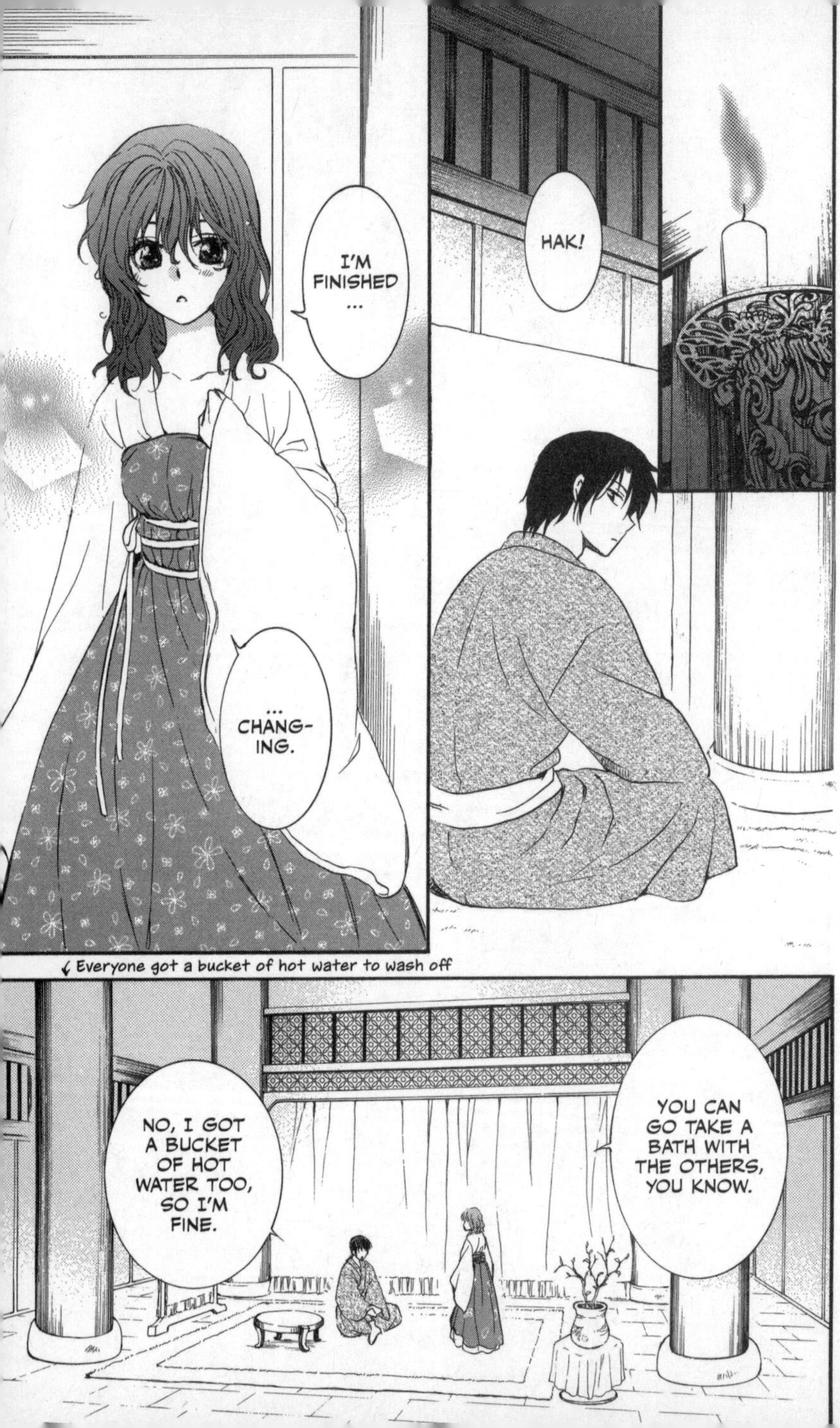
HAK!
I'M FINISHED ...
... CHANGING.
Everyone got a bucket of hot water to wash off
YOU CAN GO TAKE A BATH WITH THE OTHERS, YOU KNOW.
NO, I GOT A BUCKET OF HOT WATER TOO, SO I'M FINE.

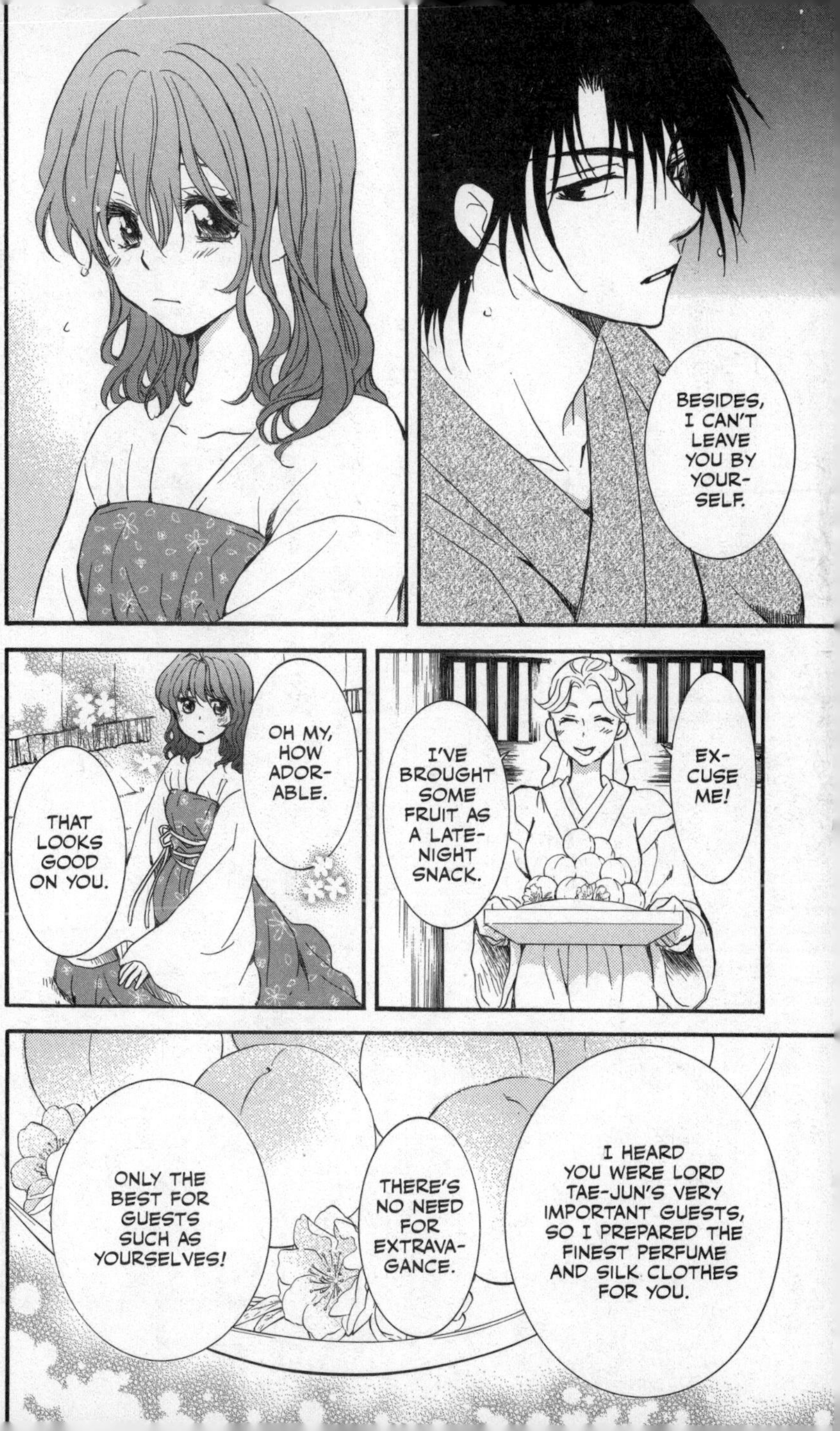
BESIDES, I CAN'T LEAVE YOU BY YOURSELF.
EXCUSE ME!
I'VE BROUGHT SOME FRUIT AS A LATE-NIGHT SNACK.
OH MY, HOW ADORABLE.
THAT LOOKS GOOD ON YOU.
I HEARD YOU WERE LORD TAE-JUN'S VERY IMPORTANT GUESTS, SO I PREPARED THE FINEST PERFUME AND SILK CLOTHES FOR YOU.
THERE'S NO NEED FOR EXTRAVAGANCE.
ONLY THE BEST FOR GUESTS SUCH AS YOURSELVES!

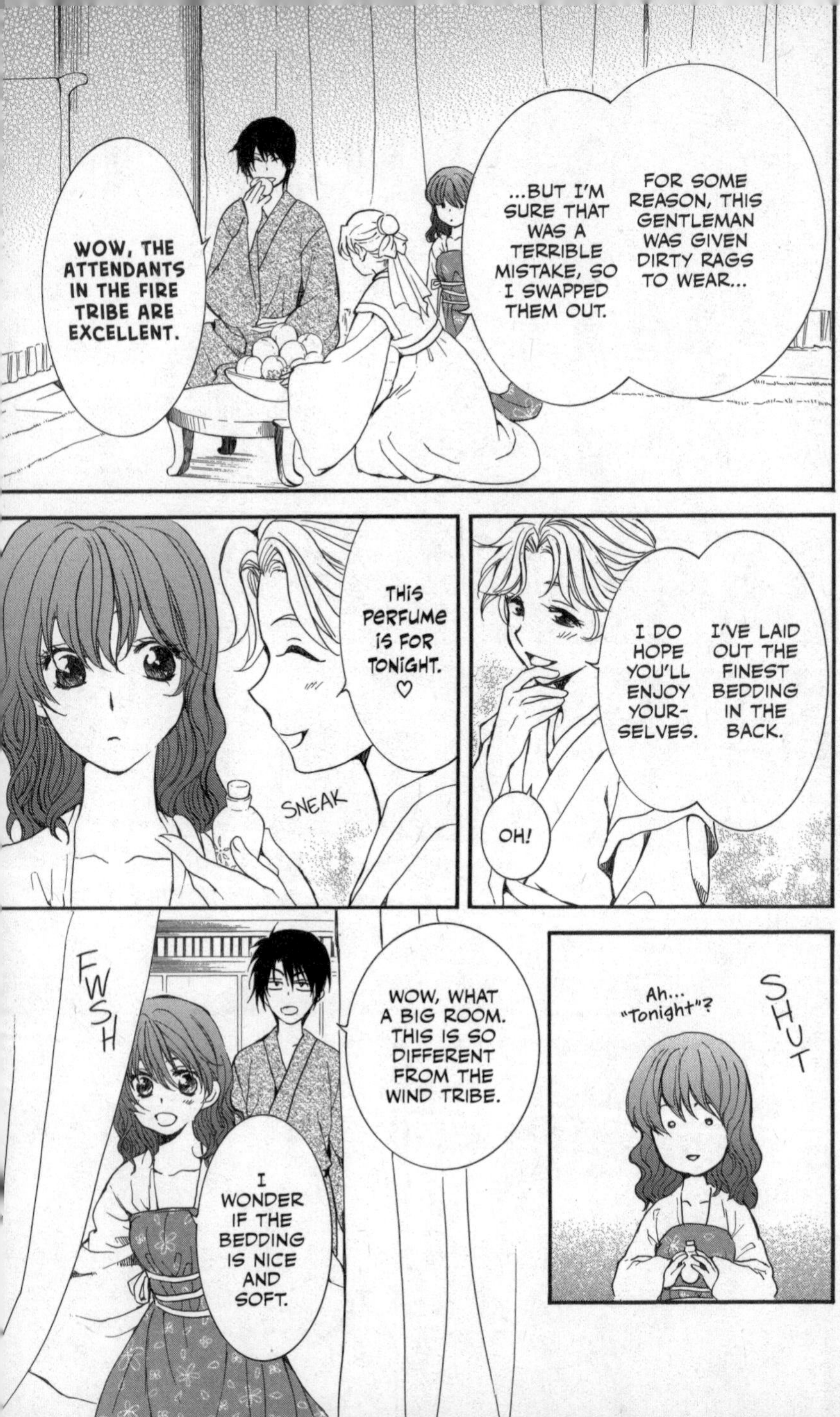

FOR SOME REASON, THIS GENTLEMAN WAS GIVEN DIRTY RAGS TO WEAR...
...BUT I'M SURE THAT WAS A TERRIBLE MISTAKE, SO I SWAPPED THEM OUT.
WOW, THE ATTENDANTS IN THE FIRE TRIBE ARE EXCELLENT.
I'VE LAID OUT THE FINEST BEDDING IN THE BACK.
I DO HOPE YOU'LL ENJOY YOUR-SELVES.
OH!
THIS PERFUME IS FOR TONIGHT. ♡
SNEAK
SHUT
Ah... "Tonight"?
FWSH
WOW, WHAT A BIG ROOM. THIS IS SO DIFFERENT FROM THE WIND TRIBE.
I WONDER IF THE BEDDING IS NICE AND SOFT.

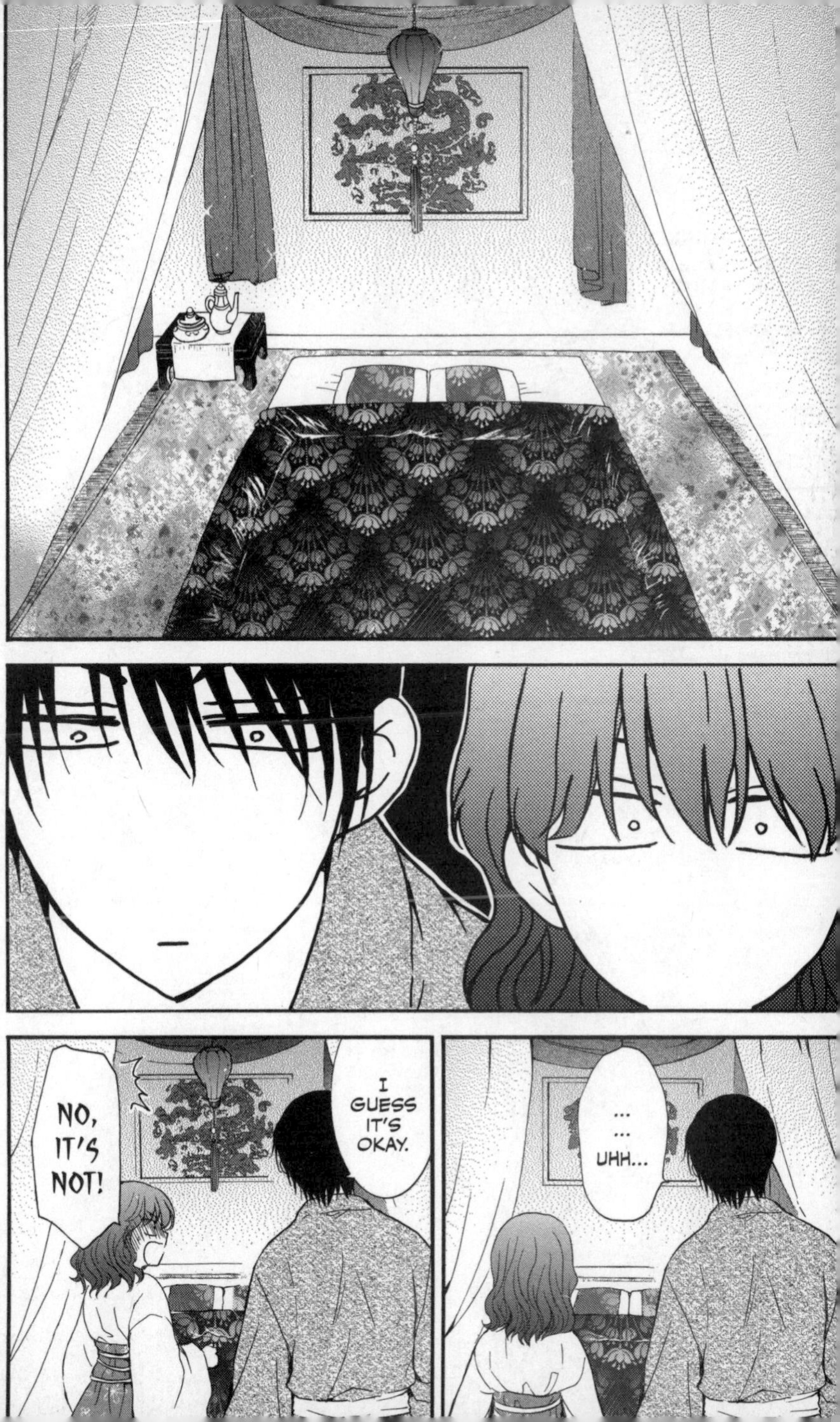
... ... UHH...
I GUESS IT'S OKAY.
NO, IT'S NOT!

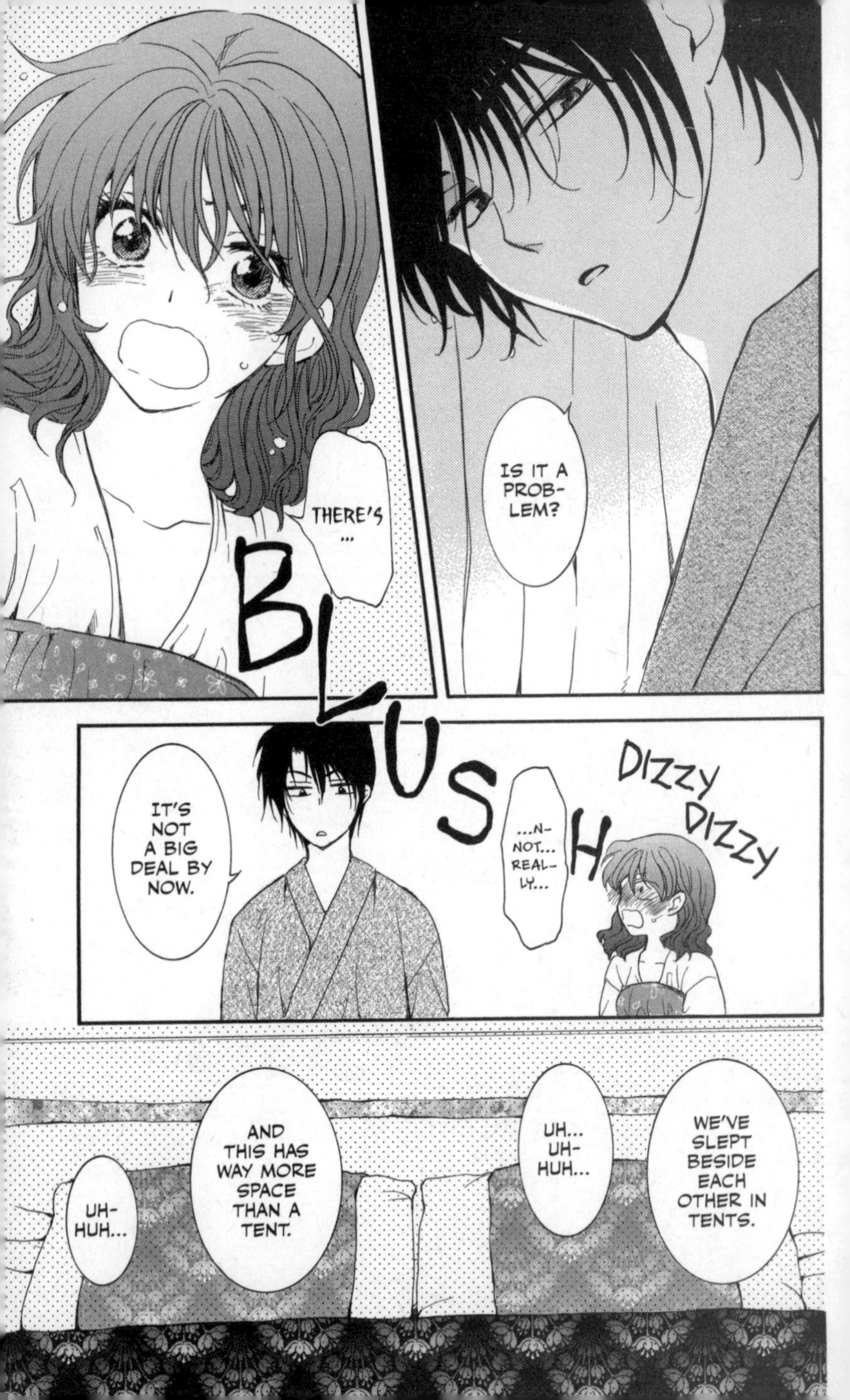
IS IT A PROBLEM?
THERE'S...
BLUSH
DIZZY DIZZY
...N-NOT... REALLY...
IT'S NOT A BIG DEAL BY NOW.
WE'VE SLEPT BESIDE EACH OTHER IN TENTS.
UH... UH-HUH...
AND THIS HAS WAY MORE SPACE THAN A TENT.
UH-HUH...

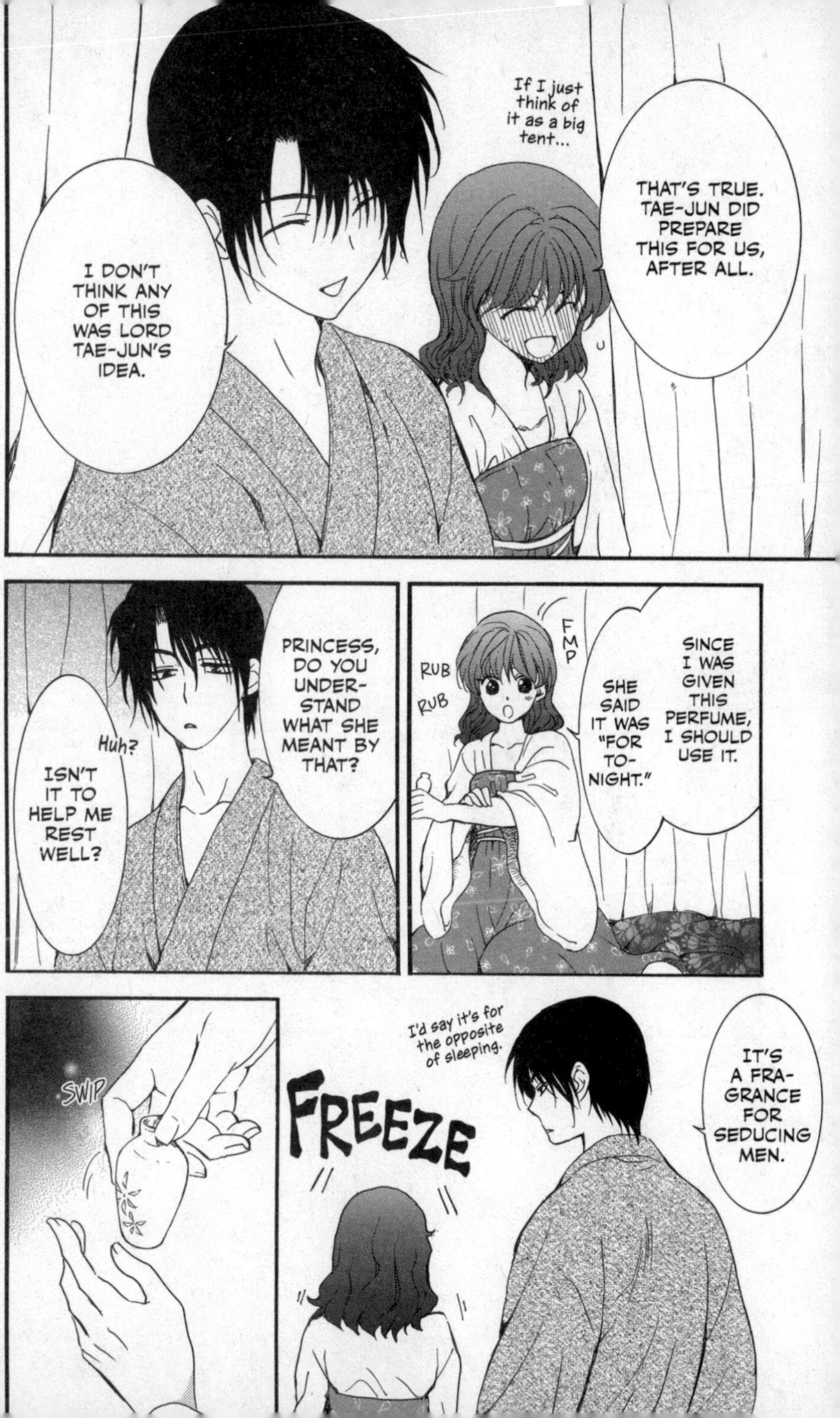
If I just think of it as a big tent...
THAT'S TRUE. TAE-JUN DID PREPARE THIS FOR US, AFTER ALL.
I DON'T THINK ANY OF THIS WAS LORD TAE-JUN'S IDEA.
FMP
SINCE I WAS GIVEN THIS PERFUME, I SHOULD USE IT.
SHE SAID IT WAS "FOR TO-NIGHT."
RUB
RUB
PRINCESS, DO YOU UNDER-STAND WHAT SHE MEANT BY THAT?
Huh?
ISN'T IT TO HELP ME REST WELL?
IT'S A FRA-GRANCE FOR SEDUCING MEN.
I'd say it's for the opposite of sleeping.
FREEZE
SWIP

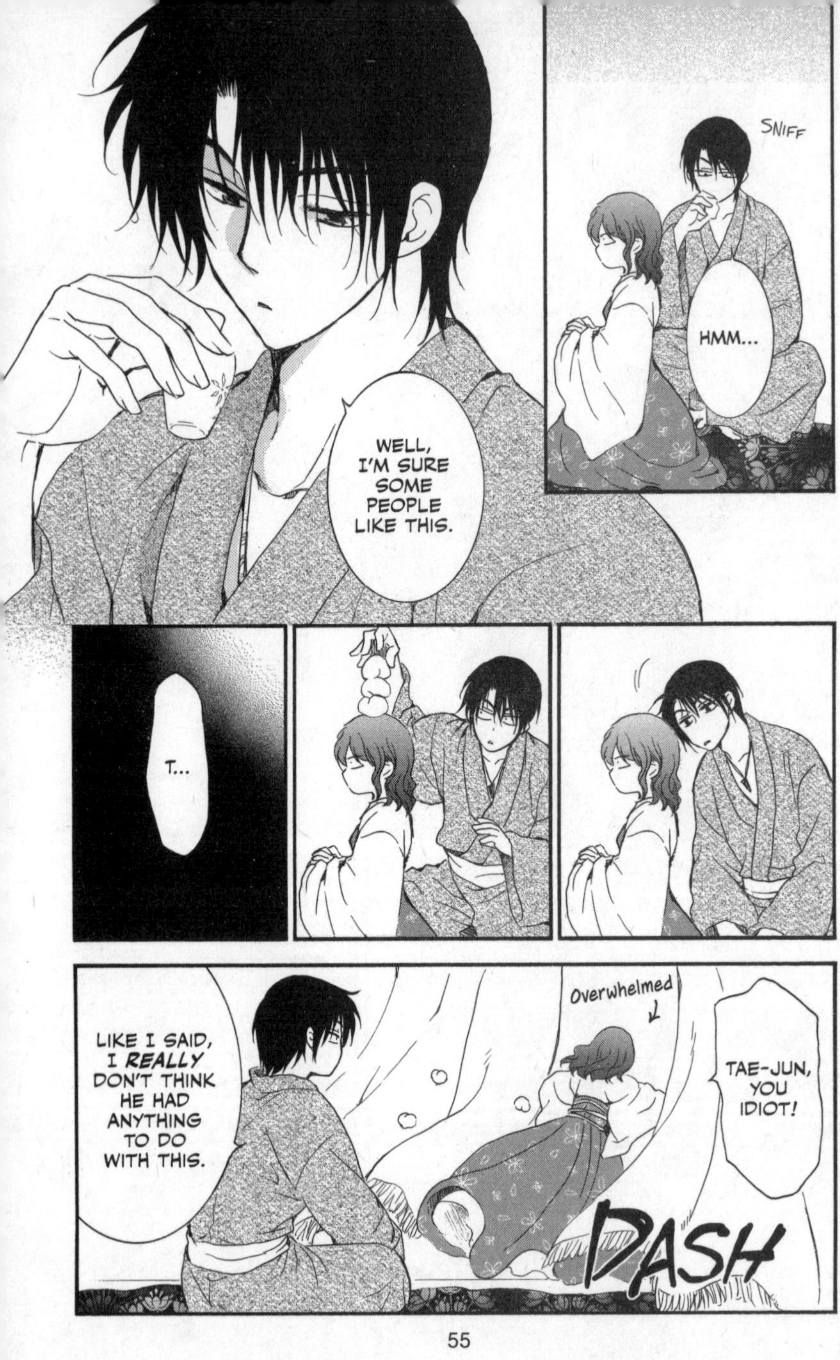
SNIFF
HMM...
WELL, I'M SURE SOME PEOPLE LIKE THIS.
T...
TAE-JUN, YOU IDIOT!
Overwhelmed
DASH
LIKE I SAID, I *REALLY* DON'T THINK HE HAD ANYTHING TO DO WITH THIS.

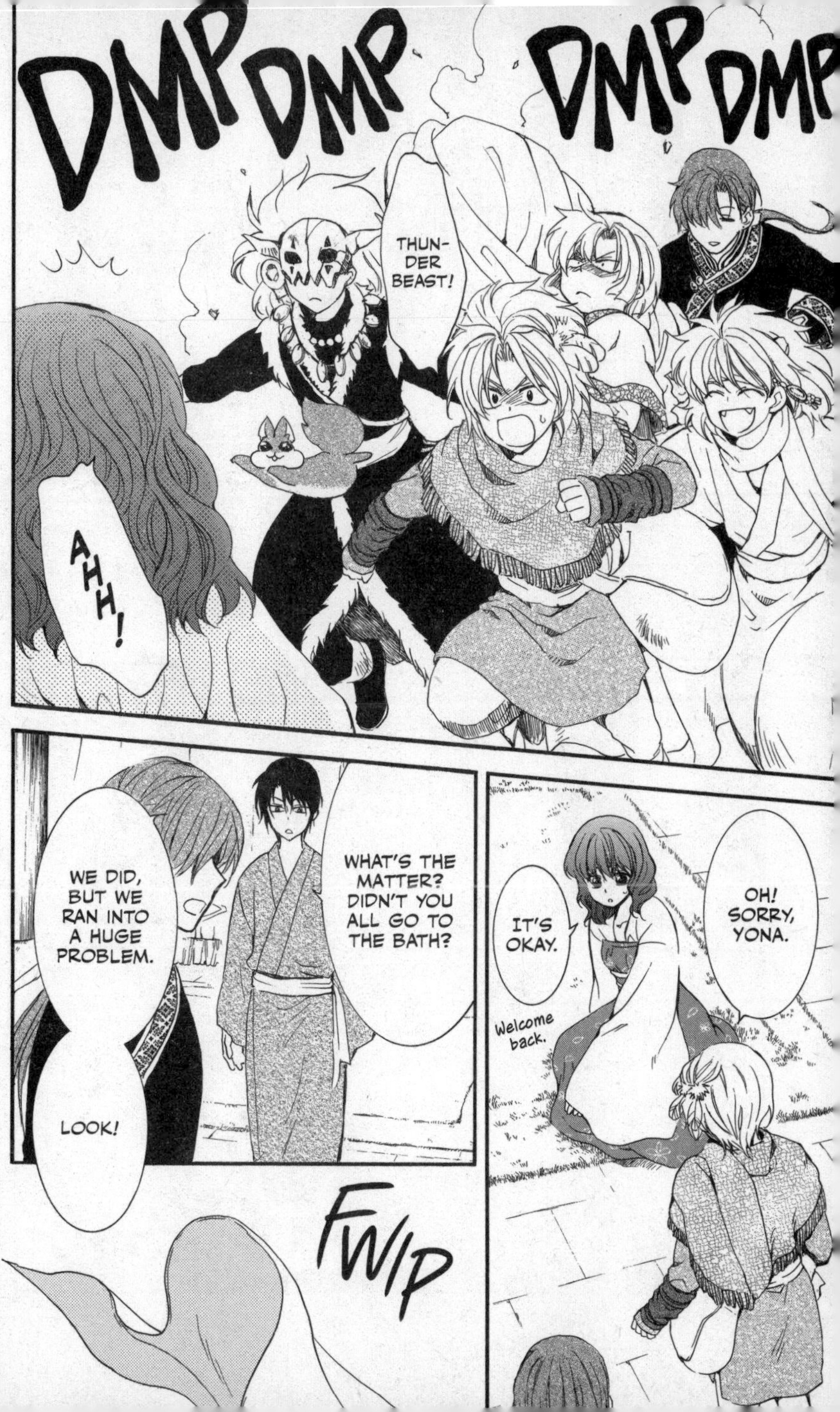
DMP DMP
DMP DMP
THUN-DER BEAST!
AHH!
OH! SORRY, YONA.
IT'S OKAY.
Welcome back.
WHAT'S THE MATTER? DIDN'T YOU ALL GO TO THE BATH?
WE DID, BUT WE RAN INTO A HUGE PROBLEM.
LOOK!
FWIP

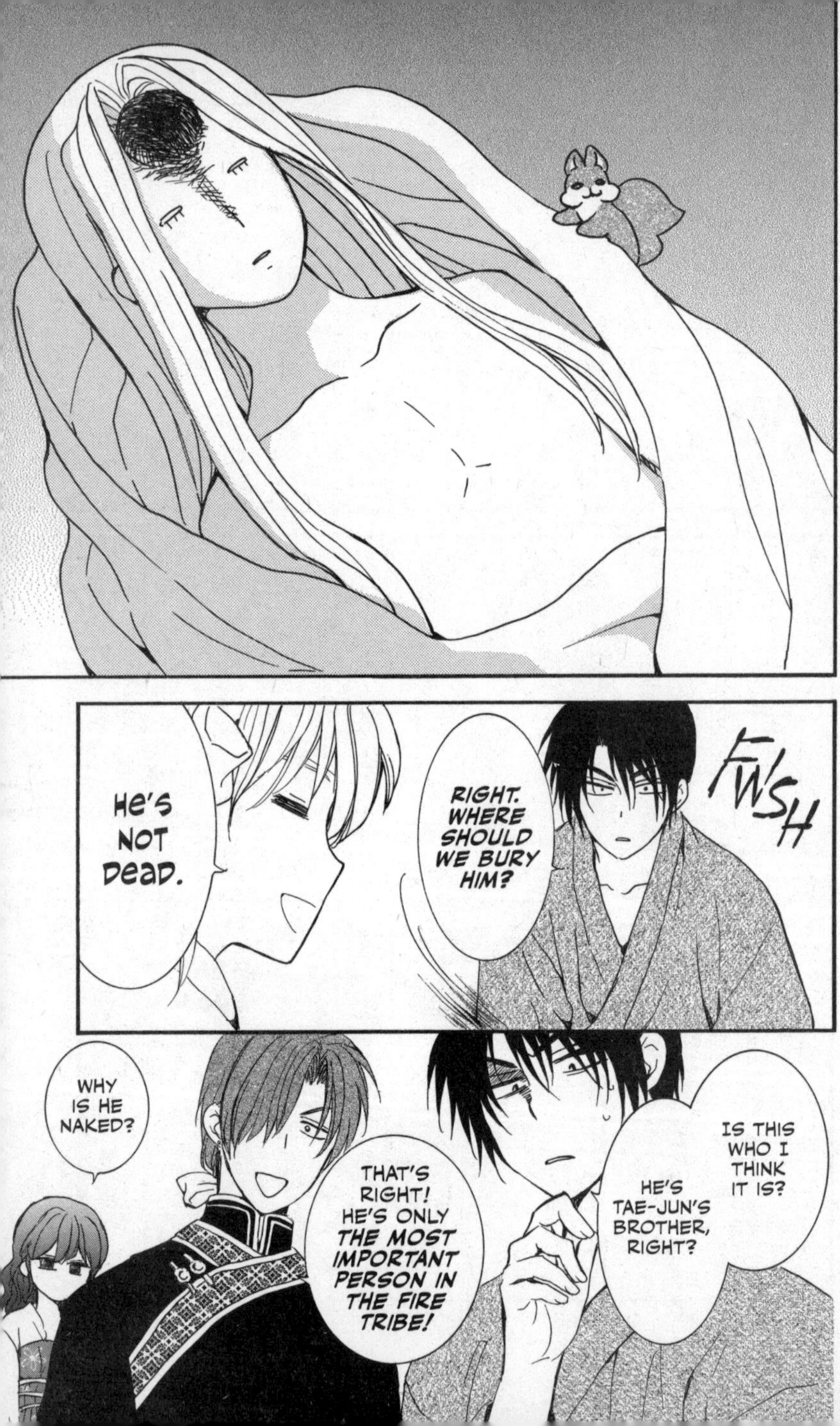
FWSH
RIGHT. WHERE SHOULD WE BURY HIM?
HE'S NOT DEAD.
IS THIS WHO I THINK IT IS?
HE'S TAE-JUN'S BROTHER, RIGHT?
THAT'S RIGHT! HE'S ONLY *THE MOST IMPORTANT PERSON IN THE FIRE TRIBE!*
WHY IS HE NAKED?

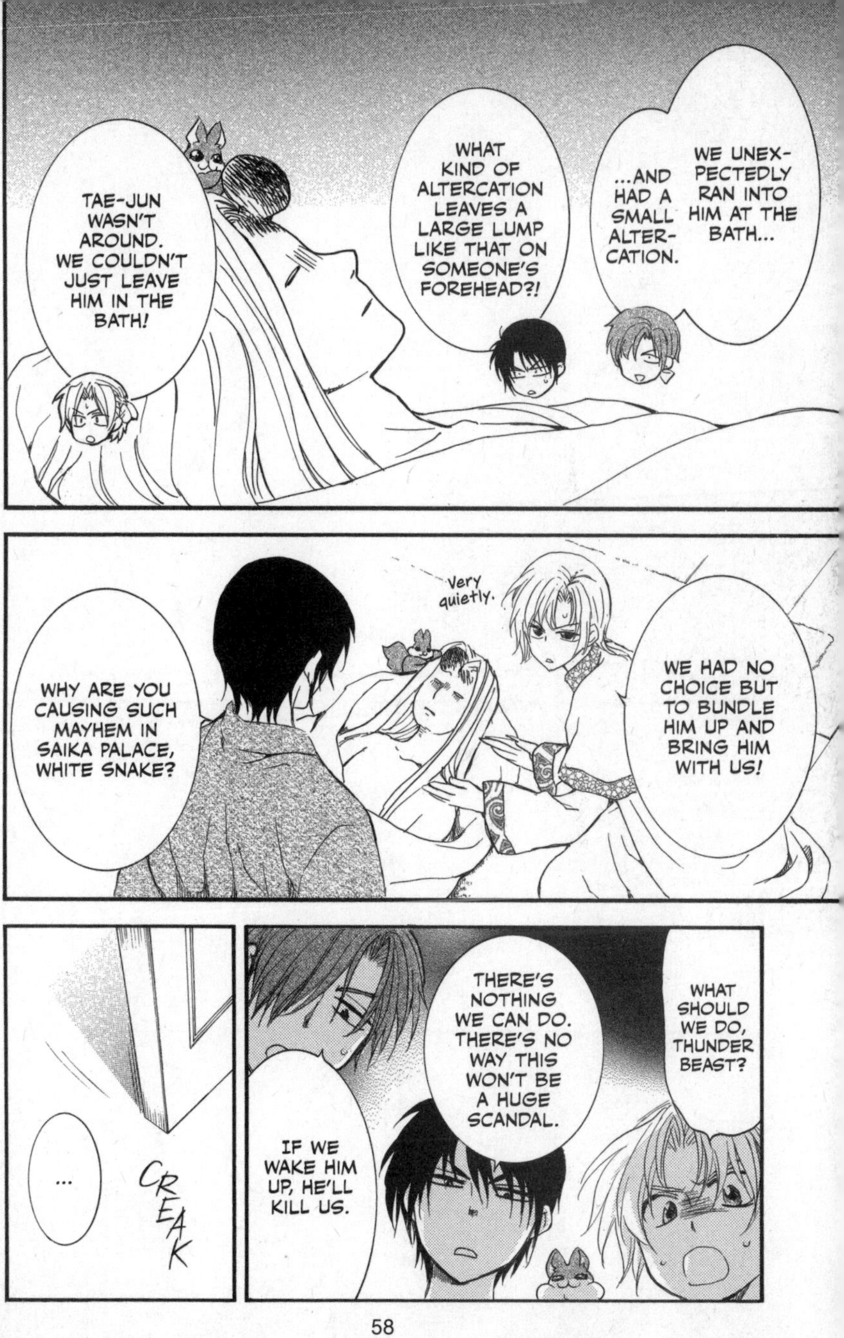
WE UNEXPECTEDLY RAN INTO HIM AT THE BATH...
...AND HAD A SMALL ALTERCATION.
WHAT KIND OF ALTERCATION LEAVES A LARGE LUMP LIKE THAT ON SOMEONE'S FOREHEAD?!
TAE-JUN WASN'T AROUND. WE COULDN'T JUST LEAVE HIM IN THE BATH!
WE HAD NO CHOICE BUT TO BUNDLE HIM UP AND BRING HIM WITH US!
Very quietly.
WHY ARE YOU CAUSING SUCH MAYHEM IN SAIKA PALACE, WHITE SNAKE?
WHAT SHOULD WE DO, THUNDER BEAST?
THERE'S NOTHING WE CAN DO. THERE'S NO WAY THIS WON'T BE A HUGE SCANDAL.
IF WE WAKE HIM UP, HE'LL KILL US.
...
CREAK

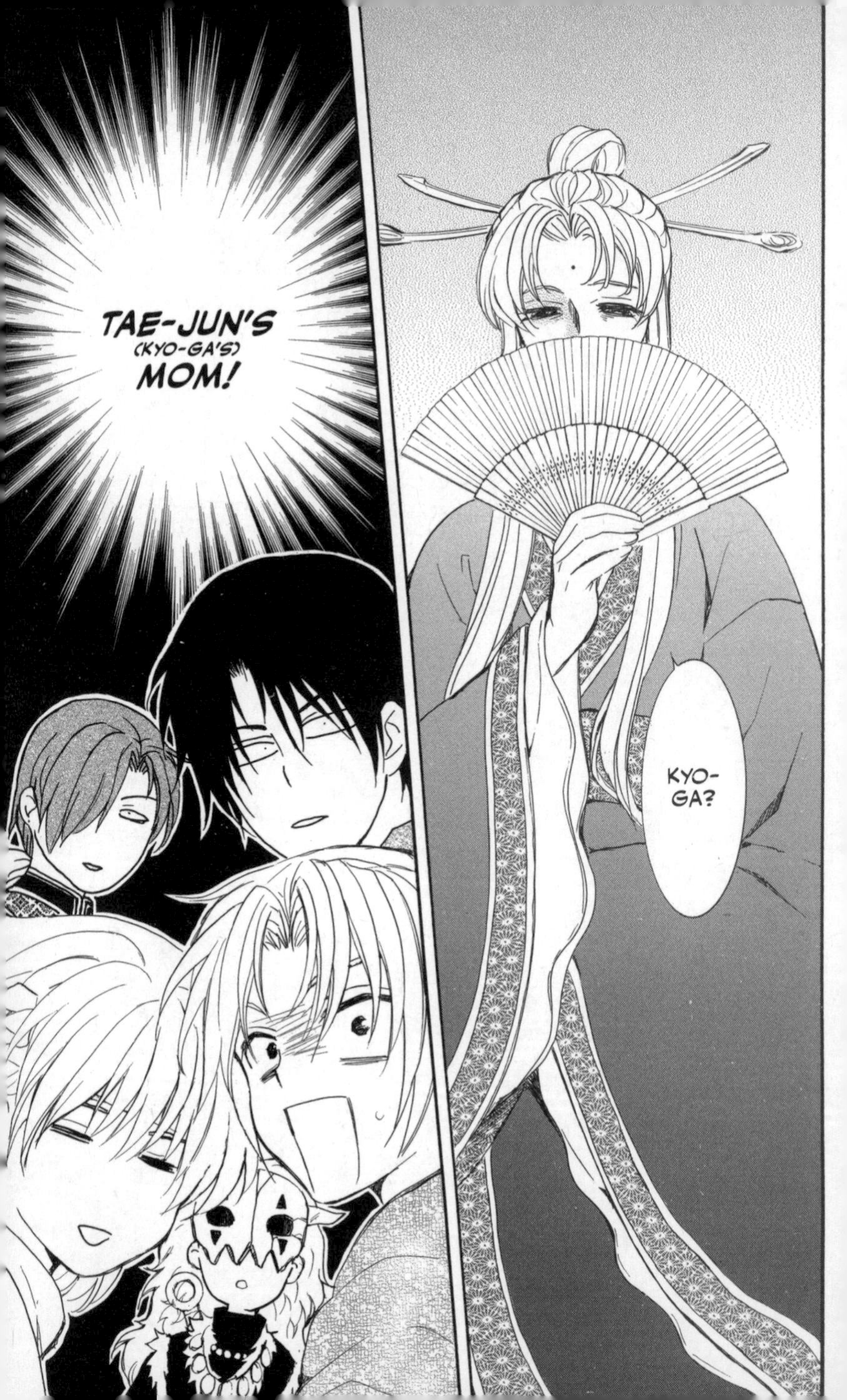
KYO-GA?
TAE-JUN'S (KYO-GA'S) MOM!

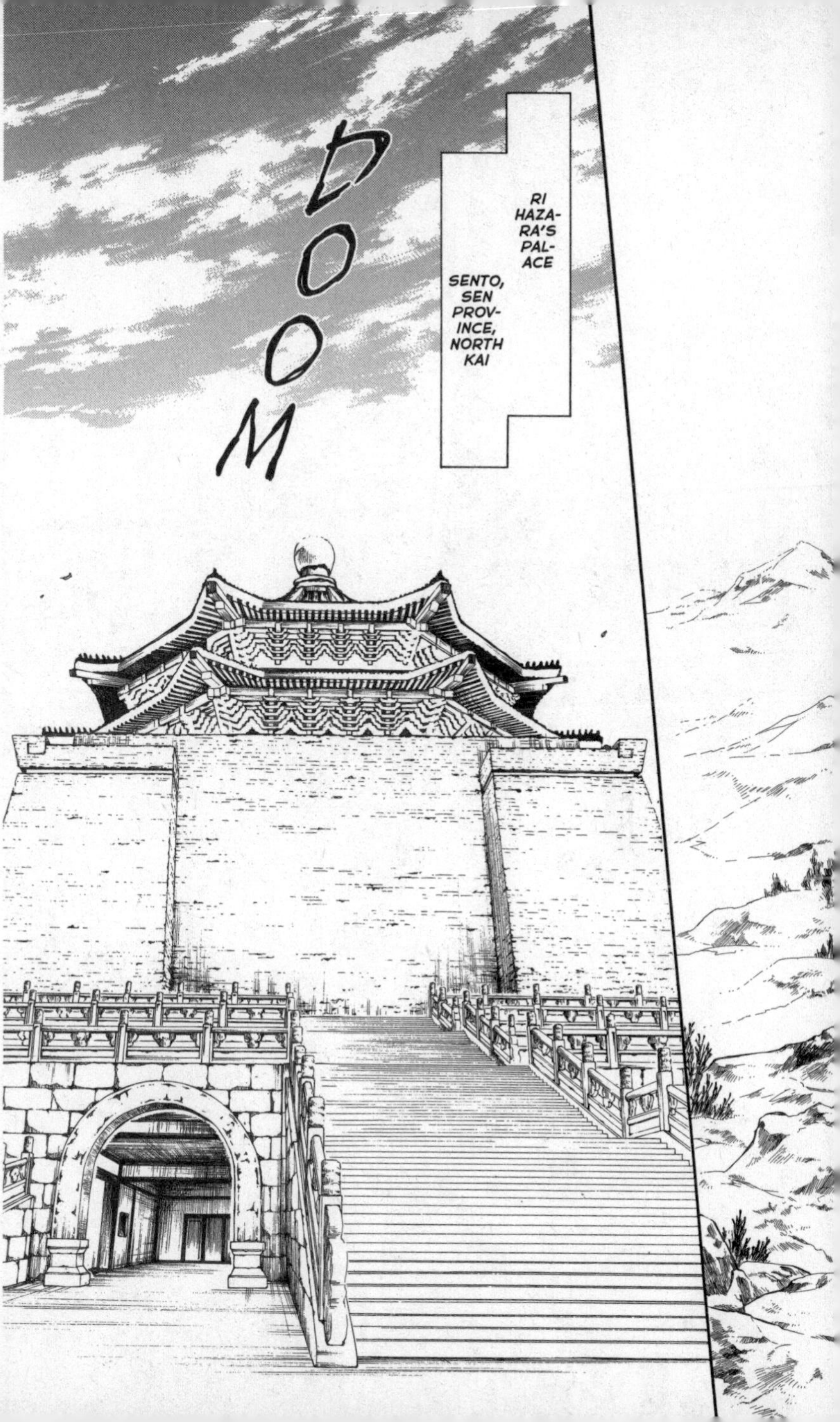
RI HAZARA'S PALACE
SENTO, SEN PROVINCE, NORTH KAI
DOOM

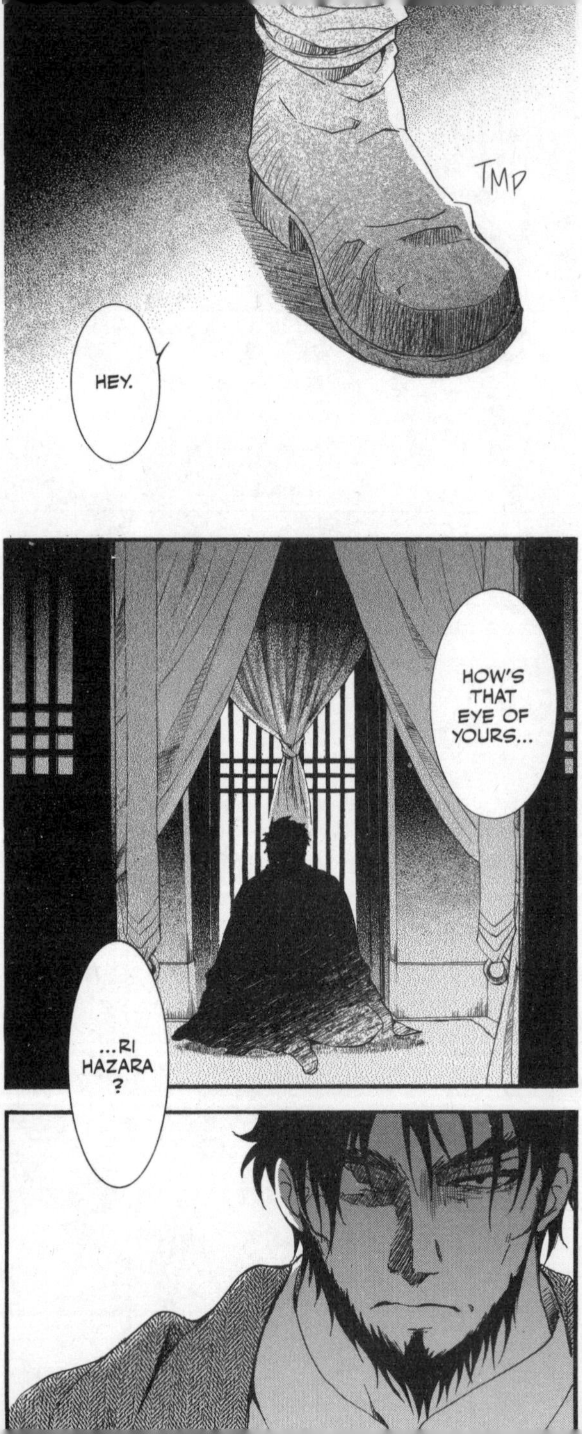
TMP
HEY.
HOW'S THAT EYE OF YOURS...
...RI HAZARA?

I've gathered questions from my readers for the fan book. Thank you for asking so many! Some of the more common ones were "Who was Ju-do's first love?", "Is Ju-do married?", "Who is Ju-do's partner?", etc. I thought only my editor (who pushes for old-men characters) was interested in such things!

Ju-do isn't the only one who's single. (*Ha ha.*) Ogi is also getting on in years. Perhaps it's a difference in popularity.

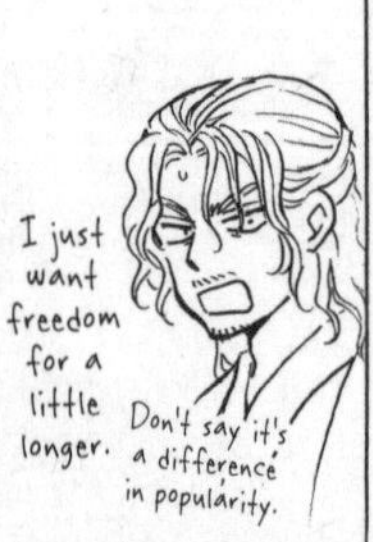
I just want freedom for a little longer.
Don't say it's a difference in popularity.

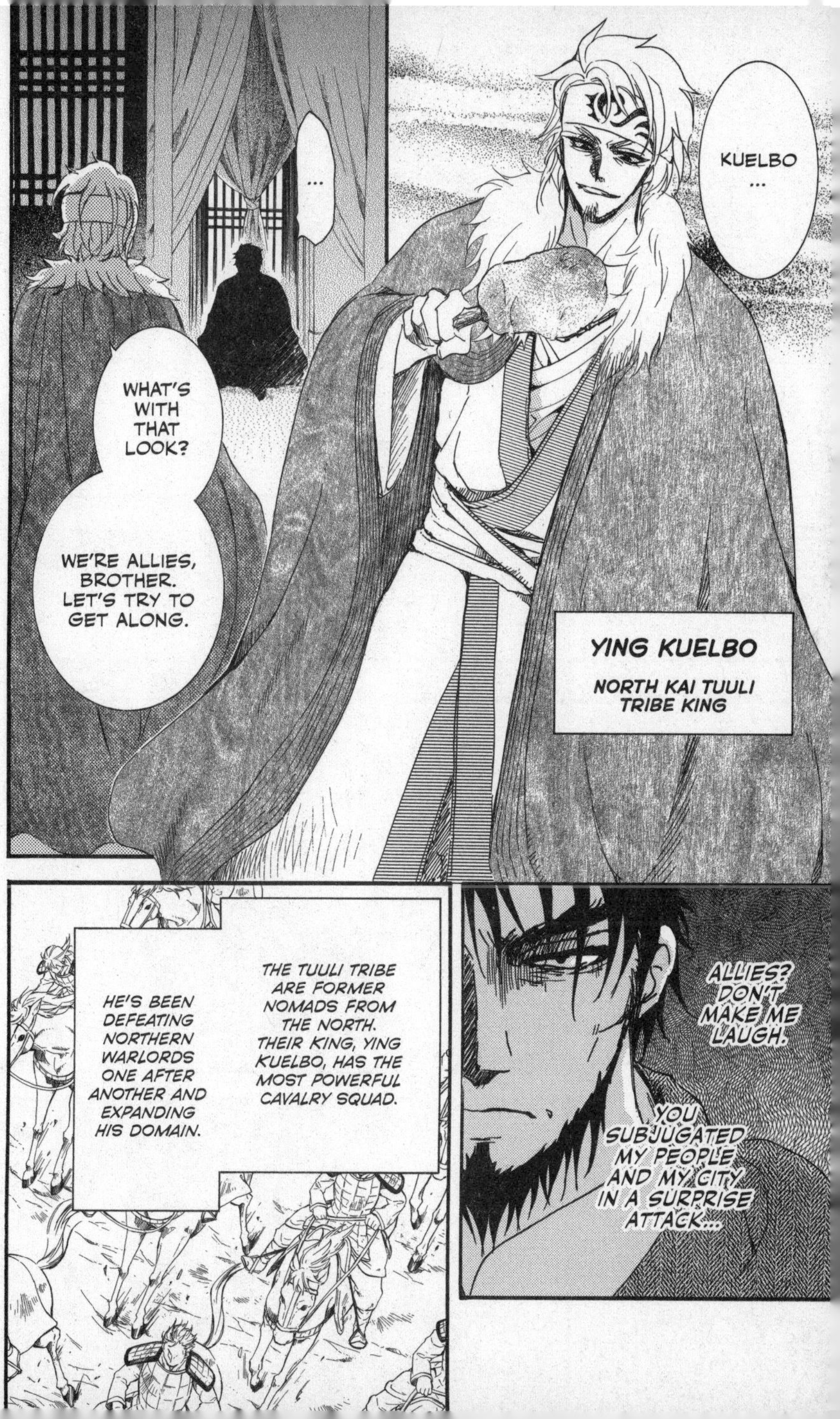
KUELBO ...
...
WHAT'S WITH THAT LOOK?
WE'RE ALLIES, BROTHER. LET'S TRY TO GET ALONG.
YING KUELBO
NORTH KAI TUULI TRIBE KING
ALLIES? DON'T MAKE ME LAUGH.
YOU SUBJUGATED MY PEOPLE AND MY CITY IN A SURPRISE ATTACK...
THE TUULI TRIBE ARE FORMER NOMADS FROM THE NORTH. THEIR KING, YING KUELBO, HAS THE MOST POWERFUL CAVALRY SQUAD.
HE'S BEEN DEFEATING NORTHERN WARLORDS ONE AFTER ANOTHER AND EXPANDING HIS DOMAIN.

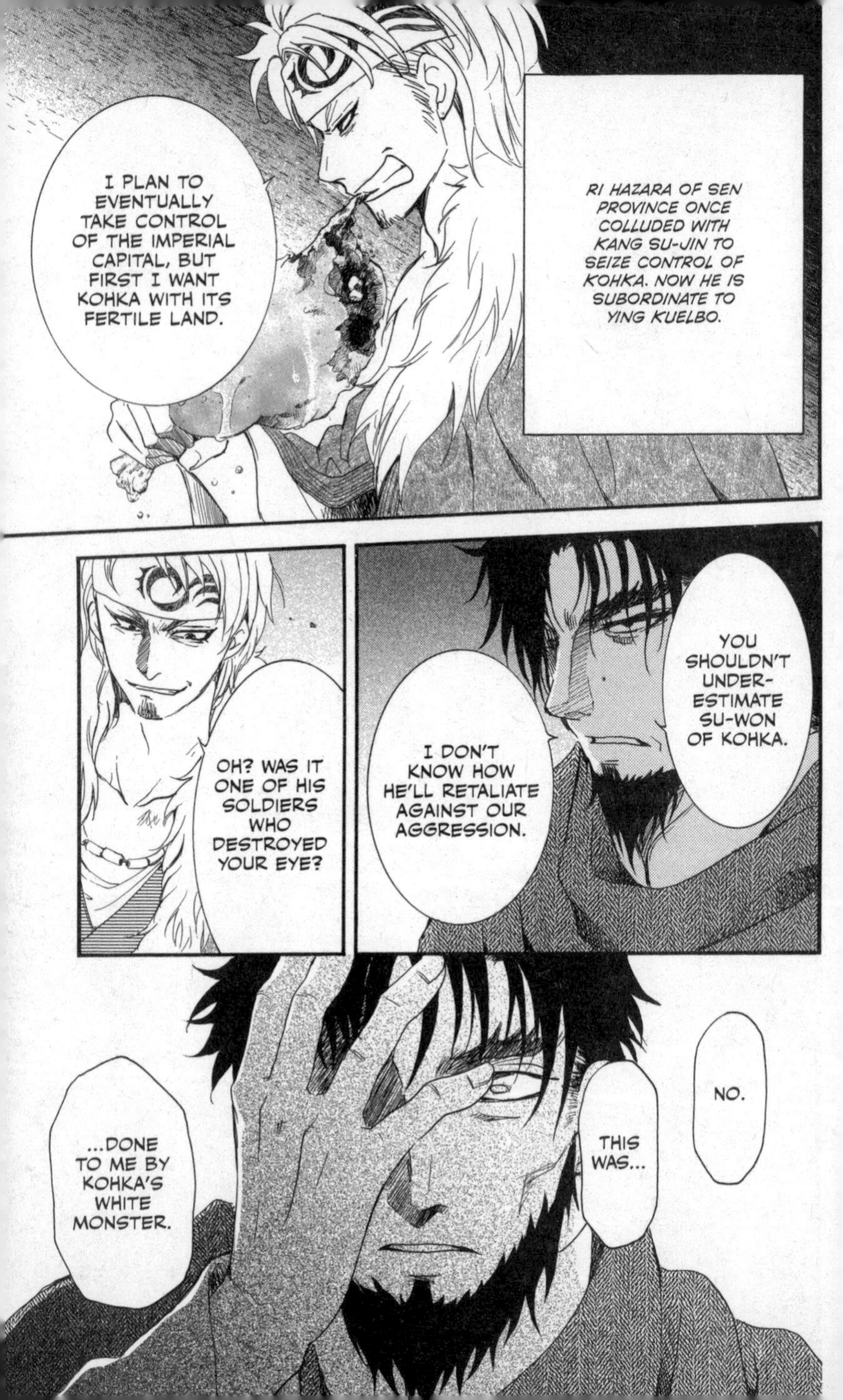
RI HAZARA OF SEN PROVINCE ONCE COLLUDED WITH KANG SU-JIN TO SEIZE CONTROL OF KOHKA. NOW HE IS SUBORDINATE TO YING KUELBO.
I PLAN TO EVENTUALLY TAKE CONTROL OF THE IMPERIAL CAPITAL, BUT FIRST I WANT KOHKA WITH ITS FERTILE LAND.
YOU SHOULDN'T UNDER-ESTIMATE SU-WON OF KOHKA.
I DON'T KNOW HOW HE'LL RETALIATE AGAINST OUR AGGRESSION.
OH? WAS IT ONE OF HIS SOLDIERS WHO DESTROYED YOUR EYE?
NO.
THIS WAS...
...DONE TO ME BY KOHKA'S WHITE MONSTER.

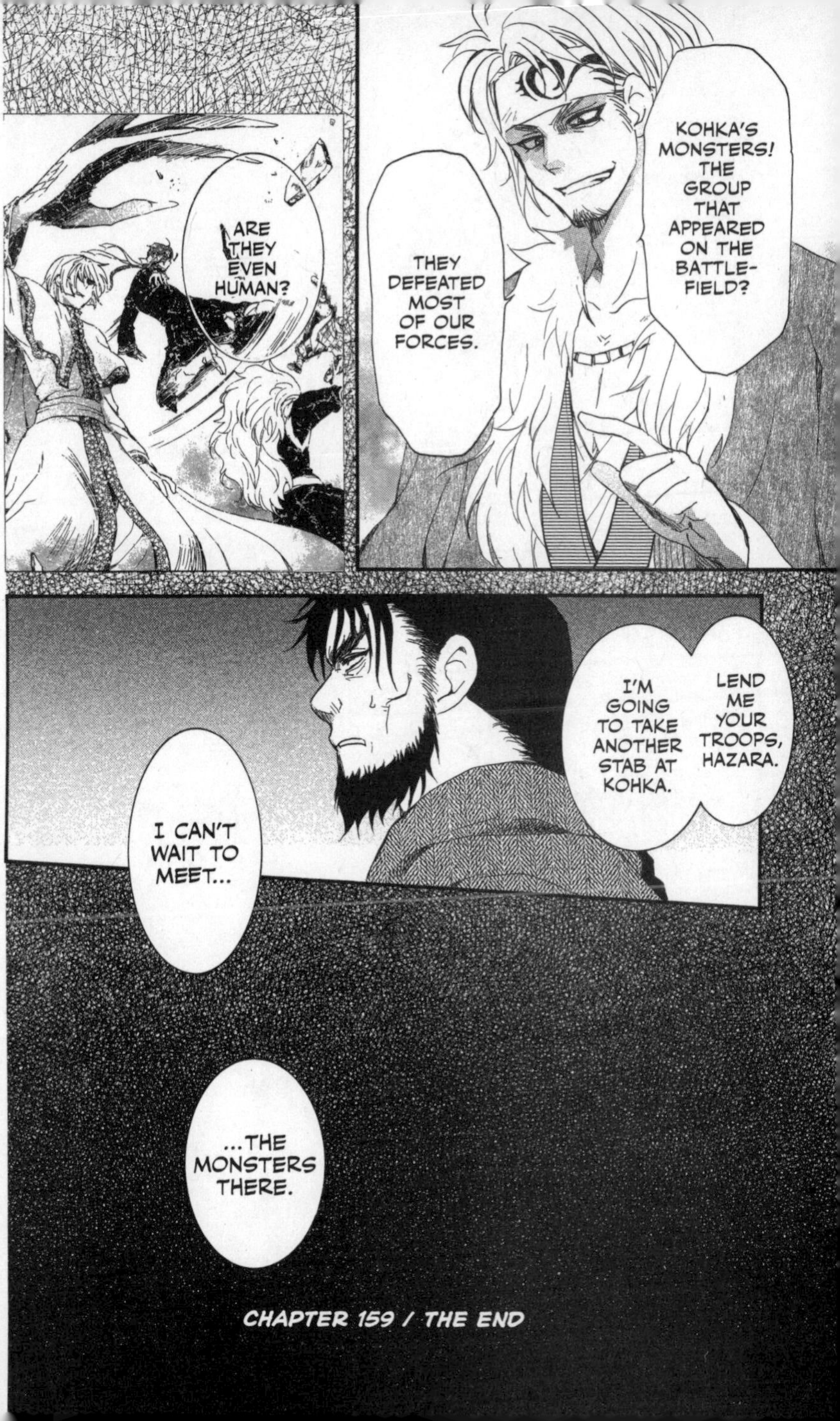
KOHKA'S MONSTERS! THE GROUP THAT APPEARED ON THE BATTLE-FIELD?
THEY DEFEATED MOST OF OUR FORCES.
ARE THEY EVEN HUMAN?
LEND ME YOUR TROOPS, HAZARA.
I'M GOING TO TAKE ANOTHER STAB AT KOHKA.
I CAN'T WAIT TO MEET...
...THE MONSTERS THERE.
CHAPTER 159 / THE END

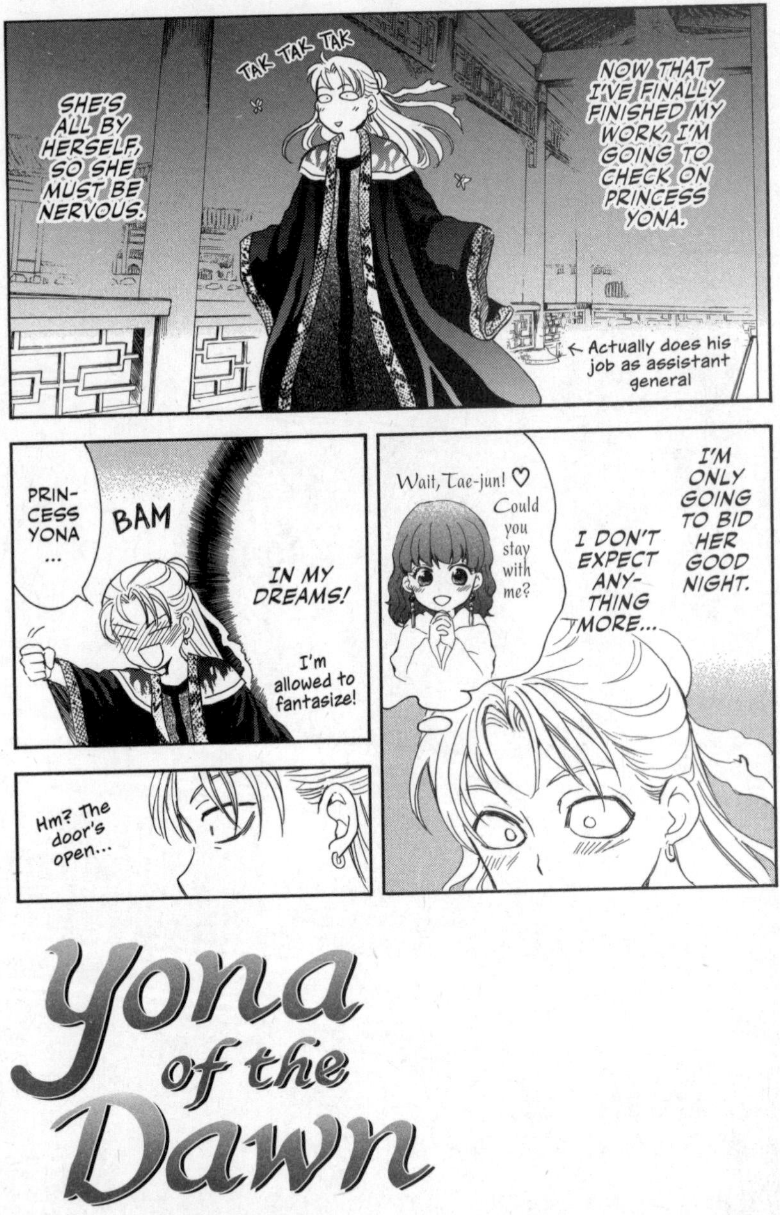
NOW THAT I'VE FINALLY FINISHED MY WORK, I'M GOING TO CHECK ON PRINCESS YONA.
TAK TAK TAK
SHE'S ALL BY HERSELF, SO SHE MUST BE NERVOUS.
← Actually does his job as assistant general
I'M ONLY GOING TO BID HER GOOD NIGHT.
I DON'T EXPECT ANYTHING MORE...
Wait, Tae-jun! ♡ Could you stay with me?
PRINCESS YONA...
BAM
IN MY DREAMS!
I'm allowed to fantasize!
Hm? The door's open...

Yona of the Dawn

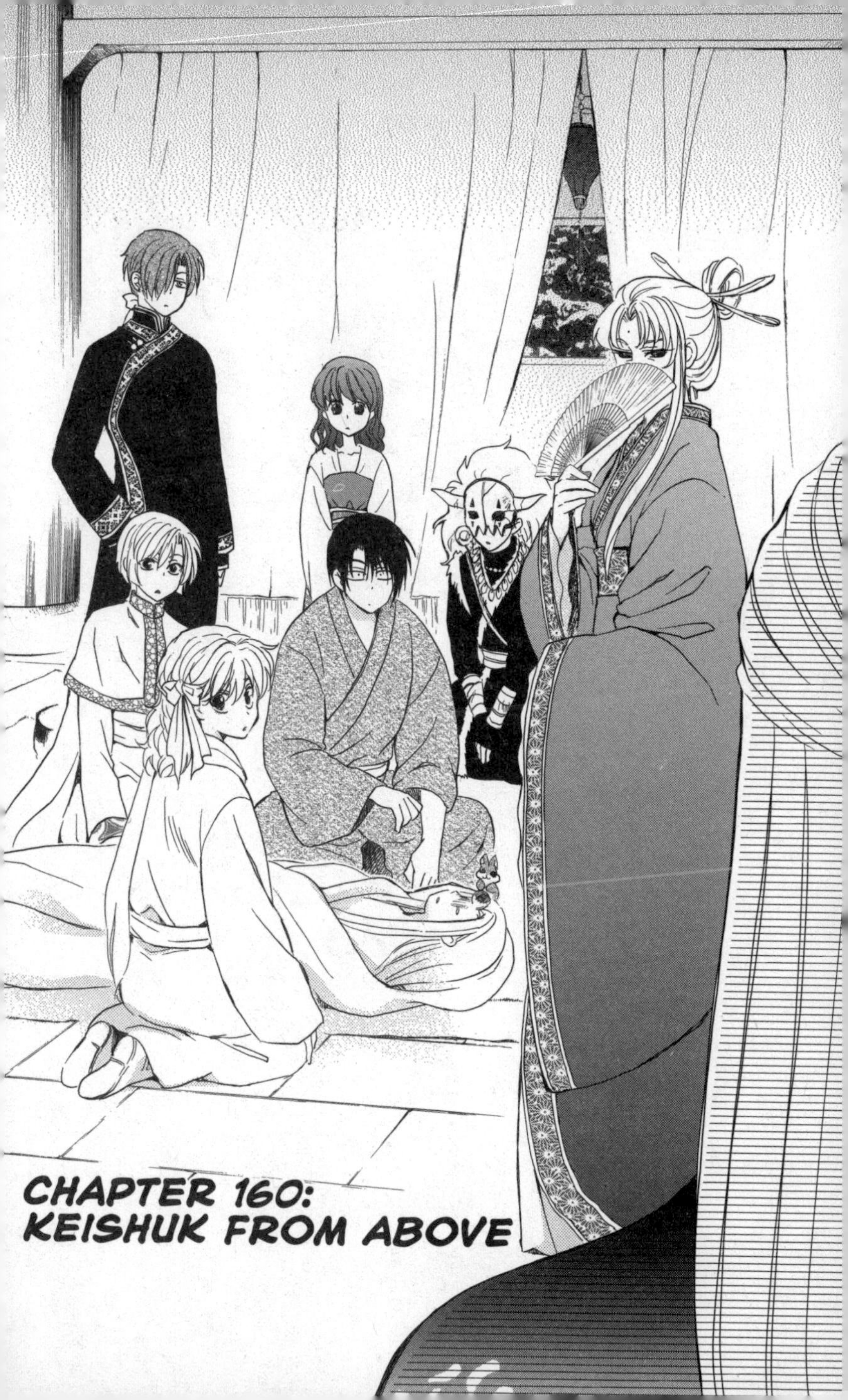

CHAPTER 160: KEISHUK FROM ABOVE

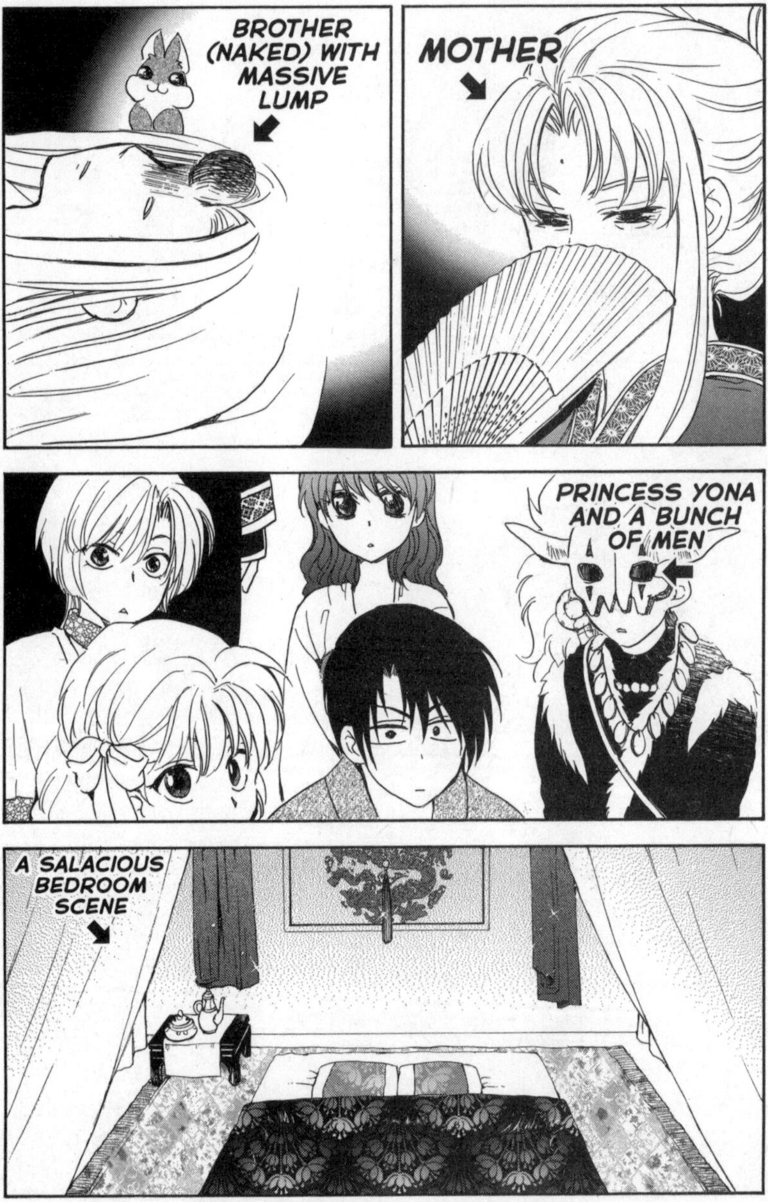
MOTHER
BROTHER (NAKED) WITH MASSIVE LUMP
PRINCESS YONA AND A BUNCH OF MEN
A SALACIOUS BEDROOM SCENE

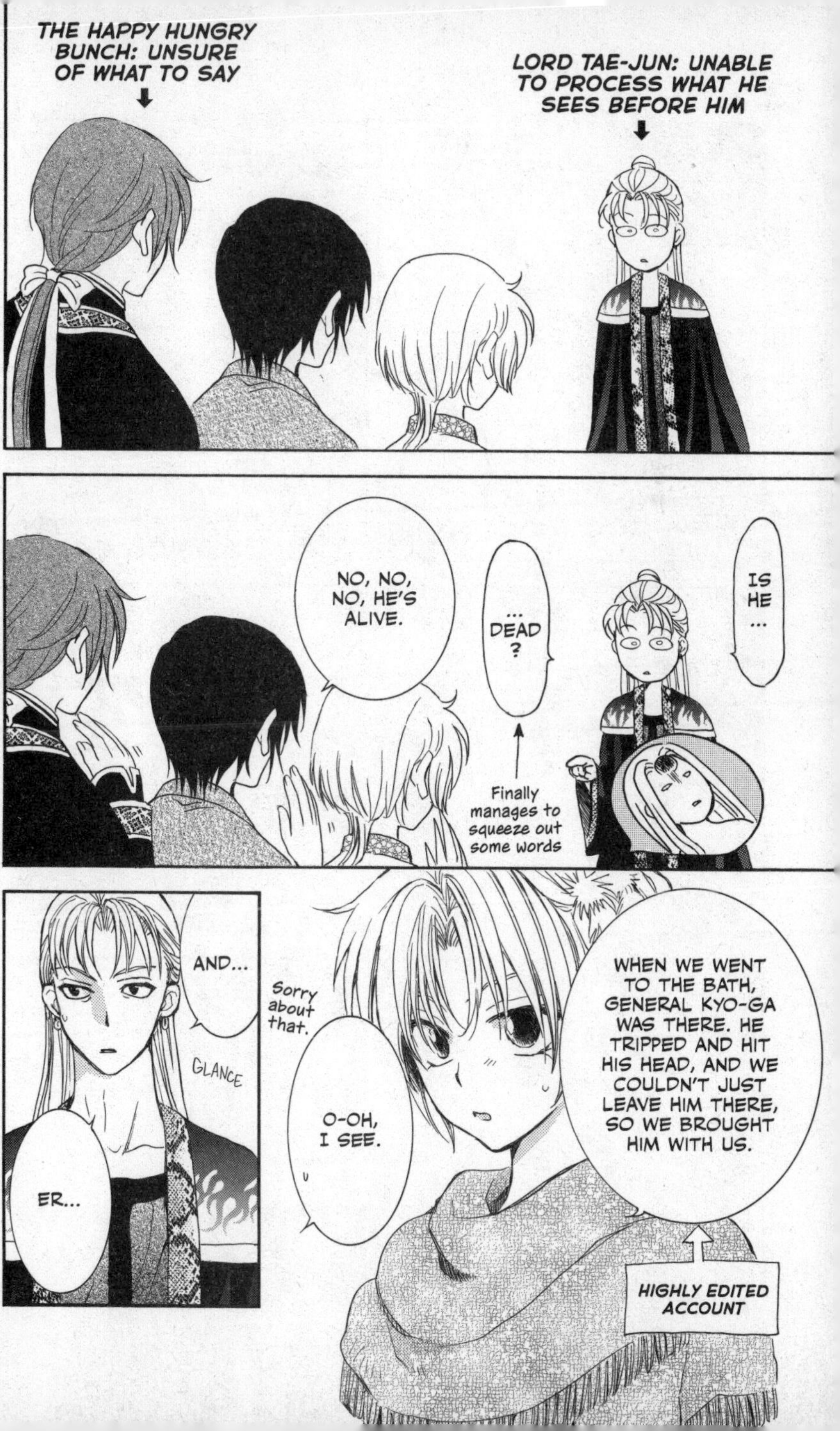
LORD TAE-JUN: UNABLE TO PROCESS WHAT HE SEES BEFORE HIM
THE HAPPY HUNGRY BUNCH: UNSURE OF WHAT TO SAY
IS HE ...
... DEAD ?
Finally manages to squeeze out some words
NO, NO, NO, HE'S ALIVE.
WHEN WE WENT TO THE BATH, GENERAL KYO-GA WAS THERE. HE TRIPPED AND HIT HIS HEAD, AND WE COULDN'T JUST LEAVE HIM THERE, SO WE BROUGHT HIM WITH US.
HIGHLY EDITED ACCOUNT
O-OH, I SEE.
Sorry about that.
AND...
GLANCE
ER...

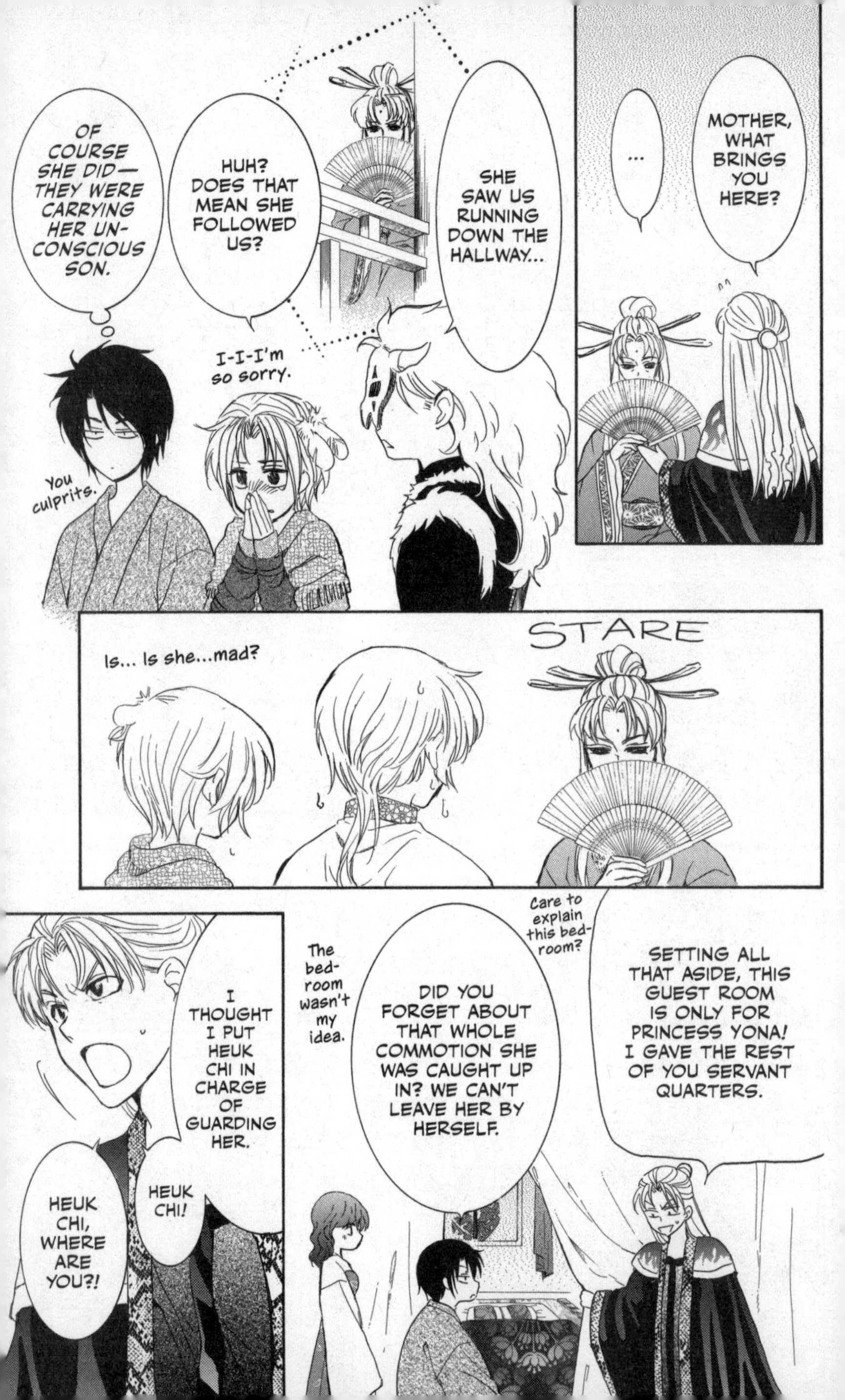
MOTHER, WHAT BRINGS YOU HERE?
...
SHE SAW US RUNNING DOWN THE HALLWAY...
HUH? DOES THAT MEAN SHE FOLLOWED US?
OF COURSE SHE DID— THEY WERE CARRYING HER UN-CONSCIOUS SON.
I-I-I'm so sorry.
You culprits.
STARE
Is... Is she...mad?
SETTING ALL THAT ASIDE, THIS GUEST ROOM IS ONLY FOR PRINCESS YONA! I GAVE THE REST OF YOU SERVANT QUARTERS.
Care to explain this bed-room?
DID YOU FORGET ABOUT THAT WHOLE COMMOTION SHE WAS CAUGHT UP IN? WE CAN'T LEAVE HER BY HERSELF.
The bed-room wasn't my idea.
I THOUGHT I PUT HEUK CHI IN CHARGE OF GUARDING HER.
HEUK CHI!
HEUK CHI, WHERE ARE YOU?!

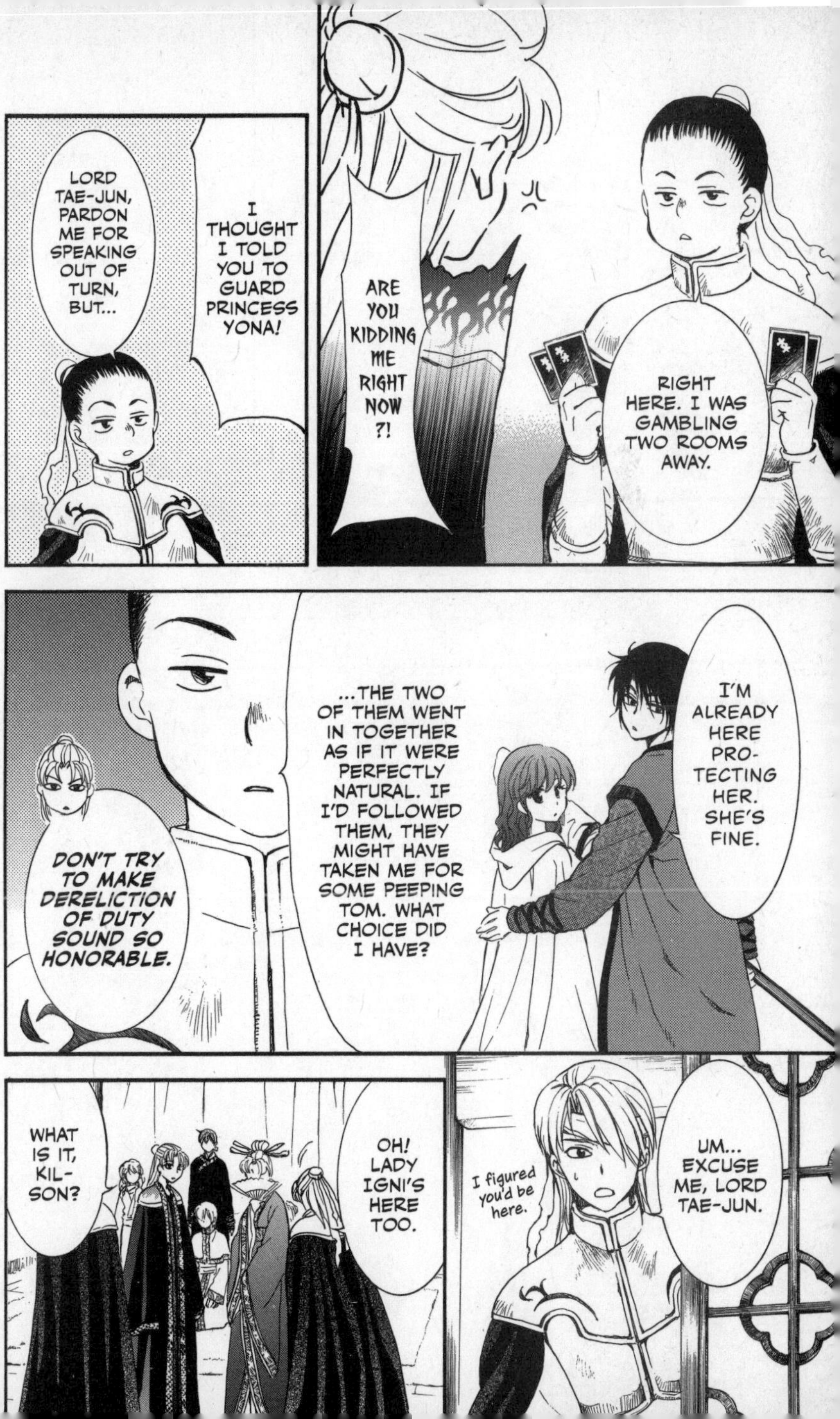
RIGHT HERE. I WAS GAMBLING TWO ROOMS AWAY.
ARE YOU KIDDING ME RIGHT NOW?!
I THOUGHT I TOLD YOU TO GUARD PRINCESS YONA!
LORD TAE-JUN, PARDON ME FOR SPEAKING OUT OF TURN, BUT...
I'M ALREADY HERE PROTECTING HER. SHE'S FINE.
...THE TWO OF THEM WENT IN TOGETHER AS IF IT WERE PERFECTLY NATURAL. IF I'D FOLLOWED THEM, THEY MIGHT HAVE TAKEN ME FOR SOME PEEPING TOM. WHAT CHOICE DID I HAVE?
DON'T TRY TO MAKE DERELICTION OF DUTY SOUND SO HONORABLE.
UM... EXCUSE ME, LORD TAE-JUN.
I figured you'd be here.
OH! LADY IGNI'S HERE TOO.
WHAT IS IT, KIL-SON?

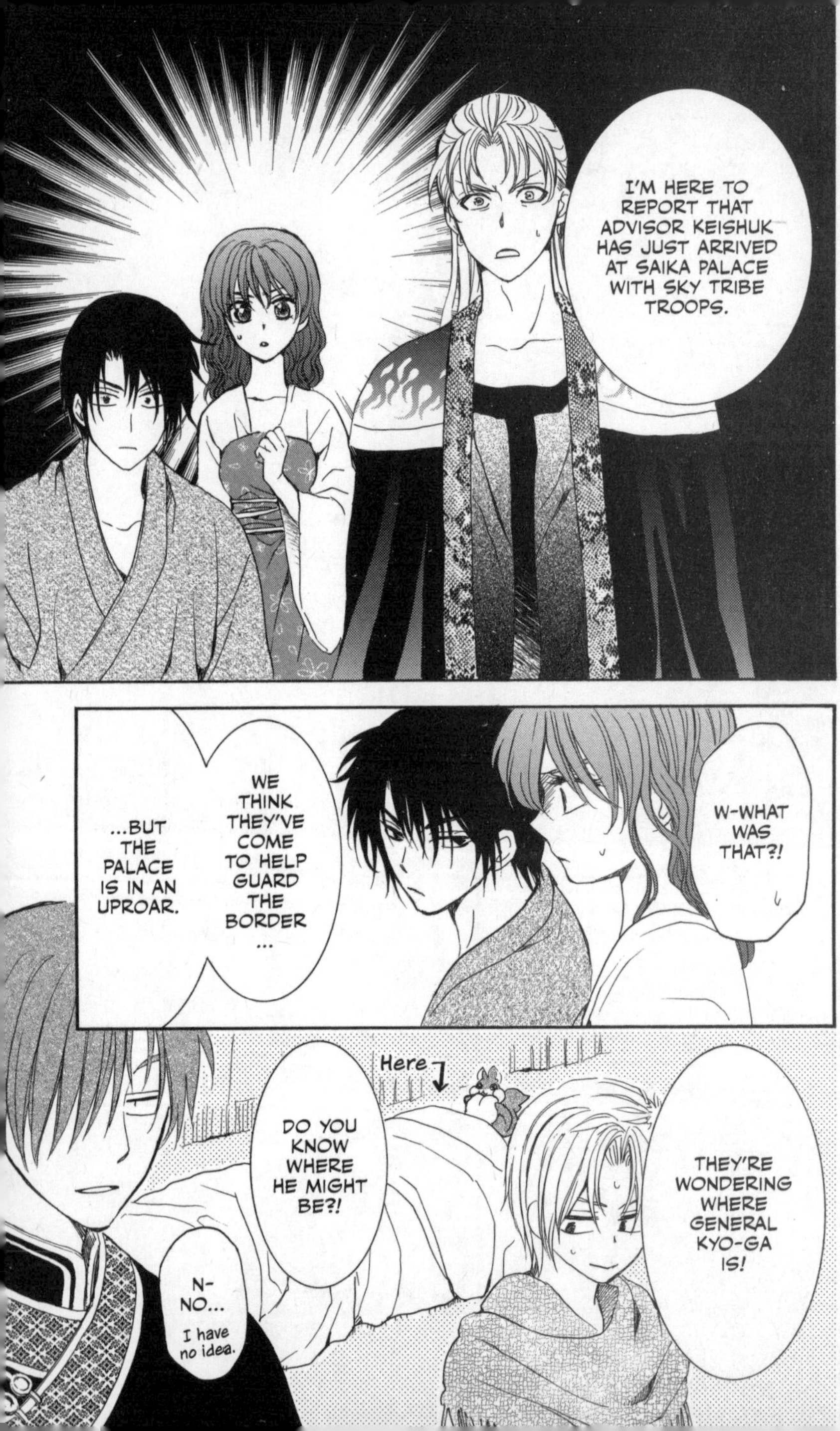
I'M HERE TO REPORT THAT ADVISOR KEISHUK HAS JUST ARRIVED AT SAIKA PALACE WITH SKY TRIBE TROOPS.
W-WHAT WAS THAT?!
WE THINK THEY'VE COME TO HELP GUARD THE BORDER...
...BUT THE PALACE IS IN AN UPROAR.
THEY'RE WONDERING WHERE GENERAL KYO-GA IS!
Here
DO YOU KNOW WHERE HE MIGHT BE?!
N-NO... I have no idea.

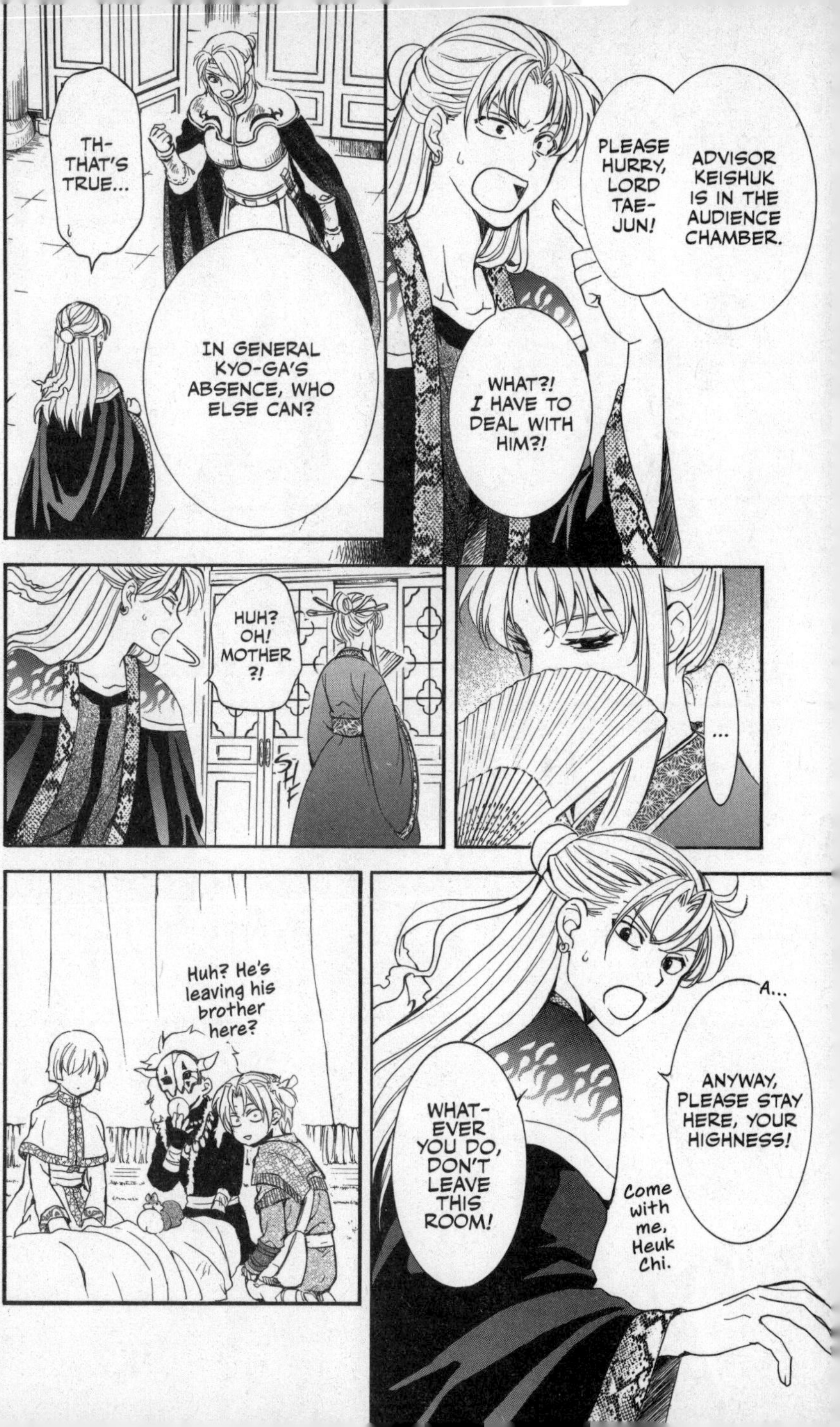
ADVISOR KEISHUK IS IN THE AUDIENCE CHAMBER.
PLEASE HURRY, LORD TAE-JUN!
WHAT?! I HAVE TO DEAL WITH HIM?!
IN GENERAL KYO-GA'S ABSENCE, WHO ELSE CAN?
TH-THAT'S TRUE...
...
HUH? OH! MOTHER?!
SHF
A...
ANYWAY, PLEASE STAY HERE, YOUR HIGHNESS!
Come with me, Heuk Chi.
WHATEVER YOU DO, DON'T LEAVE THIS ROOM!
Huh? He's leaving his brother here?

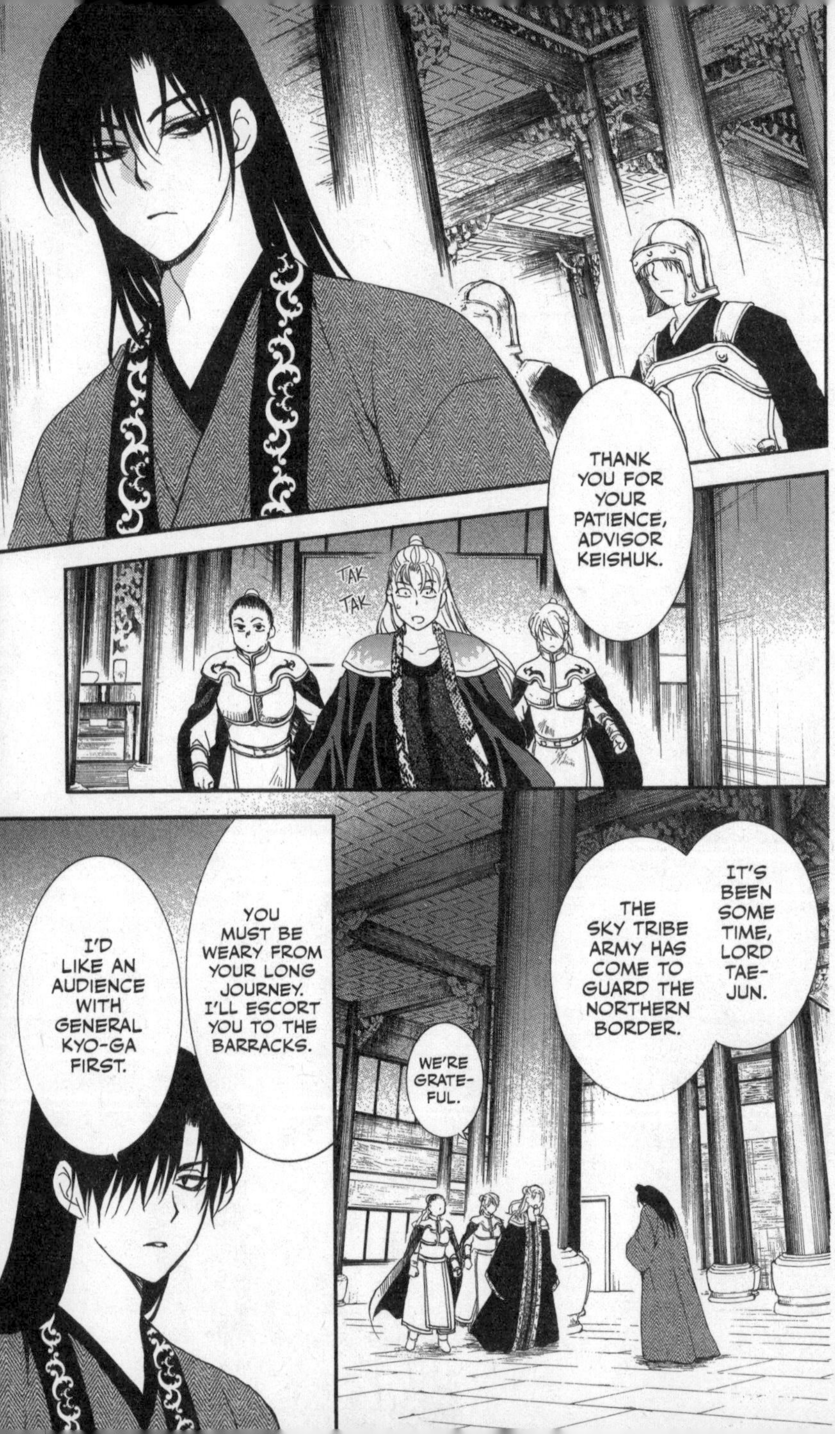
THANK YOU FOR YOUR PATIENCE, ADVISOR KEISHUK.
TAK TAK
IT'S BEEN SOME TIME, LORD TAE-JUN.
THE SKY TRIBE ARMY HAS COME TO GUARD THE NORTHERN BORDER.
WE'RE GRATE-FUL.
YOU MUST BE WEARY FROM YOUR LONG JOURNEY. I'LL ESCORT YOU TO THE BARRACKS.
I'D LIKE AN AUDIENCE WITH GENERAL KYO-GA FIRST.

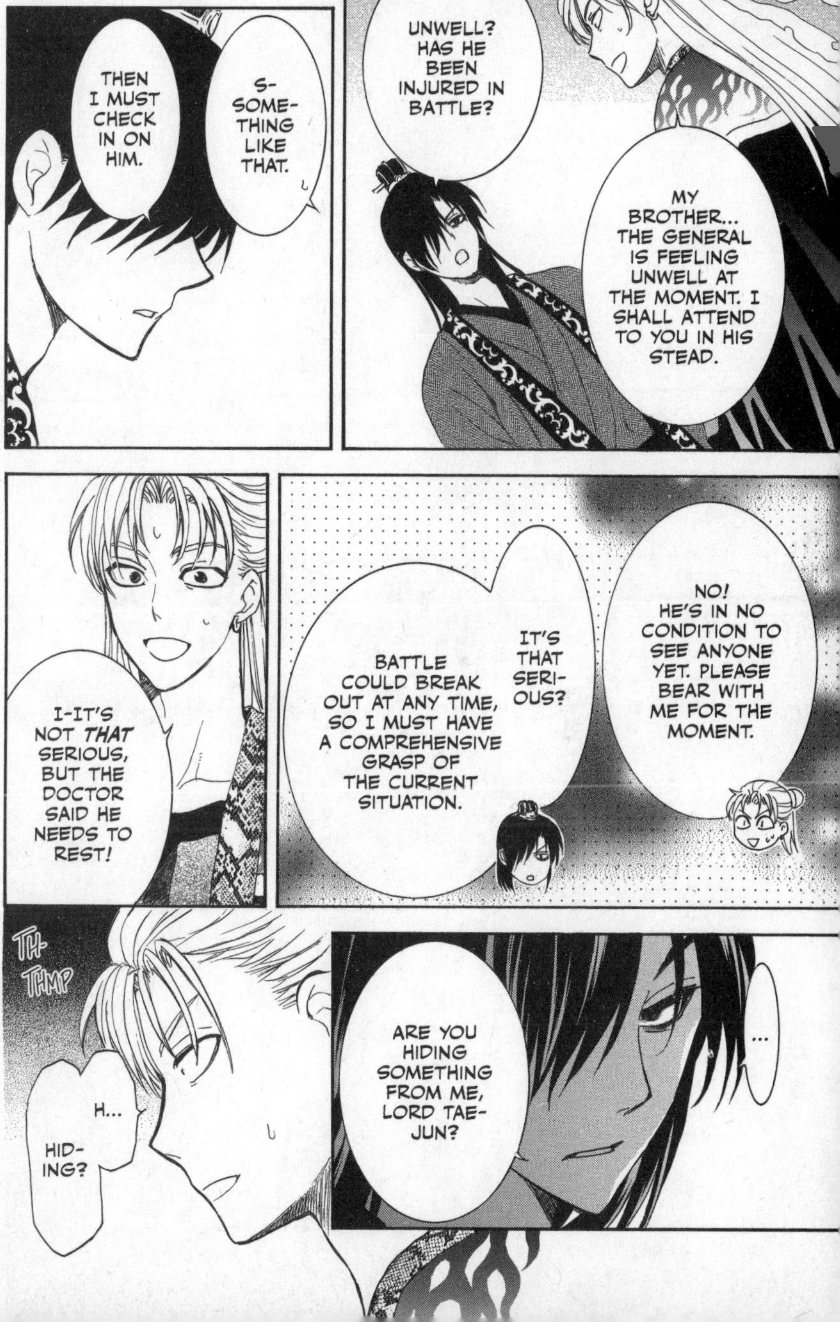
MY BROTHER... THE GENERAL IS FEELING UNWELL AT THE MOMENT. I SHALL ATTEND TO YOU IN HIS STEAD.
UNWELL? HAS HE BEEN INJURED IN BATTLE?
S-SOMETHING LIKE THAT.
THEN I MUST CHECK IN ON HIM.
NO! HE'S IN NO CONDITION TO SEE ANYONE YET. PLEASE BEAR WITH ME FOR THE MOMENT.
IT'S THAT SERIOUS?
BATTLE COULD BREAK OUT AT ANY TIME, SO I MUST HAVE A COMPREHENSIVE GRASP OF THE CURRENT SITUATION.
I-IT'S NOT *THAT* SERIOUS, BUT THE DOCTOR SAID HE NEEDS TO REST!
...
ARE YOU HIDING SOMETHING FROM ME, LORD TAE-JUN?
TH-THMP
H... HIDING?

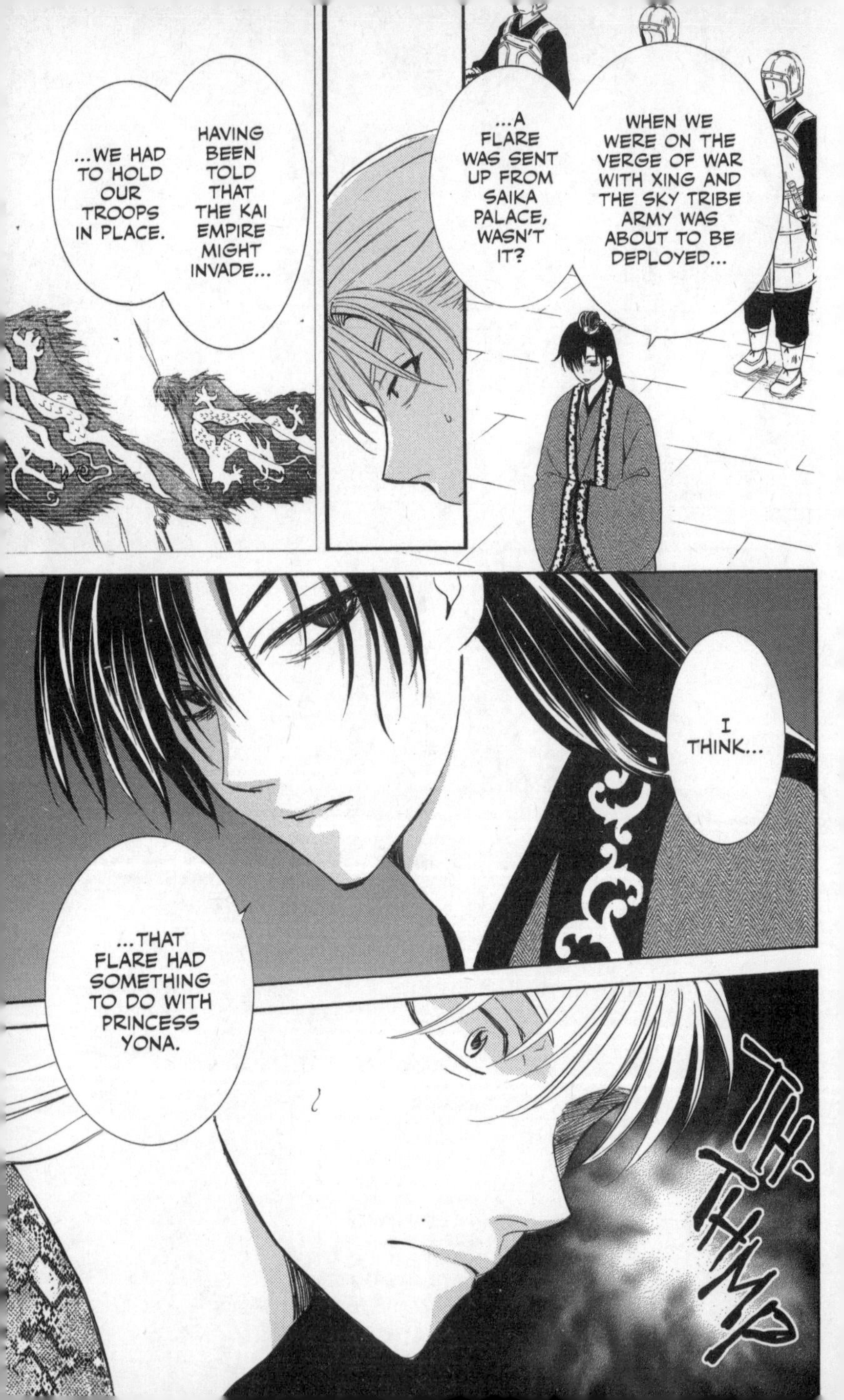
WHEN WE WERE ON THE VERGE OF WAR WITH XING AND THE SKY TRIBE ARMY WAS ABOUT TO BE DEPLOYED...
...A FLARE WAS SENT UP FROM SAIKA PALACE, WASN'T IT?
HAVING BEEN TOLD THAT THE KAI EMPIRE MIGHT INVADE...
...WE HAD TO HOLD OUR TROOPS IN PLACE.
I THINK...
...THAT FLARE HAD SOMETHING TO DO WITH PRINCESS YONA.
TH-THMP

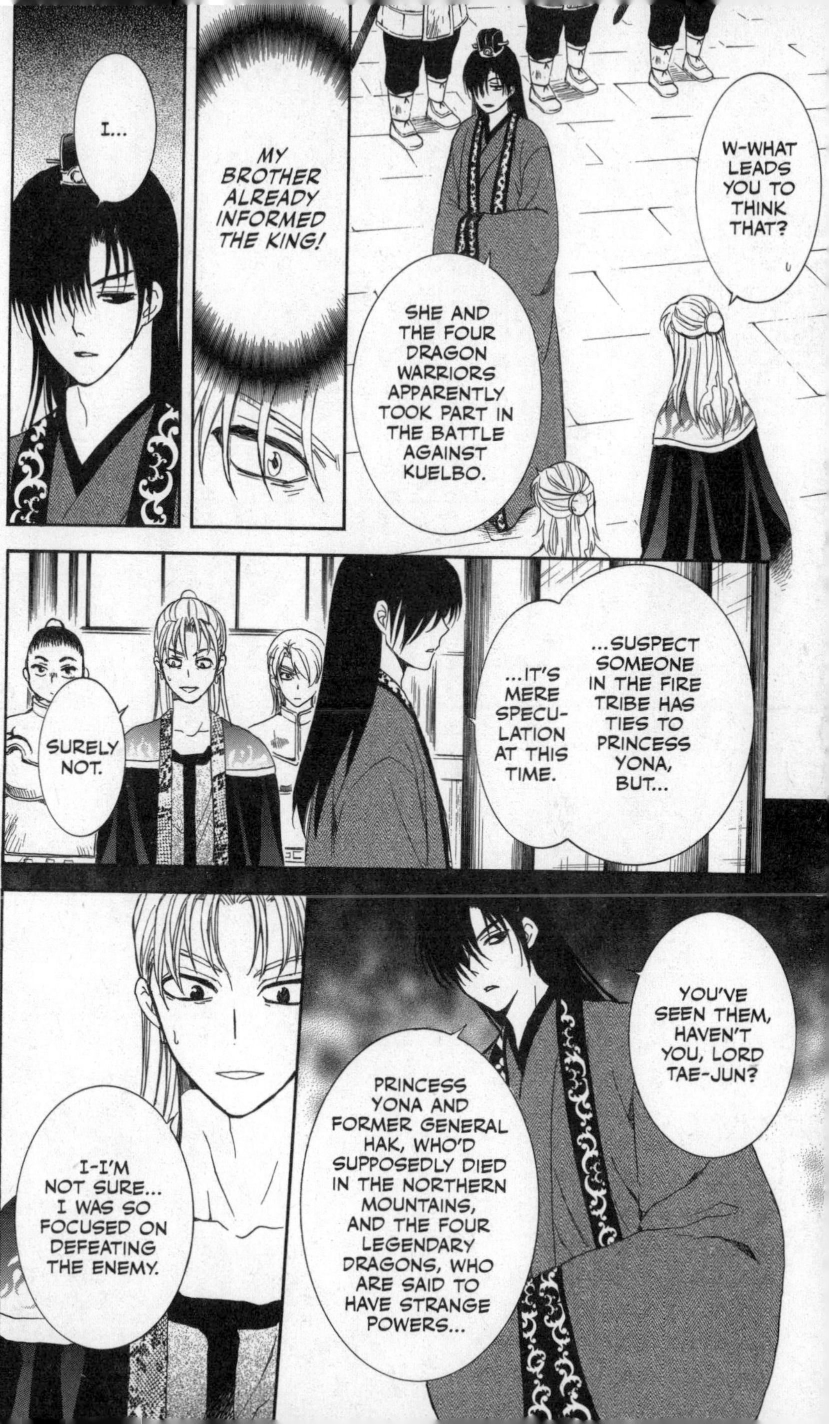
W-WHAT LEADS YOU TO THINK THAT?
SHE AND THE FOUR DRAGON WARRIORS APPARENTLY TOOK PART IN THE BATTLE AGAINST KUELBO.
MY BROTHER ALREADY INFORMED THE KING!
I...
...SUSPECT SOMEONE IN THE FIRE TRIBE HAS TIES TO PRINCESS YONA, BUT...
...IT'S MERE SPECULATION AT THIS TIME.
SURELY NOT.
YOU'VE SEEN THEM, HAVEN'T YOU, LORD TAE-JUN?
PRINCESS YONA AND FORMER GENERAL HAK, WHO'D SUPPOSEDLY DIED IN THE NORTHERN MOUNTAINS, AND THE FOUR LEGENDARY DRAGONS, WHO ARE SAID TO HAVE STRANGE POWERS...
I-I'M NOT SURE... I WAS SO FOCUSED ON DEFEATING THE ENEMY.

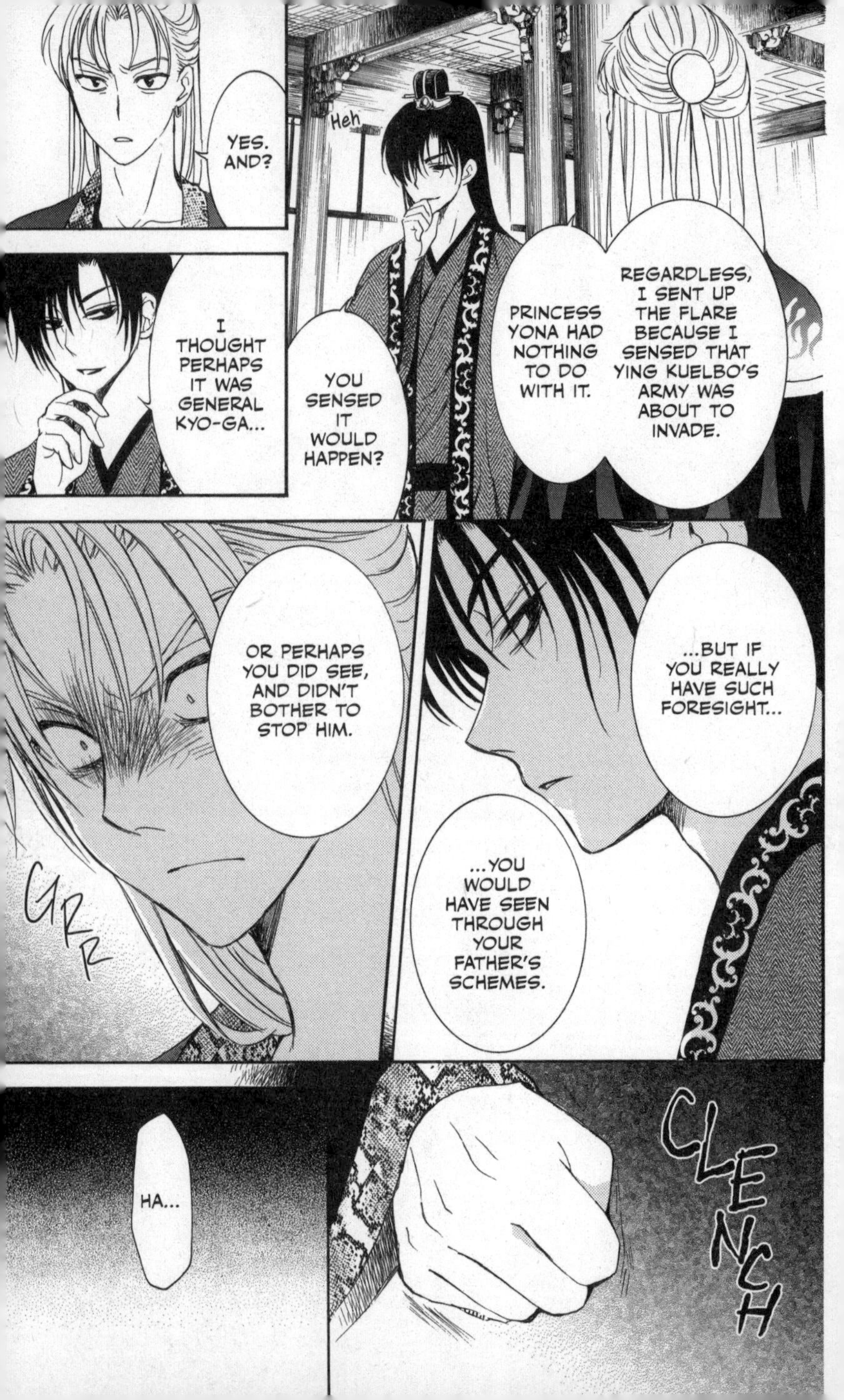
REGARDLESS, I SENT UP THE FLARE BECAUSE I SENSED THAT YING KUELBO'S ARMY WAS ABOUT TO INVADE.
PRINCESS YONA HAD NOTHING TO DO WITH IT.
Heh
YOU SENSED IT WOULD HAPPEN?
YES. AND?
I THOUGHT PERHAPS IT WAS GENERAL KYO-GA...
...BUT IF YOU REALLY HAVE SUCH FORESIGHT...
...YOU WOULD HAVE SEEN THROUGH YOUR FATHER'S SCHEMES.
OR PERHAPS YOU DID SEE, AND DIDN'T BOTHER TO STOP HIM.
GRR
CLENCH
HA...

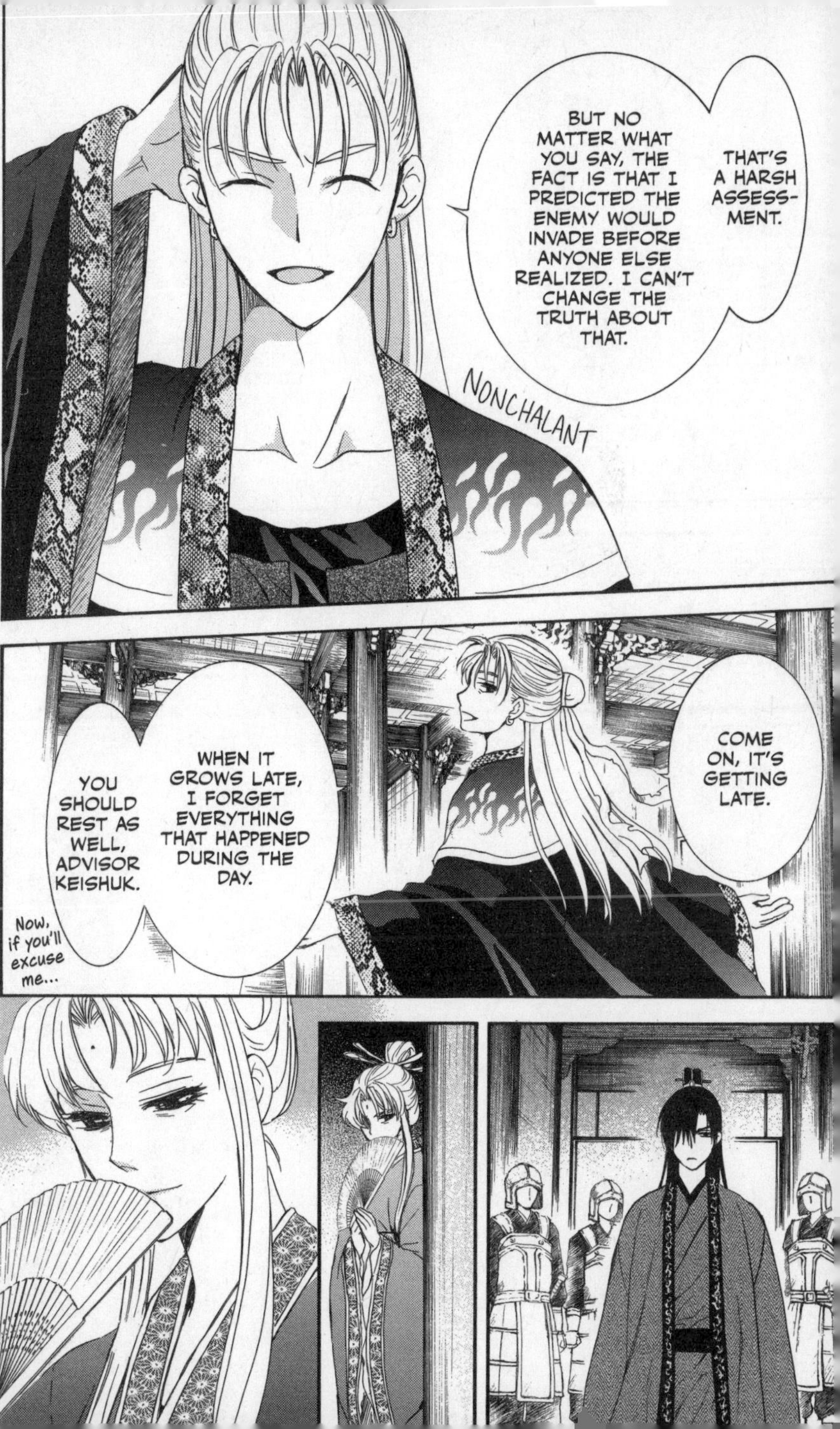
THAT'S A HARSH ASSESS-MENT.
BUT NO MATTER WHAT YOU SAY, THE FACT IS THAT I PREDICTED THE ENEMY WOULD INVADE BEFORE ANYONE ELSE REALIZED. I CAN'T CHANGE THE TRUTH ABOUT THAT.
NONCHALANT
COME ON, IT'S GETTING LATE.
WHEN IT GROWS LATE, I FORGET EVERYTHING THAT HAPPENED DURING THE DAY.
YOU SHOULD REST AS WELL, ADVISOR KEISHUK.
Now, if you'll excuse me...

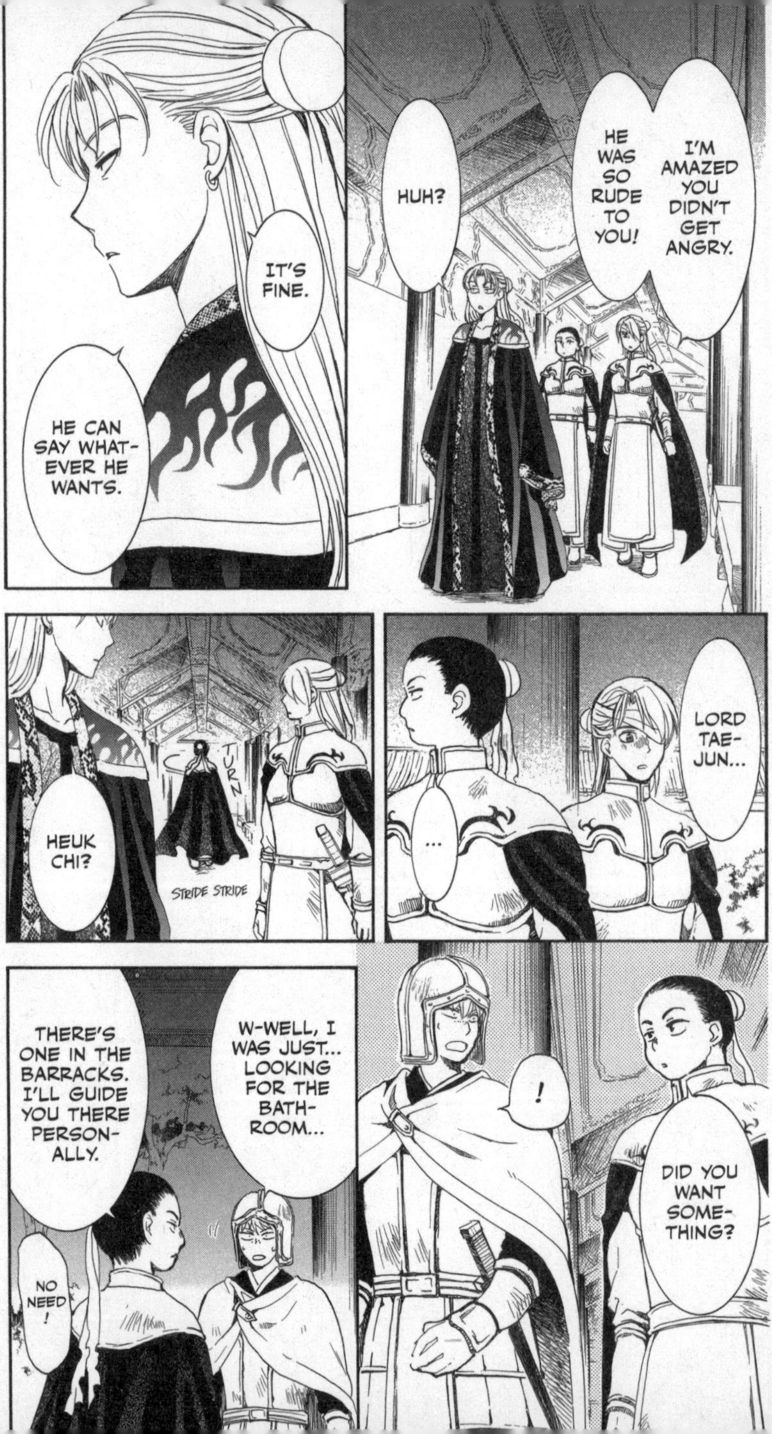
I'M AMAZED YOU DIDN'T GET ANGRY.
HE WAS SO RUDE TO YOU!
HUH?
IT'S FINE.
HE CAN SAY WHATEVER HE WANTS.
LORD TAE-JUN...
...
TURN
HEUK CHI?
STRIDE STRIDE
DID YOU WANT SOMETHING?
!
W-WELL, I WAS JUST... LOOKING FOR THE BATHROOM...
THERE'S ONE IN THE BARRACKS. I'LL GUIDE YOU THERE PERSONALLY.
NO NEED!

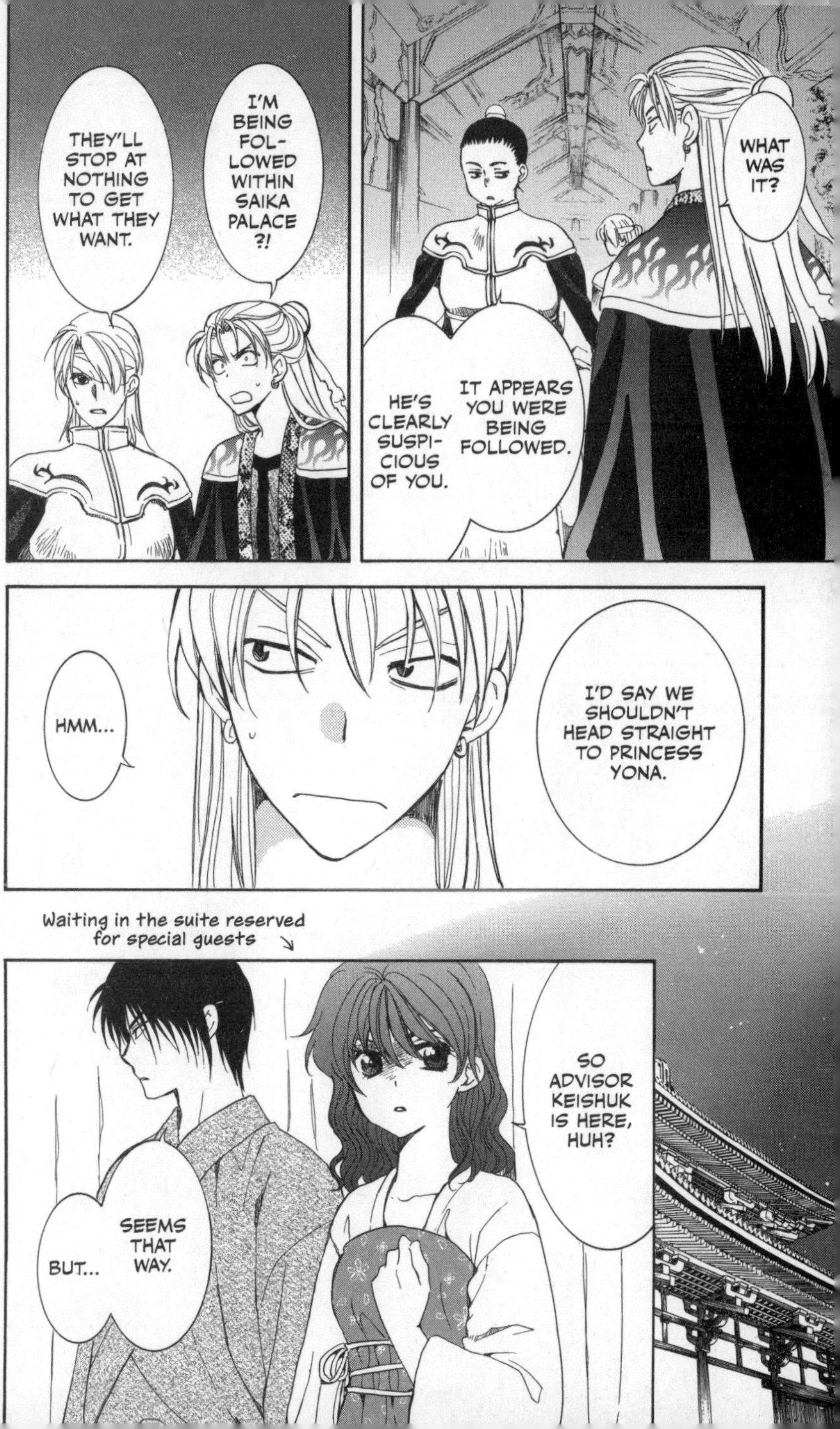
WHAT WAS IT?
IT APPEARS YOU WERE BEING FOLLOWED.
HE'S CLEARLY SUSPICIOUS OF YOU.
I'M BEING FOL-LOWED WITHIN SAIKA PALACE?!
THEY'LL STOP AT NOTHING TO GET WHAT THEY WANT.
I'D SAY WE SHOULDN'T HEAD STRAIGHT TO PRINCESS YONA.
HMM...
Waiting in the suite reserved for special guests
SO ADVISOR KEISHUK IS HERE, HUH?
SEEMS THAT WAY.
BUT...

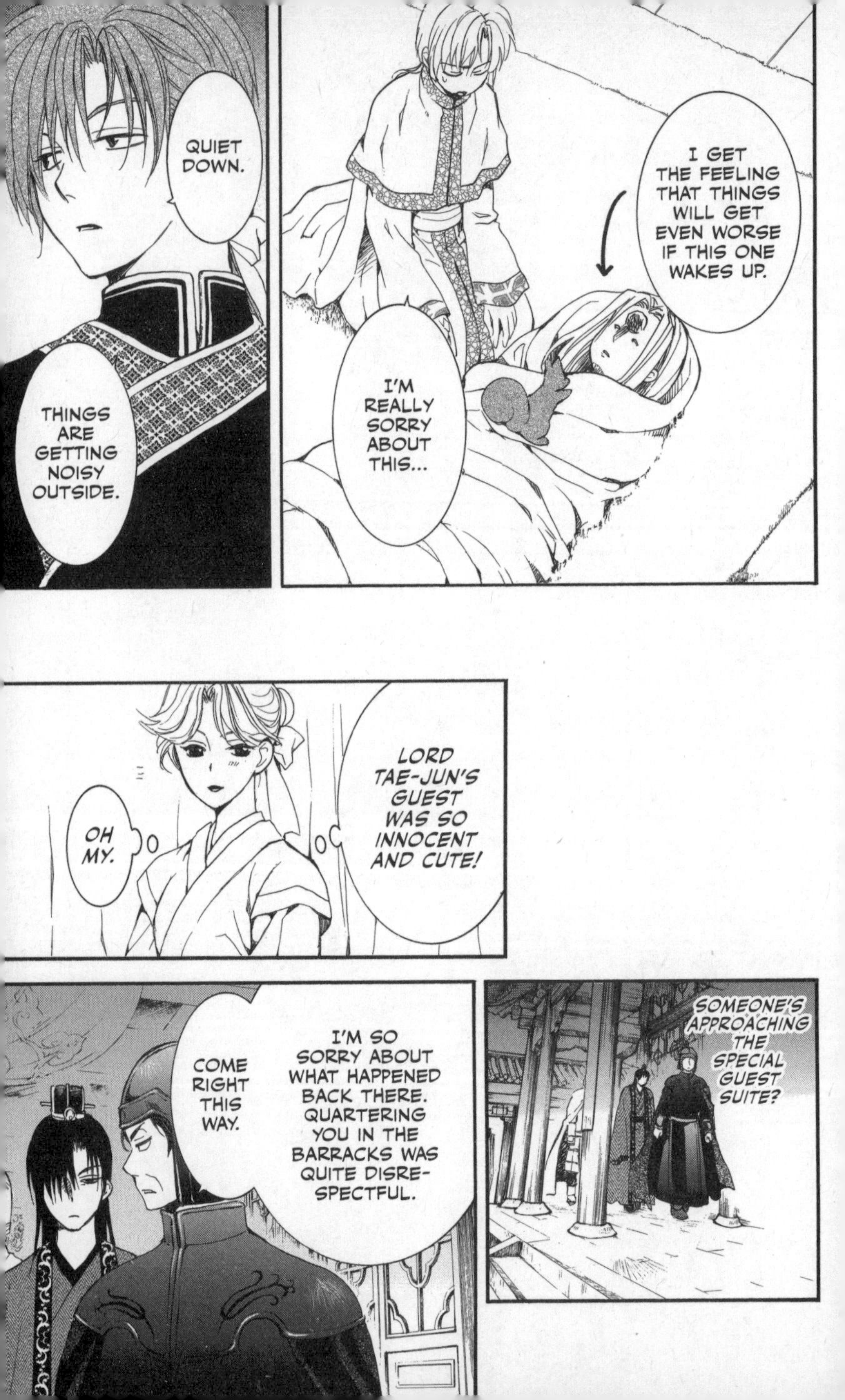
I GET THE FEELING THAT THINGS WILL GET EVEN WORSE IF THIS ONE WAKES UP.
I'M REALLY SORRY ABOUT THIS...
QUIET DOWN.
THINGS ARE GETTING NOISY OUTSIDE.
LORD TAE-JUN'S GUEST WAS SO INNOCENT AND CUTE!
OH MY.
SOMEONE'S APPROACHING THE SPECIAL GUEST SUITE?
I'M SO SORRY ABOUT WHAT HAPPENED BACK THERE. QUARTERING YOU IN THE BARRACKS WAS QUITE DISRESPECTFUL.
COME RIGHT THIS WAY.

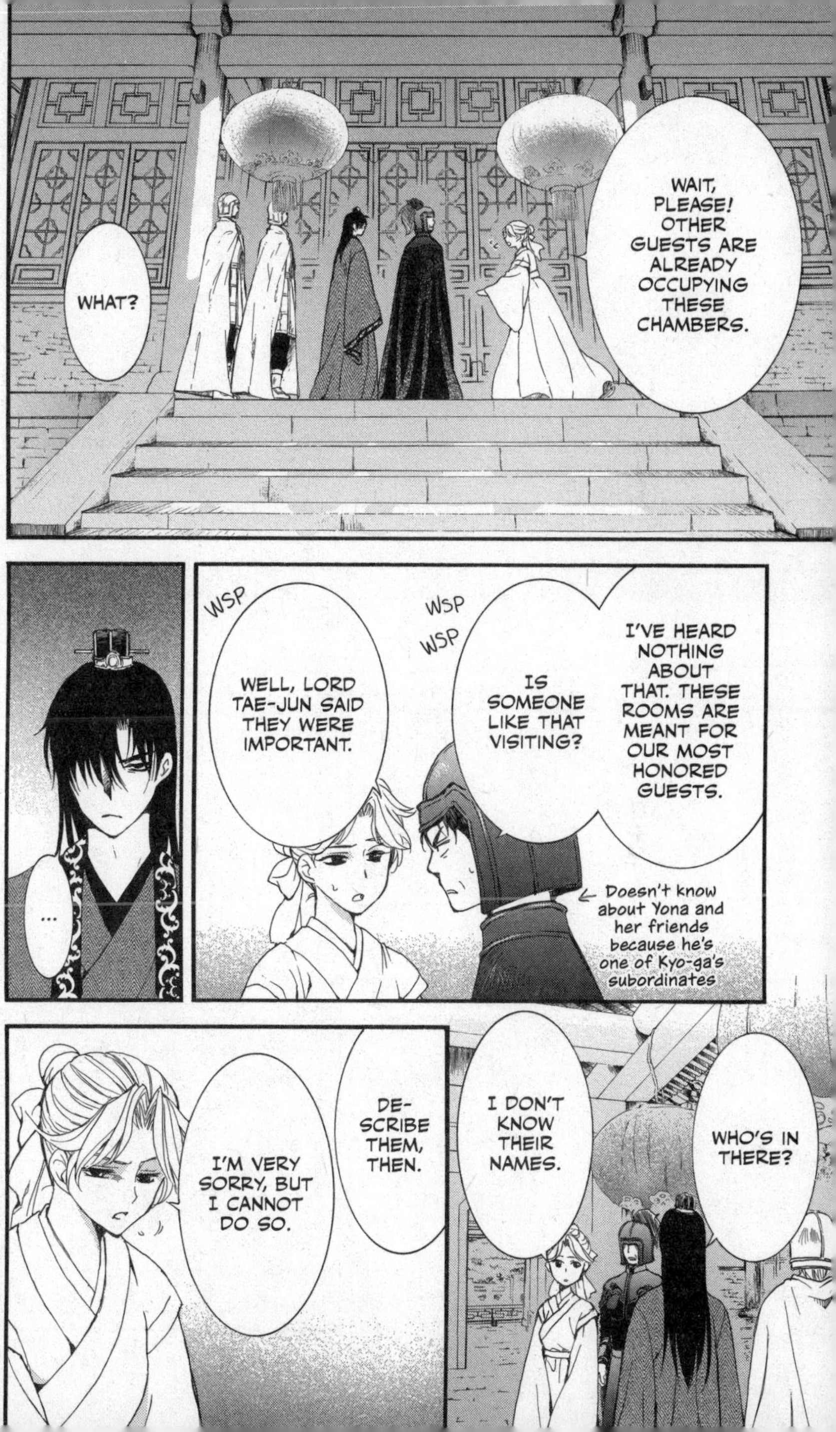
WAIT, PLEASE! OTHER GUESTS ARE ALREADY OCCUPYING THESE CHAMBERS.
WHAT?
I'VE HEARD NOTHING ABOUT THAT. THESE ROOMS ARE MEANT FOR OUR MOST HONORED GUESTS.
WSP
WSP
IS SOMEONE LIKE THAT VISITING?
WSP
WELL, LORD TAE-JUN SAID THEY WERE IMPORTANT.
Doesn't know about Yona and her friends because he's one of Kyo-ga's subordinates
...
WHO'S IN THERE?
I DON'T KNOW THEIR NAMES.
DE-SCRIBE THEM, THEN.
I'M VERY SORRY, BUT I CANNOT DO SO.

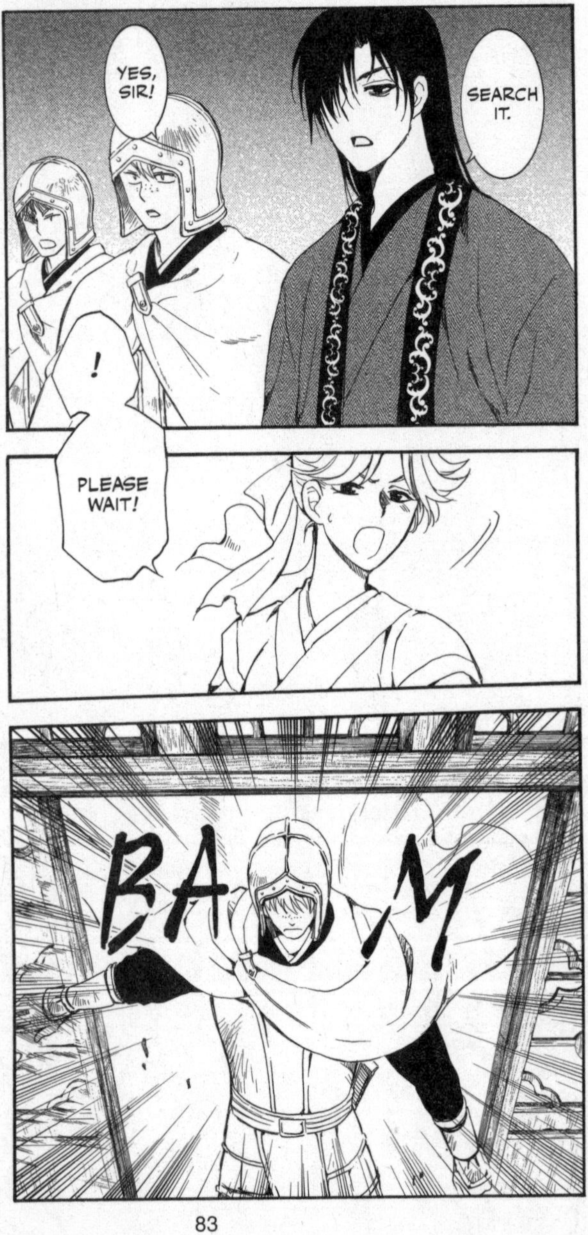
SEARCH IT.
YES, SIR!
!
PLEASE WAIT!
BAM
!

Letters to me! Sometimes I receive gifts for both me and my characters. Thank you so very much! I gladly read all of the messages left on my Twitter and my blog.
I'm so sorry I can't reply to you! But please don't spend too much money on your gifts. I really appreciate the sentiment.
I'm just so glad you choose Yona out of all the other books.
I'm also incredibly grateful for letters from overseas.

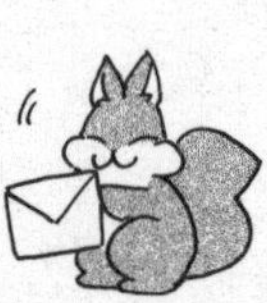

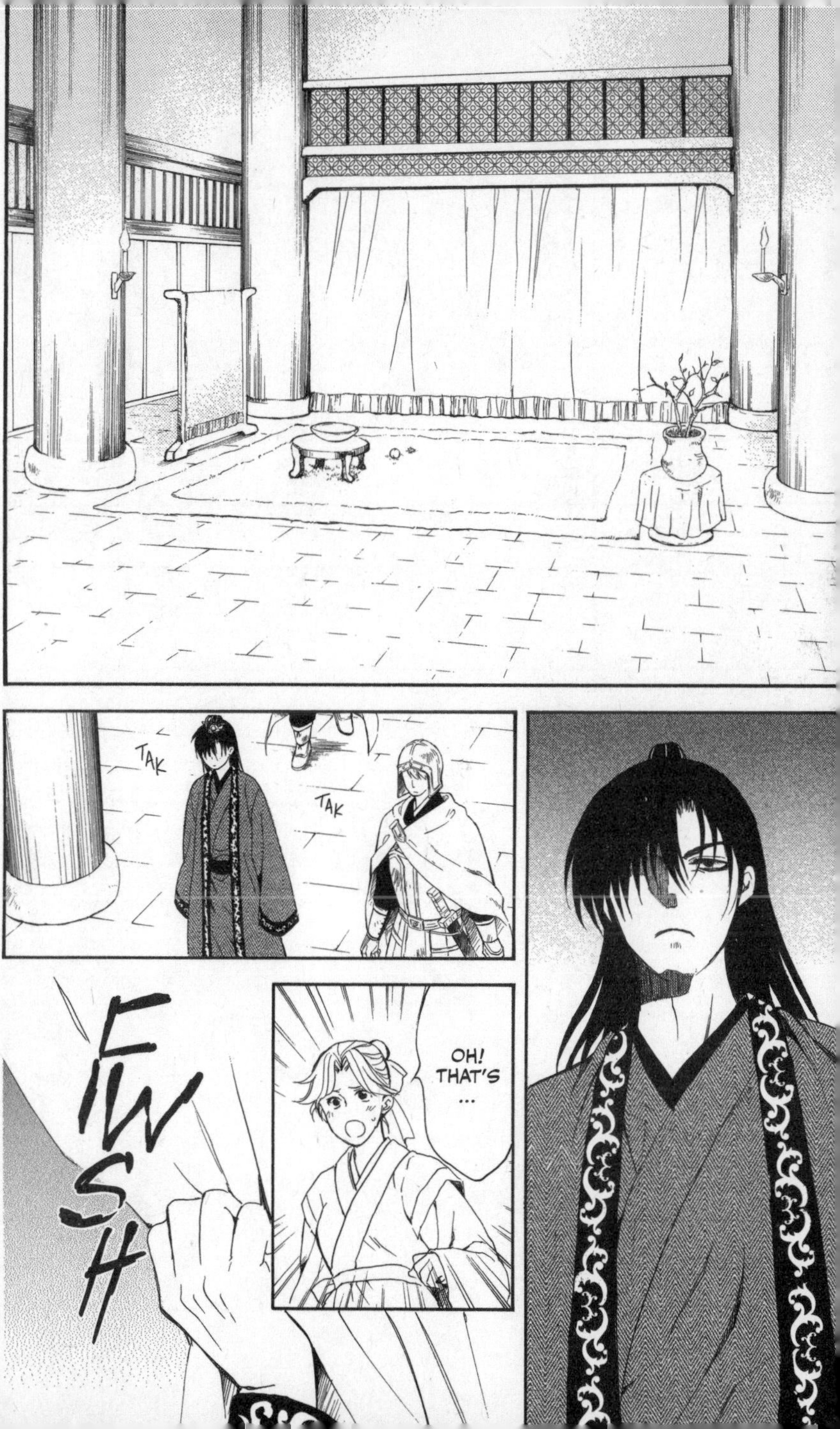
TAK
TAK
OH! THAT'S ...
FWSH

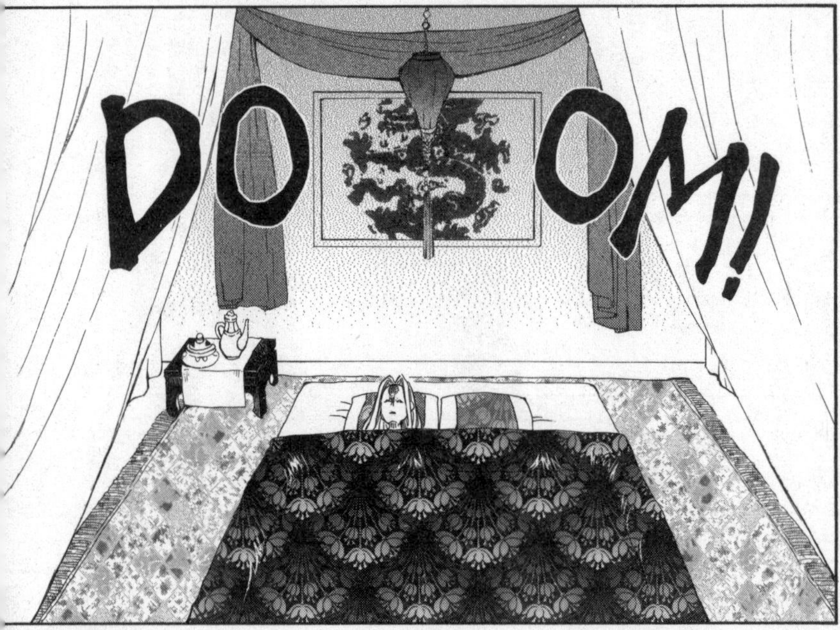
DOOOM!!
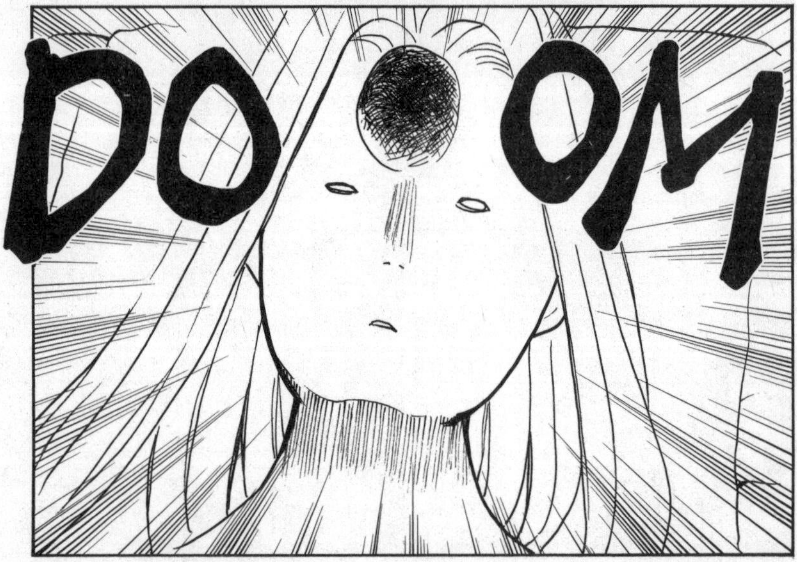
DOOOM

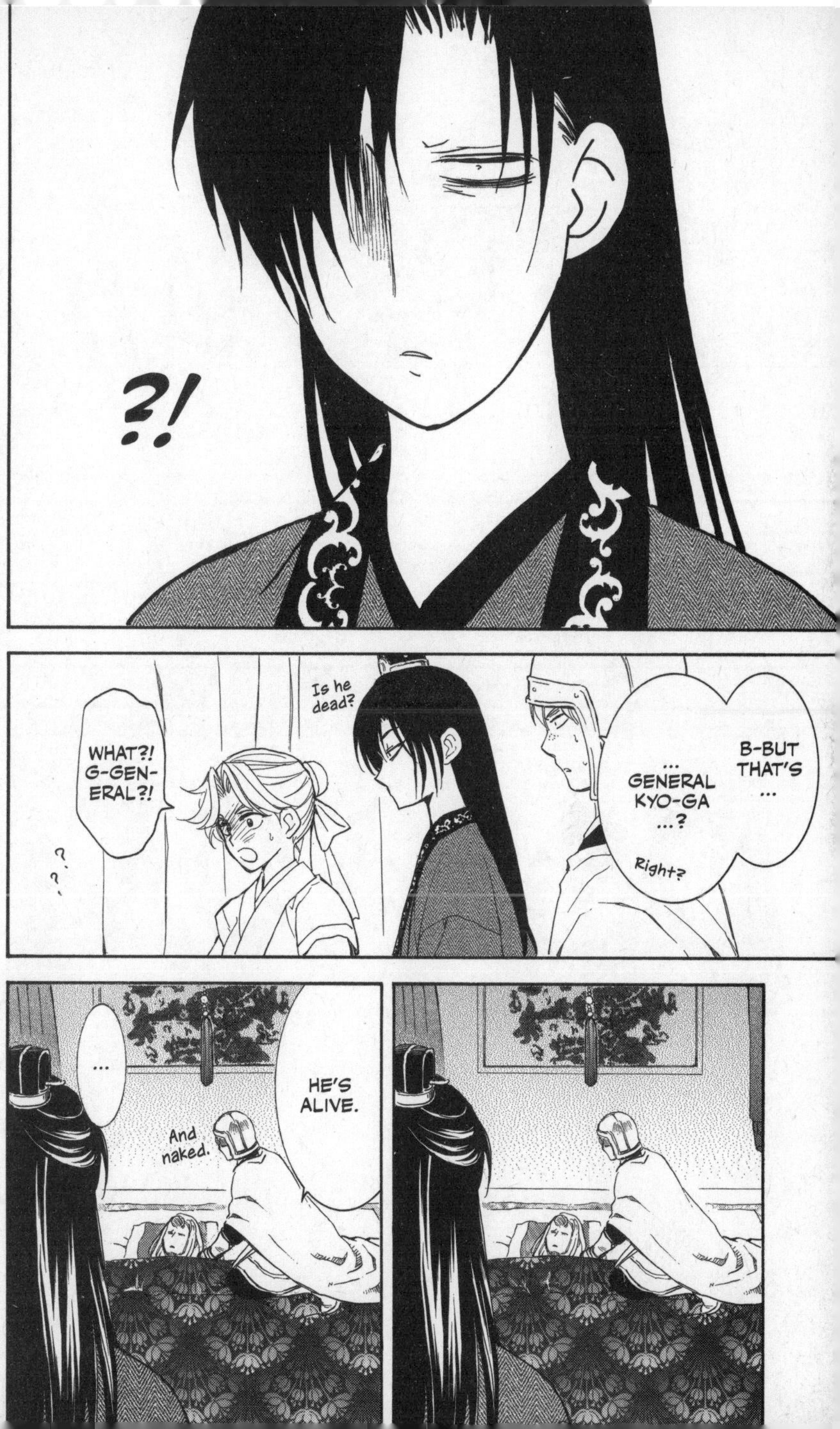
?!
B-BUT THAT'S ...
... GENERAL KYO-GA ...?
Right?
Is he dead?
WHAT?! G-GENERAL?!
? ?
HE'S ALIVE.
...
And naked.

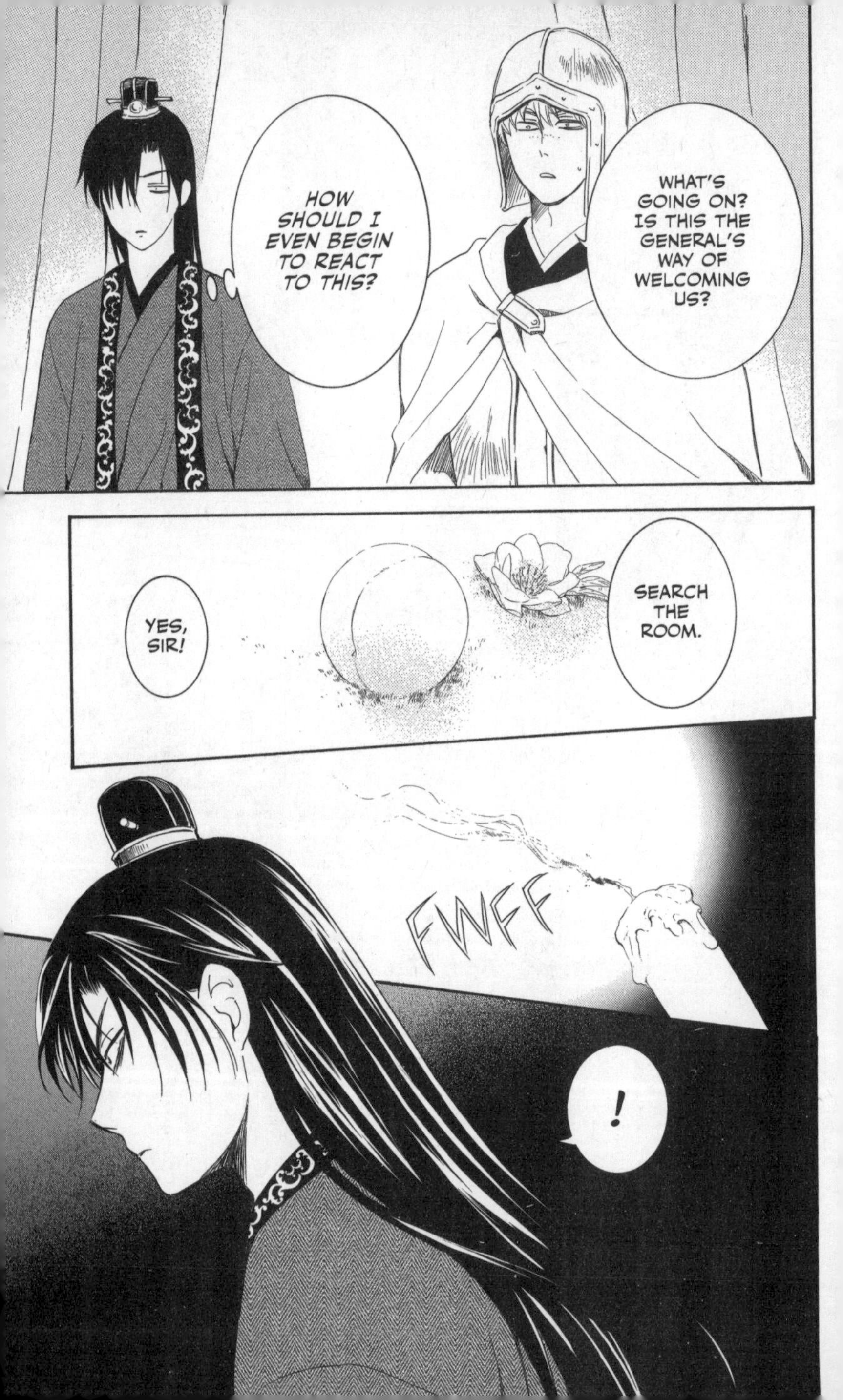
WHAT'S GOING ON? IS THIS THE GENERAL'S WAY OF WELCOMING US?
HOW SHOULD I EVEN BEGIN TO REACT TO THIS?
SEARCH THE ROOM.
YES, SIR!
FWFF
!

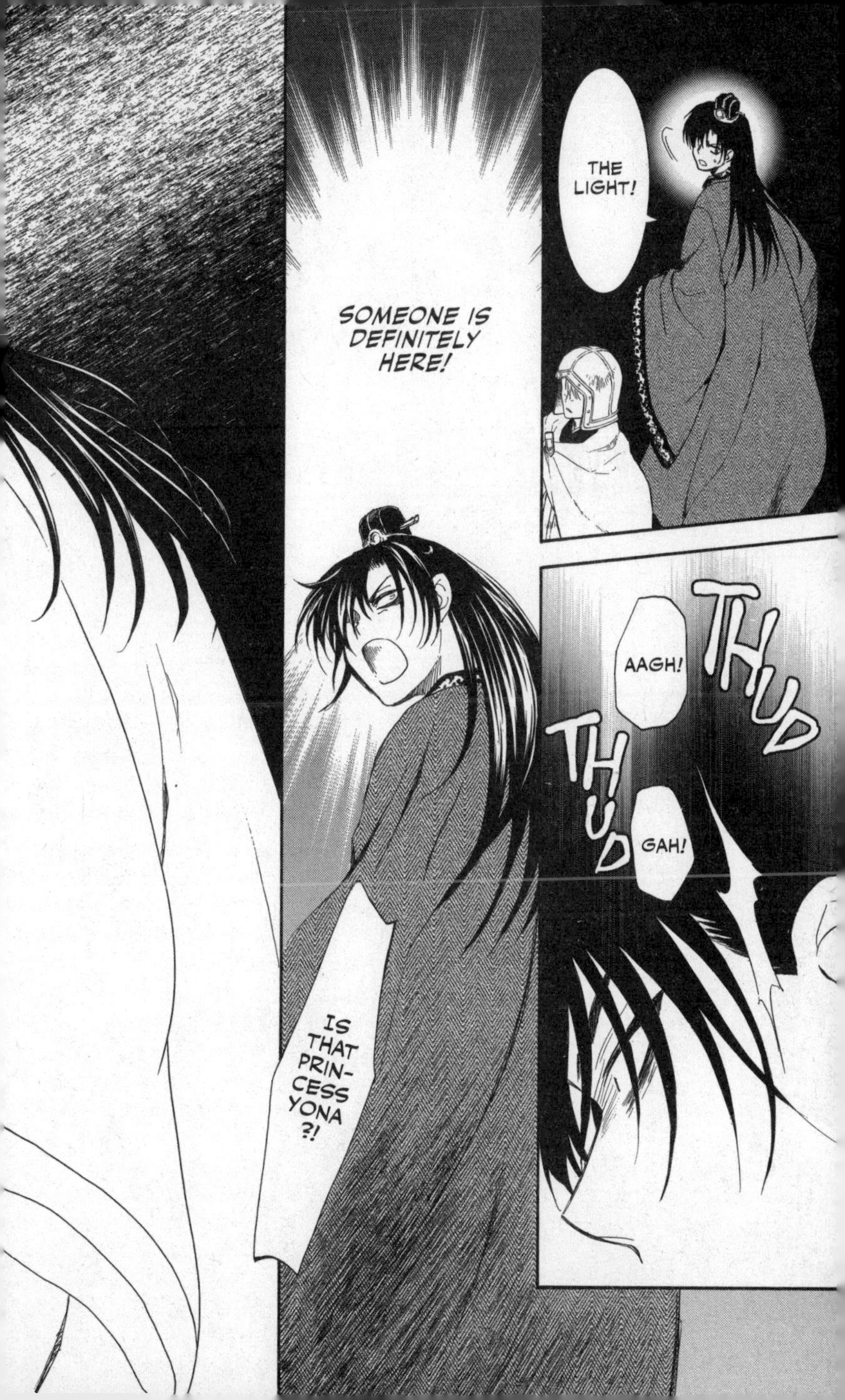
THE LIGHT!
AAGH!
THUD
THUD
GAH!
SOMEONE IS DEFINITELY HERE!
IS THAT PRIN-CESS YONA ?!

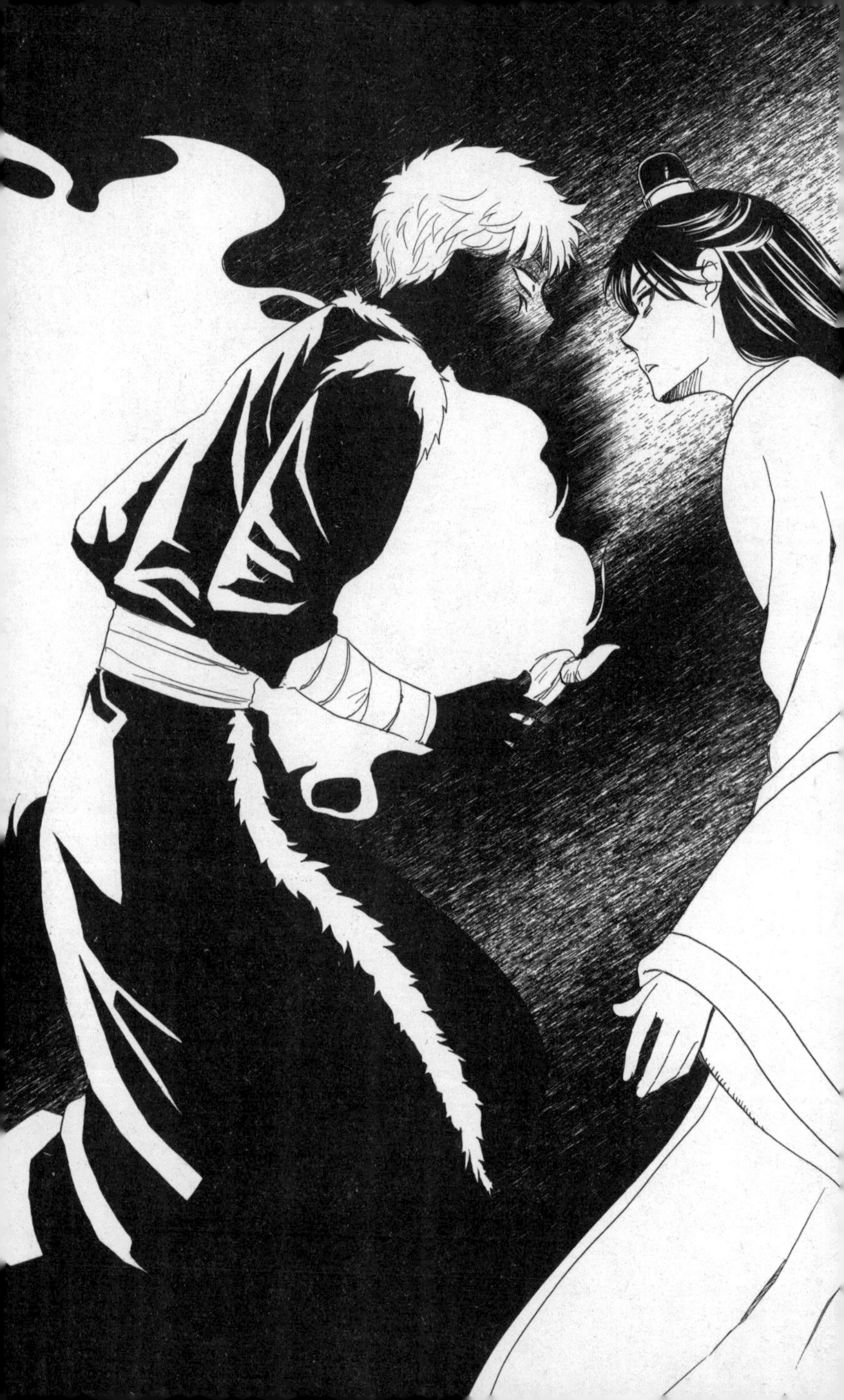

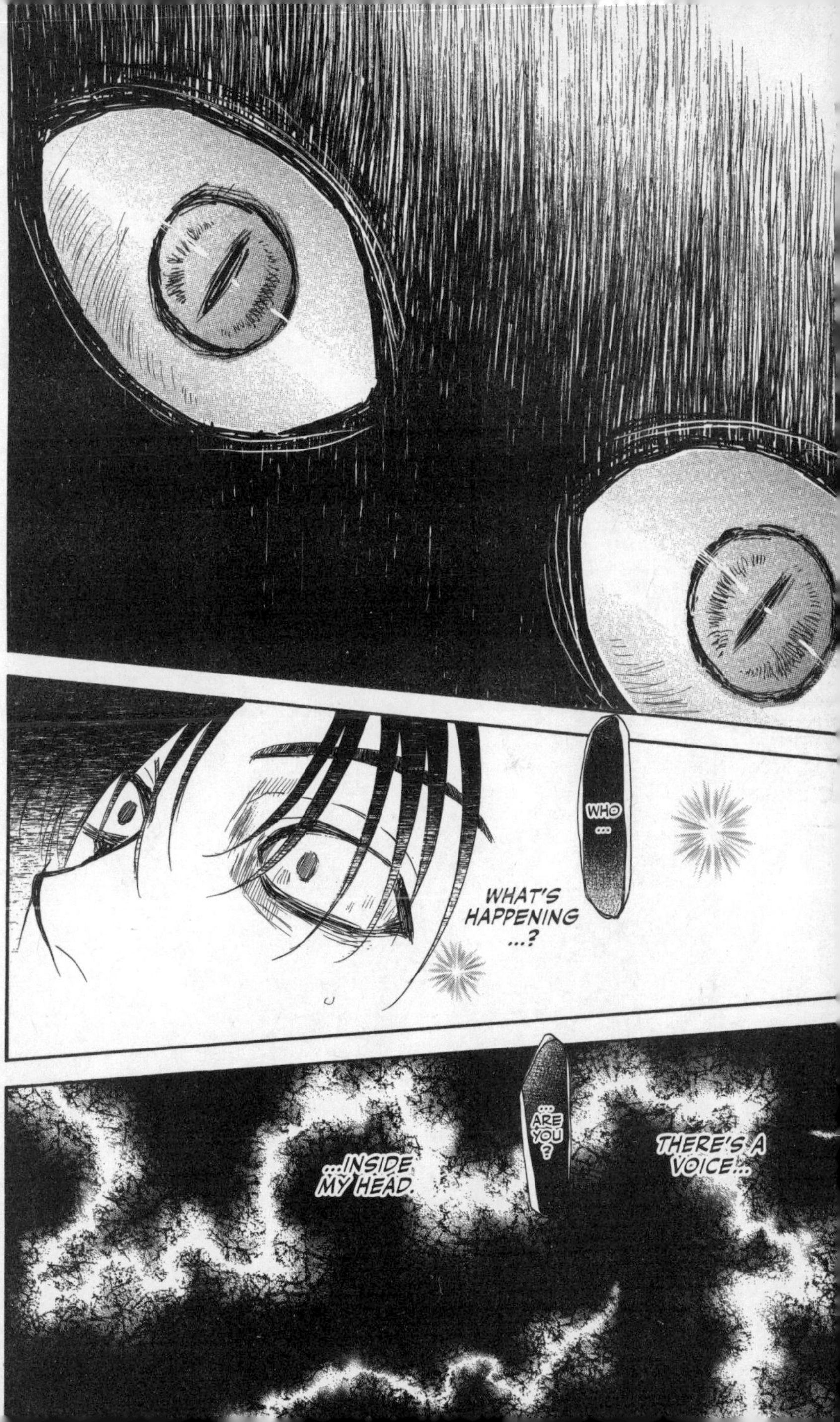
WHO ...
WHAT'S HAPPENING ...?
THERE'S A VOICE...
... ARE YOU ?
...INSIDE MY HEAD.

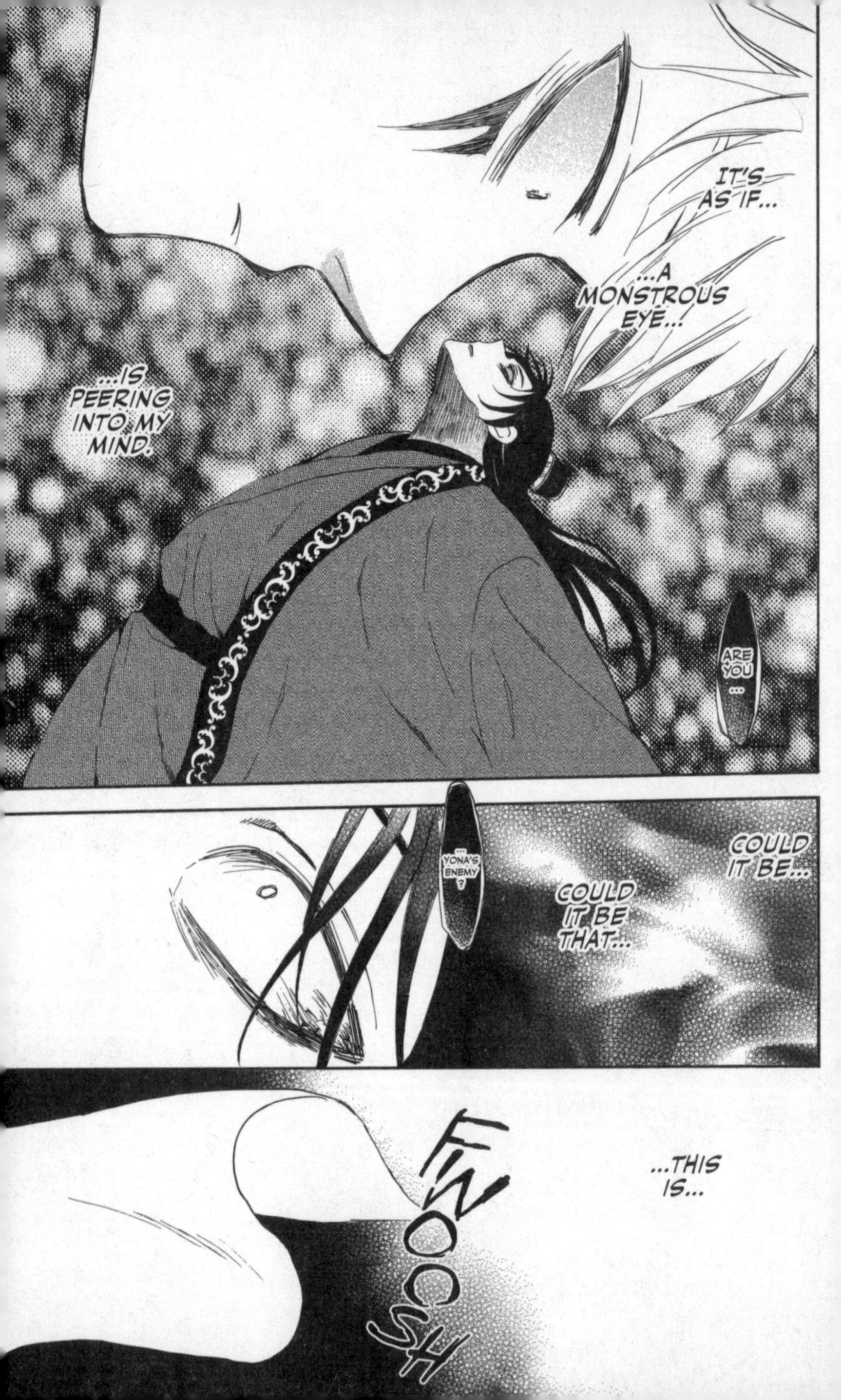
IT'S AS IF...
...A MONSTROUS EYE...
...IS PEERING INTO MY MIND.
ARE YOU ...
COULD IT BE...
COULD IT BE THAT...
...YONA'S ENEMY?
...THIS IS...
FWOOSH

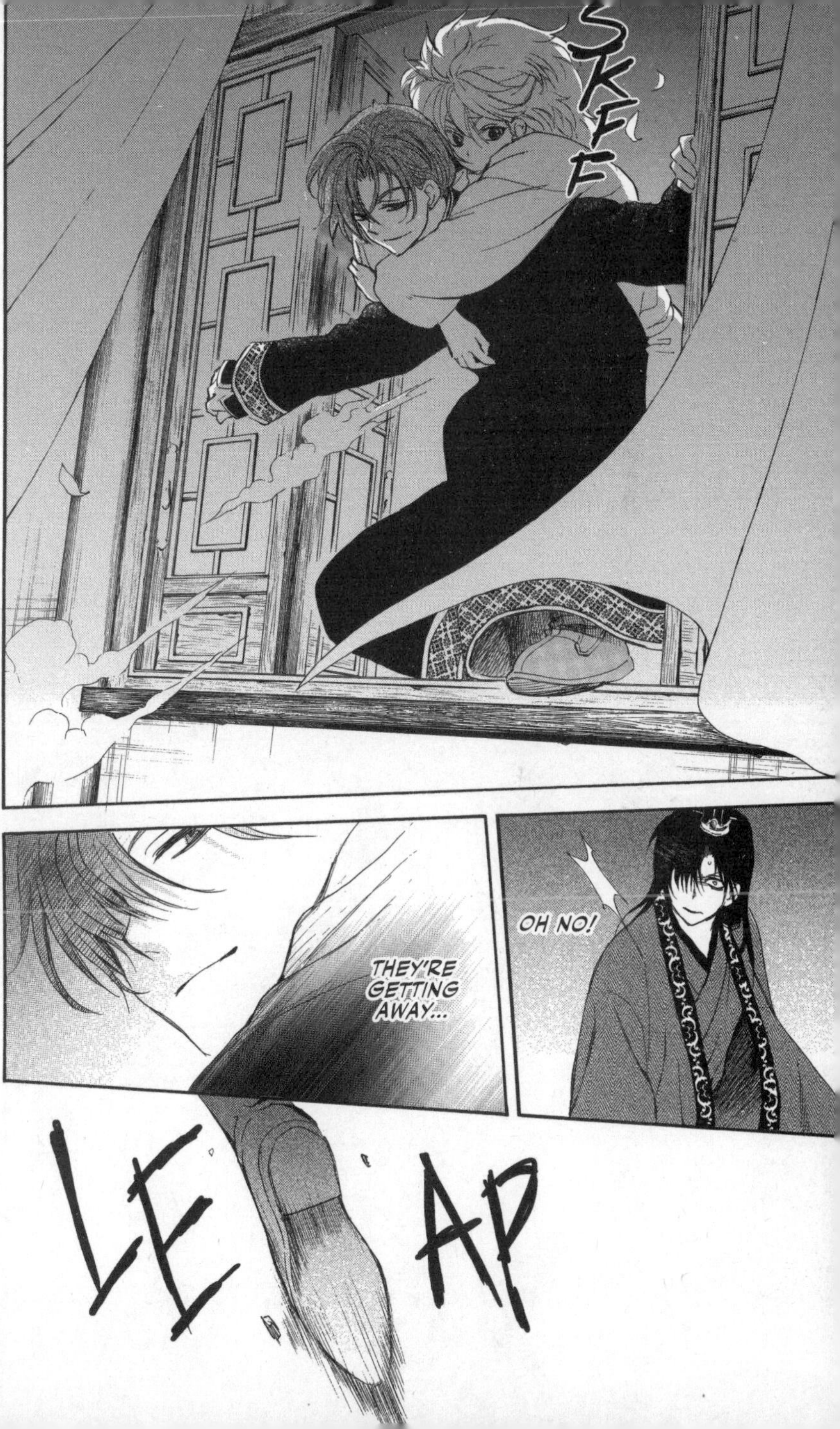
SKFF
OH NO!
THEY'RE GETTING AWAY...
LEAP

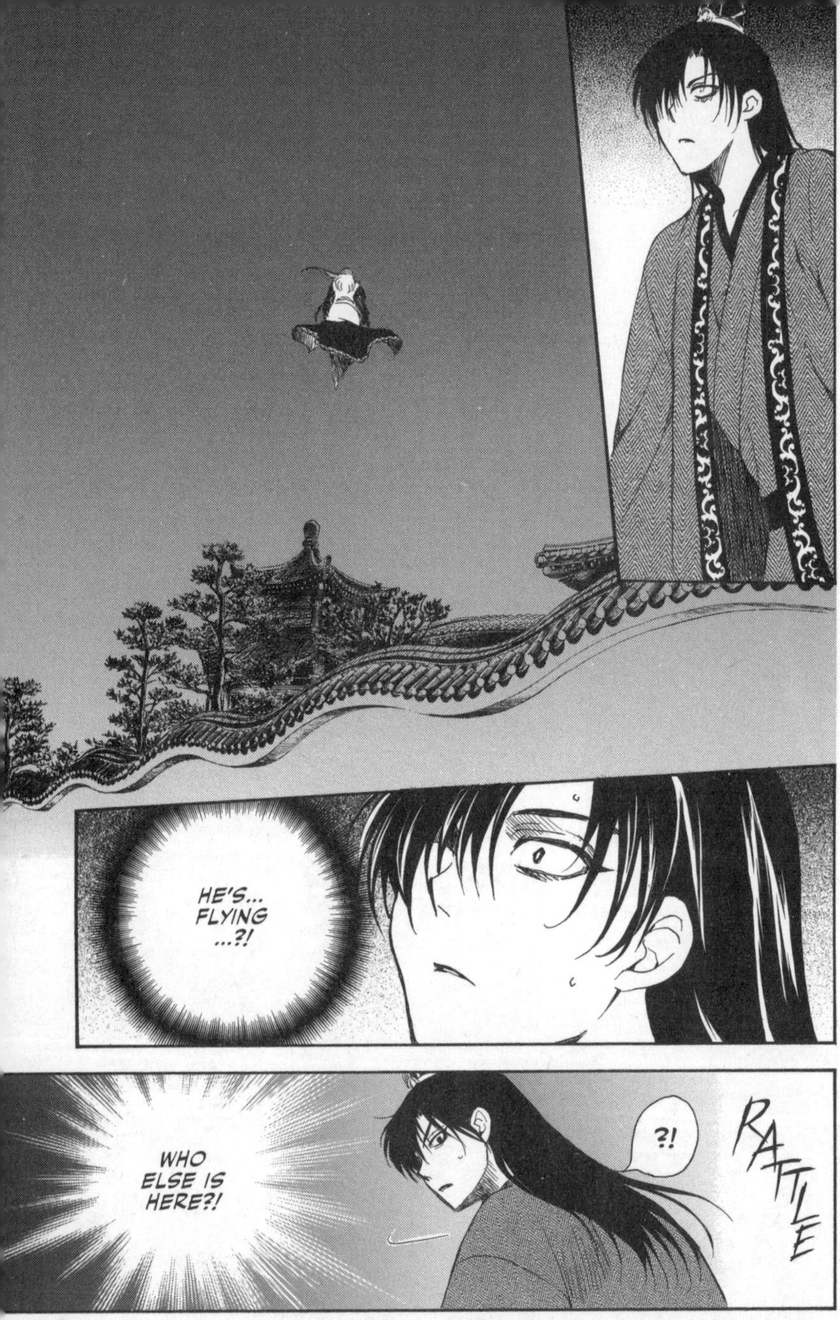
HE'S... FLYING ...?!
?!
RATTLE
WHO ELSE IS HERE?!

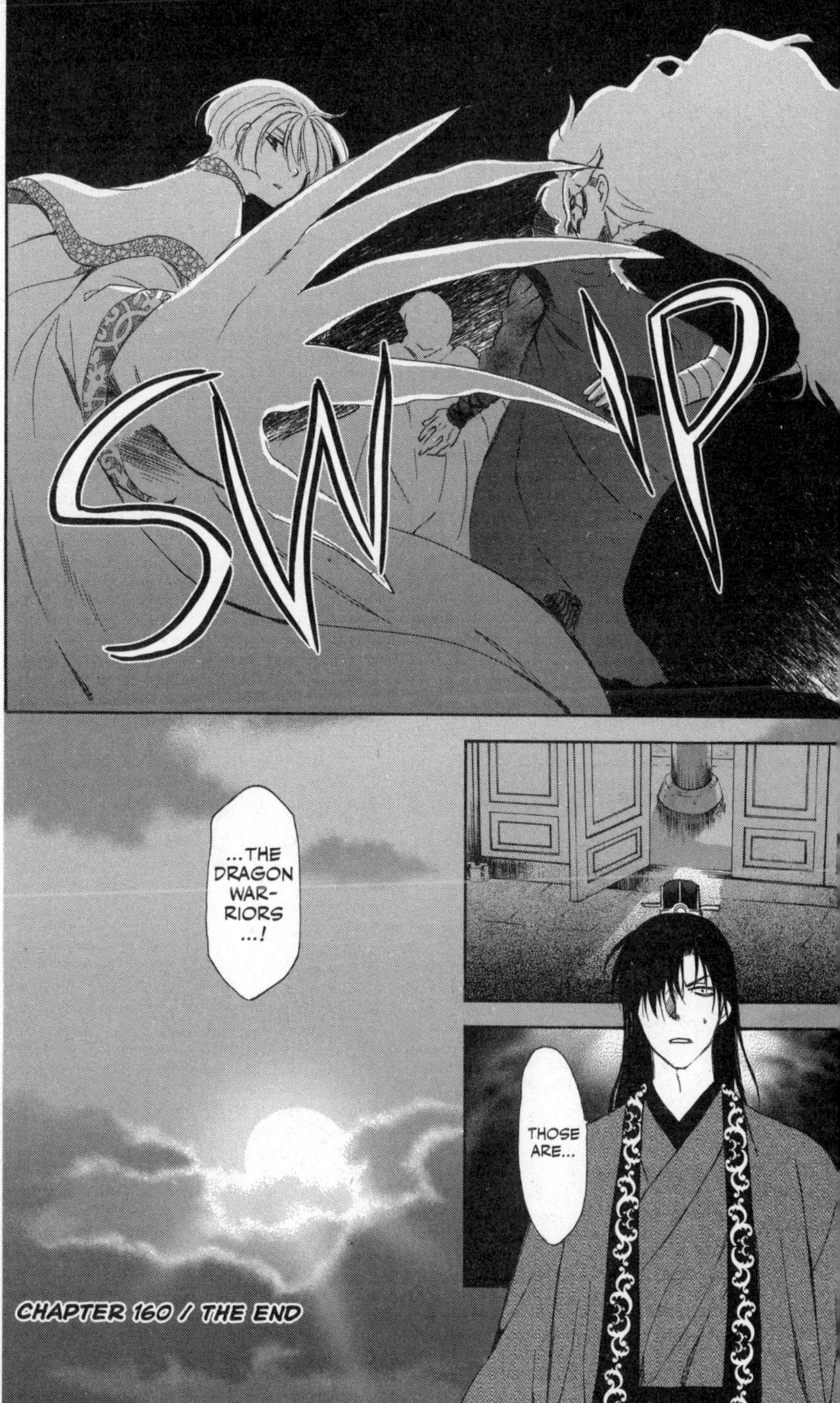
SWIP
THOSE ARE...
...THE DRAGON WARRIORS ...!
CHAPTER 160 / THE END

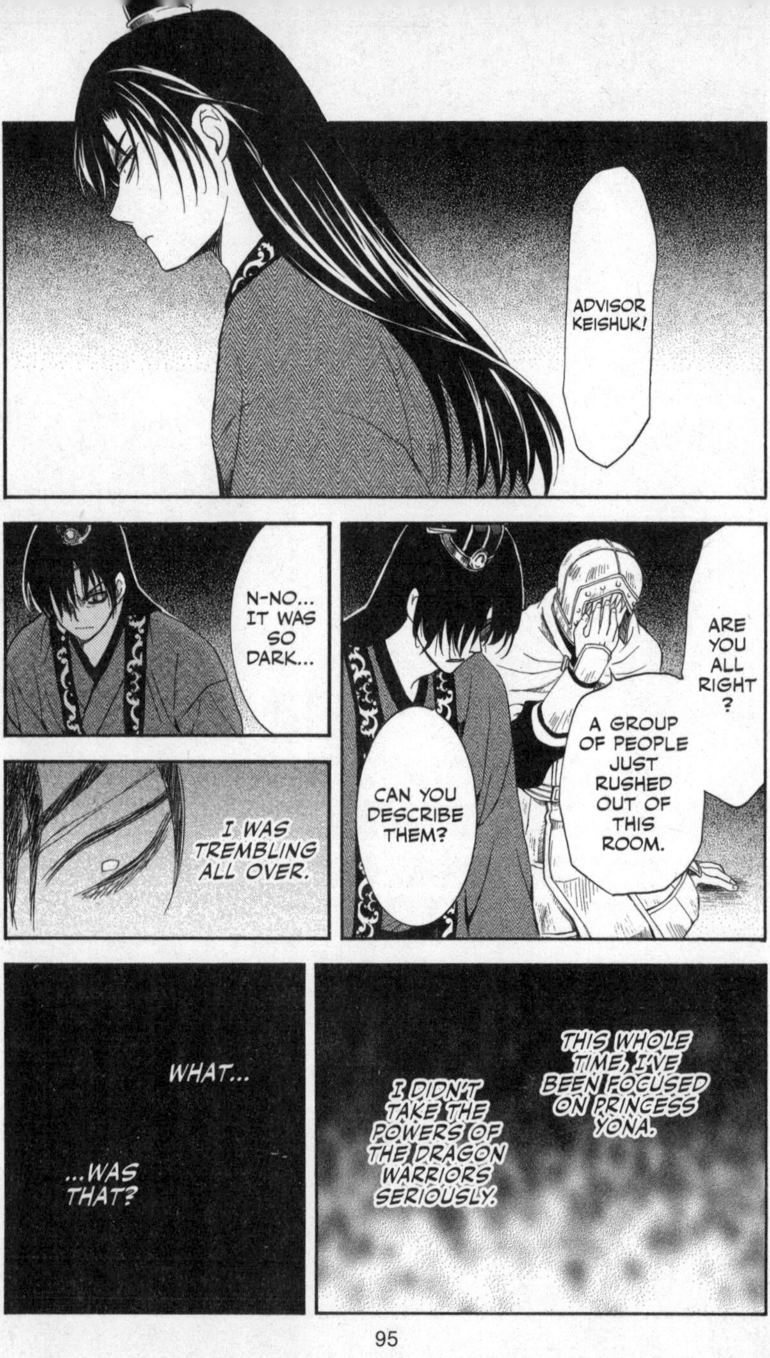
ADVISOR KEISHUK!
ARE YOU ALL RIGHT?
A GROUP OF PEOPLE JUST RUSHED OUT OF THIS ROOM.
CAN YOU DESCRIBE THEM?
N-NO... IT WAS SO DARK...
I WAS TREMBLING ALL OVER.
THIS WHOLE TIME, I'VE BEEN FOCUSED ON PRINCESS YONA.
I DIDN'T TAKE THE POWERS OF THE DRAGON WARRIORS SERIOUSLY.
WHAT...
...WAS THAT?

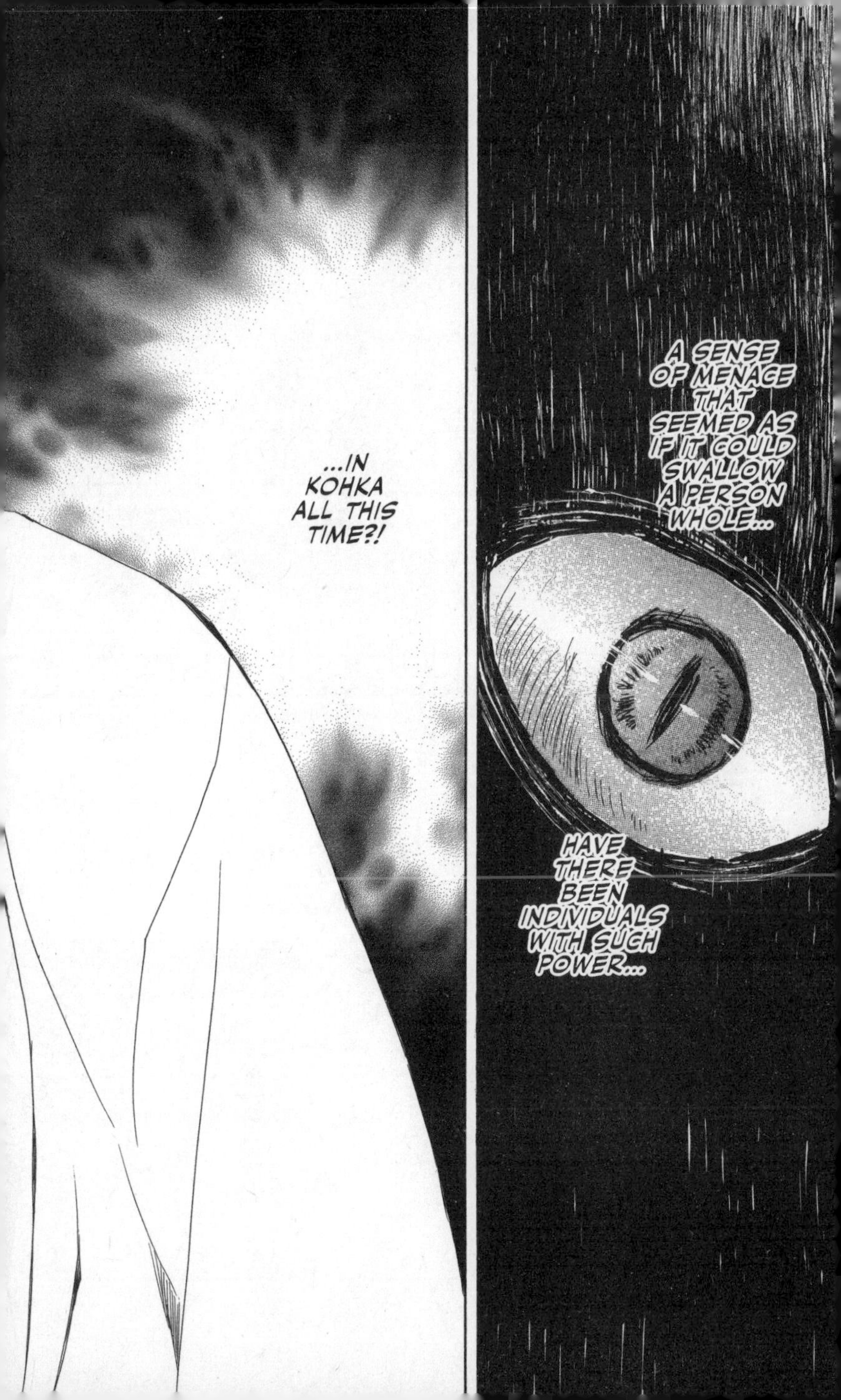
A SENSE OF MENACE THAT SEEMED AS IF IT COULD SWALLOW A PERSON WHOLE...
HAVE THERE BEEN INDIVIDUALS WITH SUCH POWER...
...IN KOHKA ALL THIS TIME?!

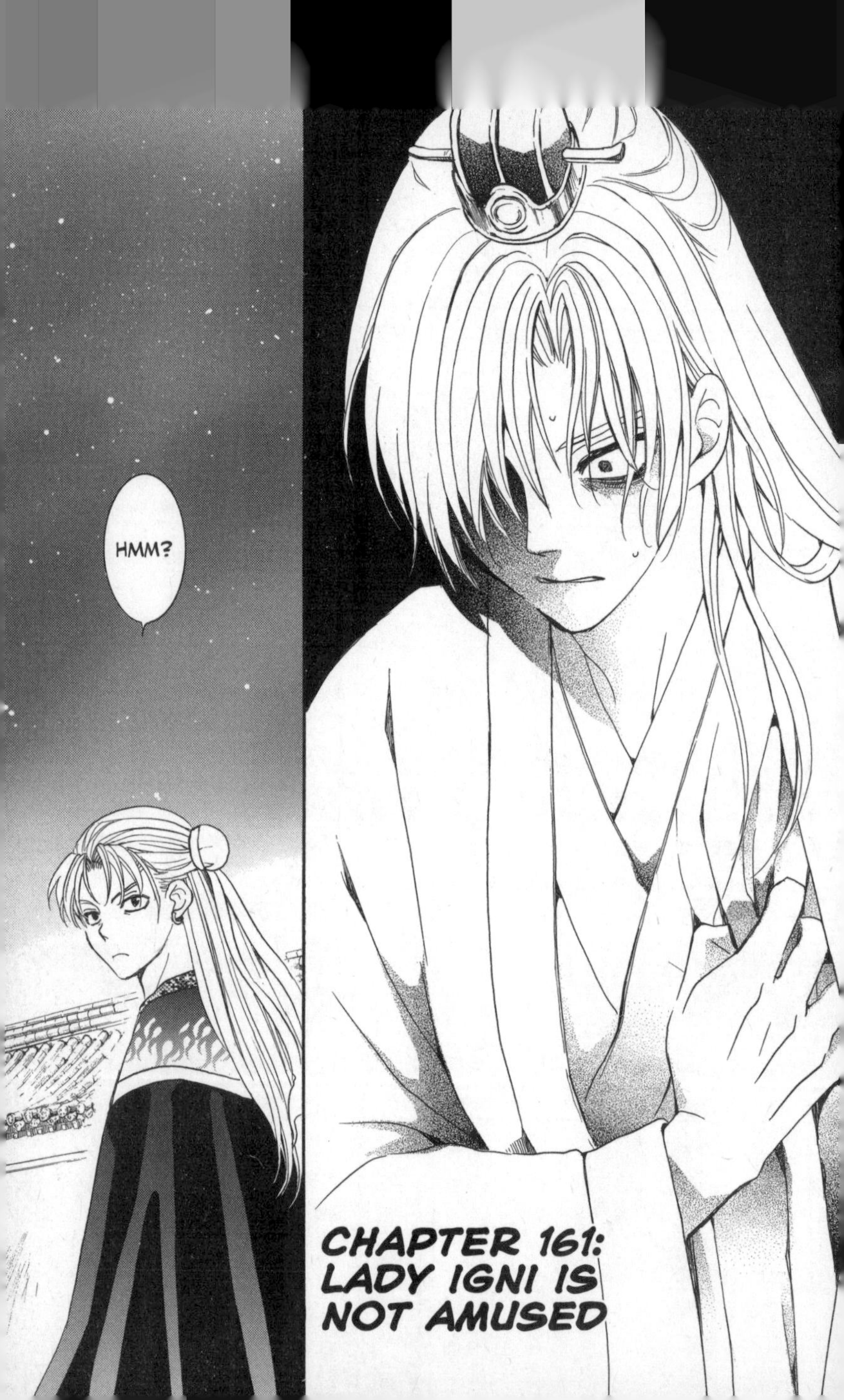
CHAPTER 161: LADY IGNI IS NOT AMUSED
HMM?

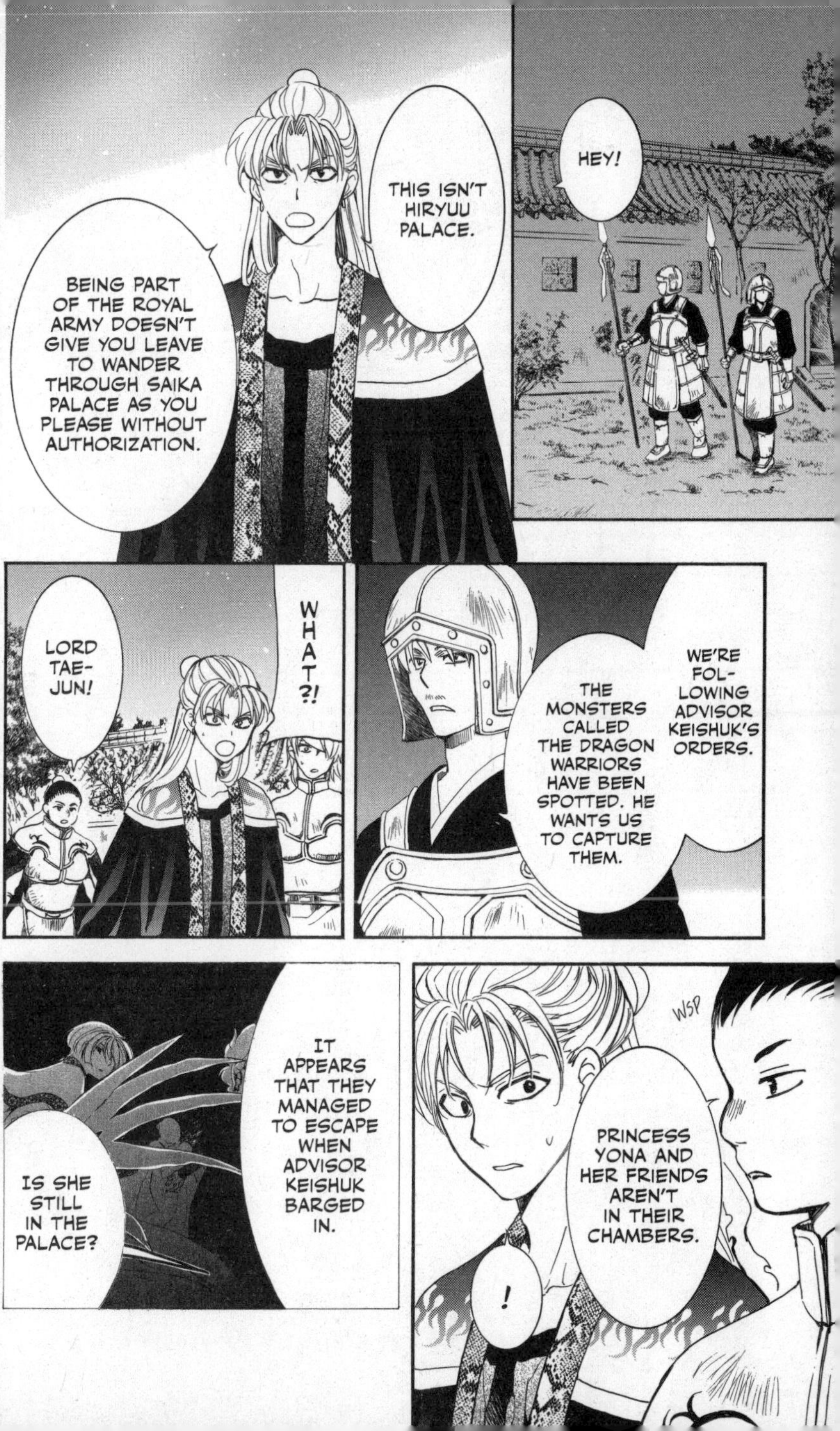
HEY!
THIS ISN'T HIRYUU PALACE.
BEING PART OF THE ROYAL ARMY DOESN'T GIVE YOU LEAVE TO WANDER THROUGH SAIKA PALACE AS YOU PLEASE WITHOUT AUTHORIZATION.
WE'RE FOL-LOWING ADVISOR KEISHUK'S ORDERS.
THE MONSTERS CALLED THE DRAGON WARRIORS HAVE BEEN SPOTTED. HE WANTS US TO CAPTURE THEM.
WHAT?!
LORD TAE-JUN!
WSP
PRINCESS YONA AND HER FRIENDS AREN'T IN THEIR CHAMBERS.
!
IT APPEARS THAT THEY MANAGED TO ESCAPE WHEN ADVISOR KEISHUK BARGED IN.
IS SHE STILL IN THE PALACE?

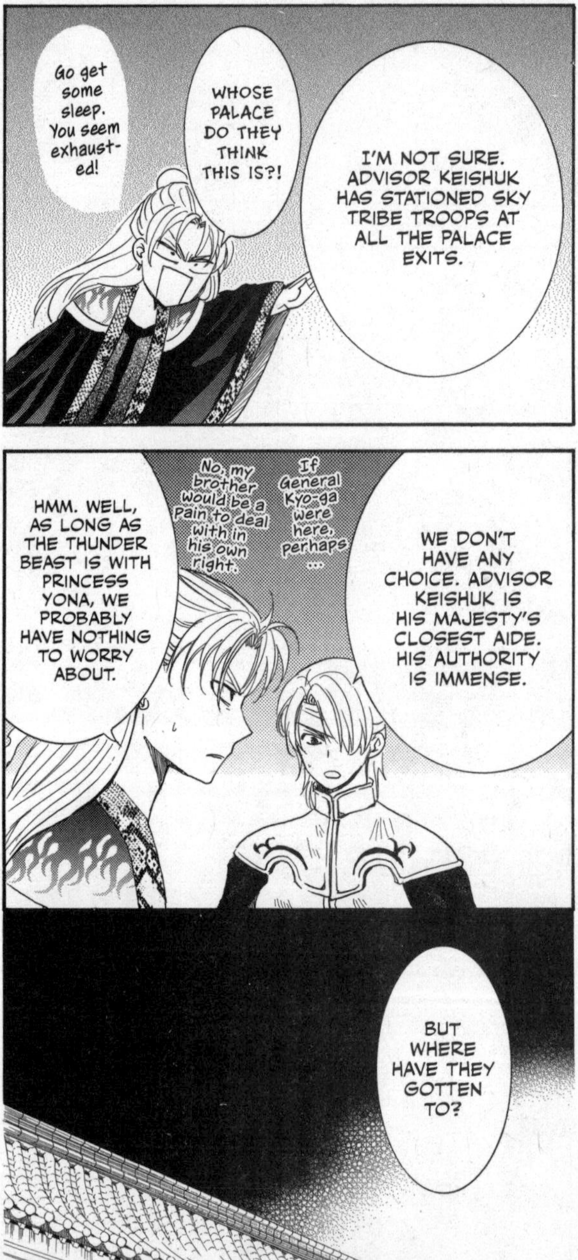
I'M NOT SURE. ADVISOR KEISHUK HAS STATIONED SKY TRIBE TROOPS AT ALL THE PALACE EXITS.
WHOSE PALACE DO THEY THINK THIS IS?!
Go get some sleep. You seem exhaust-ed!
WE DON'T HAVE ANY CHOICE. ADVISOR KEISHUK IS HIS MAJESTY'S CLOSEST AIDE. HIS AUTHORITY IS IMMENSE.
If General Kyo-ga were here, perhaps...
No, my brother would be a pain to deal with in his own right.
HMM. WELL, AS LONG AS THE THUNDER BEAST IS WITH PRINCESS YONA, WE PROBABLY HAVE NOTHING TO WORRY ABOUT.
BUT WHERE HAVE THEY GOTTEN TO?
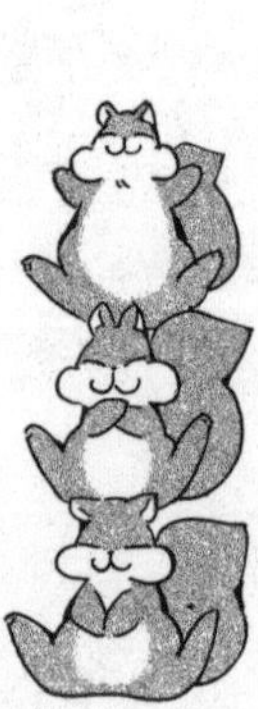

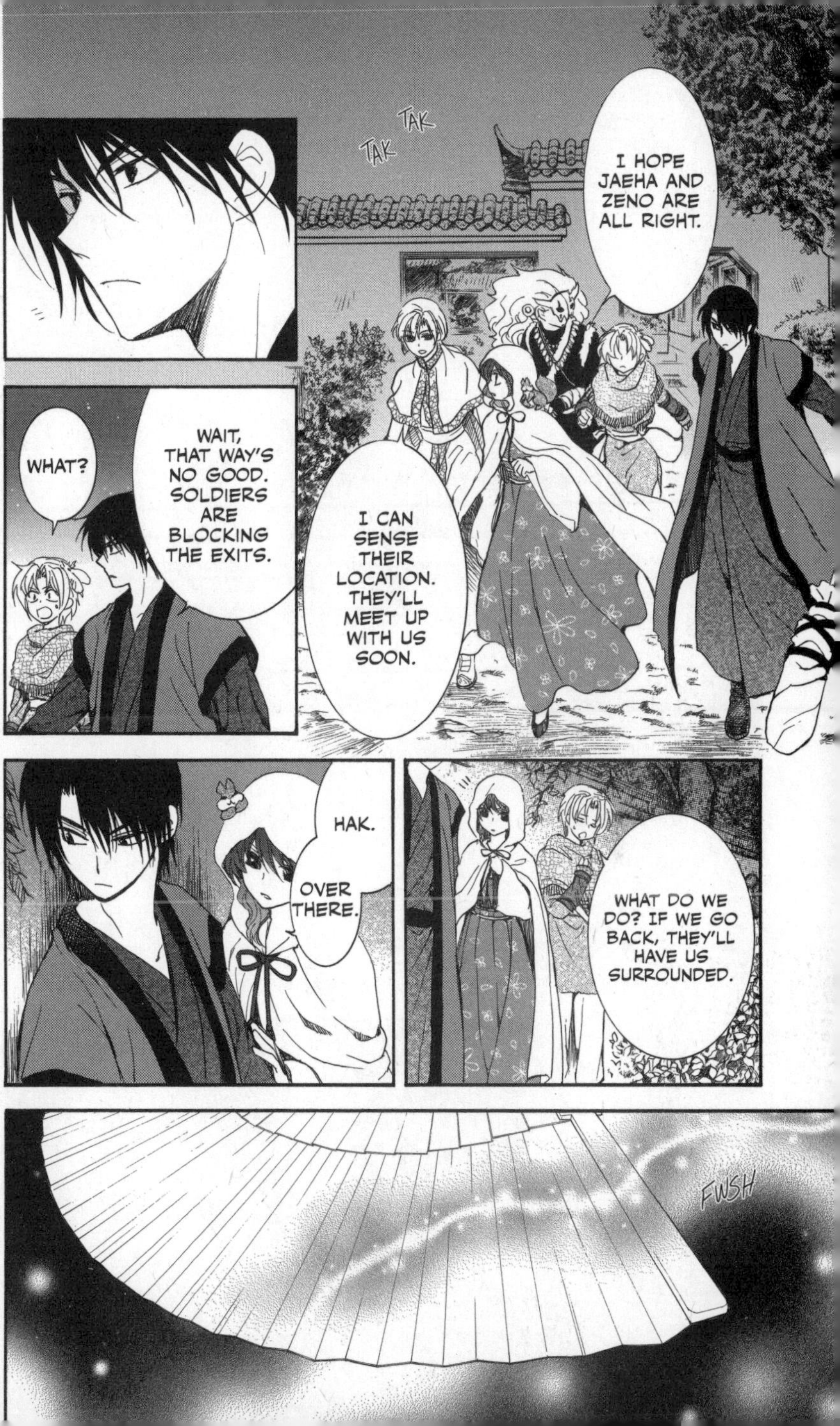
TAK
TAK
I HOPE JAEHA AND ZENO ARE ALL RIGHT.
I CAN SENSE THEIR LOCATION. THEY'LL MEET UP WITH US SOON.
WAIT, THAT WAY'S NO GOOD. SOLDIERS ARE BLOCKING THE EXITS.
WHAT?
WHAT DO WE DO? IF WE GO BACK, THEY'LL HAVE US SURROUNDED.
HAK.
OVER THERE.
FWSH

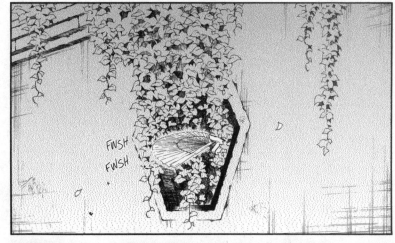

FWSH
FWSH

SKFF

ARE THEY HERE ?!

THEY WENT THIS WAY!

TAK
TAK

THEY'RE GONE...

SILENCE

HMM?

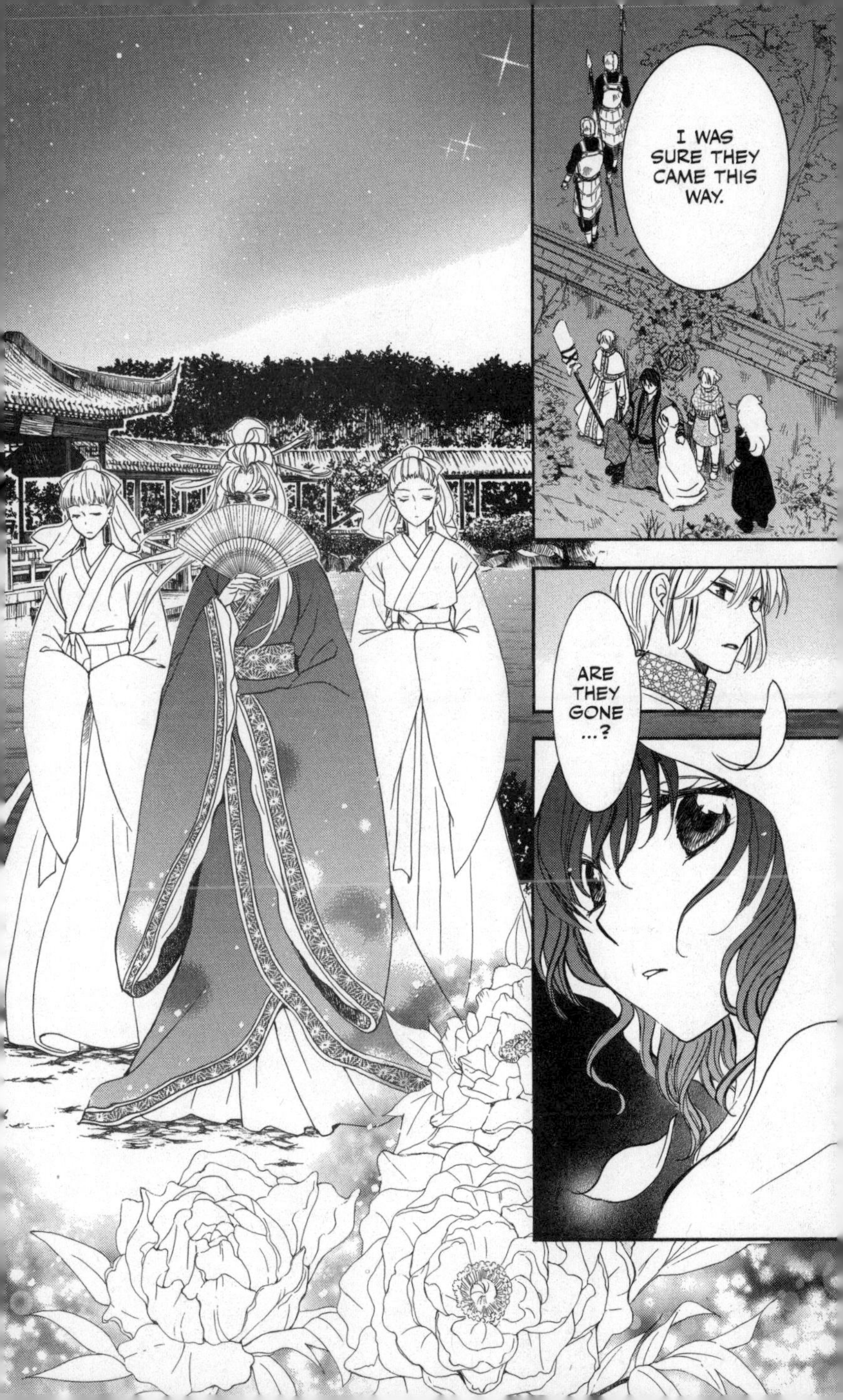
I WAS SURE THEY CAME THIS WAY.
ARE THEY GONE ...?

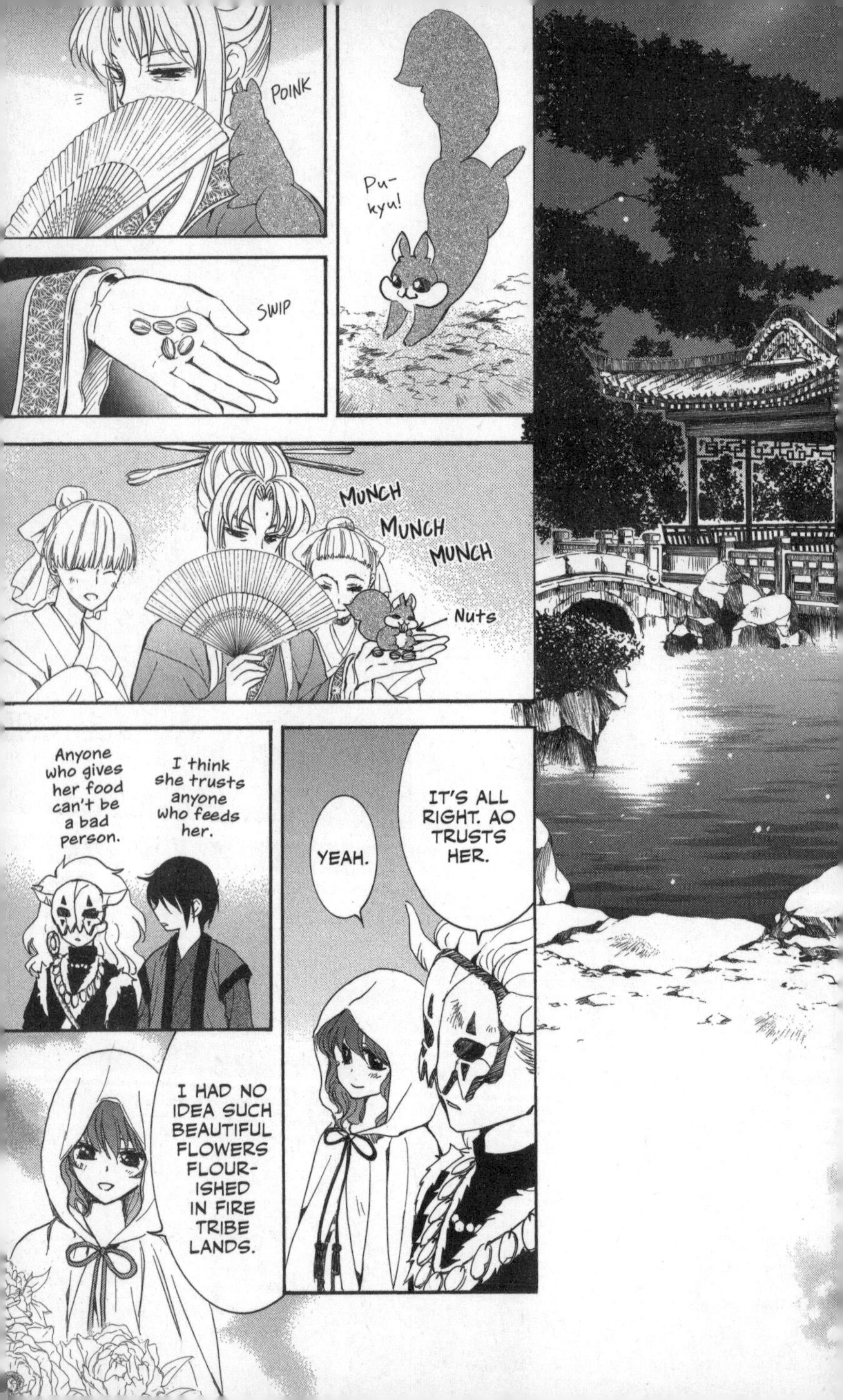
Pu-kyu!
POINK
SWIP
MUNCH MUNCH MUNCH
Nuts
IT'S ALL RIGHT. AO TRUSTS HER.
YEAH.
I think she trusts anyone who feeds her.
Anyone who gives her food can't be a bad person.
I HAD NO IDEA SUCH BEAUTIFUL FLOWERS FLOURISHED IN FIRE TRIBE LANDS.

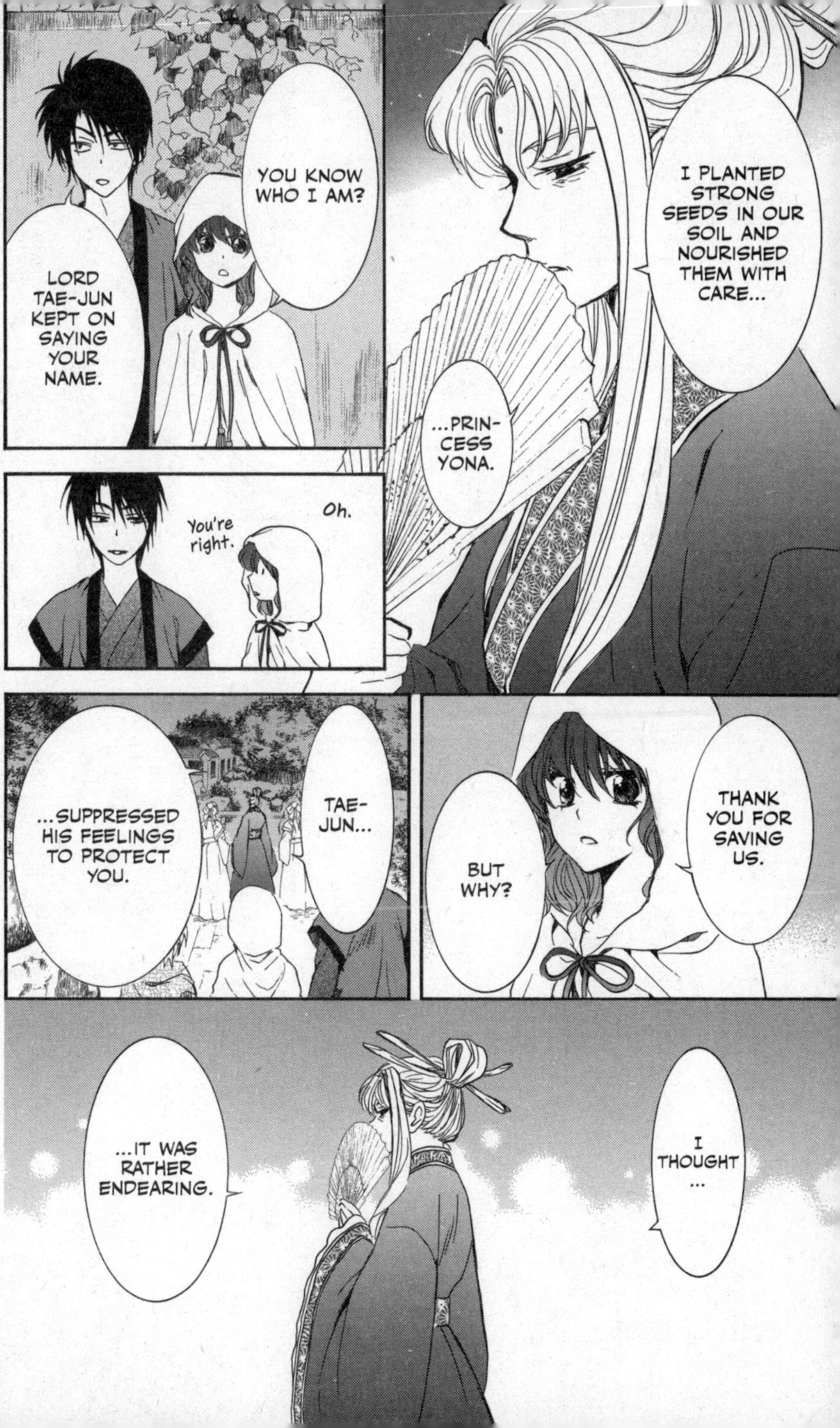
I PLANTED STRONG SEEDS IN OUR SOIL AND NOURISHED THEM WITH CARE...
...PRINCESS YONA.
YOU KNOW WHO I AM?
LORD TAE-JUN KEPT ON SAYING YOUR NAME.
Oh.
You're right.
THANK YOU FOR SAVING US.
BUT WHY?
TAE-JUN...
...SUPPRESSED HIS FEELINGS TO PROTECT YOU.
I THOUGHT...
...IT WAS RATHER ENDEARING.

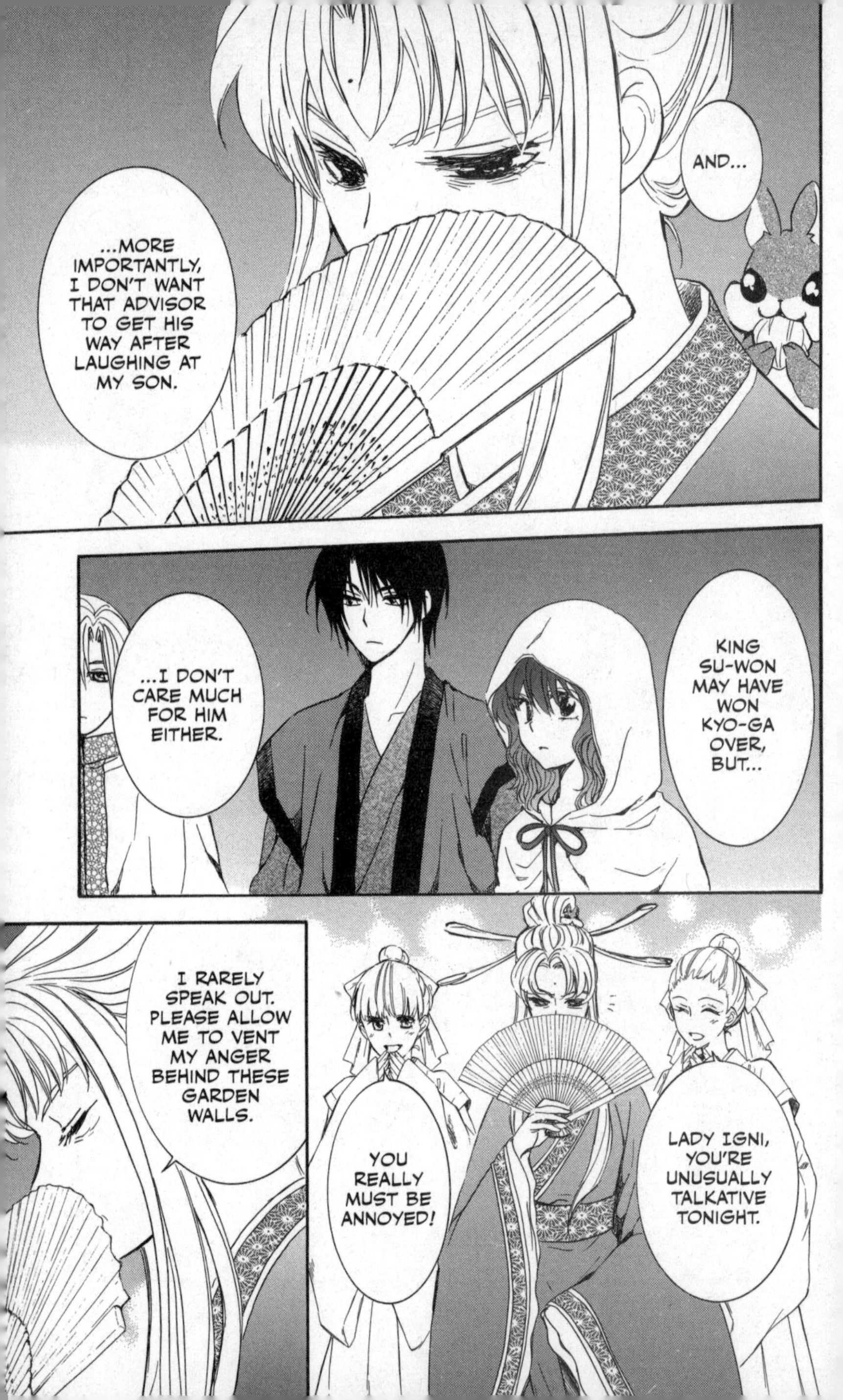
AND...
...MORE IMPORTANTLY, I DON'T WANT THAT ADVISOR TO GET HIS WAY AFTER LAUGHING AT MY SON.
KING SU-WON MAY HAVE WON KYO-GA OVER, BUT...
...I DON'T CARE MUCH FOR HIM EITHER.
LADY IGNI, YOU'RE UNUSUALLY TALKATIVE TONIGHT.
YOU REALLY MUST BE ANNOYED!
I RARELY SPEAK OUT. PLEASE ALLOW ME TO VENT MY ANGER BEHIND THESE GARDEN WALLS.

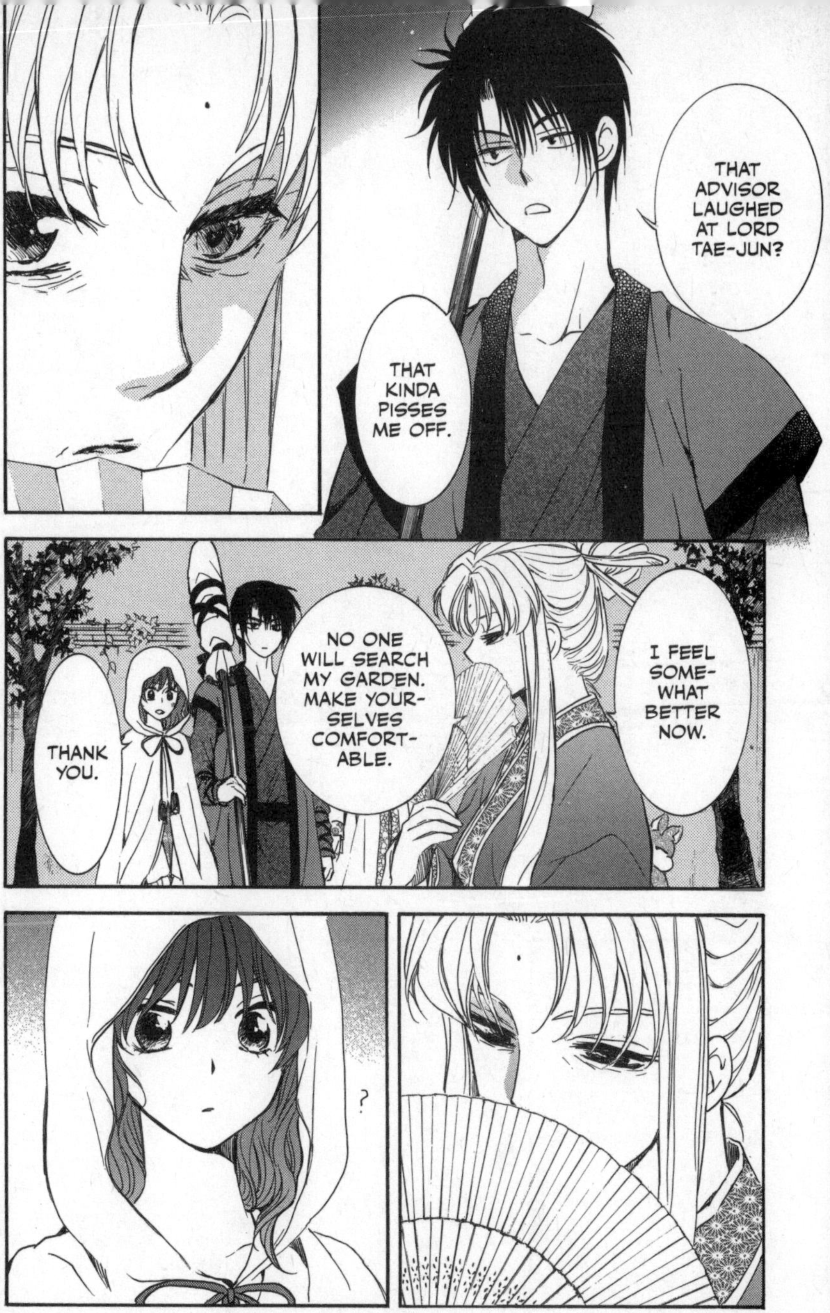
THAT ADVISOR LAUGHED AT LORD TAE-JUN?
THAT KINDA PISSES ME OFF.
I FEEL SOMEWHAT BETTER NOW.
NO ONE WILL SEARCH MY GARDEN. MAKE YOURSELVES COMFORTABLE.
THANK YOU.
?

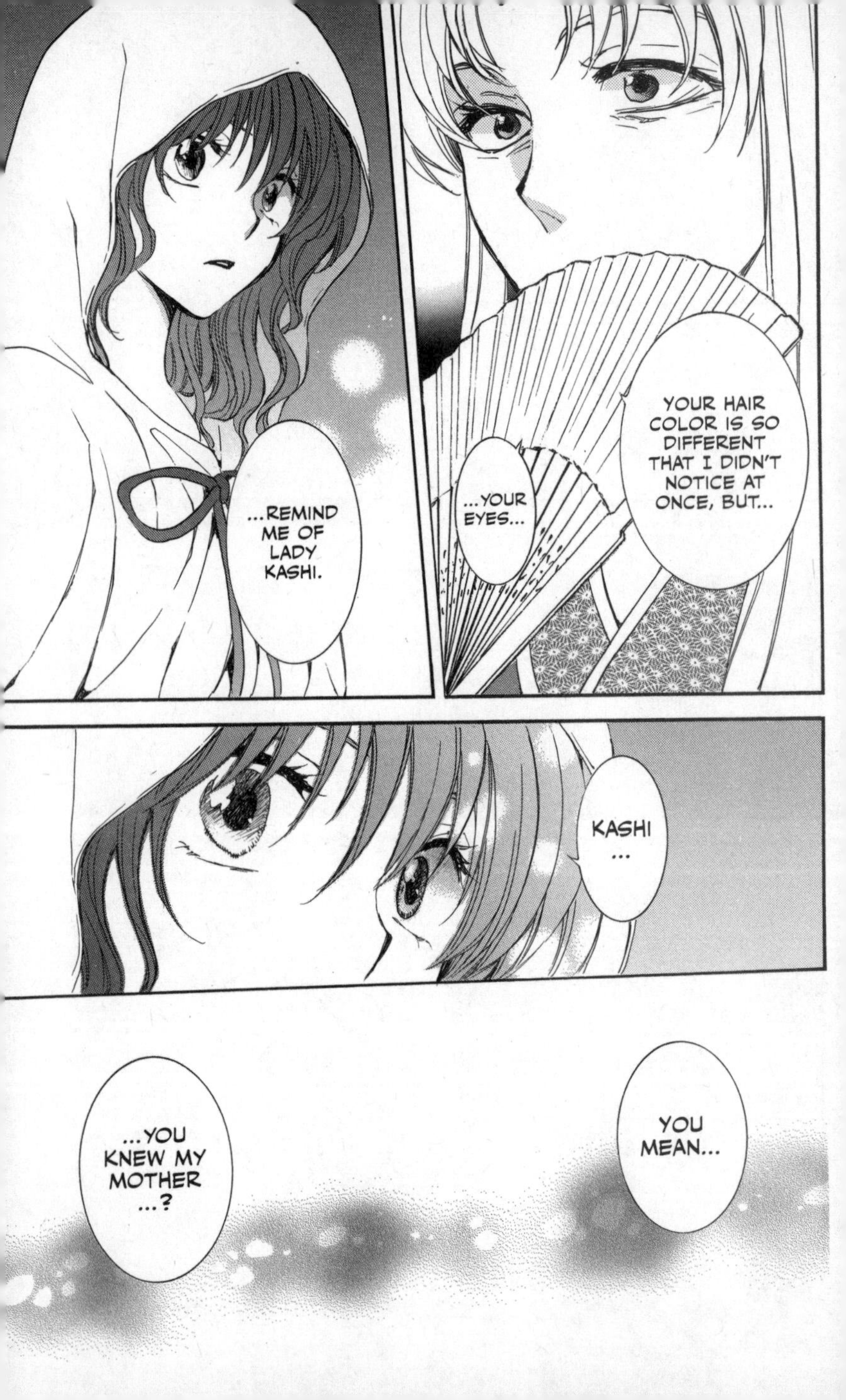
YOUR HAIR COLOR IS SO DIFFERENT THAT I DIDN'T NOTICE AT ONCE, BUT...
...YOUR EYES...
...REMIND ME OF LADY KASHI.
KASHI ...
YOU MEAN...
...YOU KNEW MY MOTHER ...?

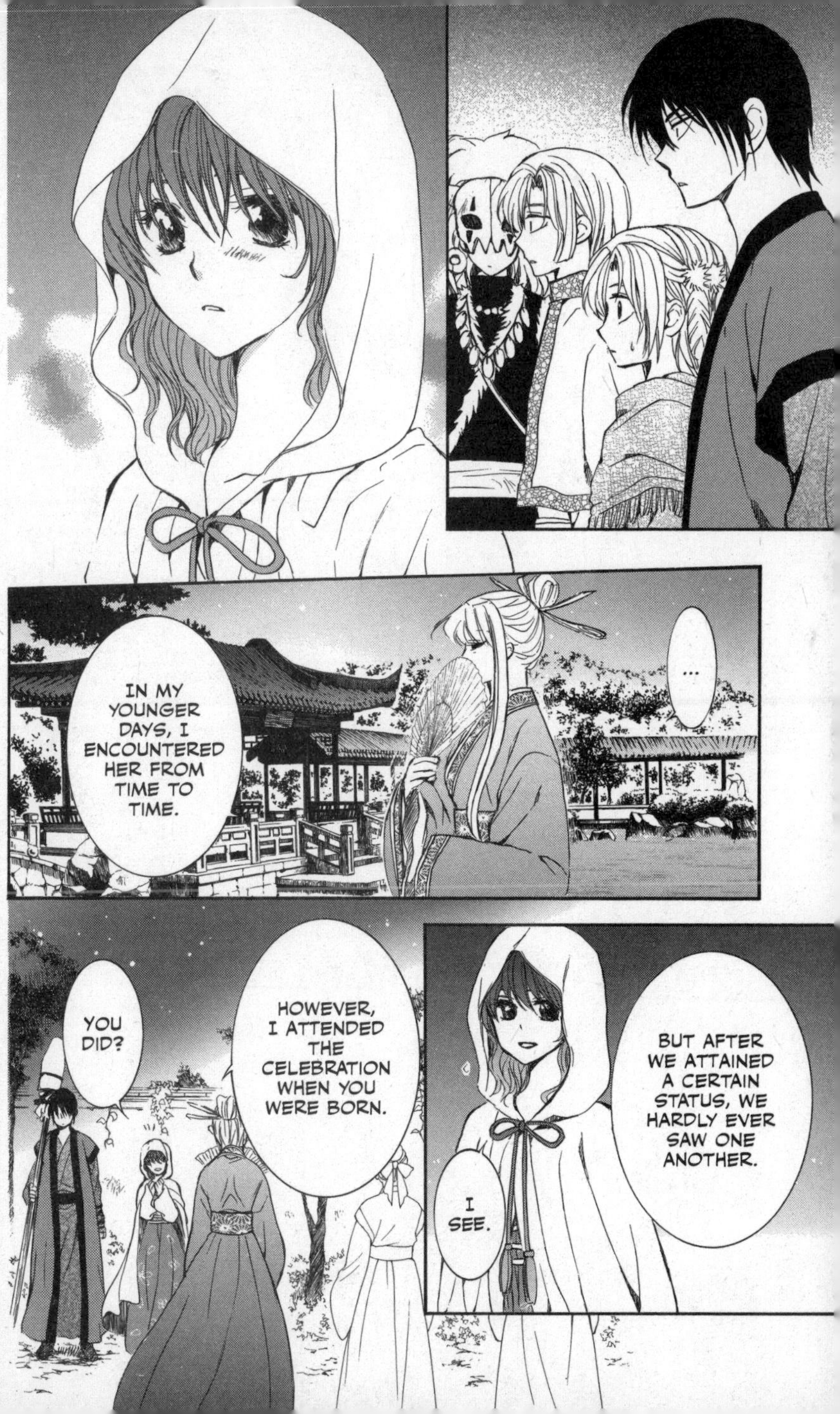
...
IN MY YOUNGER DAYS, I ENCOUNTERED HER FROM TIME TO TIME.
BUT AFTER WE ATTAINED A CERTAIN STATUS, WE HARDLY EVER SAW ONE ANOTHER.
I SEE.
HOWEVER, I ATTENDED THE CELEBRATION WHEN YOU WERE BORN.
YOU DID?

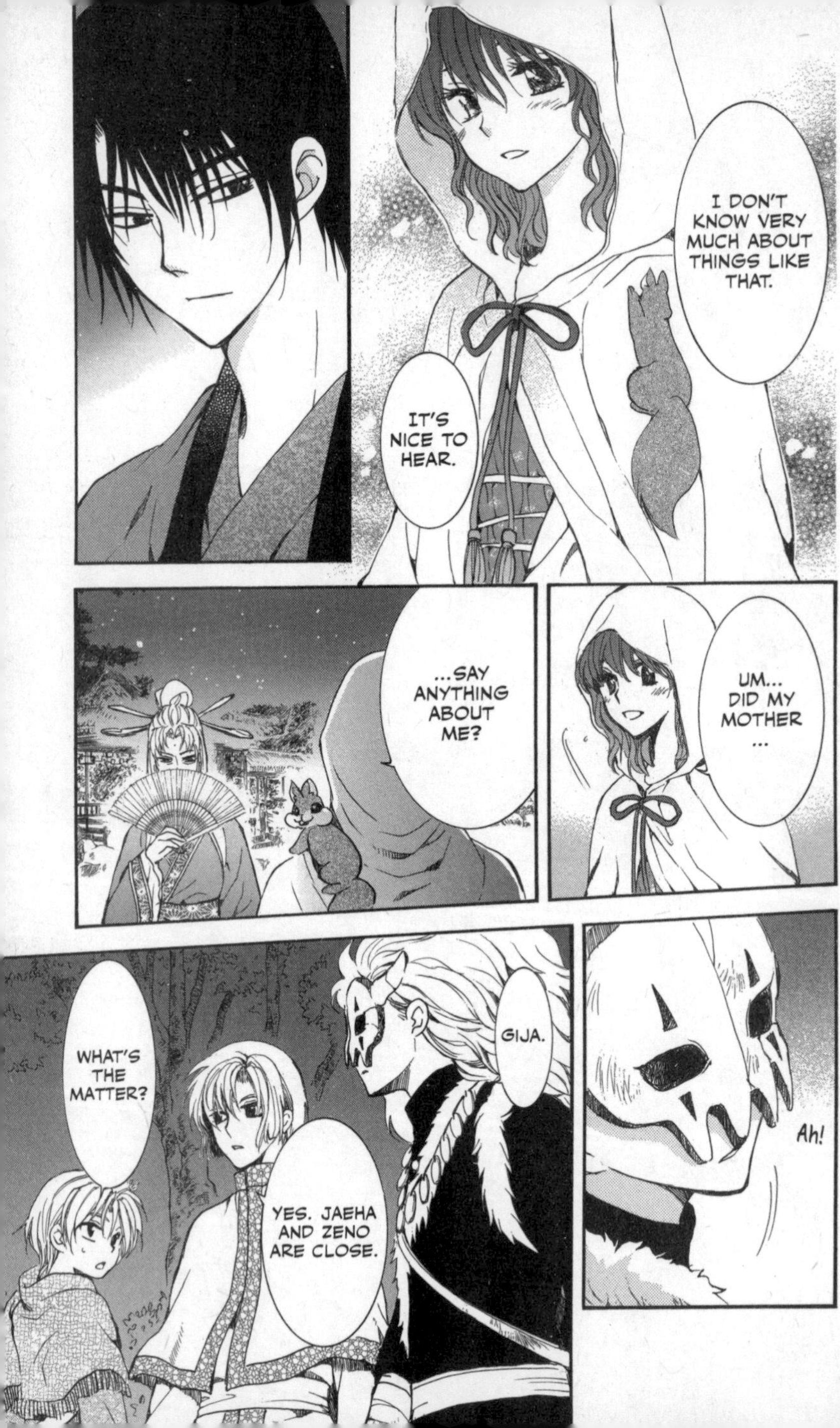
I DON'T KNOW VERY MUCH ABOUT THINGS LIKE THAT.
IT'S NICE TO HEAR.
UM... DID MY MOTHER ...
...SAY ANYTHING ABOUT ME?
Ah!
GIJA.
WHAT'S THE MATTER?
YES. JAEHA AND ZENO ARE CLOSE.

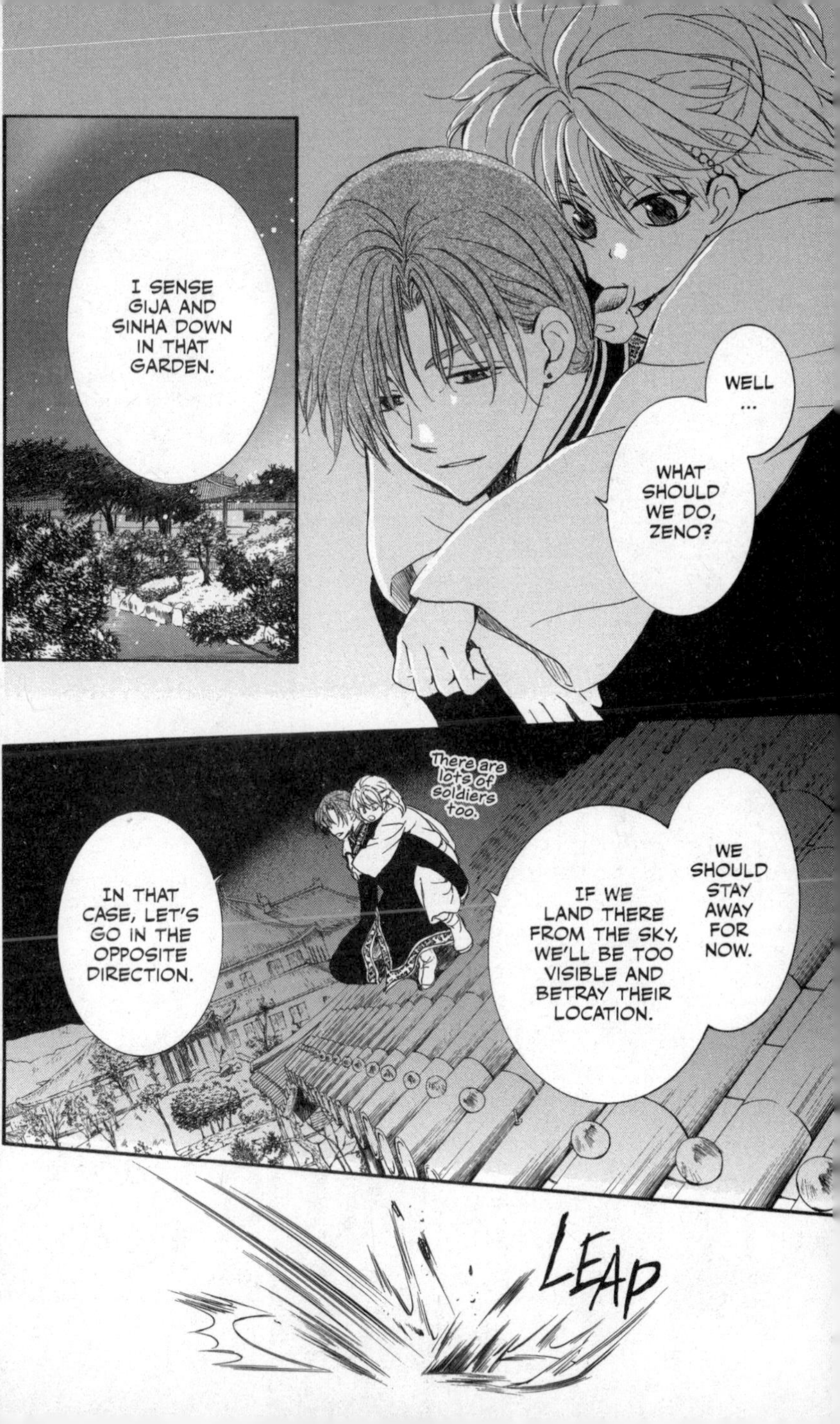
WELL ...
WHAT SHOULD WE DO, ZENO?
I SENSE GIJA AND SINHA DOWN IN THAT GARDEN.
WE SHOULD STAY AWAY FOR NOW.
IF WE LAND THERE FROM THE SKY, WE'LL BE TOO VISIBLE AND BETRAY THEIR LOCATION.
There are lots of soldiers too.
IN THAT CASE, LET'S GO IN THE OPPOSITE DIRECTION.
LEAP

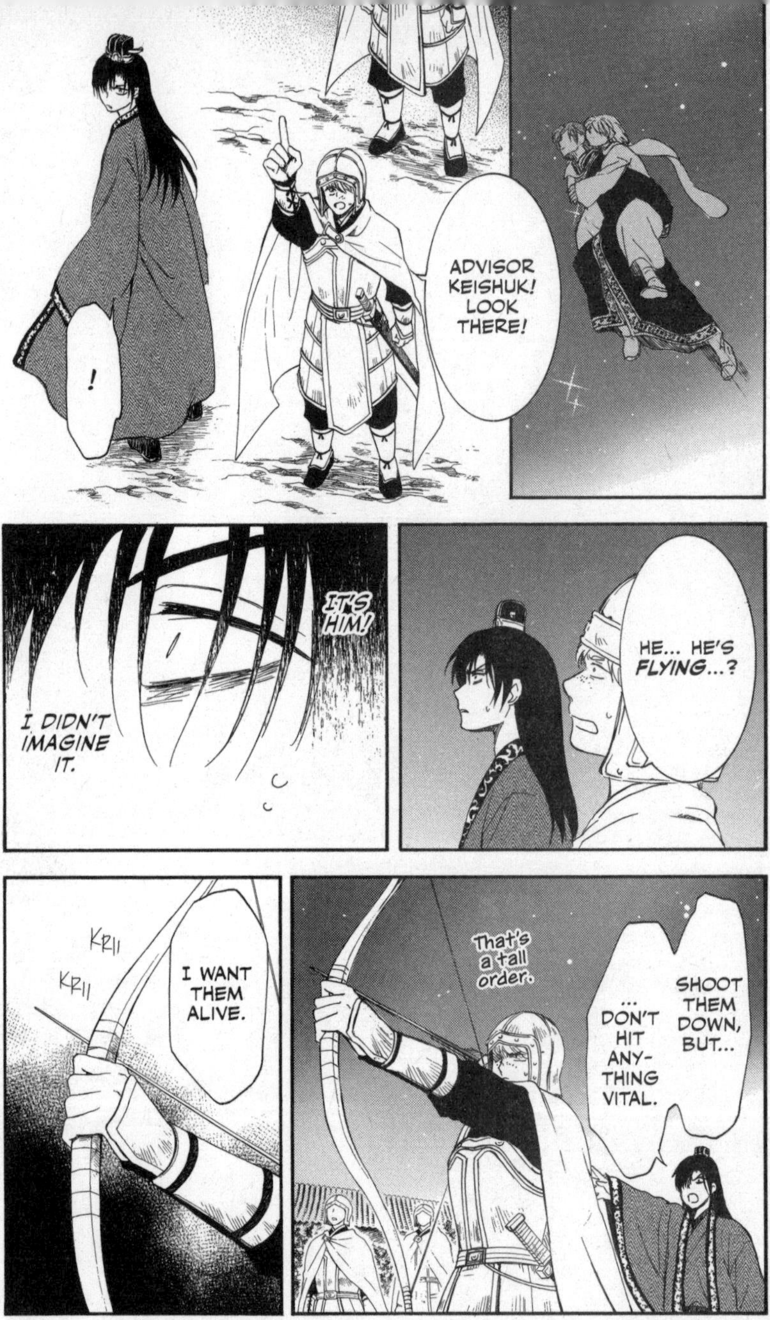
ADVISOR KEISHUK! LOOK THERE!
!
HE... HE'S *FLYING*...?
IT'S HIM!
I DIDN'T IMAGINE IT.
SHOOT THEM DOWN, BUT...
...DON'T HIT ANY-THING VITAL.
That's a tall order.
I WANT THEM ALIVE.
KRII
KRII

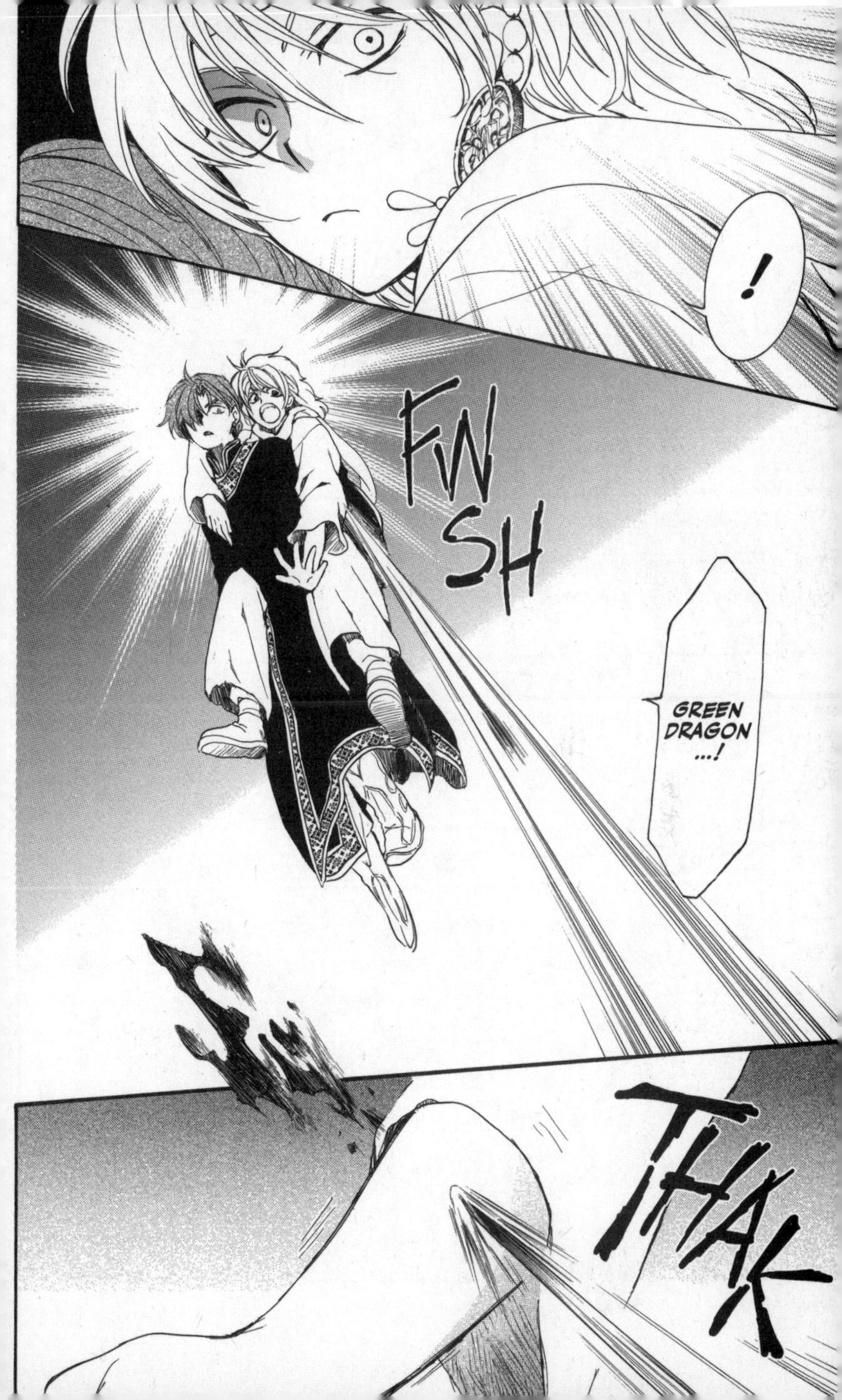
!
FWSH
GREEN DRAGON ...!
THAK

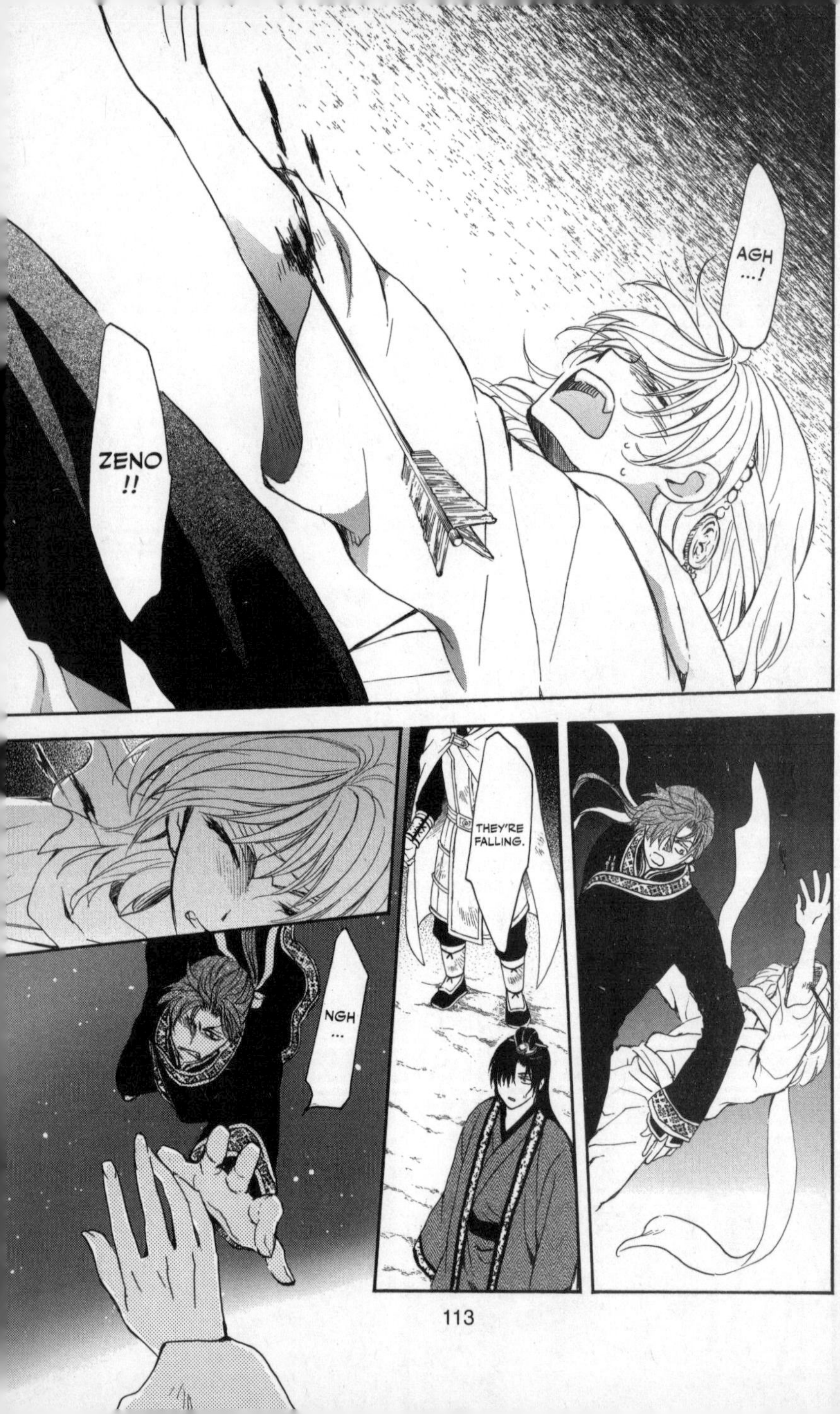
AGH ...!
ZENO !!
THEY'RE FALLING.
NGH ...

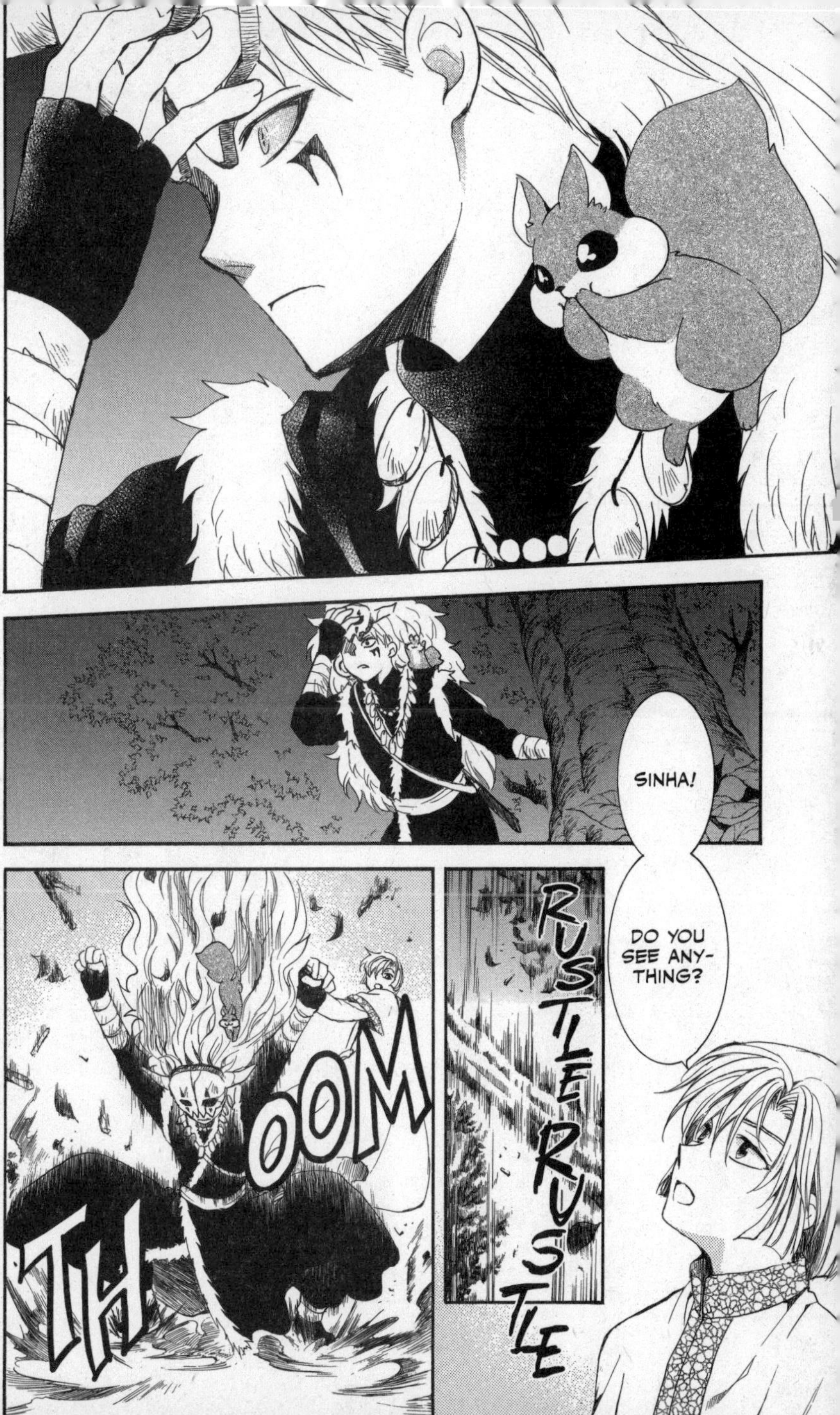
SINHA!
DO YOU SEE ANY-THING?
RUSTLE RUSTLE
THOOM

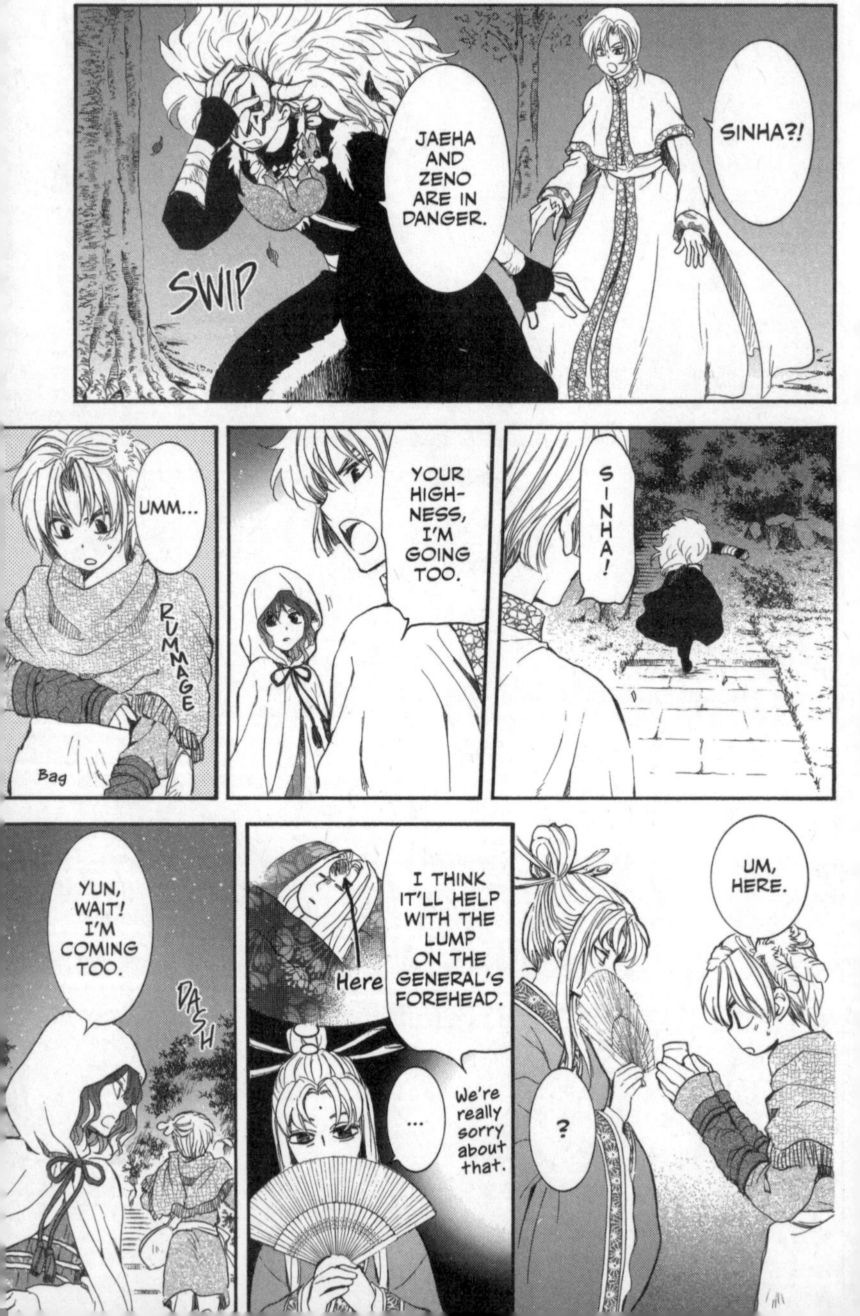
SINHA?!
JAEHA AND ZENO ARE IN DANGER.
SWIP
SINHA!
YOUR HIGH-NESS, I'M GOING TOO.
UMM...
RUMMAGE
Bag
UM, HERE.
?
I THINK IT'LL HELP WITH THE LUMP ON THE GENERAL'S FOREHEAD.
Here
...
We're really sorry about that.
YUN, WAIT! I'M COMING TOO.
DASH

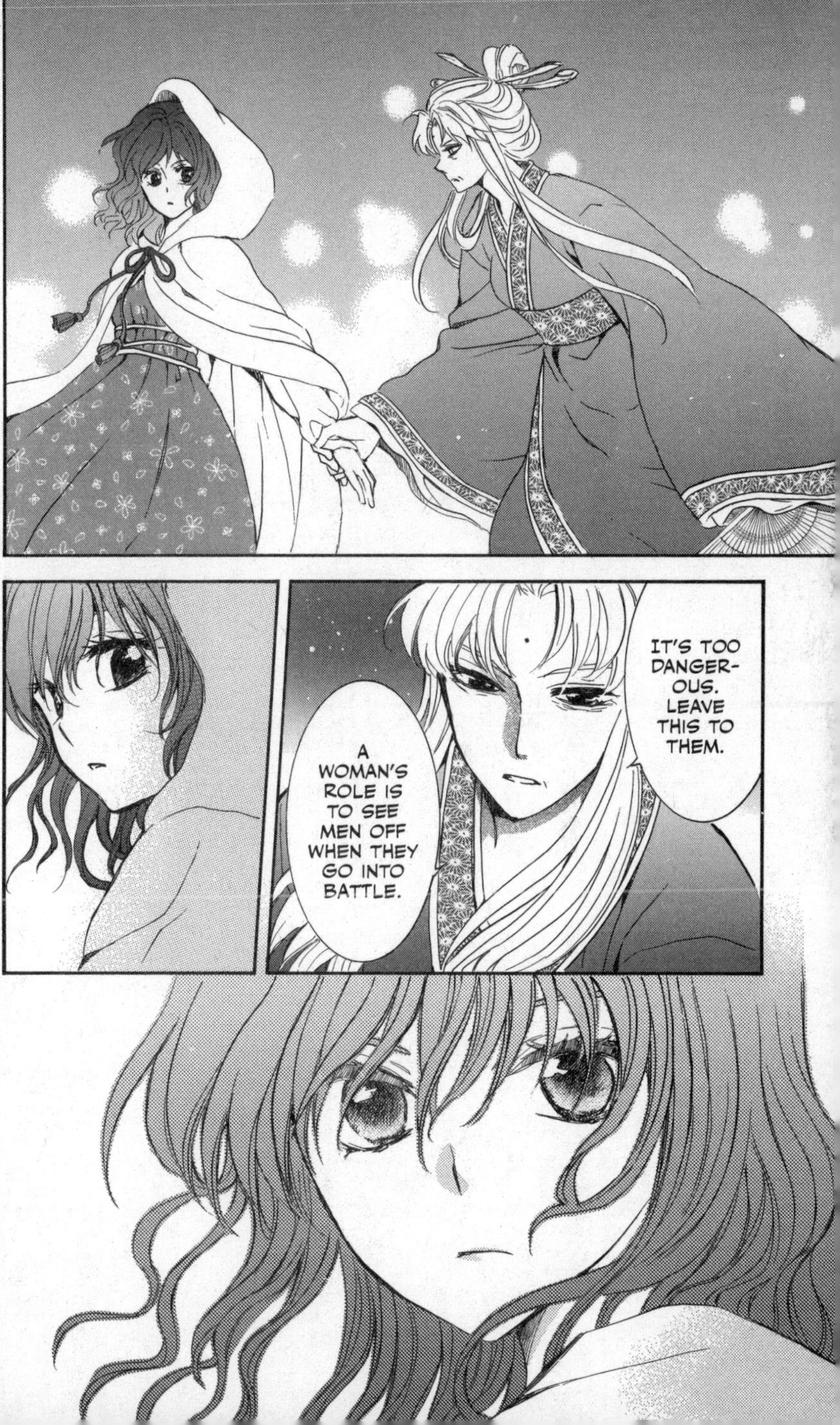
IT'S TOO DANGEROUS. LEAVE THIS TO THEM.
A WOMAN'S ROLE IS TO SEE MEN OFF WHEN THEY GO INTO BATTLE.

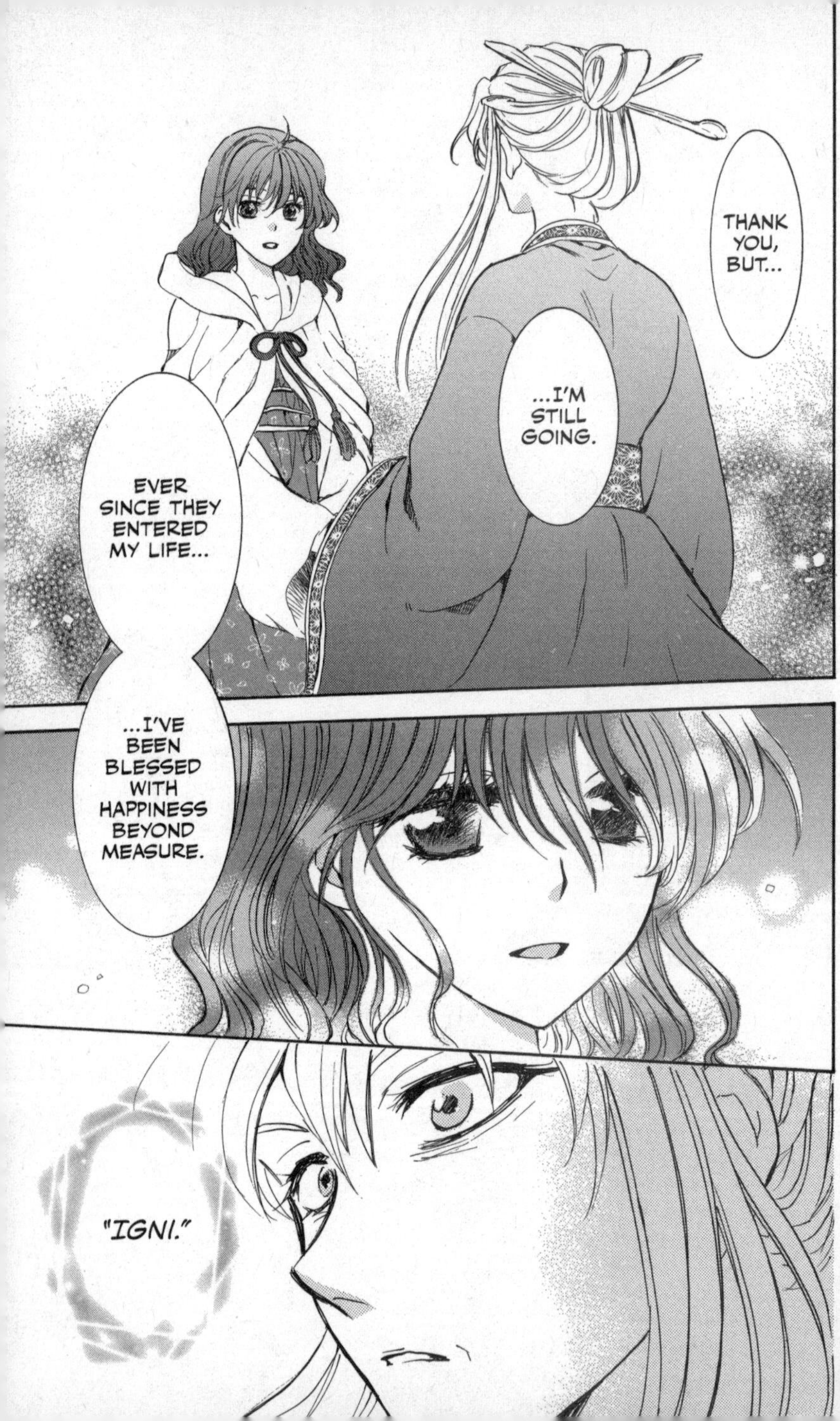
THANK YOU, BUT...
...I'M STILL GOING.
EVER SINCE THEY ENTERED MY LIFE...
...I'VE BEEN BLESSED WITH HAPPINESS BEYOND MEASURE.
"IGNI."

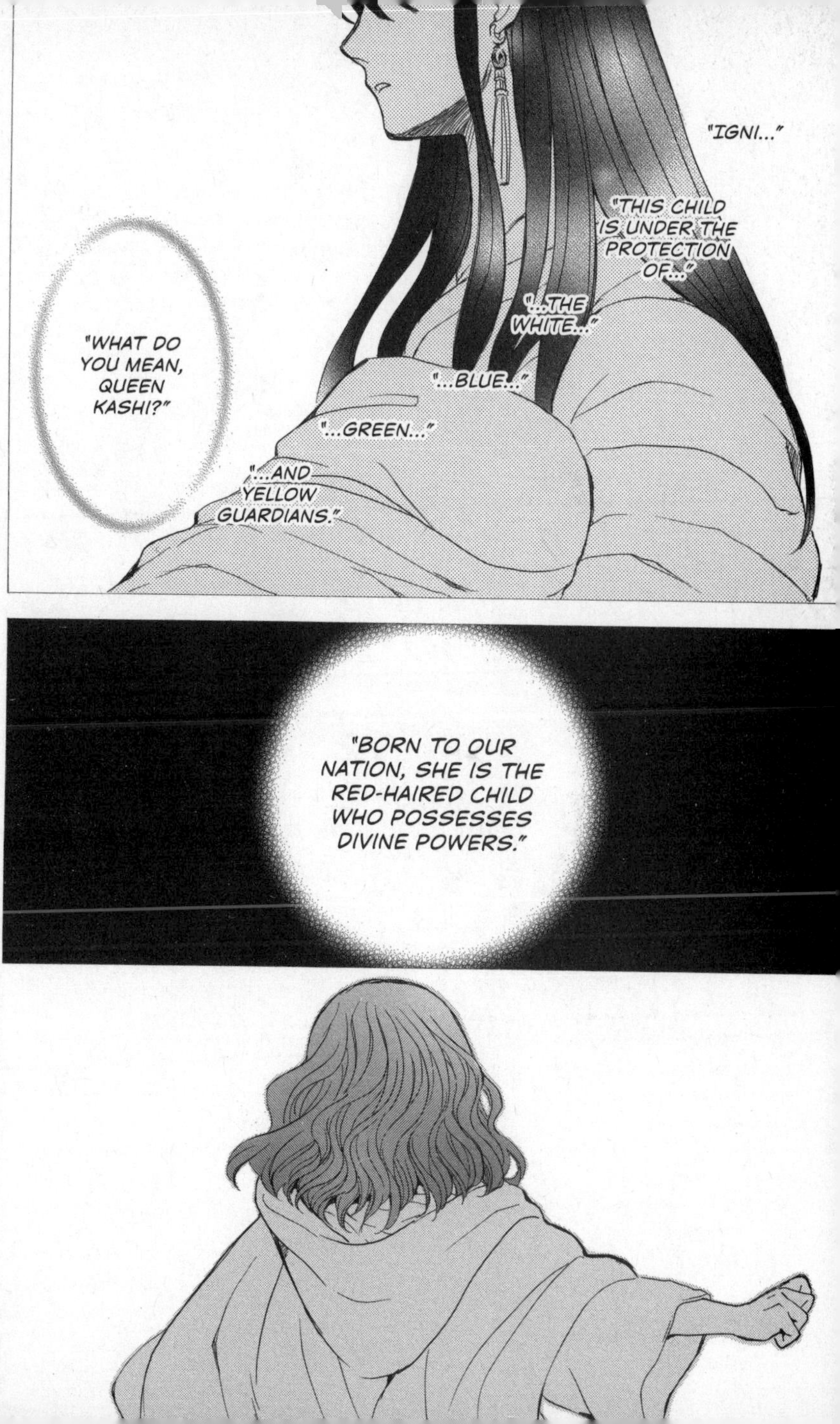
"IGNI..."
"THIS CHILD IS UNDER THE PROTECTION OF..."
"...THE WHITE..."
"...BLUE..."
"...GREEN..."
"...AND YELLOW GUARDIANS."
"WHAT DO YOU MEAN, QUEEN KASHI?"
"BORN TO OUR NATION, SHE IS THE RED-HAIRED CHILD WHO POSSESSES DIVINE POWERS."

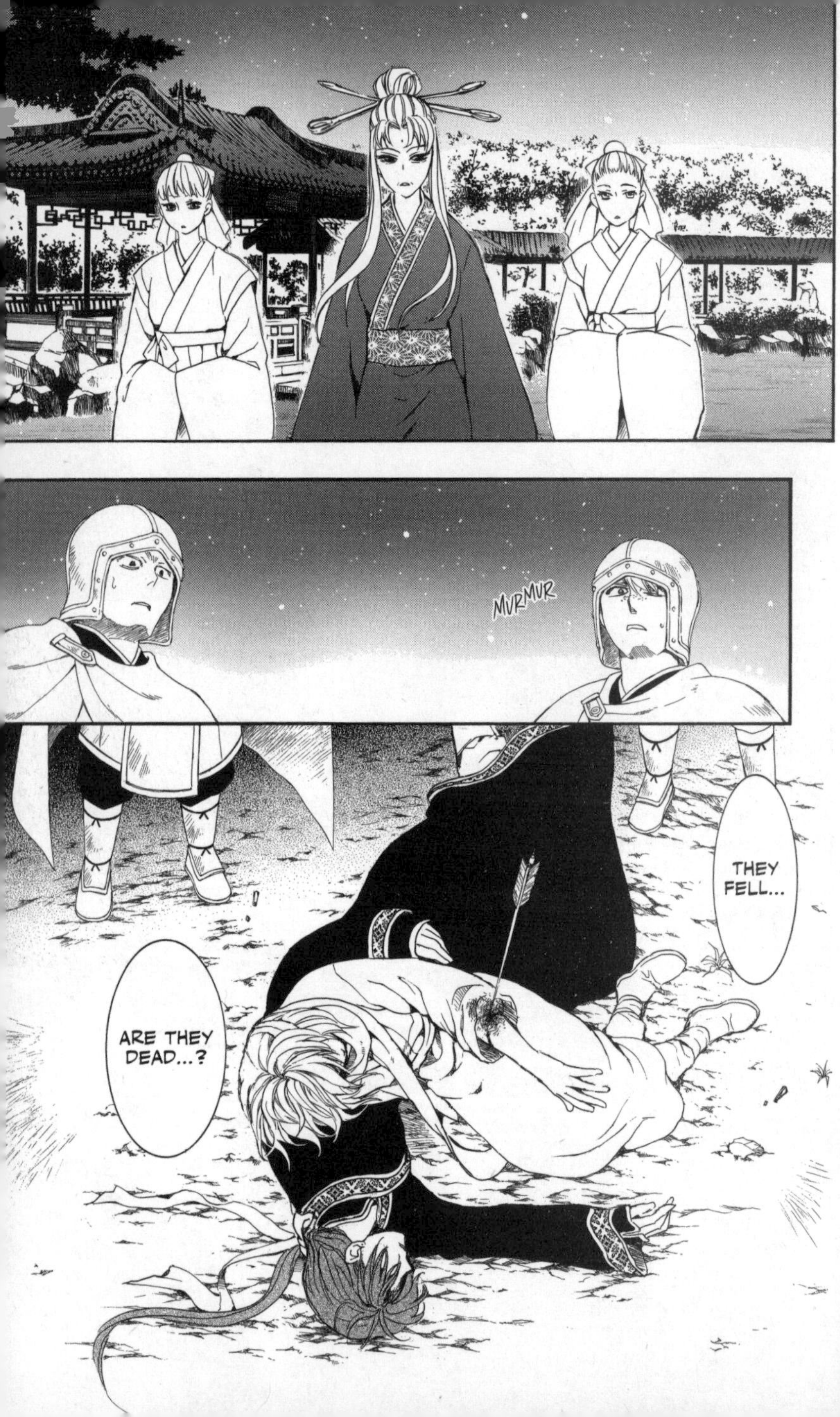
MURMUR
THEY FELL...
ARE THEY DEAD...?

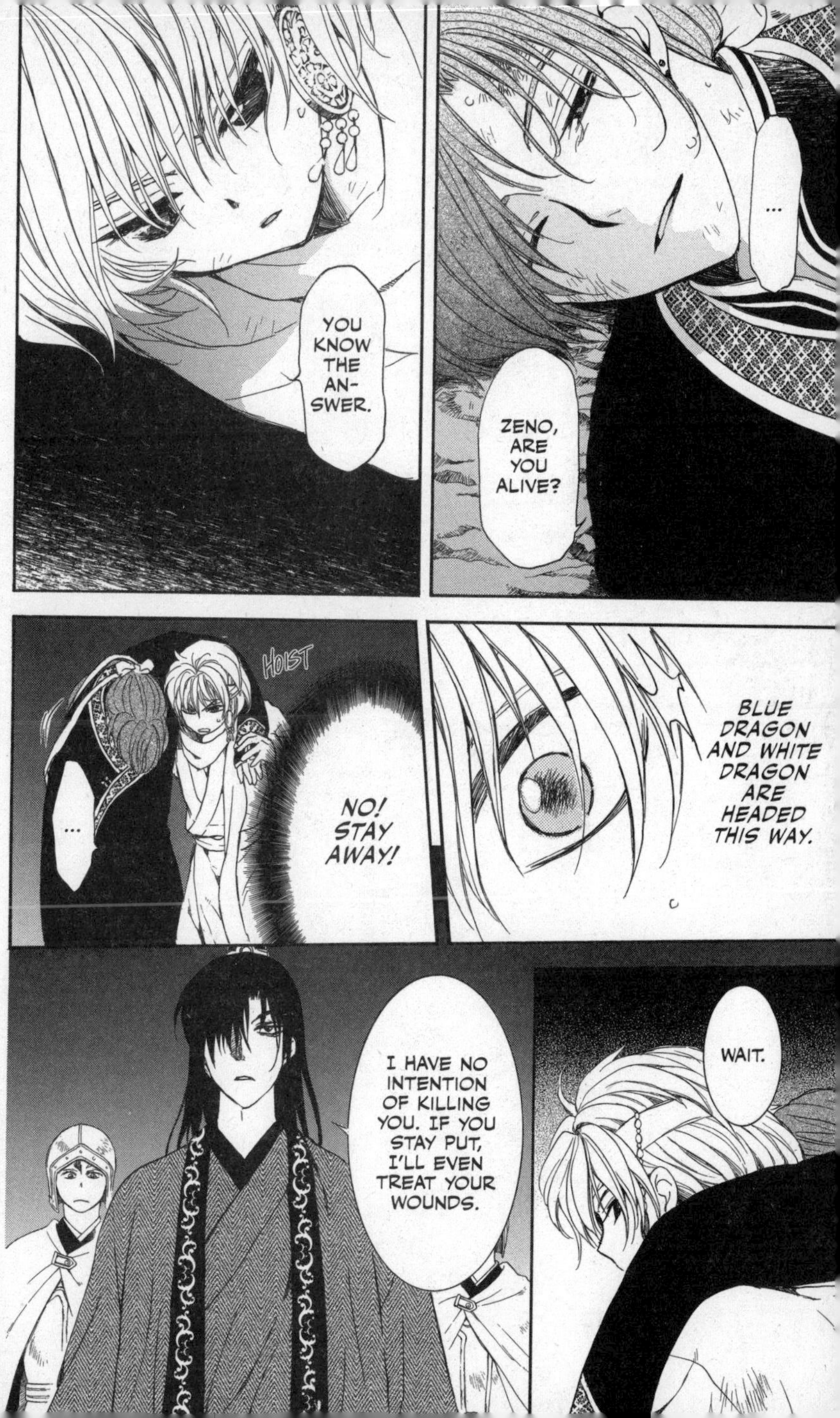
...
ZENO, ARE YOU ALIVE?
YOU KNOW THE AN-SWER.
BLUE DRAGON AND WHITE DRAGON ARE HEADED THIS WAY.
HOIST
NO! STAY AWAY!
...
WAIT.
I HAVE NO INTENTION OF KILLING YOU. IF YOU STAY PUT, I'LL EVEN TREAT YOUR WOUNDS.

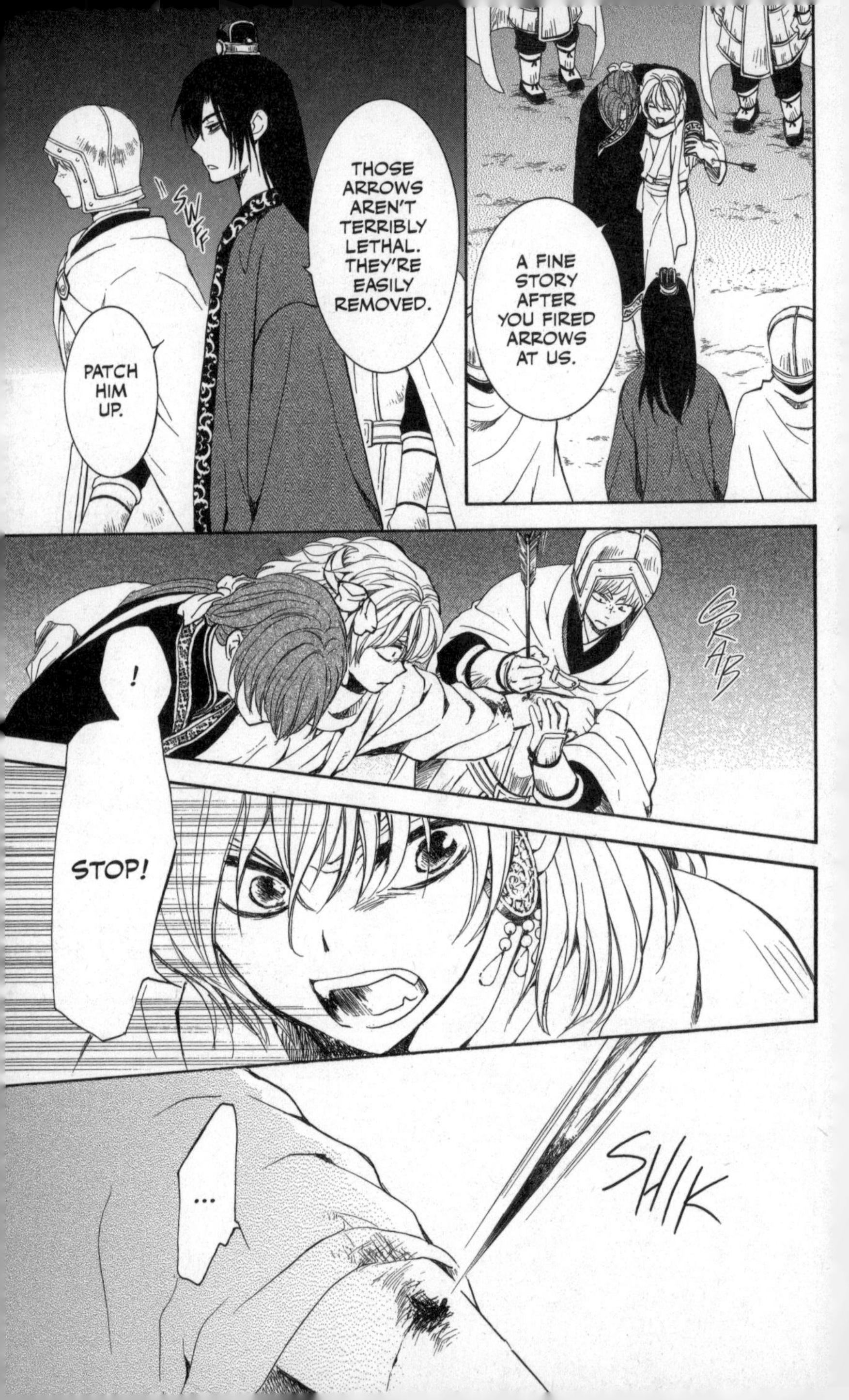
A FINE STORY AFTER YOU FIRED ARROWS AT US.
SWFF
THOSE ARROWS AREN'T TERRIBLY LETHAL. THEY'RE EASILY REMOVED.
PATCH HIM UP.
GRAB
!
STOP!
SHIK
...

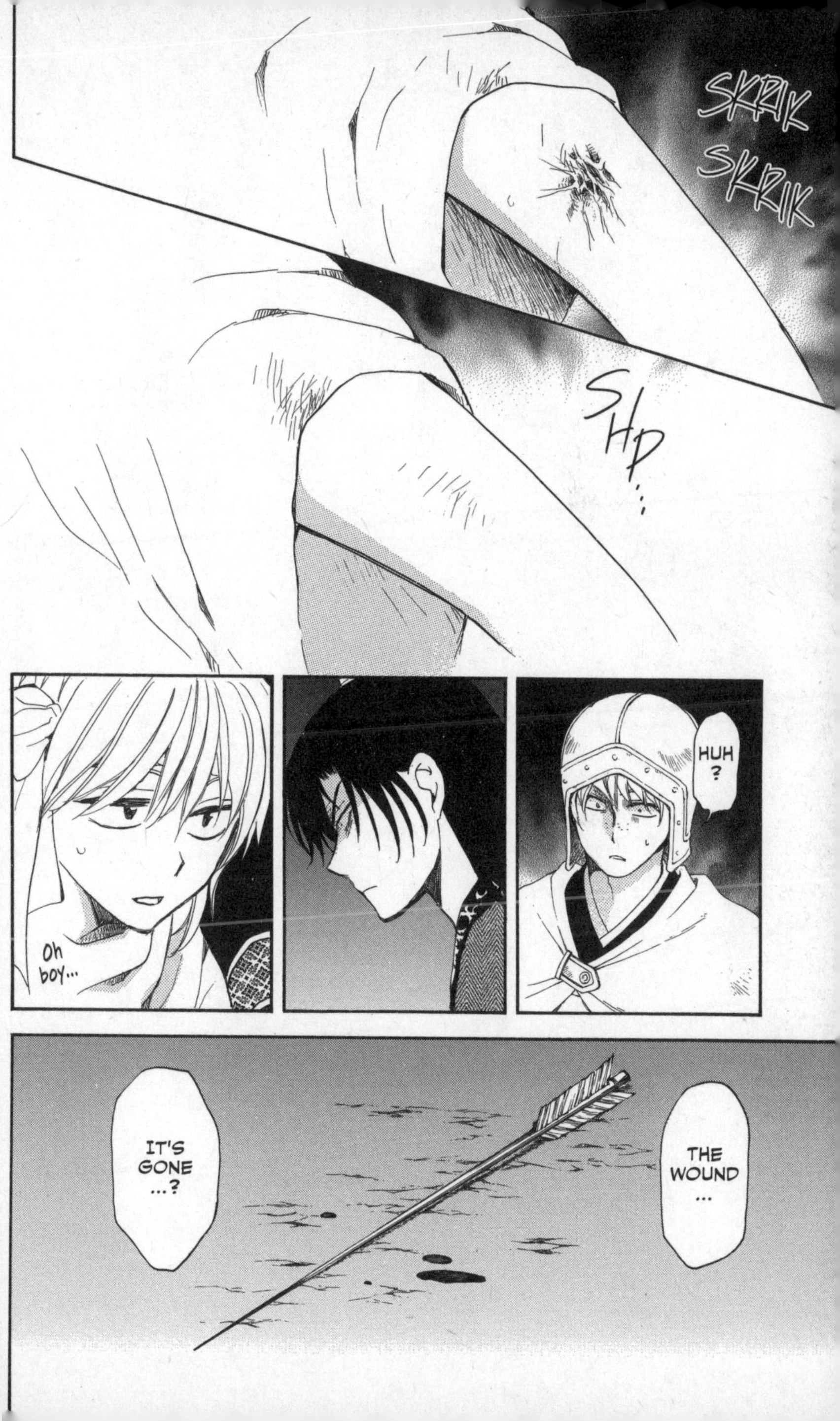
SKRIK
SKRIK
SHP...
HUH?
Oh boy...
THE WOUND ...
IT'S GONE ...?

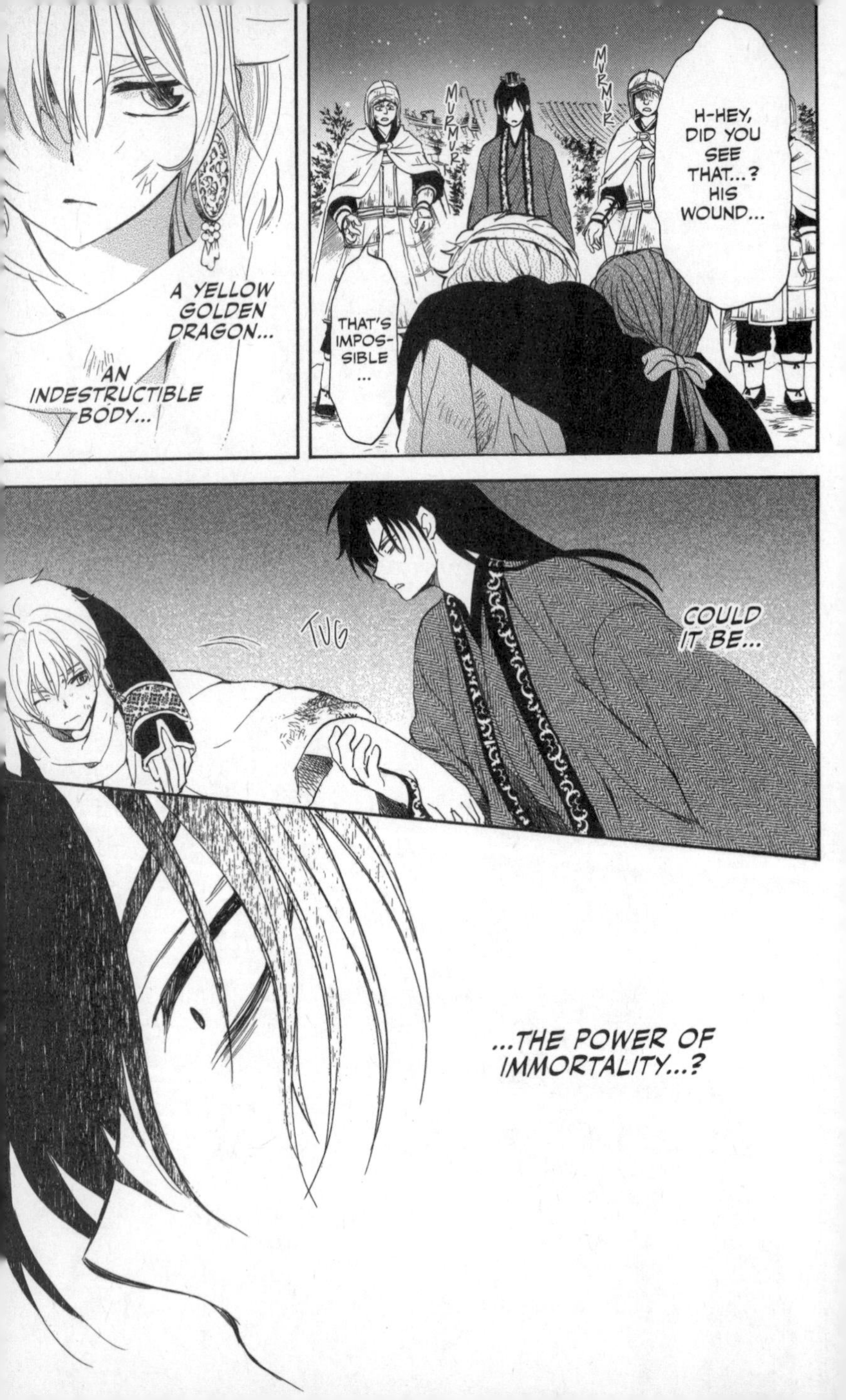
H-HEY, DID YOU SEE THAT...? HIS WOUND...
MURMUR
MURMUR
THAT'S IMPOS-SIBLE...
A YELLOW GOLDEN DRAGON...
AN INDESTRUCTIBLE BODY...
COULD IT BE...
TUG
...THE POWER OF IMMORTALITY...?

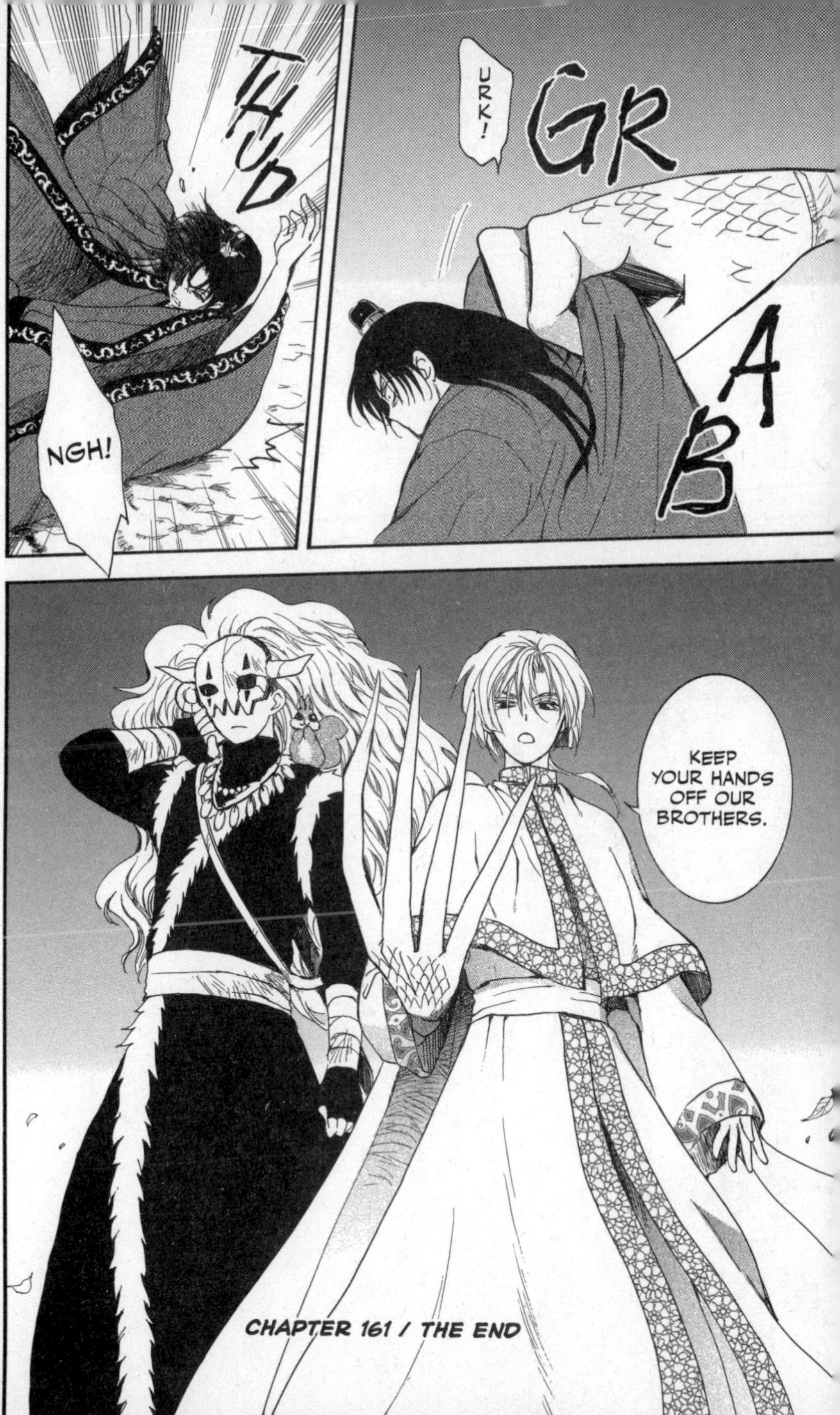
URK!
GRAB
THUD
NGH!
KEEP YOUR HANDS OFF OUR BROTHERS.
CHAPTER 161 / THE END

CHAPTER 162: A BARGAIN

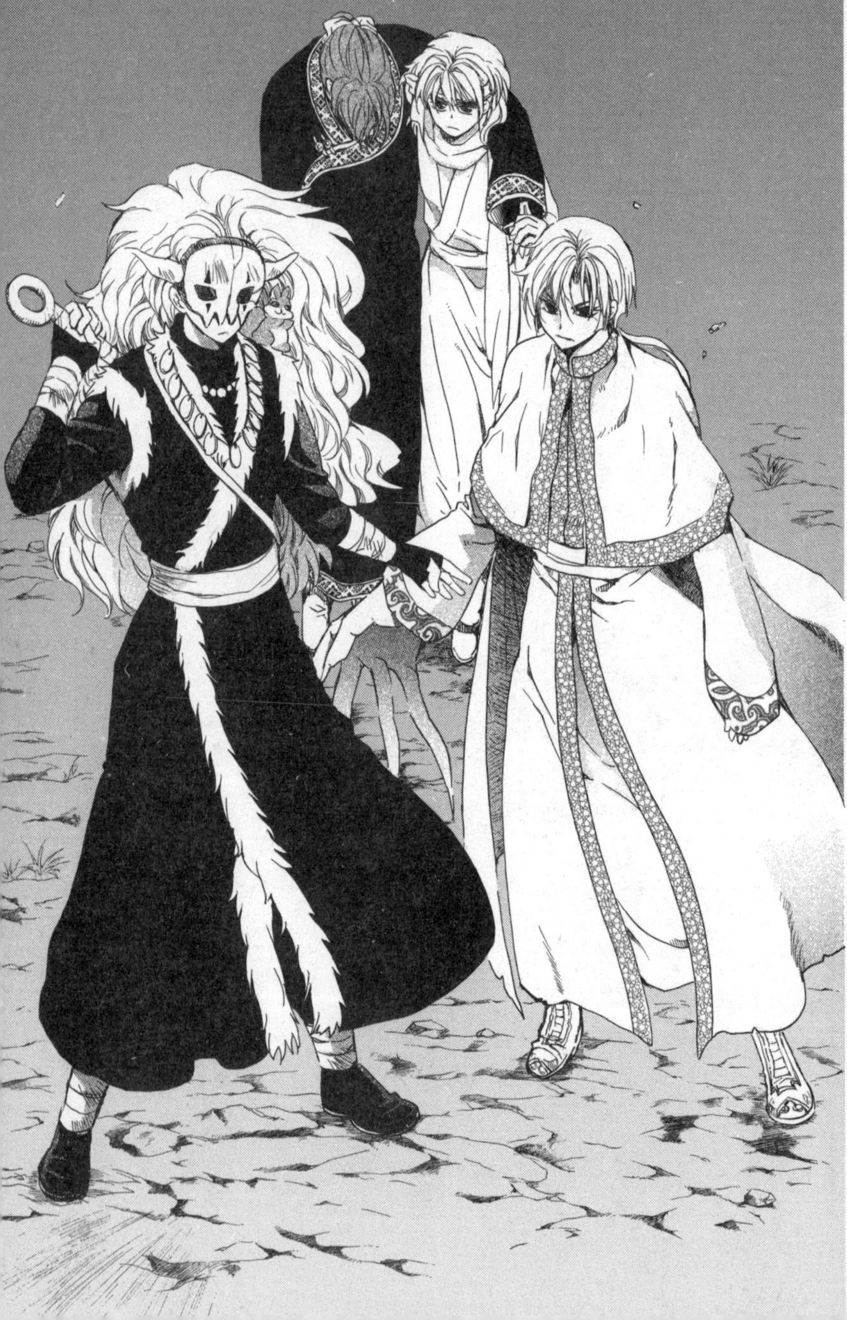

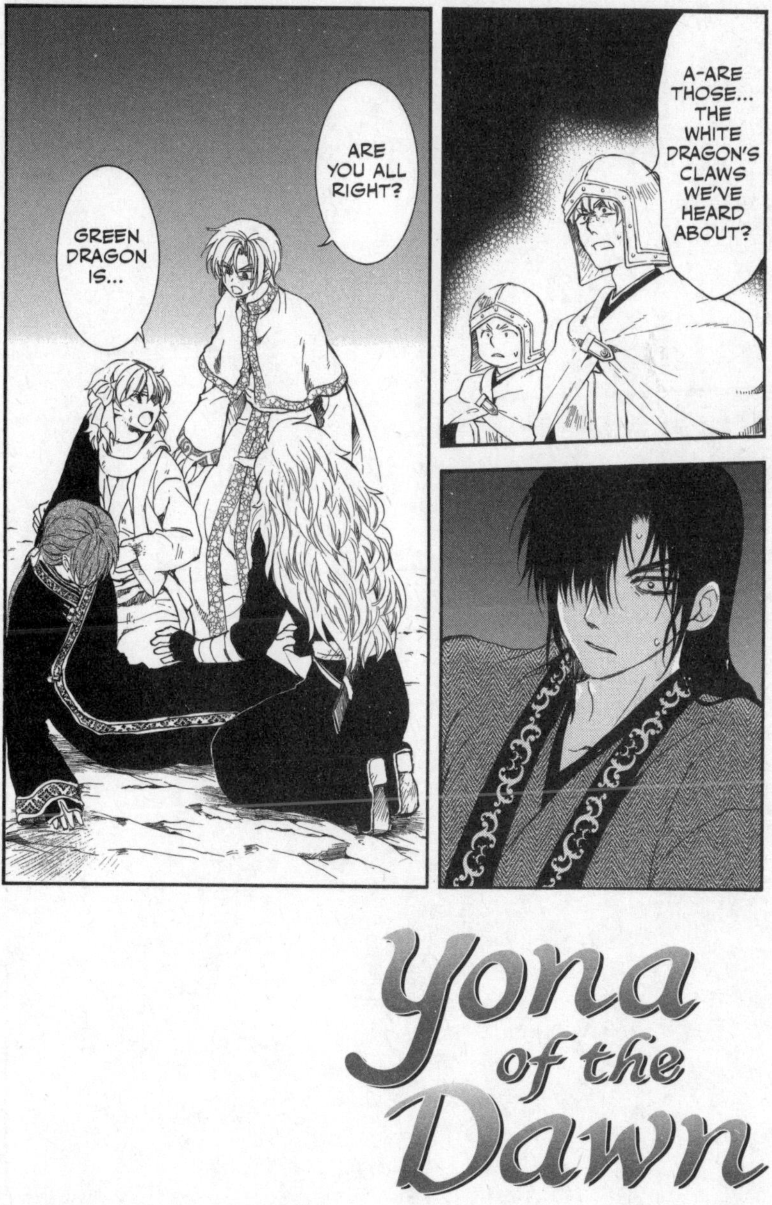
A-ARE THOSE... THE WHITE DRAGON'S CLAWS WE'VE HEARD ABOUT?
ARE YOU ALL RIGHT?
GREEN DRAGON IS...

Yona of the Dawn

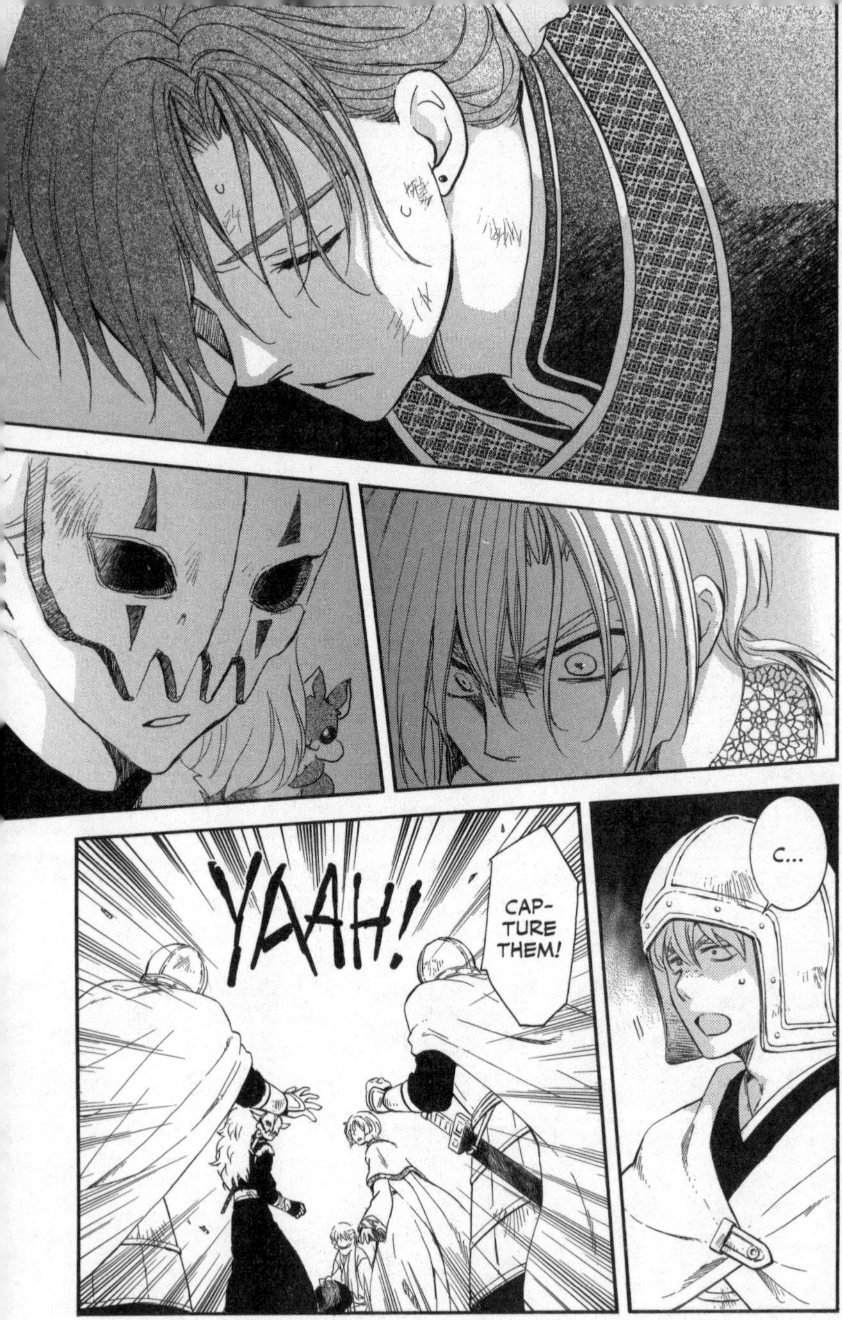
C...
CAP-TURE THEM!
YAAH!

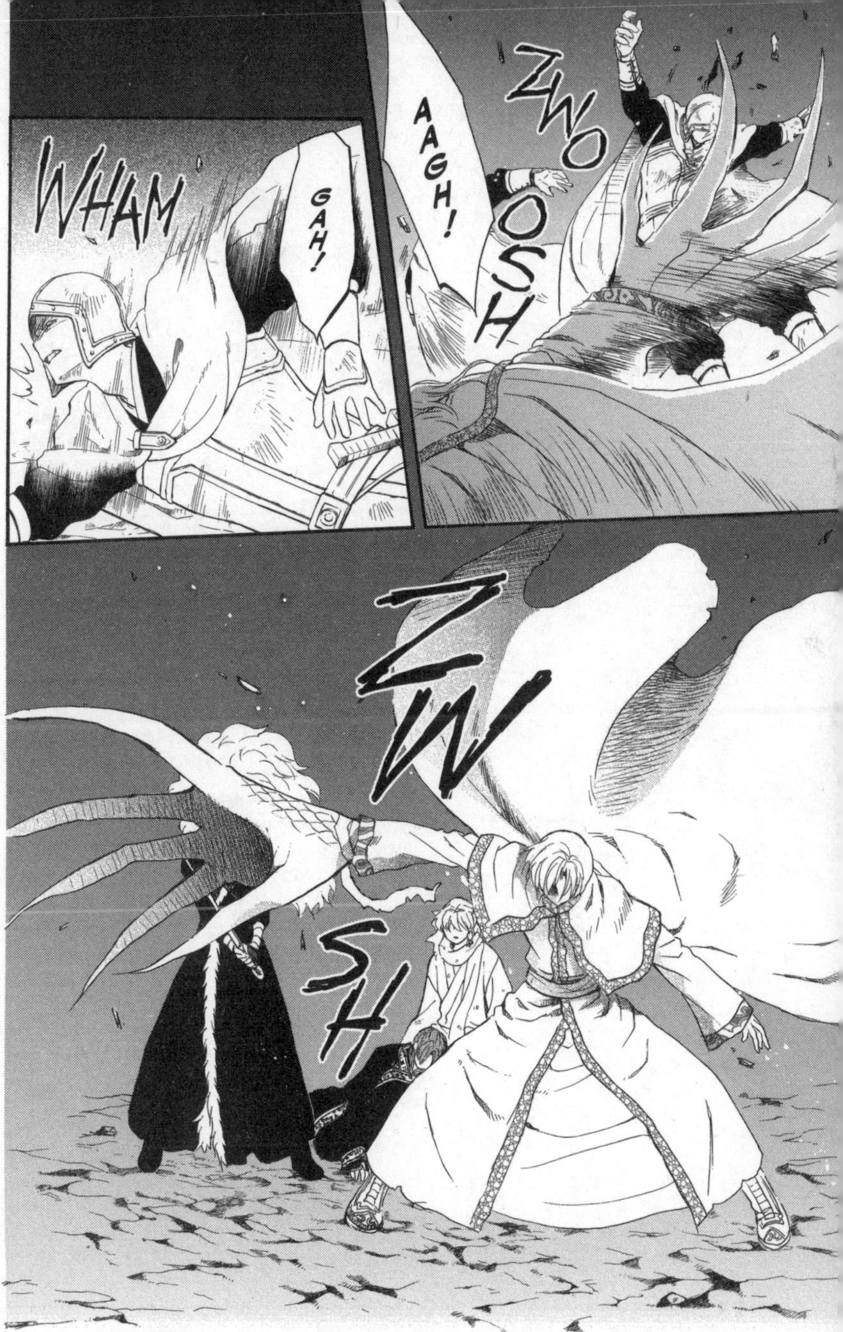
ZWOOSH
AAGH!
WHAM
GAH!
ZWSH

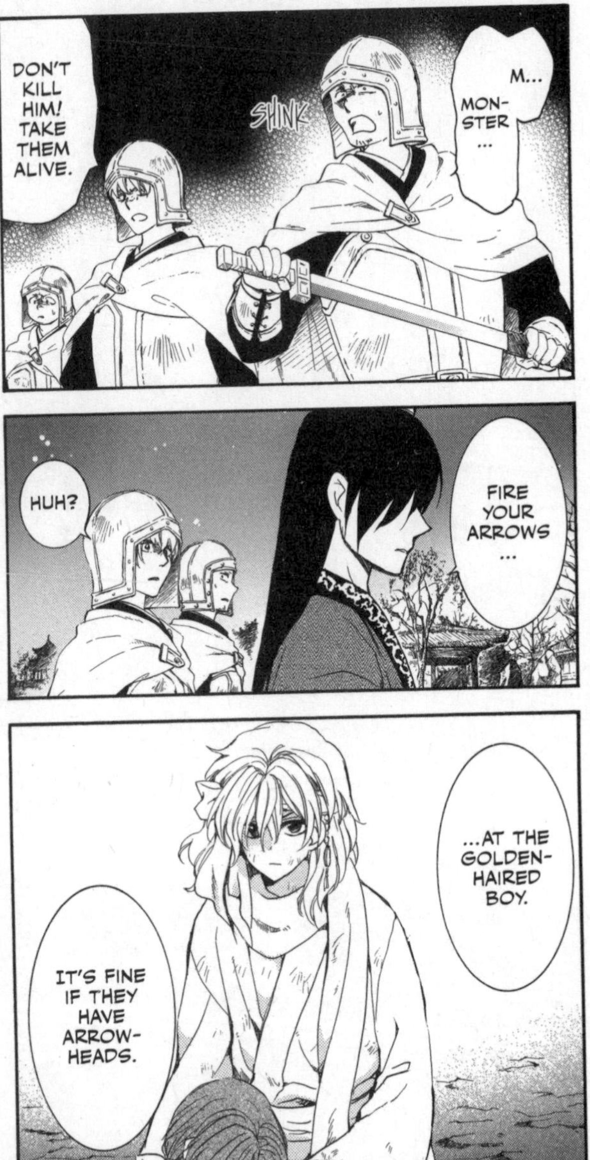
M... MONSTER...
SHINK
DON'T KILL HIM! TAKE THEM ALIVE.
FIRE YOUR ARROWS...
HUH?
...AT THE GOLDEN-HAIRED BOY.
IT'S FINE IF THEY HAVE ARROWHEADS.

A Special Thanks!

Everyone who has been helping me:

My assistants
Mikorun
C.F.
Ryo Sakura
Ryo
Awafuji
Oka
My little sister

My editor
Tokushige

The *Hana to Yume* editorial office.

Everyone who's involved in creating and selling Yona-related merchandise.

My family, friends and readers who always give me support and strength.

Thank you for allowing me to draw manga.

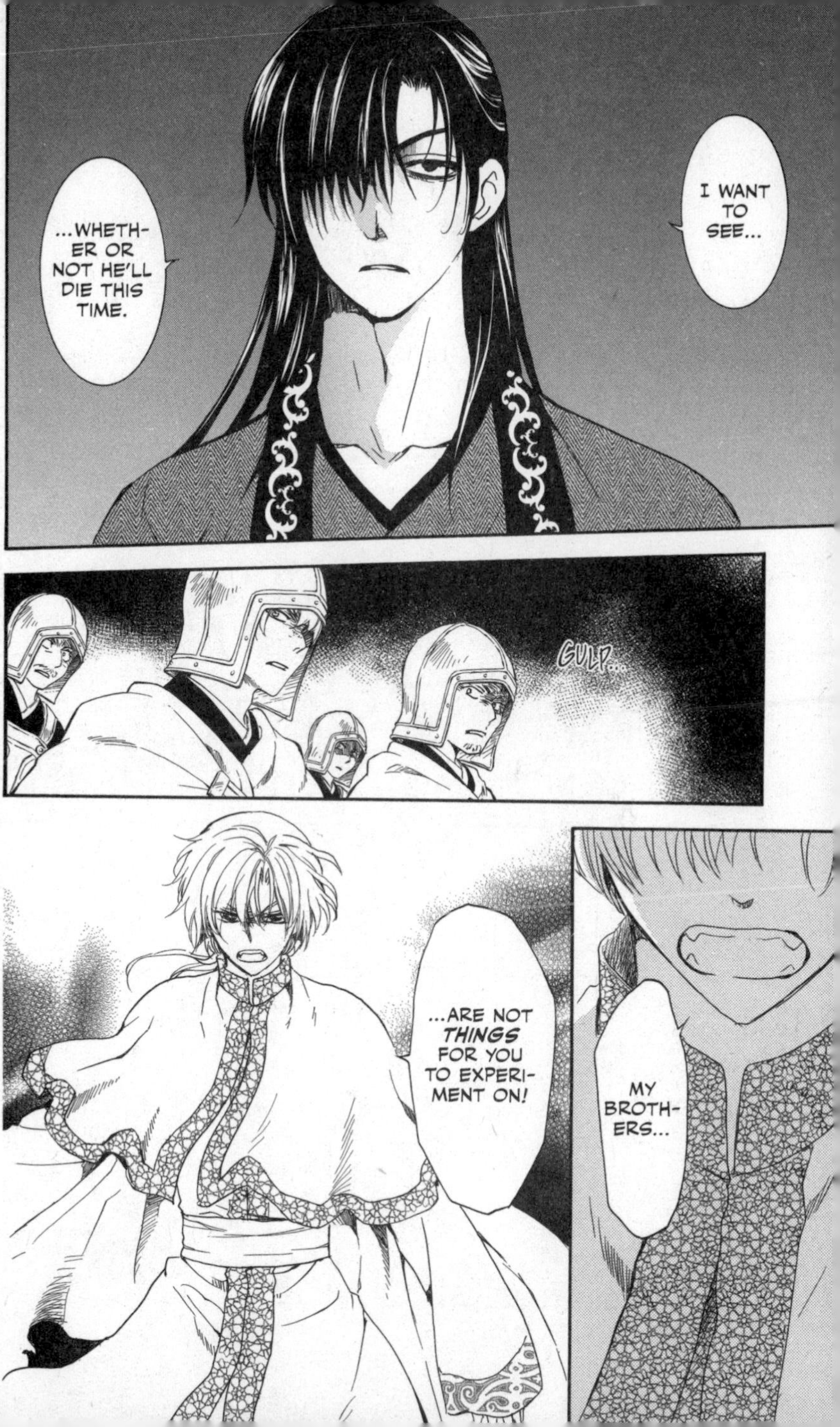
I WANT TO SEE...
...WHETHER OR NOT HE'LL DIE THIS TIME.
GULP...
MY BROTHERS...
...ARE NOT *THINGS* FOR YOU TO EXPERIMENT ON!

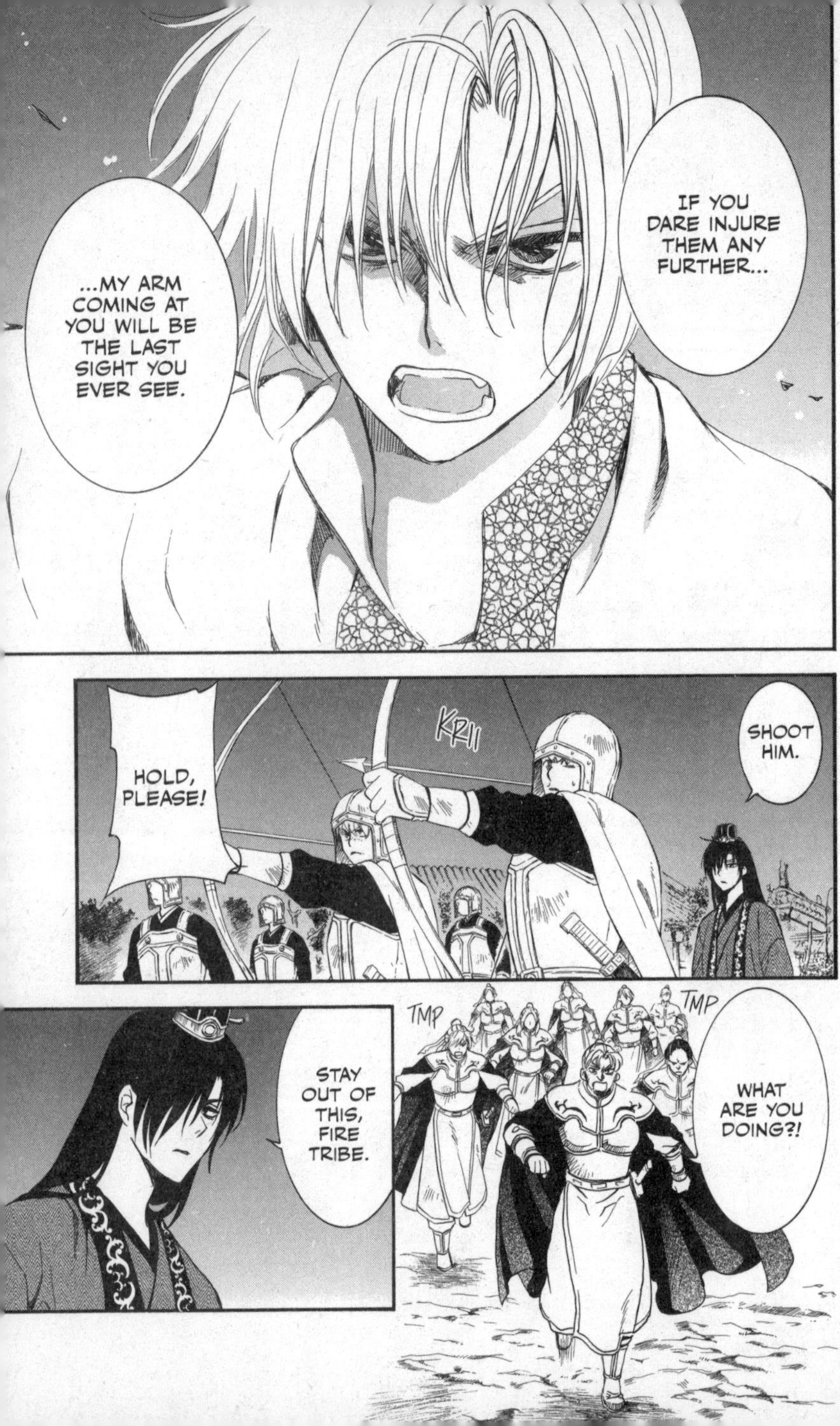
IF YOU DARE INJURE THEM ANY FURTHER...
...MY ARM COMING AT YOU WILL BE THE LAST SIGHT YOU EVER SEE.
SHOOT HIM.
KRII
HOLD, PLEASE!
WHAT ARE YOU DOING?!
TMP
TMP
STAY OUT OF THIS, FIRE TRIBE.

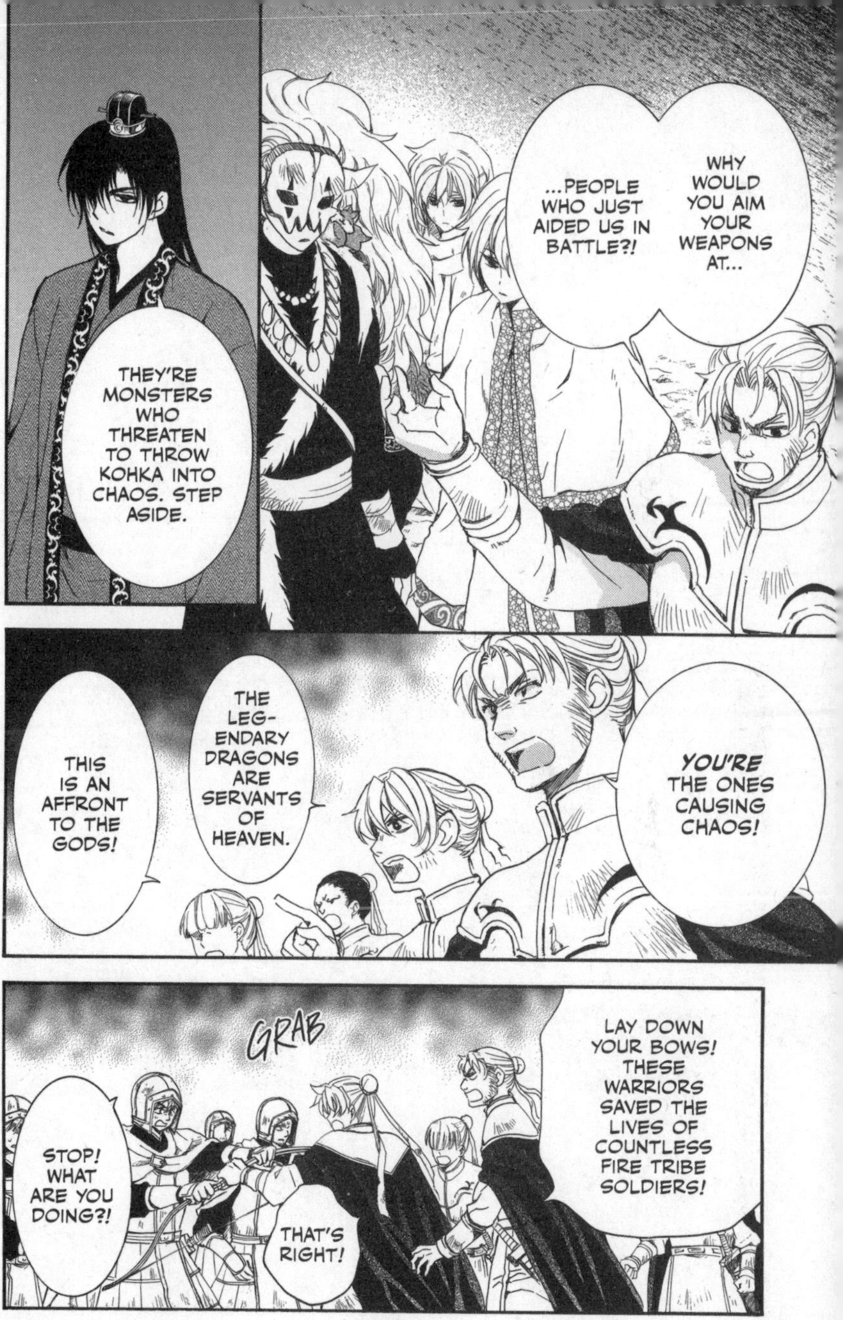
WHY WOULD YOU AIM YOUR WEAPONS AT...
...PEOPLE WHO JUST AIDED US IN BATTLE?!
THEY'RE MONSTERS WHO THREATEN TO THROW KOHKA INTO CHAOS. STEP ASIDE.
YOU'RE THE ONES CAUSING CHAOS!
THE LEG-ENDARY DRAGONS ARE SERVANTS OF HEAVEN.
THIS IS AN AFFRONT TO THE GODS!
LAY DOWN YOUR BOWS! THESE WARRIORS SAVED THE LIVES OF COUNTLESS FIRE TRIBE SOLDIERS!
GRAB
THAT'S RIGHT!
STOP! WHAT ARE YOU DOING?!

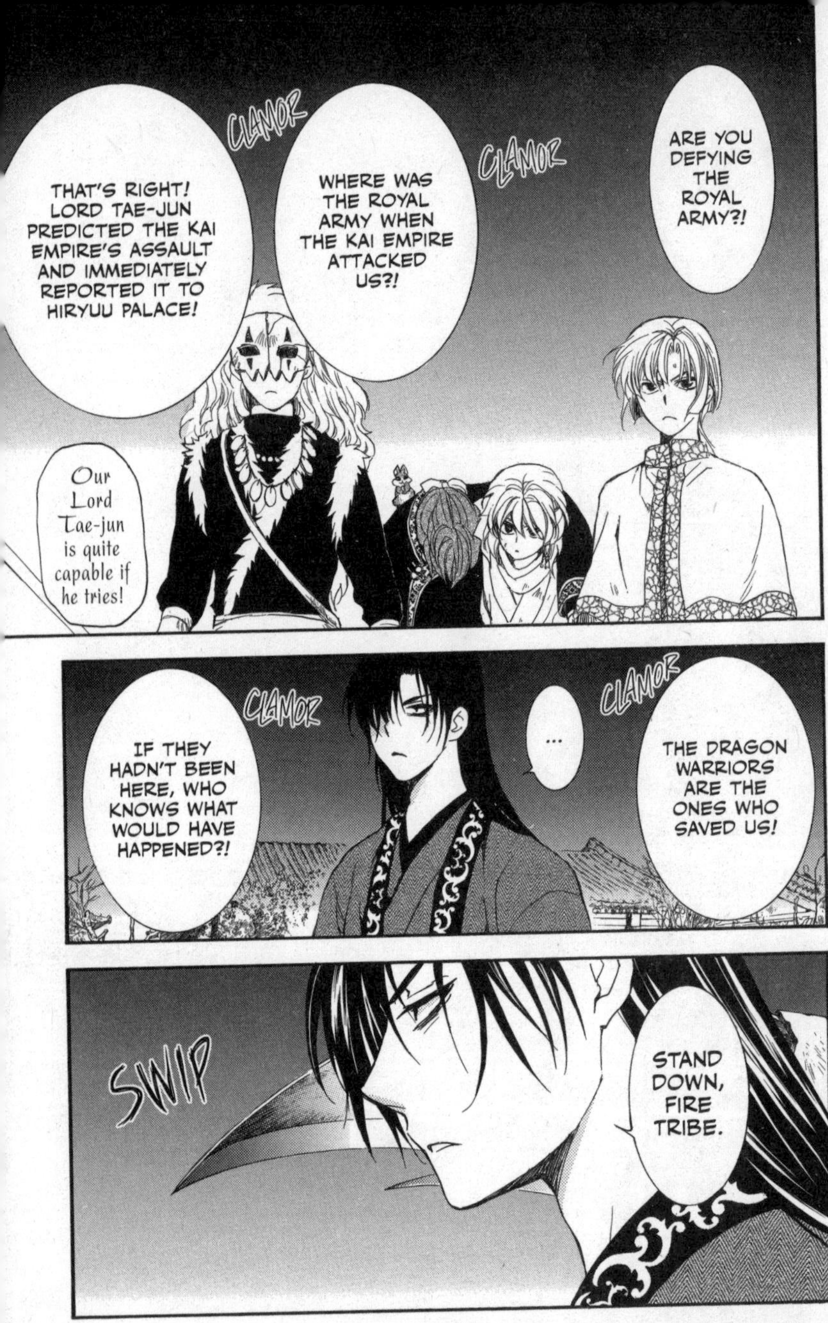
ARE YOU DEFYING THE ROYAL ARMY?!
CLAMOR
WHERE WAS THE ROYAL ARMY WHEN THE KAI EMPIRE ATTACKED US?!
CLAMOR
THAT'S RIGHT! LORD TAE-JUN PREDICTED THE KAI EMPIRE'S ASSAULT AND IMMEDIATELY REPORTED IT TO HIRYUU PALACE!
Our Lord Tae-jun is quite capable if he tries!
CLAMOR
THE DRAGON WARRIORS ARE THE ONES WHO SAVED US!
...
CLAMOR
IF THEY HADN'T BEEN HERE, WHO KNOWS WHAT WOULD HAVE HAPPENED?!
STAND DOWN, FIRE TRIBE.
SWIP

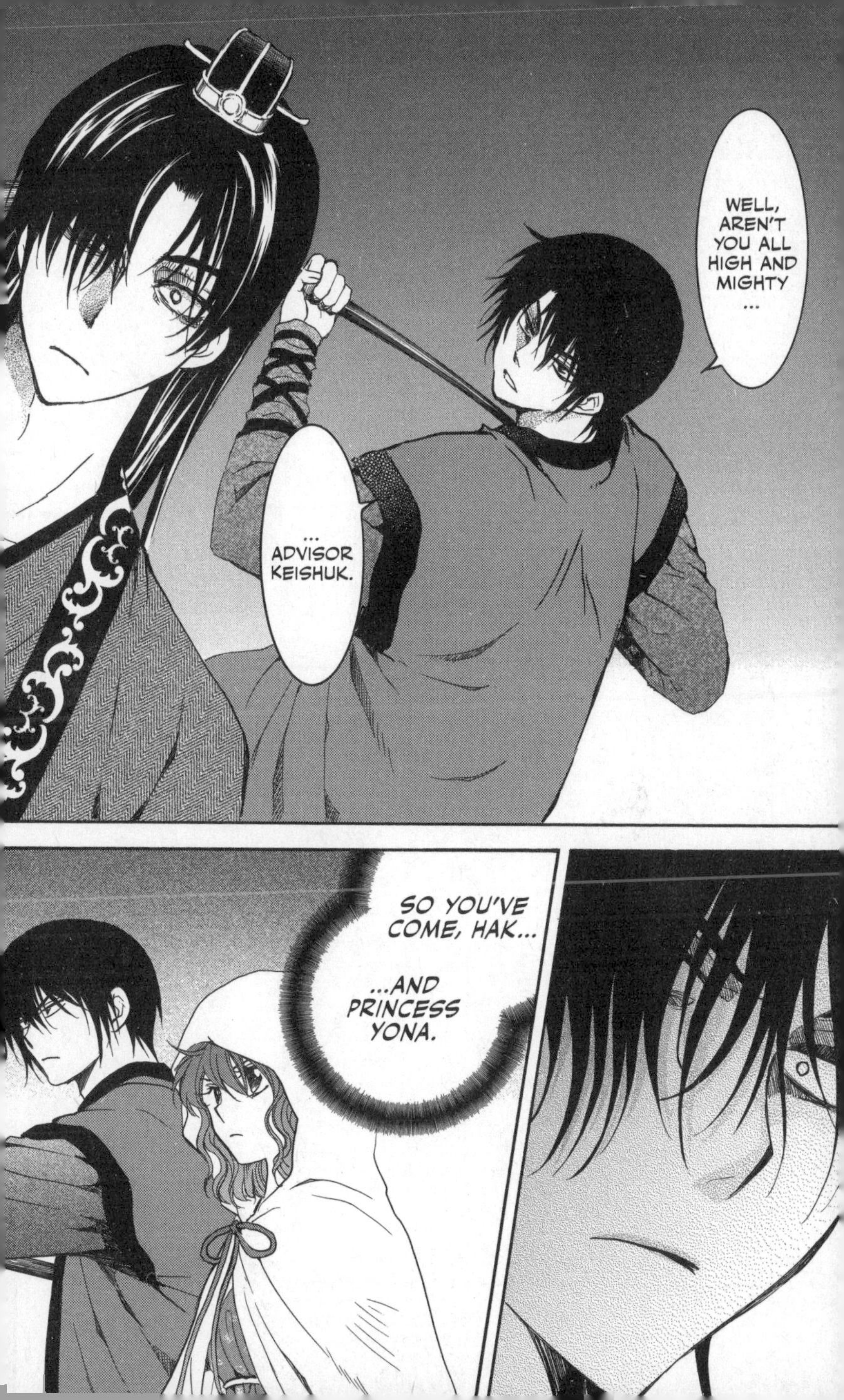
WELL, AREN'T YOU ALL HIGH AND MIGHTY...
...ADVISOR KEISHUK.
SO YOU'VE COME, HAK...
...AND PRINCESS YONA.

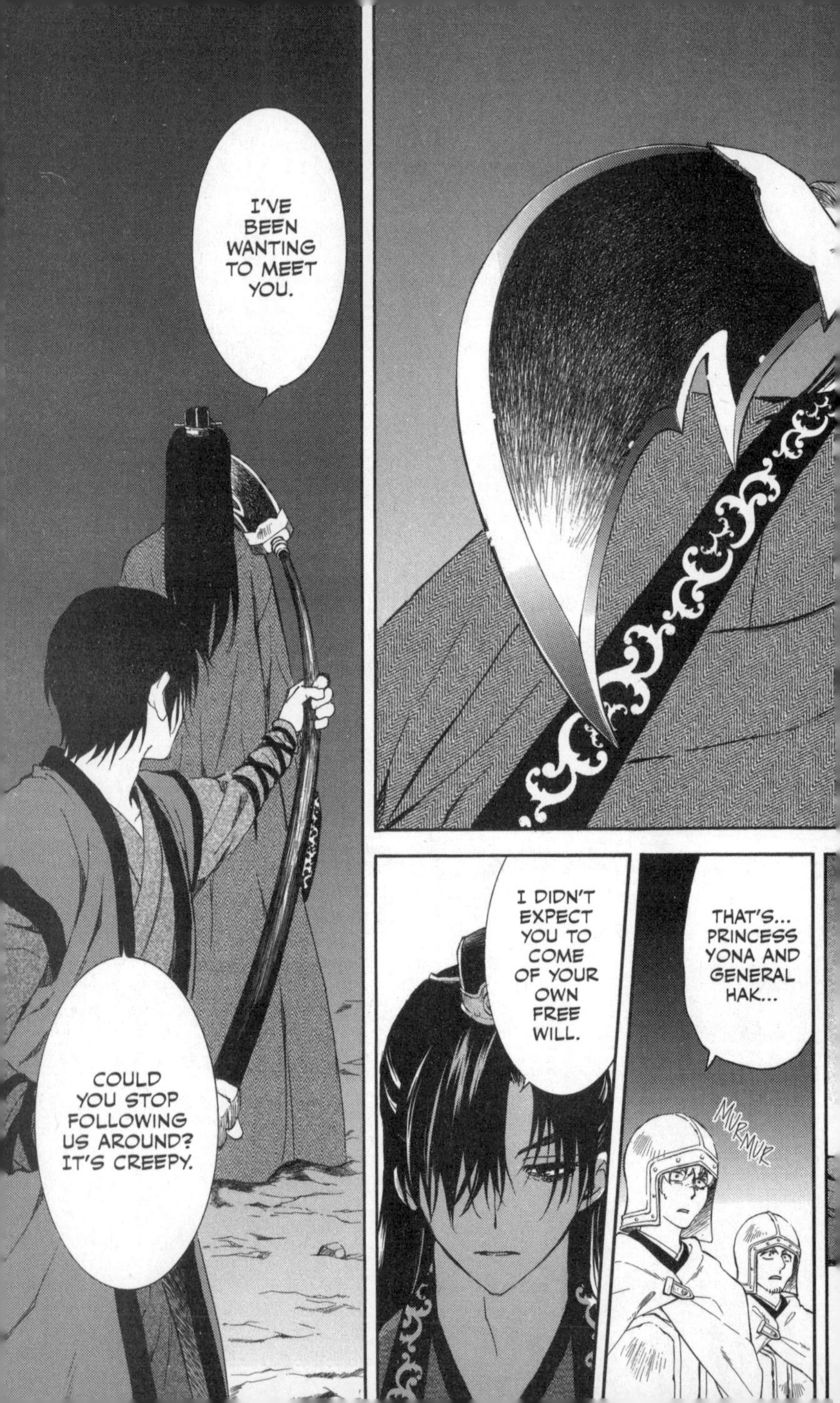
THAT'S... PRINCESS YONA AND GENERAL HAK...
MURMUR
I DIDN'T EXPECT YOU TO COME OF YOUR OWN FREE WILL.
I'VE BEEN WANTING TO MEET YOU.
COULD YOU STOP FOLLOWING US AROUND? IT'S CREEPY.

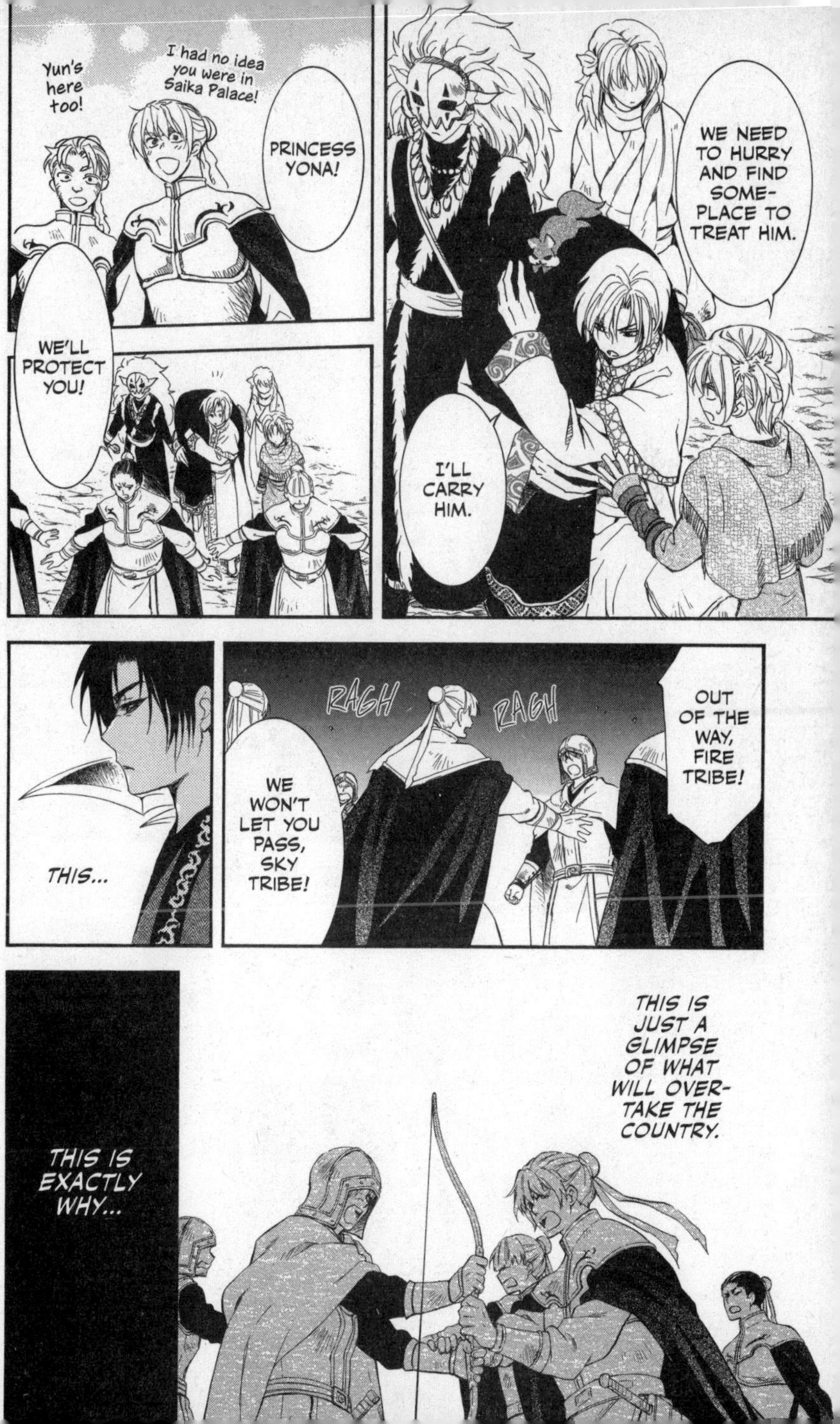
WE NEED TO HURRY AND FIND SOME-PLACE TO TREAT HIM.
I'LL CARRY HIM.
PRINCESS YONA!
I had no idea you were in Saika Palace!
Yun's here too!
WE'LL PROTECT YOU!
OUT OF THE WAY, FIRE TRIBE!
RAGH
RAGH
WE WON'T LET YOU PASS, SKY TRIBE!
THIS...
THIS IS JUST A GLIMPSE OF WHAT WILL OVER-TAKE THE COUNTRY.
THIS IS EXACTLY WHY...

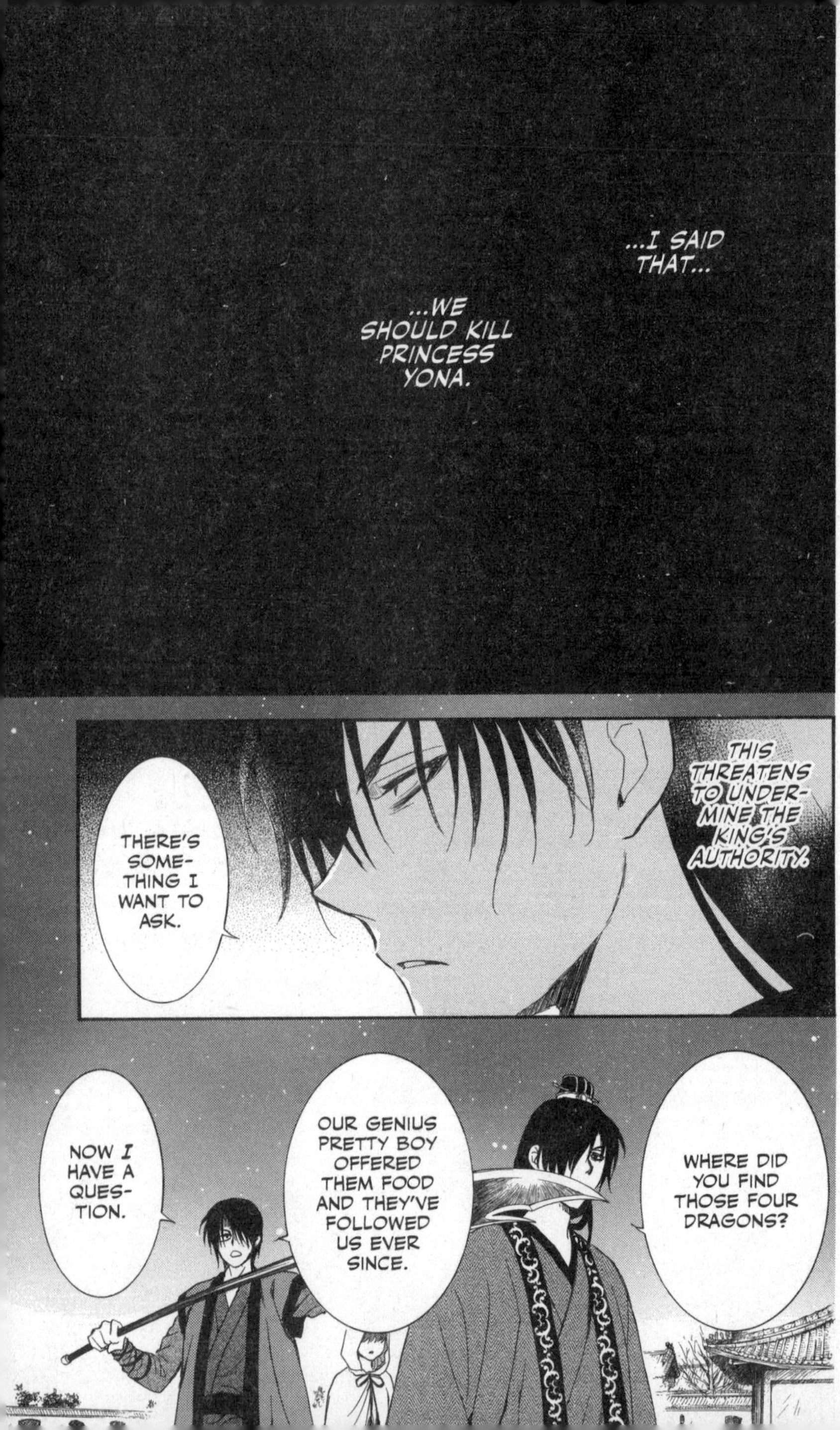
...I SAID THAT...
...WE SHOULD KILL PRINCESS YONA.
THIS THREATENS TO UNDERMINE THE KING'S AUTHORITY.
THERE'S SOMETHING I WANT TO ASK.
WHERE DID YOU FIND THOSE FOUR DRAGONS?
OUR GENIUS PRETTY BOY OFFERED THEM FOOD AND THEY'VE FOLLOWED US EVER SINCE.
NOW *I* HAVE A QUESTION.

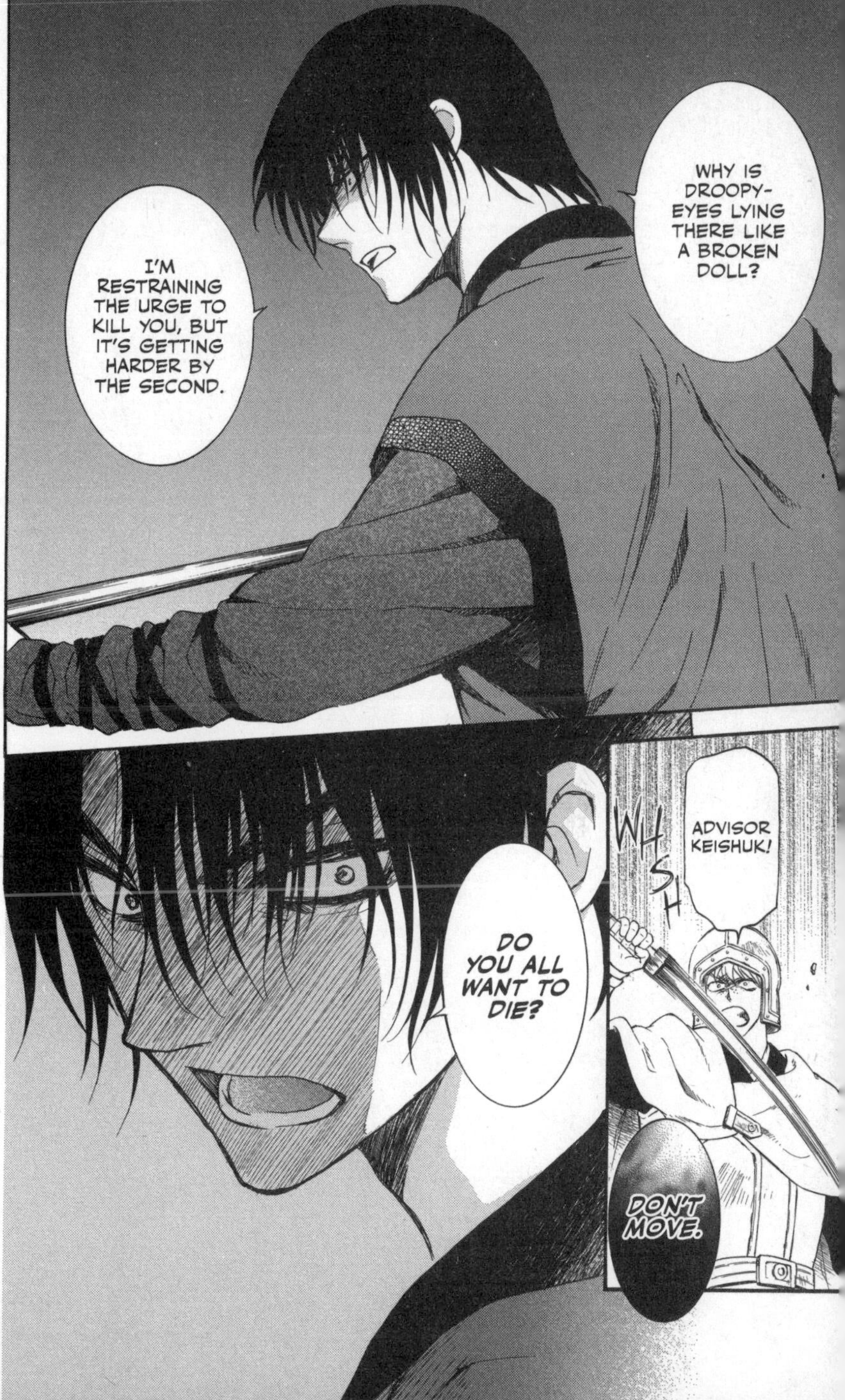
WHY IS DROOPY-EYES LYING THERE LIKE A BROKEN DOLL?
I'M RESTRAINING THE URGE TO KILL YOU, BUT IT'S GETTING HARDER BY THE SECOND.
ADVISOR KEISHUK!
WHSH
DON'T MOVE.
DO YOU ALL WANT TO DIE?

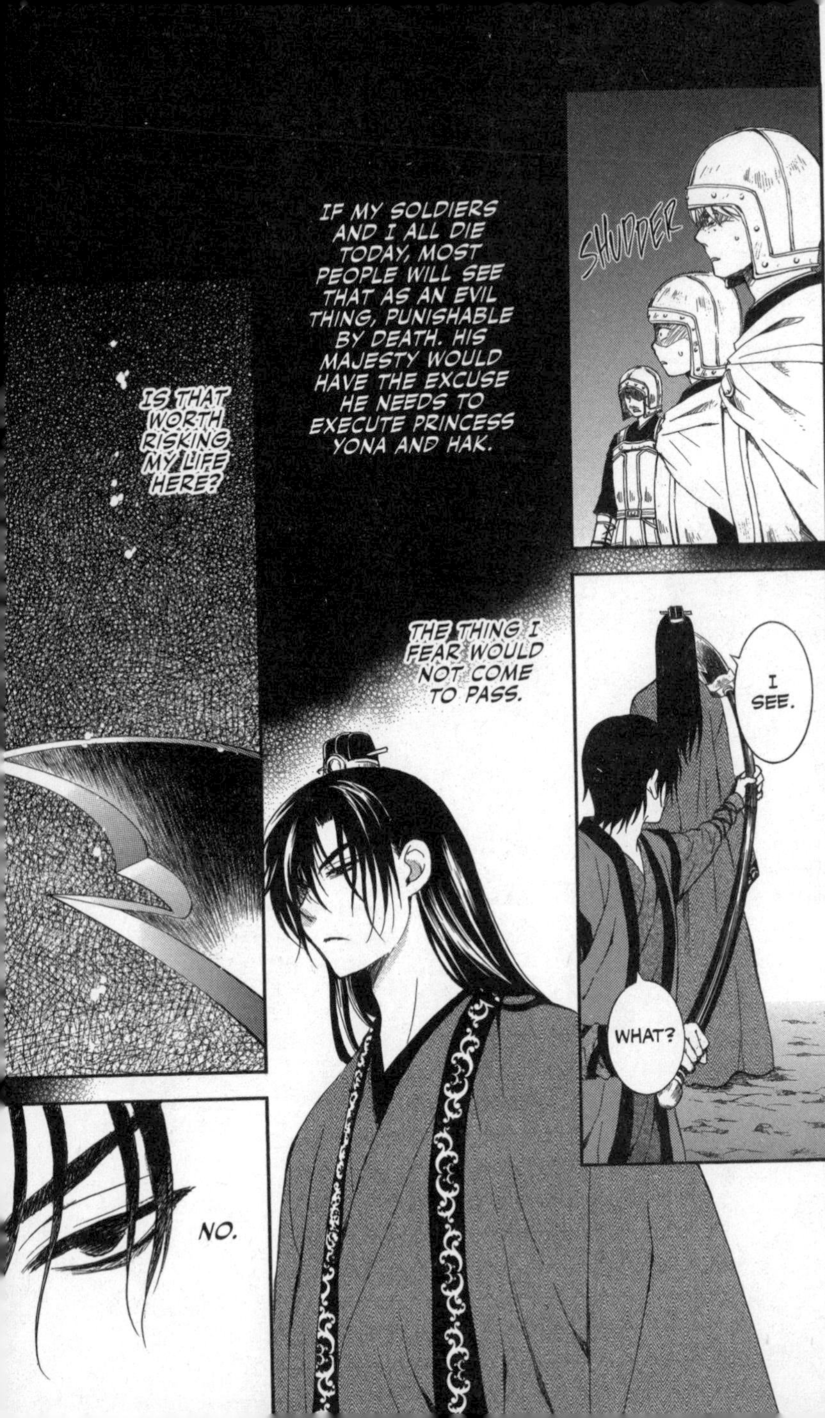
SHUDDER
IF MY SOLDIERS AND I ALL DIE TODAY, MOST PEOPLE WILL SEE THAT AS AN EVIL THING, PUNISHABLE BY DEATH. HIS MAJESTY WOULD HAVE THE EXCUSE HE NEEDS TO EXECUTE PRINCESS YONA AND HAK.
THE THING I FEAR WOULD NOT COME TO PASS.
I SEE.
WHAT?
IS THAT WORTH RISKING MY LIFE HERE?
NO.

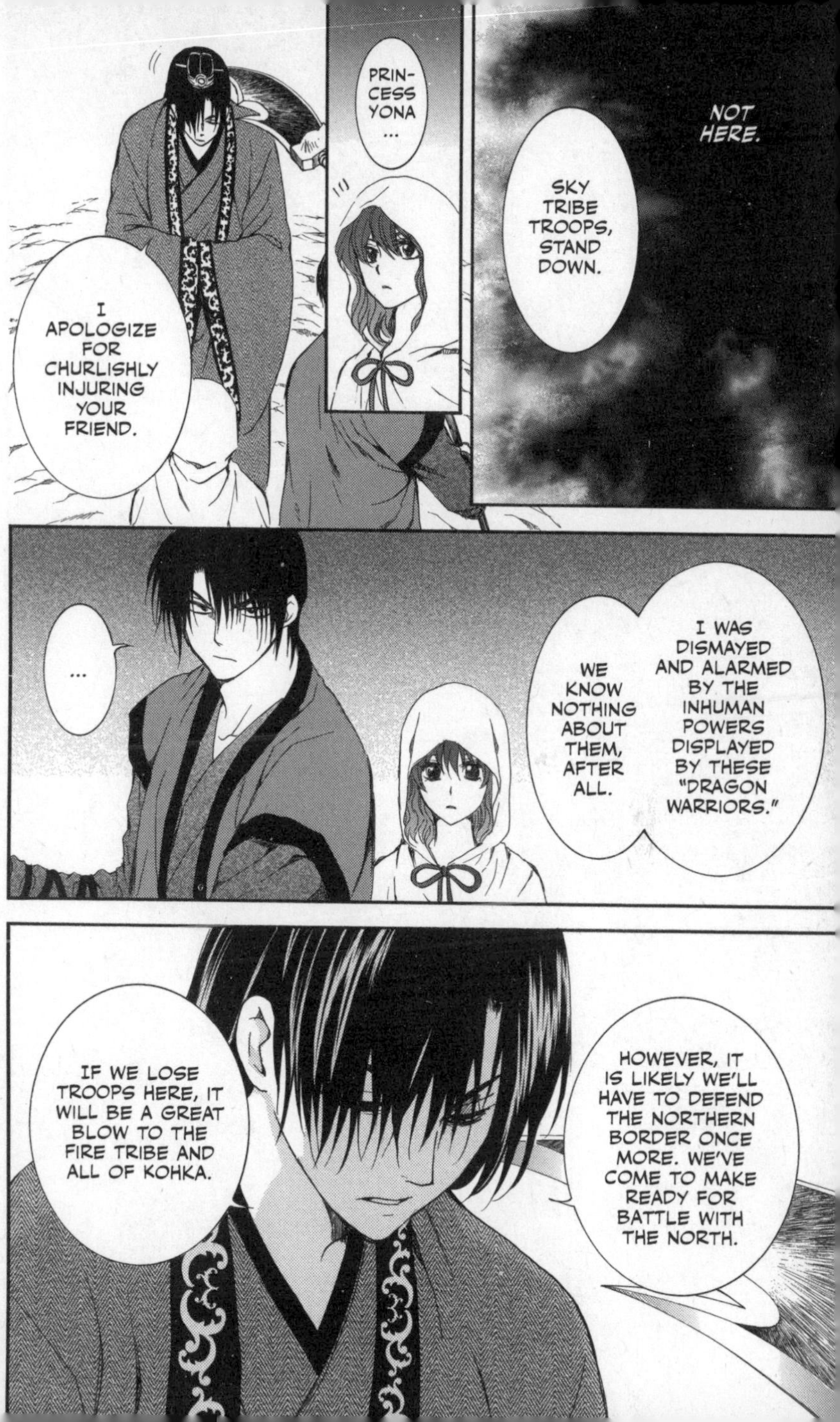
NOT HERE.
SKY TRIBE TROOPS, STAND DOWN.
PRIN-CESS YONA ...
I APOLOGIZE FOR CHURLISHLY INJURING YOUR FRIEND.
I WAS DISMAYED AND ALARMED BY THE INHUMAN POWERS DISPLAYED BY THESE "DRAGON WARRIORS."
WE KNOW NOTHING ABOUT THEM, AFTER ALL.
...
HOWEVER, IT IS LIKELY WE'LL HAVE TO DEFEND THE NORTHERN BORDER ONCE MORE. WE'VE COME TO MAKE READY FOR BATTLE WITH THE NORTH.
IF WE LOSE TROOPS HERE, IT WILL BE A GREAT BLOW TO THE FIRE TRIBE AND ALL OF KOHKA.

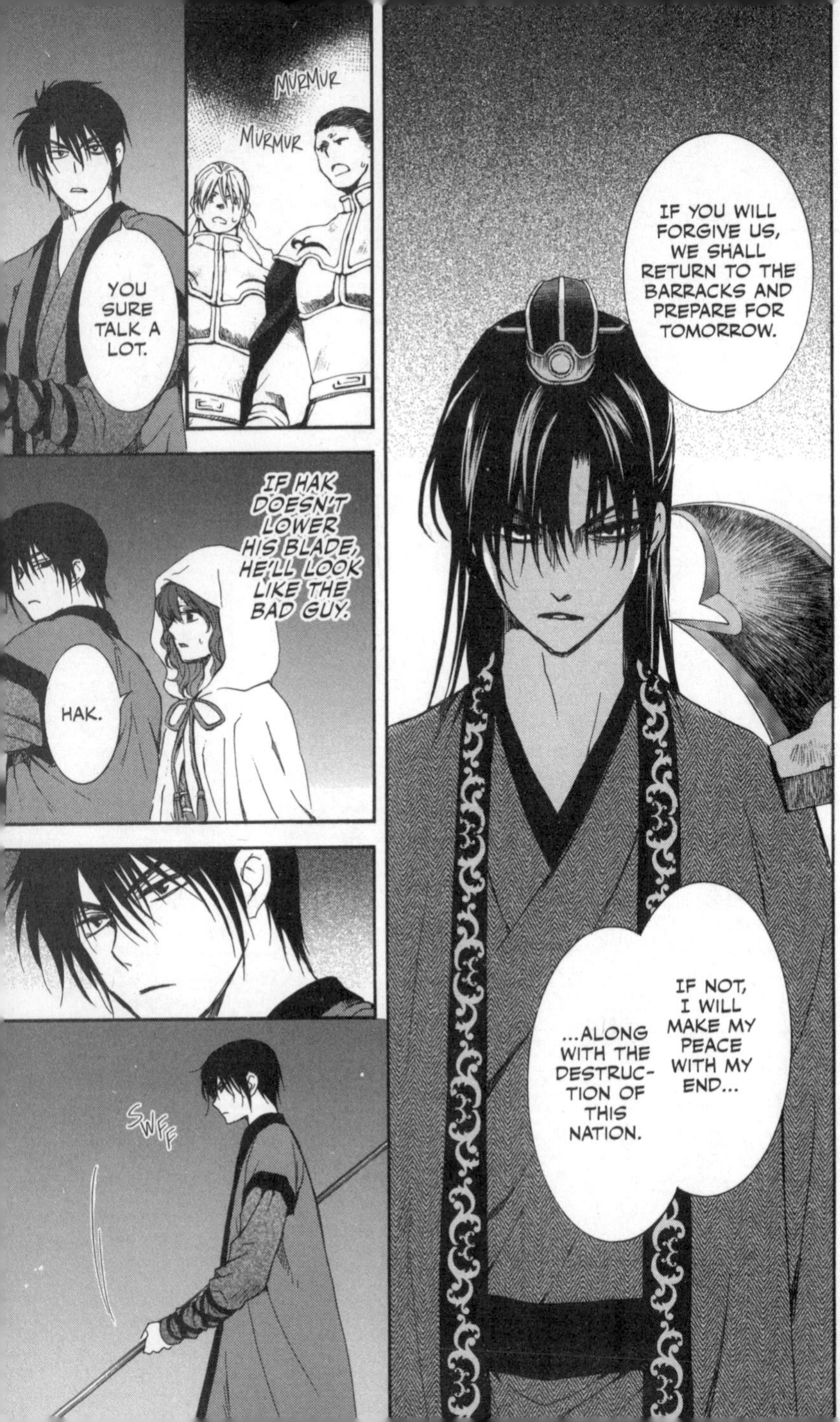
IF YOU WILL FORGIVE US, WE SHALL RETURN TO THE BARRACKS AND PREPARE FOR TOMORROW.
IF NOT, I WILL MAKE MY PEACE WITH MY END...
...ALONG WITH THE DESTRUCTION OF THIS NATION.
MURMUR
MURMUR
YOU SURE TALK A LOT.
IF HAK DOESN'T LOWER HIS BLADE, HE'LL LOOK LIKE THE BAD GUY.
HAK.
SWFF

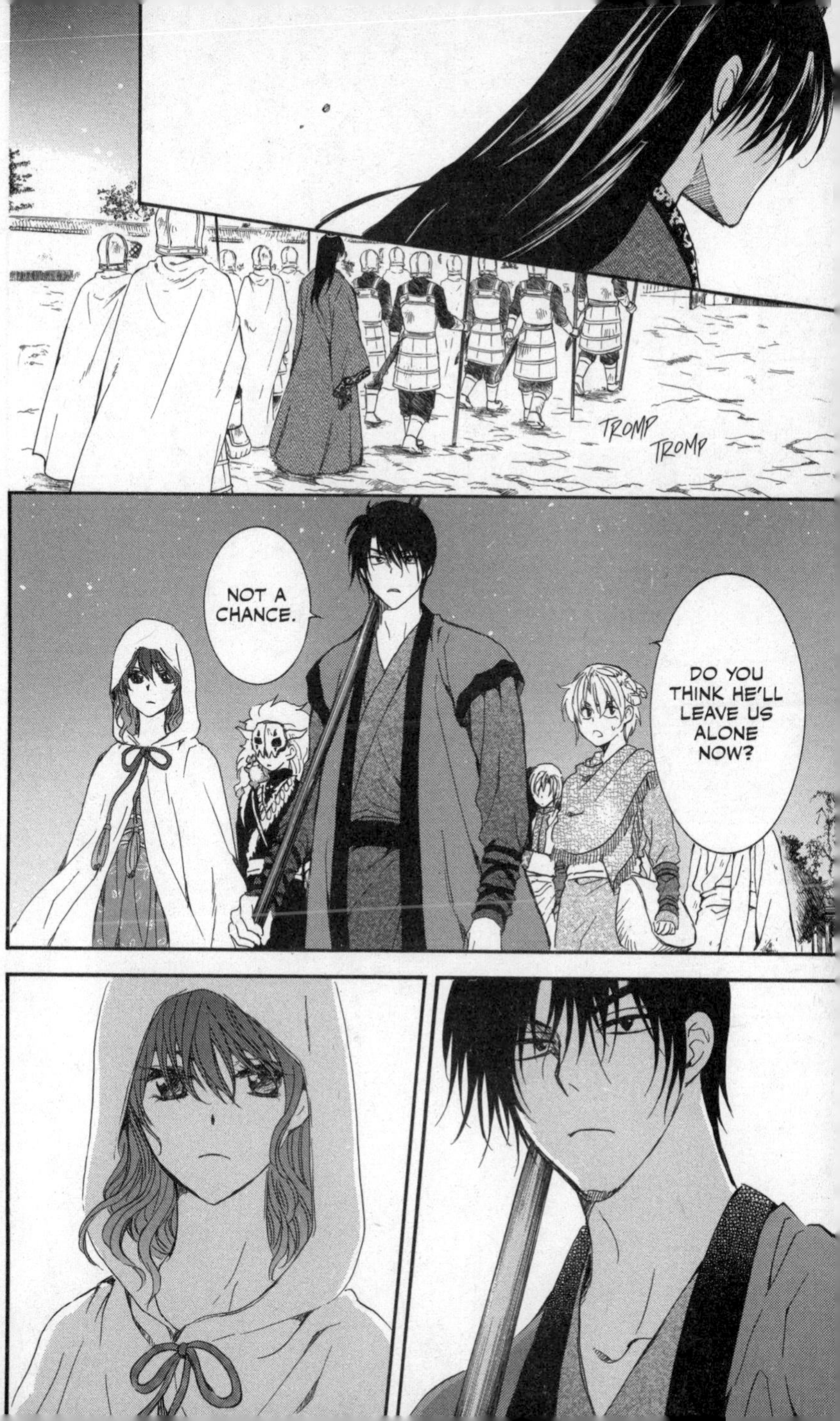
TROMP
TROMP
DO YOU THINK HE'LL LEAVE US ALONE NOW?
NOT A CHANCE.

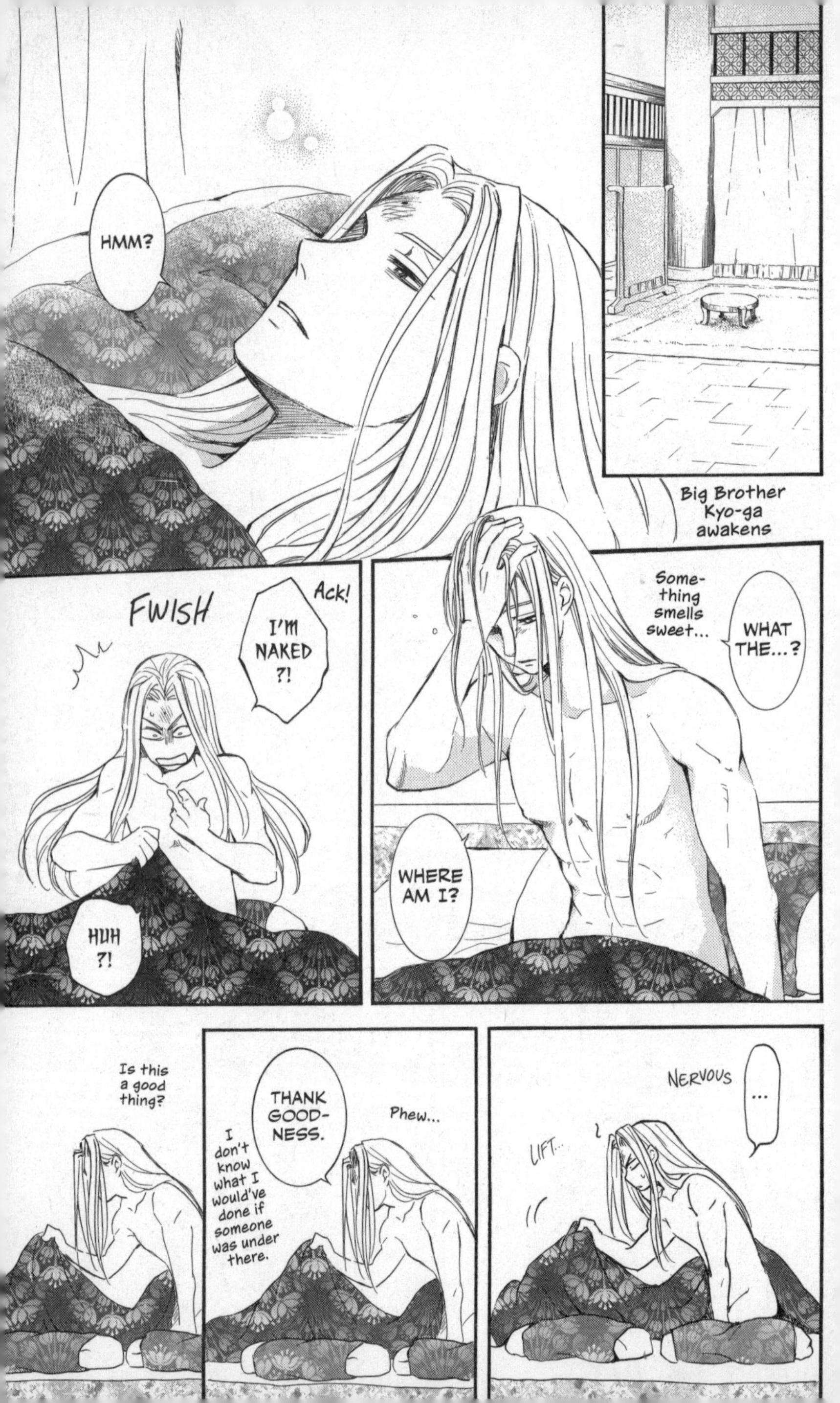
Big Brother Kyo-ga awakens
HMM?
WHAT THE...?
Something smells sweet...
WHERE AM I?
Ack!
I'M NAKED?!
FWISH
HUH?!
NERVOUS
...
LIFT...
Phew...
THANK GOODNESS.
I don't know what I would've done if someone was under there.
Is this a good thing?

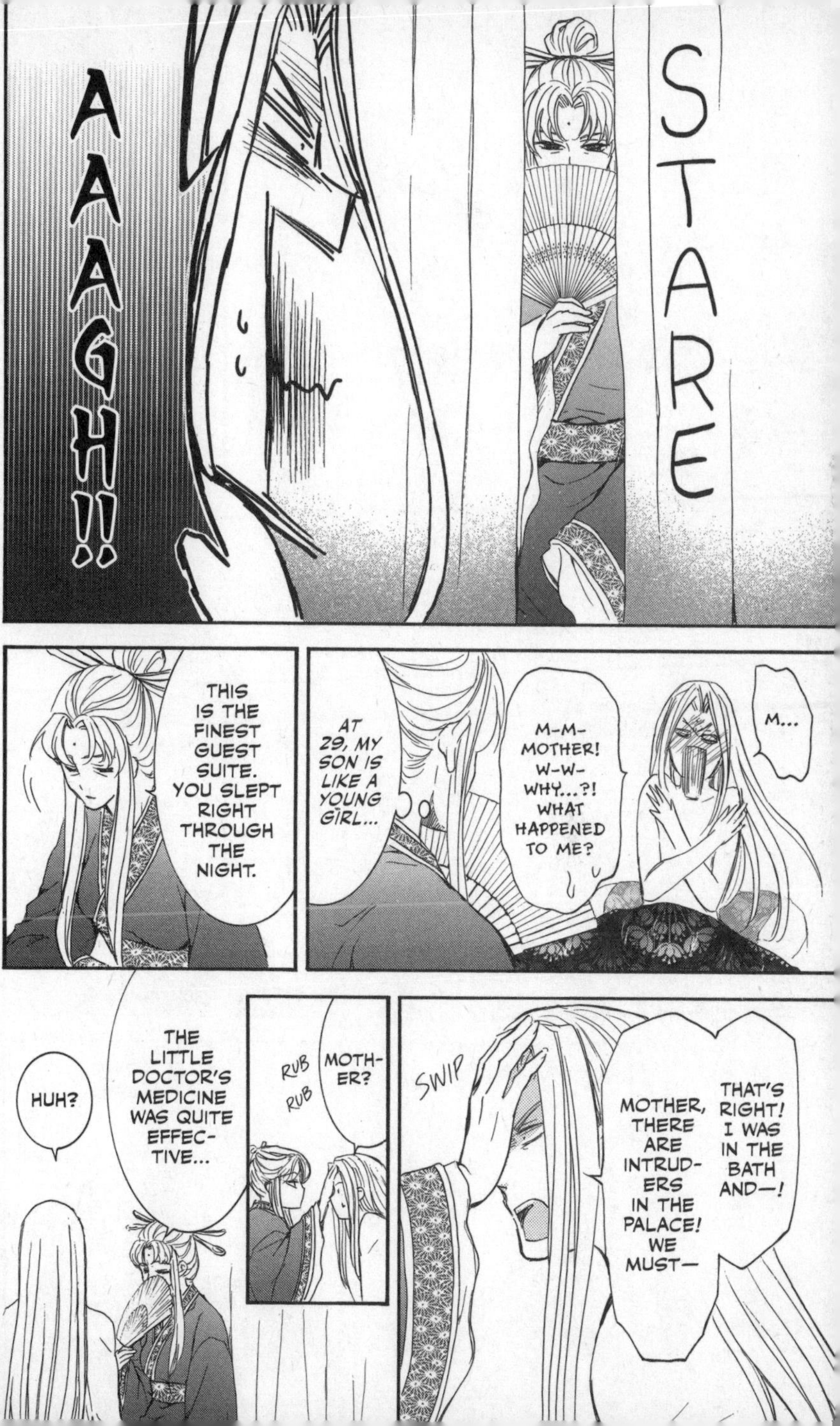
STARE
AAAGH!!
M...
M-M-MOTHER! W-W-WHY...?! WHAT HAPPENED TO ME?
AT 29, MY SON IS LIKE A YOUNG GIRL...
THIS IS THE FINEST GUEST SUITE. YOU SLEPT RIGHT THROUGH THE NIGHT.
SWIP
THAT'S RIGHT! I WAS IN THE BATH AND—!
MOTHER, THERE ARE INTRUDERS IN THE PALACE! WE MUST—
RUB RUB
MOTHER?
THE LITTLE DOCTOR'S MEDICINE WAS QUITE EFFECTIVE...
HUH?

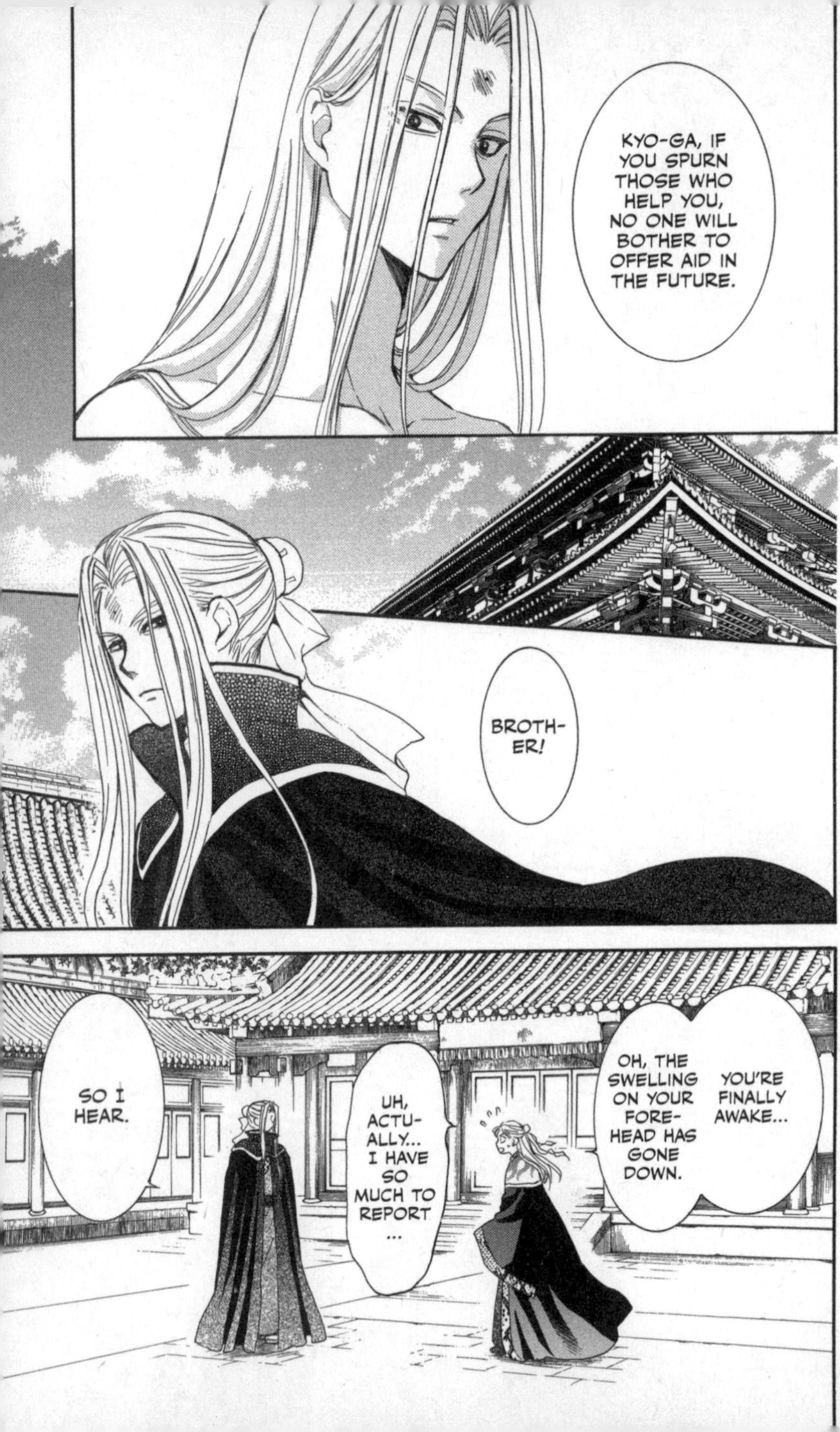
KYO-GA, IF YOU SPURN THOSE WHO HELP YOU, NO ONE WILL BOTHER TO OFFER AID IN THE FUTURE.
BROTHER!
YOU'RE FINALLY AWAKE...
OH, THE SWELLING ON YOUR FOREHEAD HAS GONE DOWN.
UH, ACTUALLY... I HAVE SO MUCH TO REPORT...
SO I HEAR.

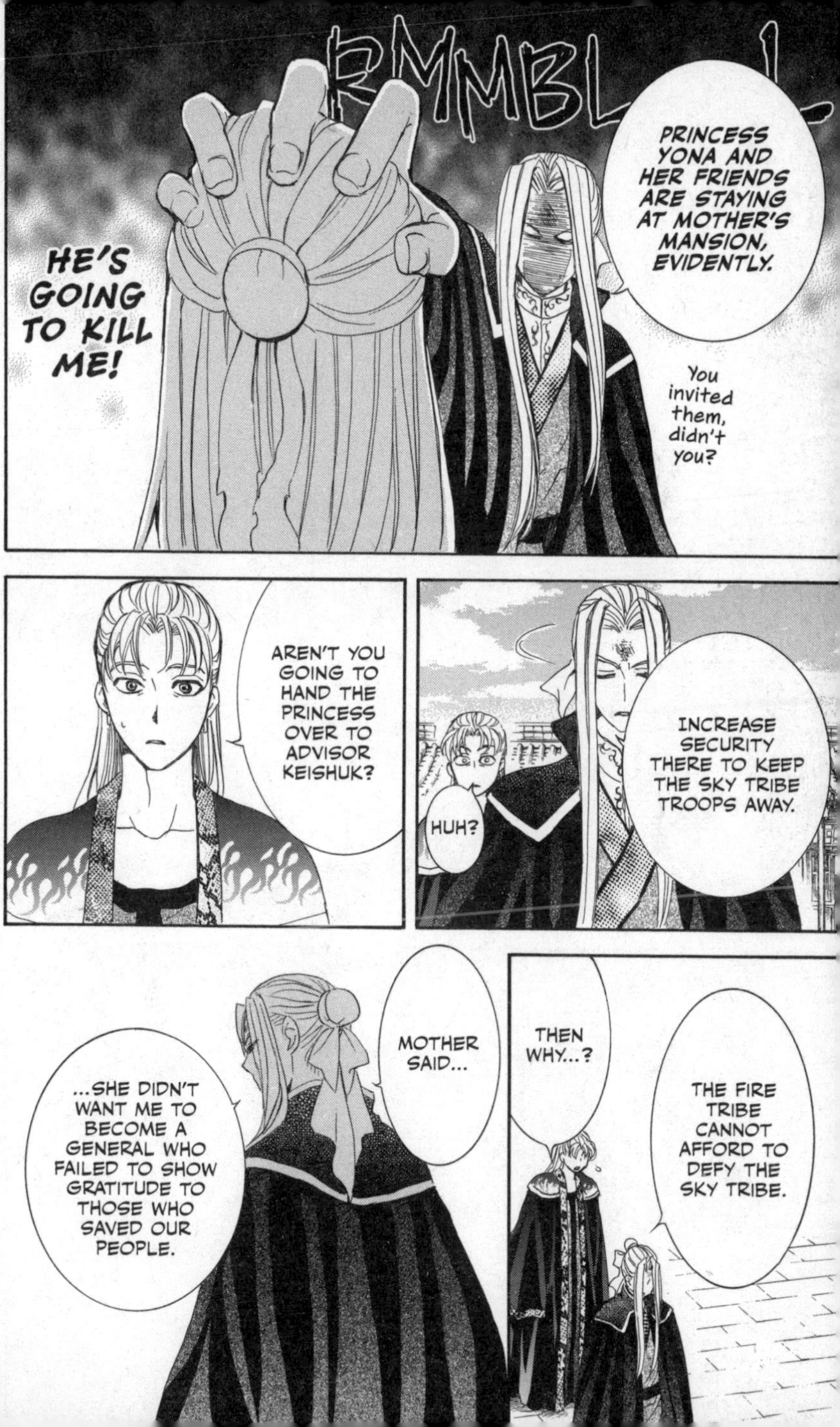
RMMBL
PRINCESS YONA AND HER FRIENDS ARE STAYING AT MOTHER'S MANSION, EVIDENTLY.
You invited them, didn't you?
HE'S GOING TO KILL ME!
INCREASE SECURITY THERE TO KEEP THE SKY TRIBE TROOPS AWAY.
HUH?
AREN'T YOU GOING TO HAND THE PRINCESS OVER TO ADVISOR KEISHUK?
THE FIRE TRIBE CANNOT AFFORD TO DEFY THE SKY TRIBE.
THEN WHY...?
MOTHER SAID...
...SHE DIDN'T WANT ME TO BECOME A GENERAL WHO FAILED TO SHOW GRATITUDE TO THOSE WHO SAVED OUR PEOPLE.

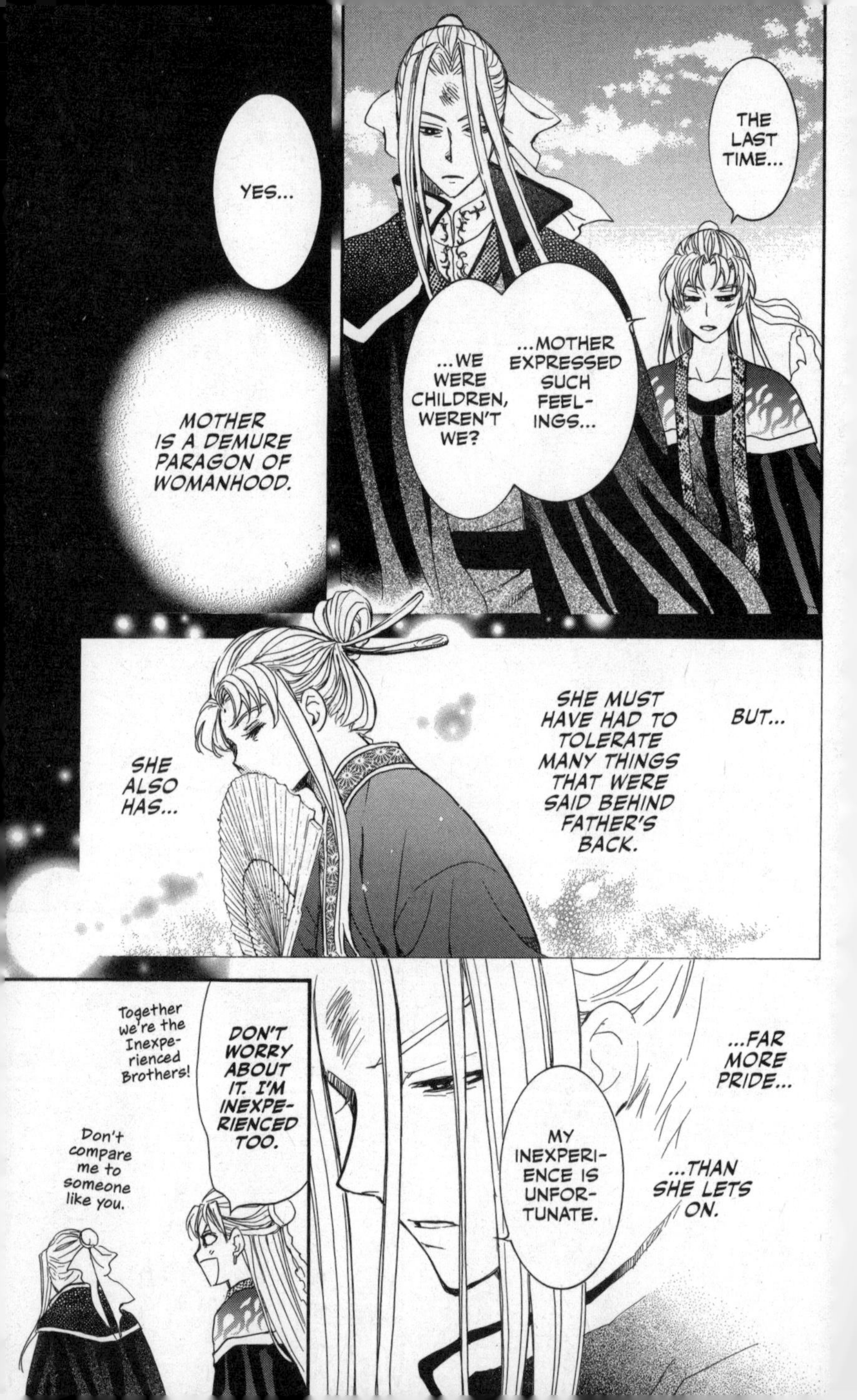
THE LAST TIME...
...MOTHER EXPRESSED SUCH FEEL- INGS...
...WE WERE CHILDREN, WEREN'T WE?
YES...
MOTHER IS A DEMURE PARAGON OF WOMANHOOD.
BUT...
SHE MUST HAVE HAD TO TOLERATE MANY THINGS THAT WERE SAID BEHIND FATHER'S BACK.
SHE ALSO HAS...
...FAR MORE PRIDE...
...THAN SHE LETS ON.
MY INEXPERI- ENCE IS UNFOR- TUNATE.
DON'T WORRY ABOUT IT. I'M INEXPE- RIENCED TOO.
Together we're the Inexpe- rienced Brothers!
Don't compare me to someone like you.

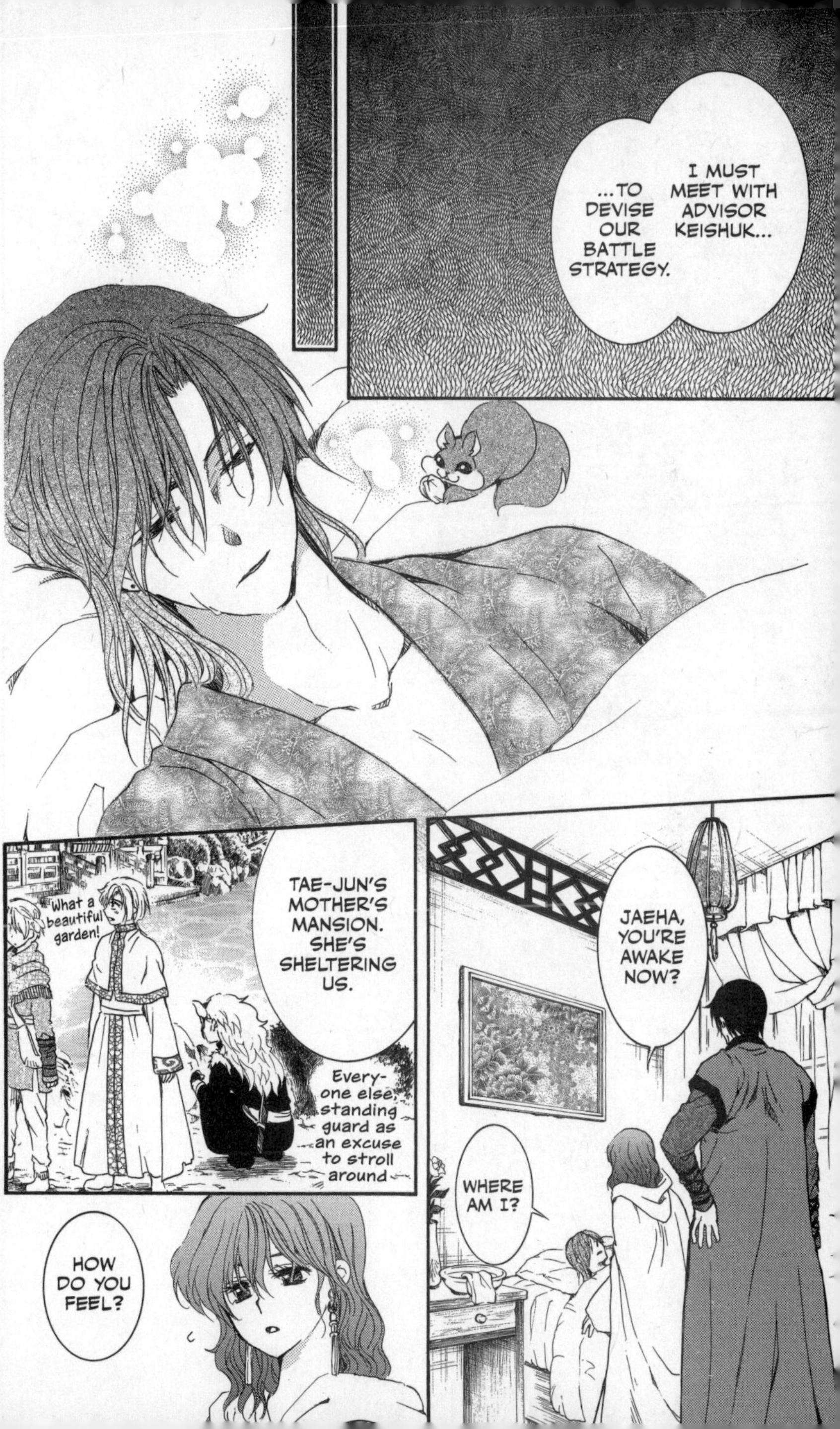
I MUST MEET WITH ADVISOR KEISHUK...
...TO DEVISE OUR BATTLE STRATEGY.
JAEHA, YOU'RE AWAKE NOW?
WHERE AM I?
TAE-JUN'S MOTHER'S MANSION. SHE'S SHELTERING US.
What a beautiful garden!
Every-one else, standing guard as an excuse to stroll around
HOW DO YOU FEEL?

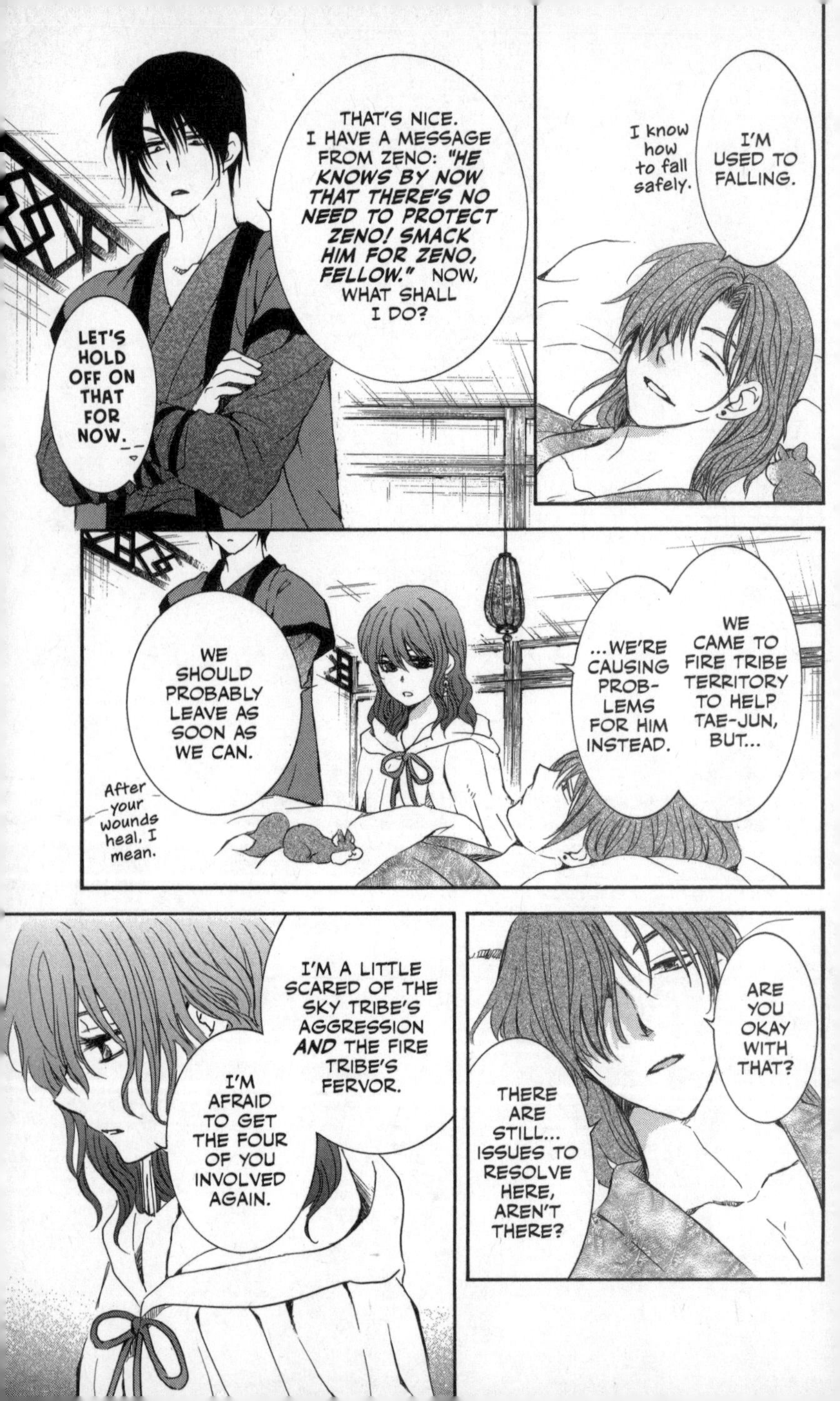
I'M USED TO FALLING.
I know how to fall safely.
THAT'S NICE. I HAVE A MESSAGE FROM ZENO: "HE KNOWS BY NOW THAT THERE'S NO NEED TO PROTECT ZENO! SMACK HIM FOR ZENO, FELLOW." NOW, WHAT SHALL I DO?
LET'S HOLD OFF ON THAT FOR NOW.
WE CAME TO FIRE TRIBE TERRITORY TO HELP TAE-JUN, BUT...
...WE'RE CAUSING PROB-LEMS FOR HIM INSTEAD.
WE SHOULD PROBABLY LEAVE AS SOON AS WE CAN.
After your wounds heal, I mean.
ARE YOU OKAY WITH THAT?
THERE ARE STILL... ISSUES TO RESOLVE HERE, AREN'T THERE?
I'M A LITTLE SCARED OF THE SKY TRIBE'S AGGRESSION AND THE FIRE TRIBE'S FERVOR.
I'M AFRAID TO GET THE FOUR OF YOU INVOLVED AGAIN.

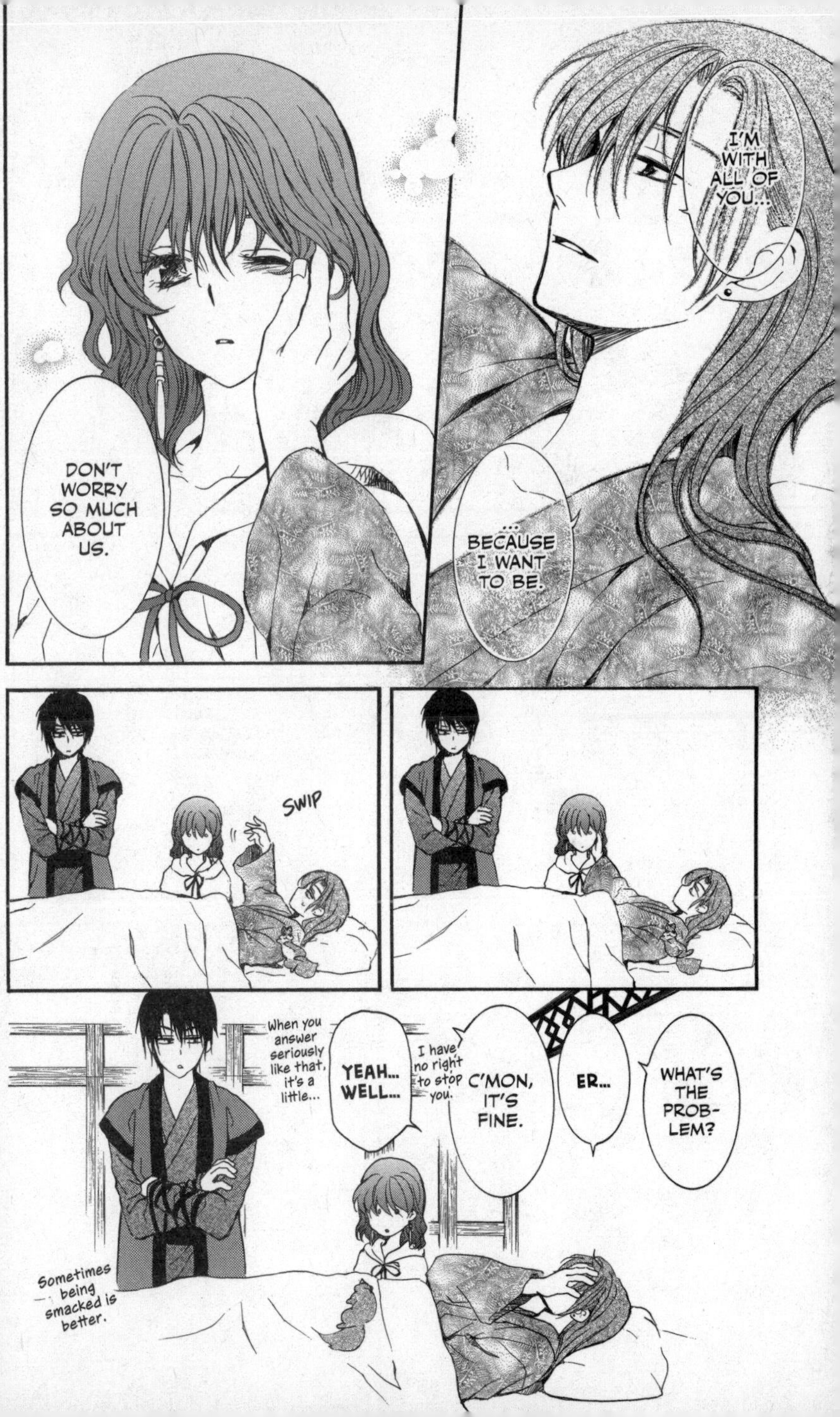
I'M WITH ALL OF YOU...
...BECAUSE I WANT TO BE.
DON'T WORRY SO MUCH ABOUT US.
SWIP
WHAT'S THE PROB-LEM?
ER...
C'MON, IT'S FINE.
I have no right to stop you.
YEAH... WELL...
When you answer seriously like that, it's a little...
Sometimes being smacked is better.

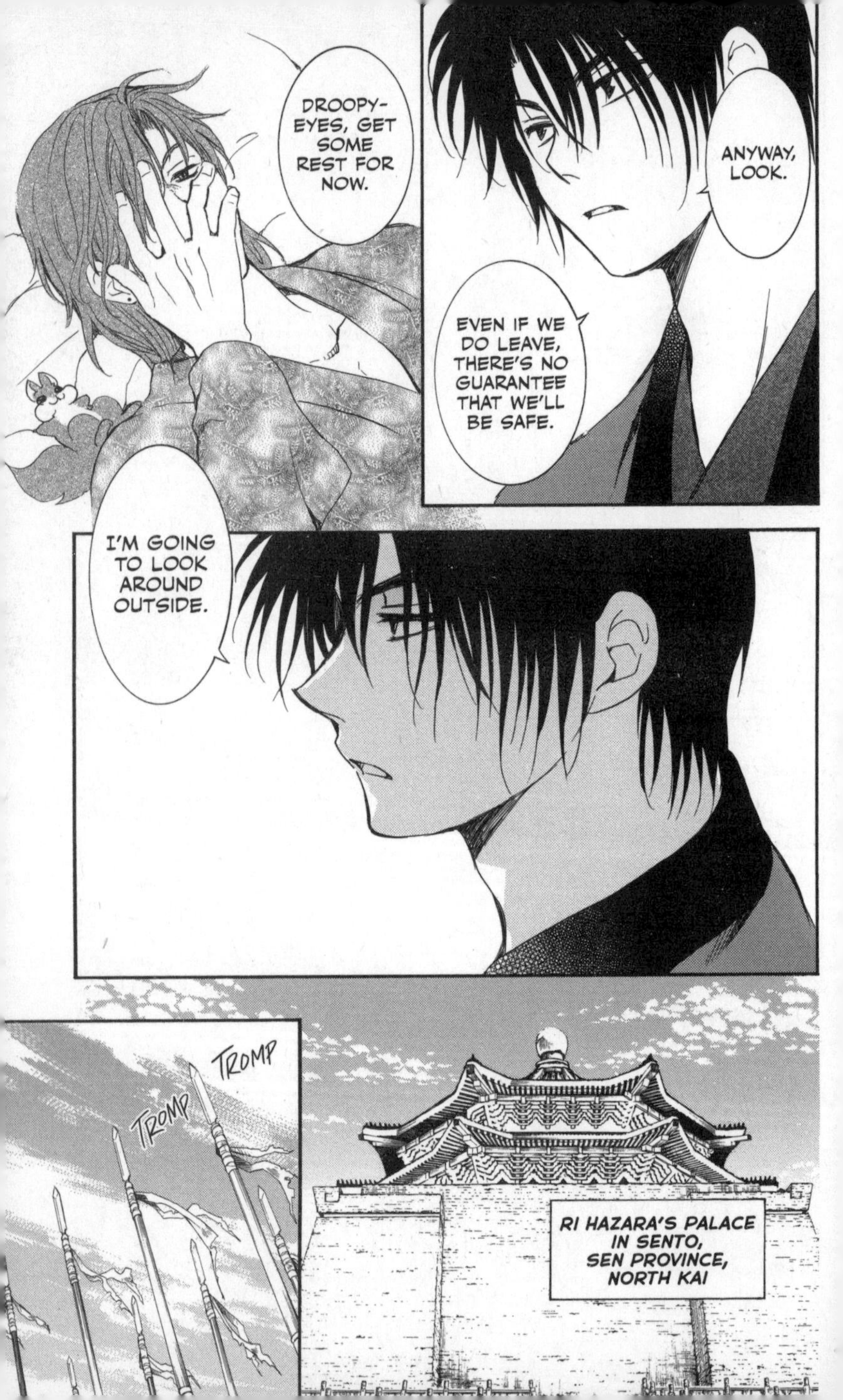
ANYWAY, LOOK.
EVEN IF WE DO LEAVE, THERE'S NO GUARANTEE THAT WE'LL BE SAFE.
DROOPY-EYES, GET SOME REST FOR NOW.
I'M GOING TO LOOK AROUND OUTSIDE.
RI HAZARA'S PALACE IN SENTO, SEN PROVINCE, NORTH KAI
TROMP
TROMP

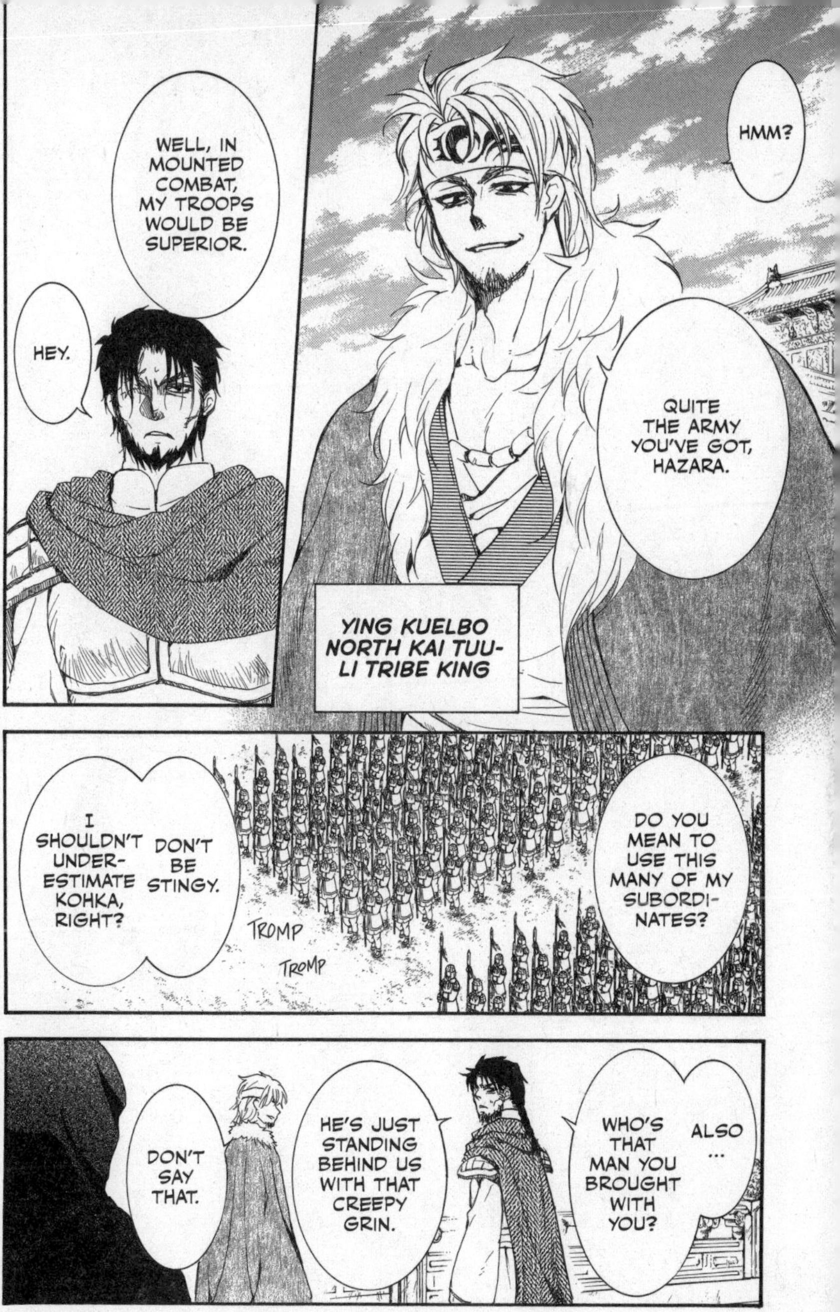
HMM?
QUITE THE ARMY YOU'VE GOT, HAZARA.
YING KUELBO NORTH KAI TUULI TRIBE KING
WELL, IN MOUNTED COMBAT, MY TROOPS WOULD BE SUPERIOR.
HEY.
DO YOU MEAN TO USE THIS MANY OF MY SUBORDINATES?
DON'T BE STINGY.
I SHOULDN'T UNDERESTIMATE KOHKA, RIGHT?
TROMP
TROMP
ALSO ...
WHO'S THAT MAN YOU BROUGHT WITH YOU?
HE'S JUST STANDING BEHIND US WITH THAT CREEPY GRIN.
DON'T SAY THAT.

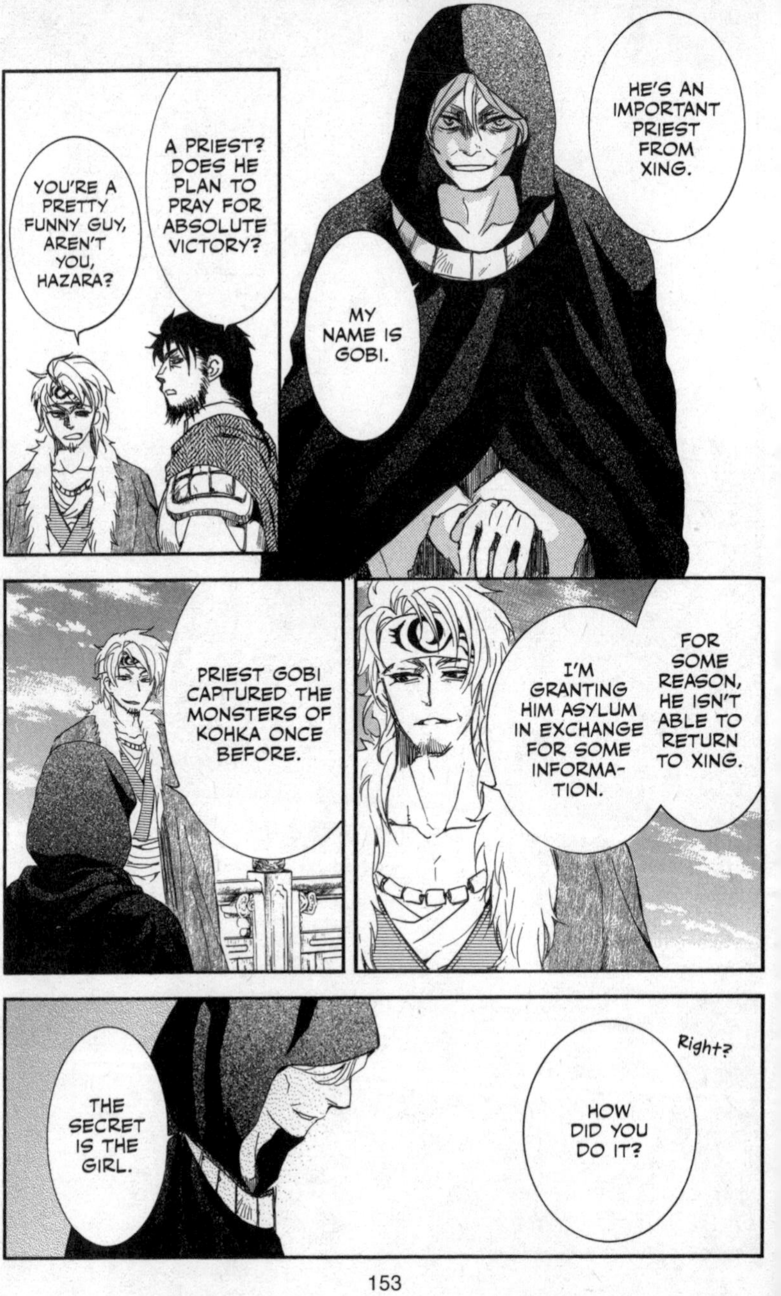
HE'S AN IMPORTANT PRIEST FROM XING.
MY NAME IS GOBI.
A PRIEST? DOES HE PLAN TO PRAY FOR ABSOLUTE VICTORY?
YOU'RE A PRETTY FUNNY GUY, AREN'T YOU, HAZARA?
FOR SOME REASON, HE ISN'T ABLE TO RETURN TO XING.
I'M GRANTING HIM ASYLUM IN EXCHANGE FOR SOME INFORMATION.
PRIEST GOBI CAPTURED THE MONSTERS OF KOHKA ONCE BEFORE.
Right?
HOW DID YOU DO IT?
THE SECRET IS THE GIRL.

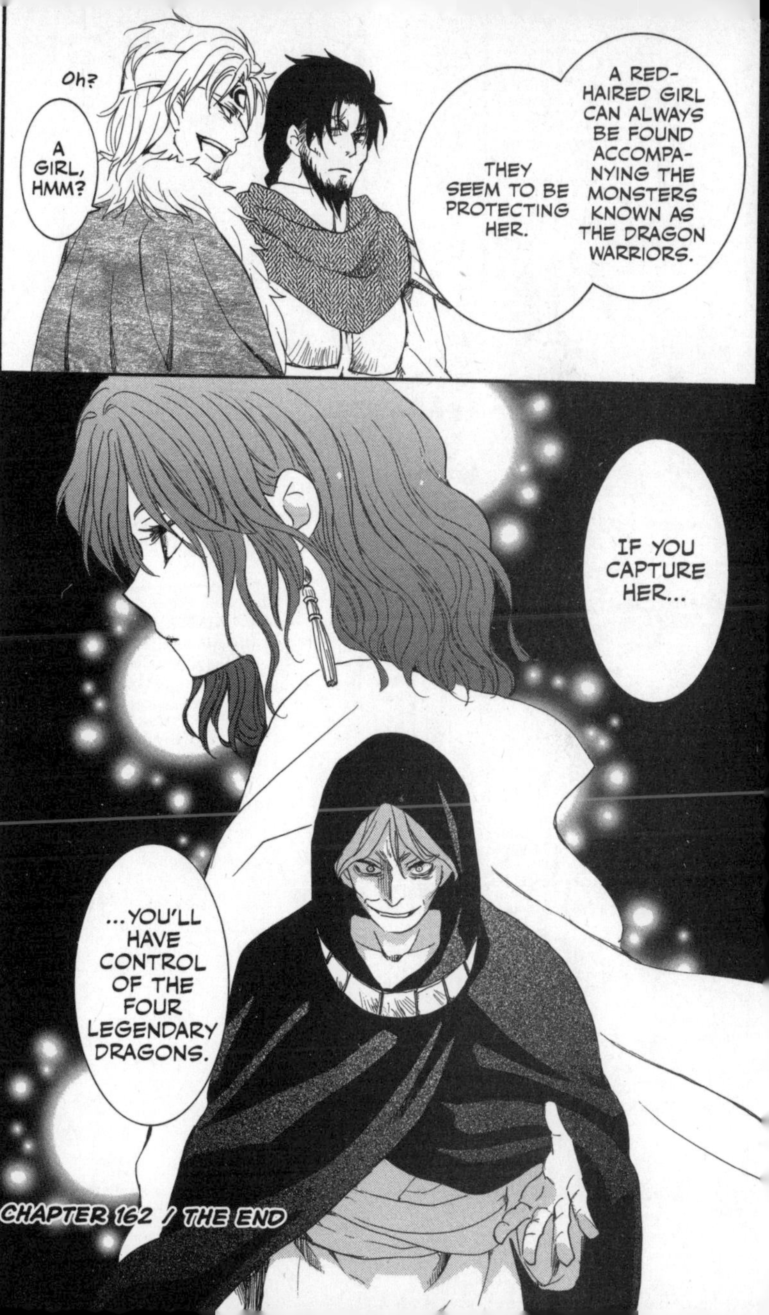
A RED-HAIRED GIRL CAN ALWAYS BE FOUND ACCOMPANYING THE MONSTERS KNOWN AS THE DRAGON WARRIORS.
THEY SEEM TO BE PROTECTING HER.
Oh?
A GIRL, HMM?
IF YOU CAPTURE HER...
...YOU'LL HAVE CONTROL OF THE FOUR LEGENDARY DRAGONS.
CHAPTER 162 / THE END

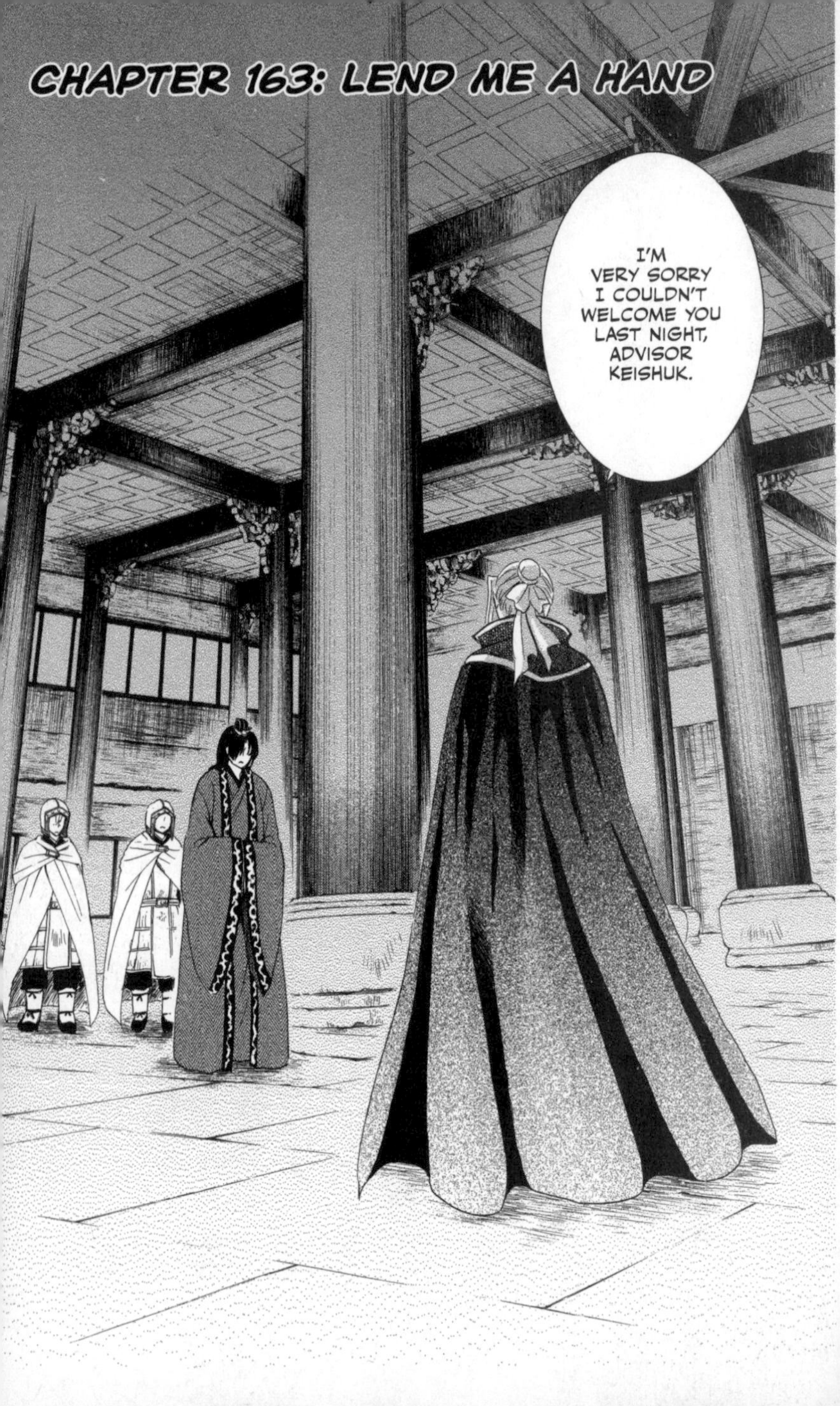
CHAPTER 163: LEND ME A HAND
I'M VERY SORRY I COULDN'T WELCOME YOU LAST NIGHT, ADVISOR KEISHUK.

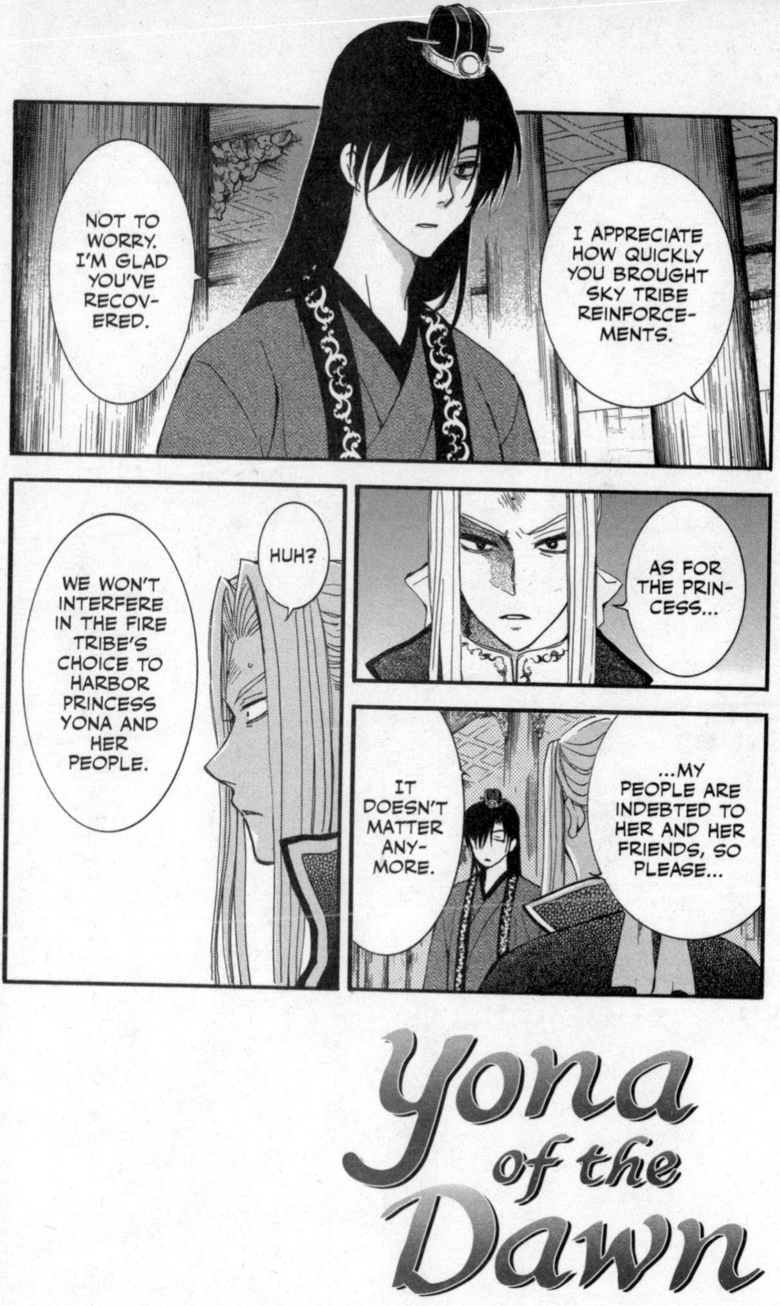
I APPRECIATE HOW QUICKLY YOU BROUGHT SKY TRIBE REINFORCEMENTS.
NOT TO WORRY. I'M GLAD YOU'VE RECOVERED.
AS FOR THE PRINCESS...
...MY PEOPLE ARE INDEBTED TO HER AND HER FRIENDS, SO PLEASE...
IT DOESN'T MATTER ANYMORE.
HUH?
WE WON'T INTERFERE IN THE FIRE TRIBE'S CHOICE TO HARBOR PRINCESS YONA AND HER PEOPLE.

Yona of the Dawn

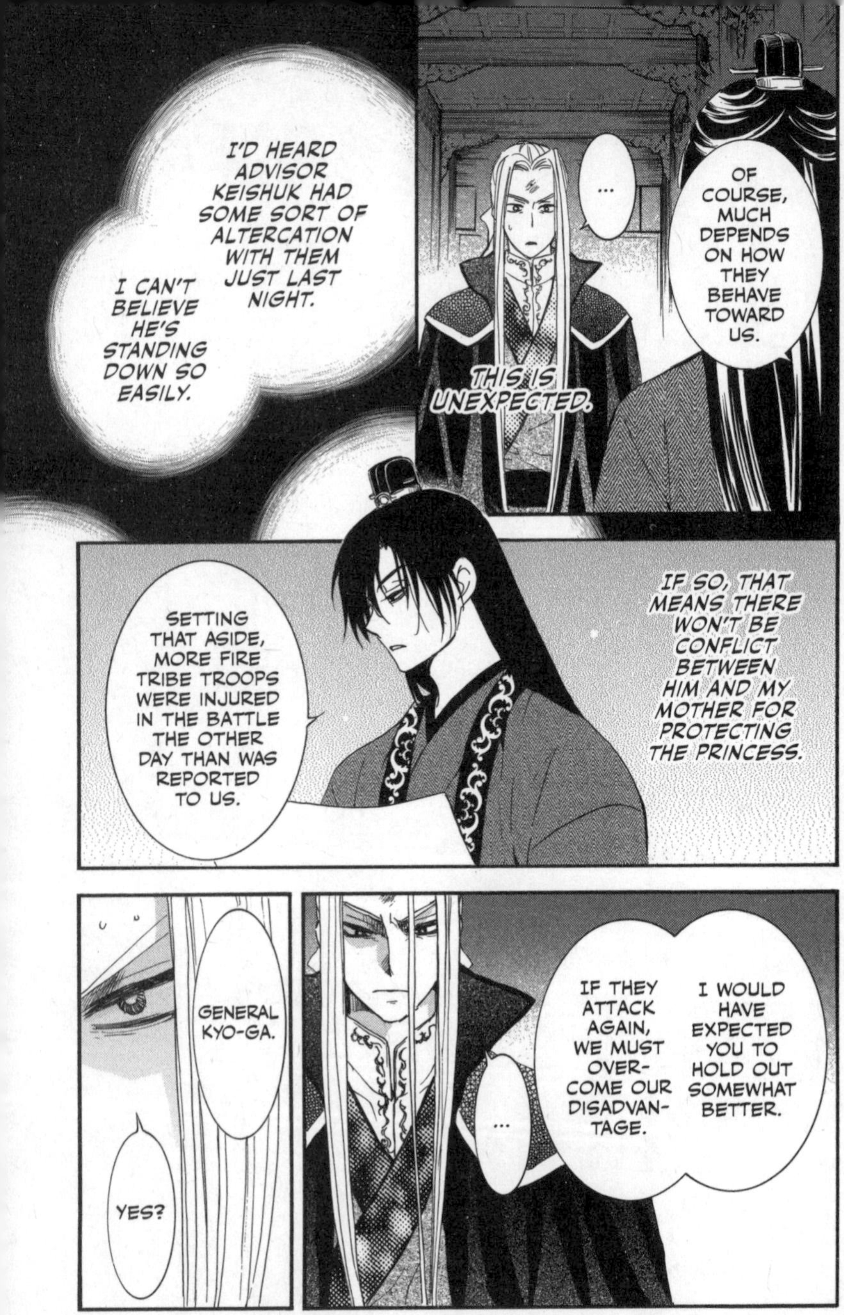
OF COURSE, MUCH DEPENDS ON HOW THEY BEHAVE TOWARD US.
...
THIS IS UNEXPECTED.
I'D HEARD ADVISOR KEISHUK HAD SOME SORT OF ALTERCATION WITH THEM JUST LAST NIGHT.
I CAN'T BELIEVE HE'S STANDING DOWN SO EASILY.
IF SO, THAT MEANS THERE WON'T BE CONFLICT BETWEEN HIM AND MY MOTHER FOR PROTECTING THE PRINCESS.
SETTING THAT ASIDE, MORE FIRE TRIBE TROOPS WERE INJURED IN THE BATTLE THE OTHER DAY THAN WAS REPORTED TO US.
I WOULD HAVE EXPECTED YOU TO HOLD OUT SOMEWHAT BETTER.
IF THEY ATTACK AGAIN, WE MUST OVER-COME OUR DISADVAN-TAGE.
...
GENERAL KYO-GA.
YES?

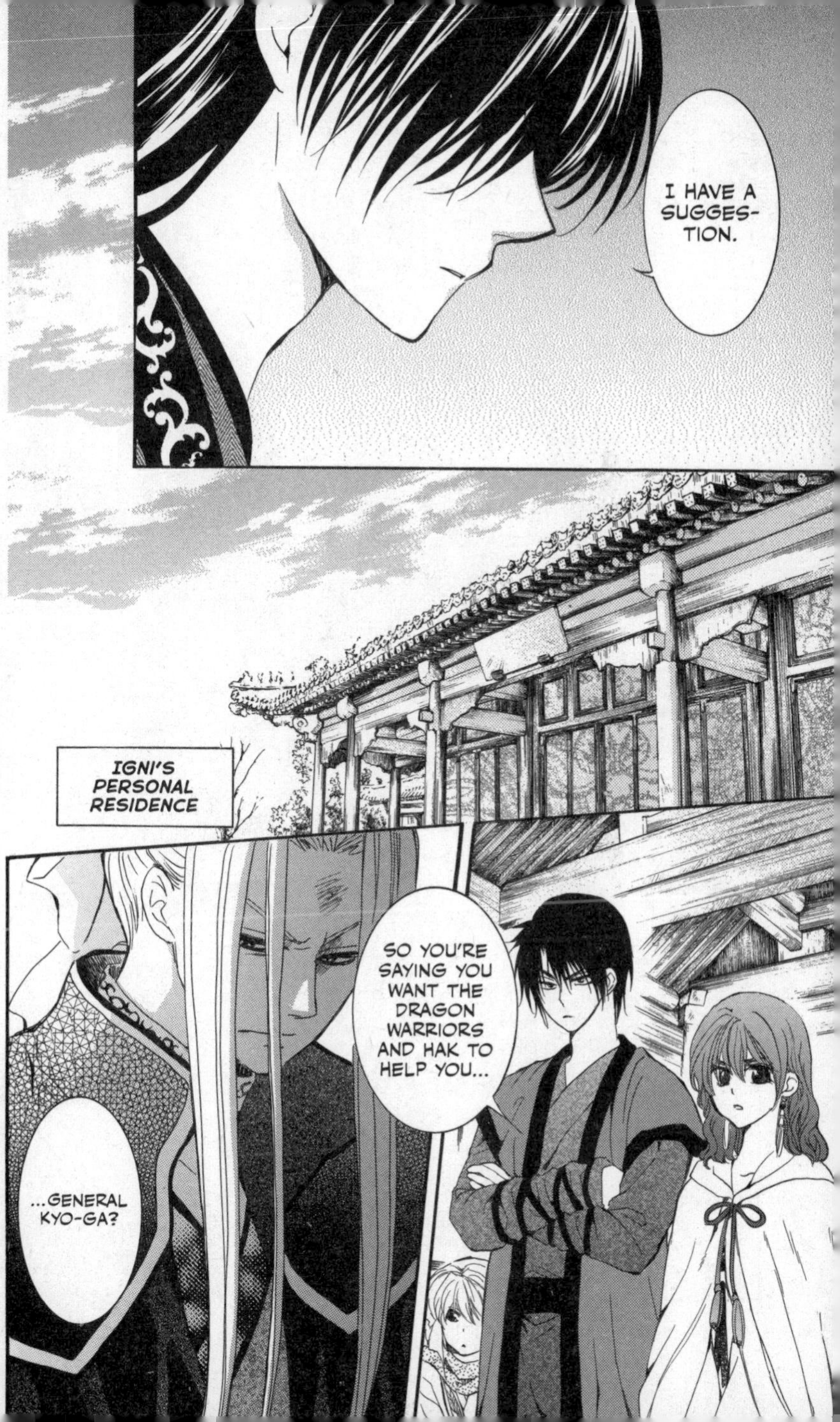
I HAVE A SUGGES- TION.
IGNI'S PERSONAL RESIDENCE
SO YOU'RE SAYING YOU WANT THE DRAGON WARRIORS AND HAK TO HELP YOU...
...GENERAL KYO-GA?

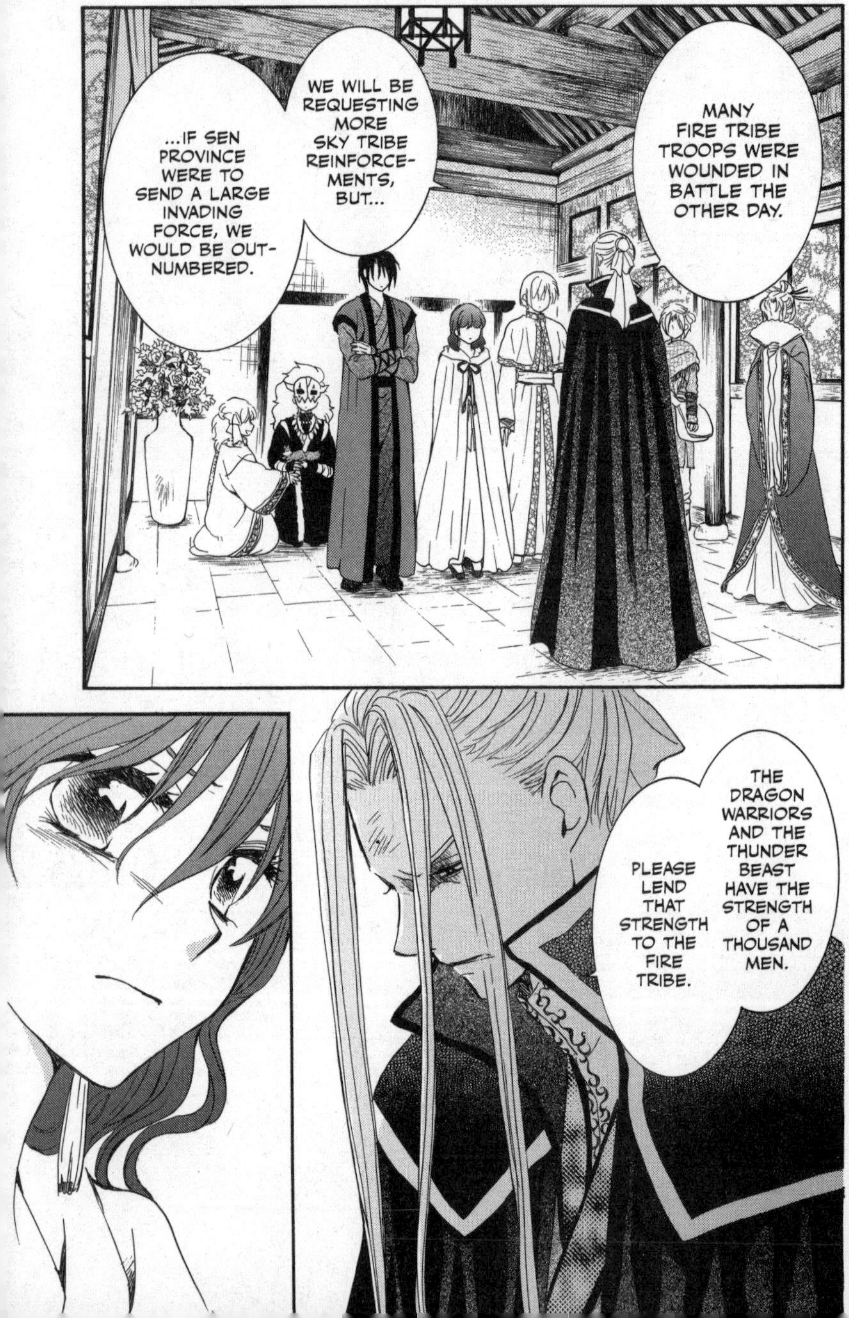
MANY FIRE TRIBE TROOPS WERE WOUNDED IN BATTLE THE OTHER DAY.
WE WILL BE REQUESTING MORE SKY TRIBE REINFORCE-MENTS, BUT...
...IF SEN PROVINCE WERE TO SEND A LARGE INVADING FORCE, WE WOULD BE OUT-NUMBERED.
THE DRAGON WARRIORS AND THE THUNDER BEAST HAVE THE STRENGTH OF A THOUSAND MEN.
PLEASE LEND THAT STRENGTH TO THE FIRE TRIBE.

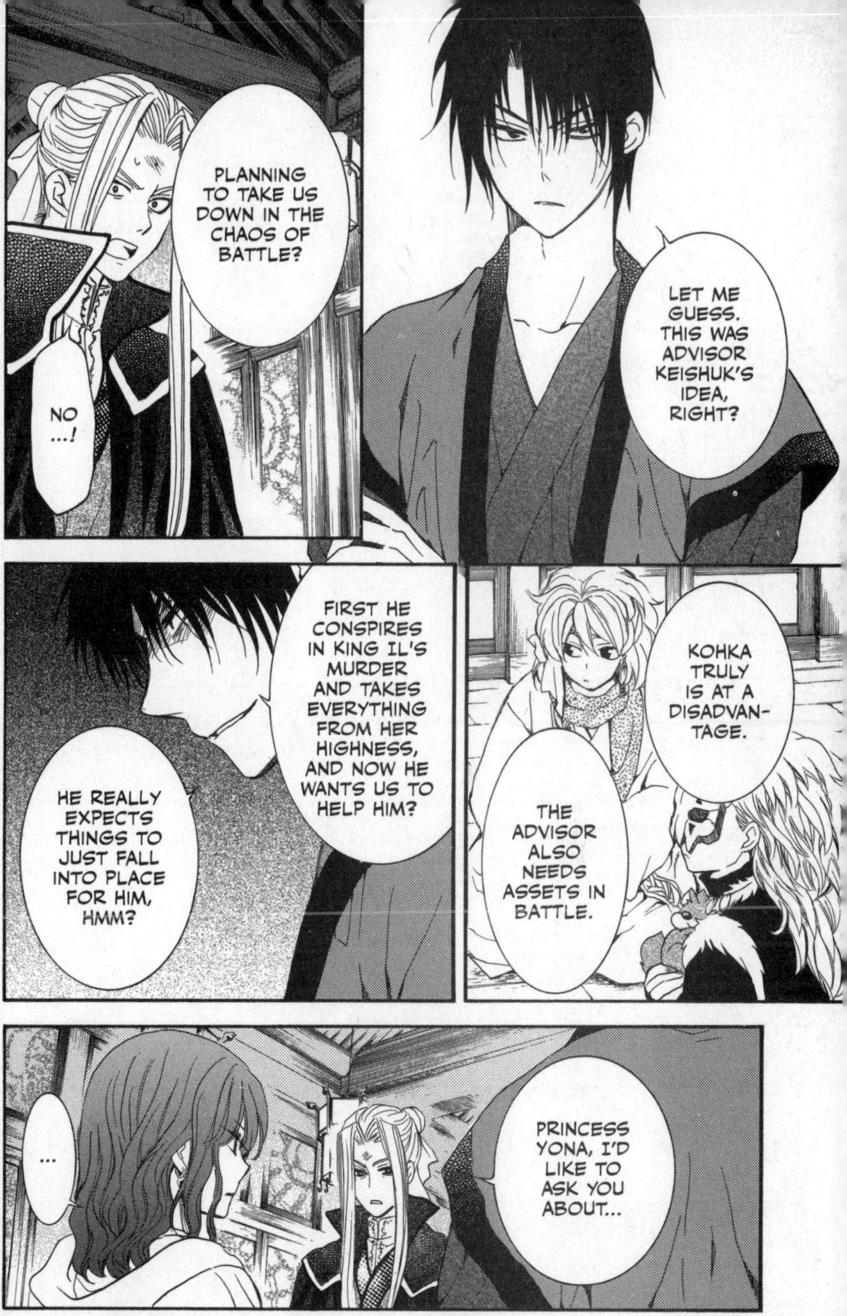
LET ME GUESS. THIS WAS ADVISOR KEISHUK'S IDEA, RIGHT?
PLANNING TO TAKE US DOWN IN THE CHAOS OF BATTLE?
NO ...!
KOHKA TRULY IS AT A DISADVANTAGE.
THE ADVISOR ALSO NEEDS ASSETS IN BATTLE.
FIRST HE CONSPIRES IN KING IL'S MURDER AND TAKES EVERYTHING FROM HER HIGHNESS, AND NOW HE WANTS US TO HELP HIM?
HE REALLY EXPECTS THINGS TO JUST FALL INTO PLACE FOR HIM, HMM?
PRINCESS YONA, I'D LIKE TO ASK YOU ABOUT...
...

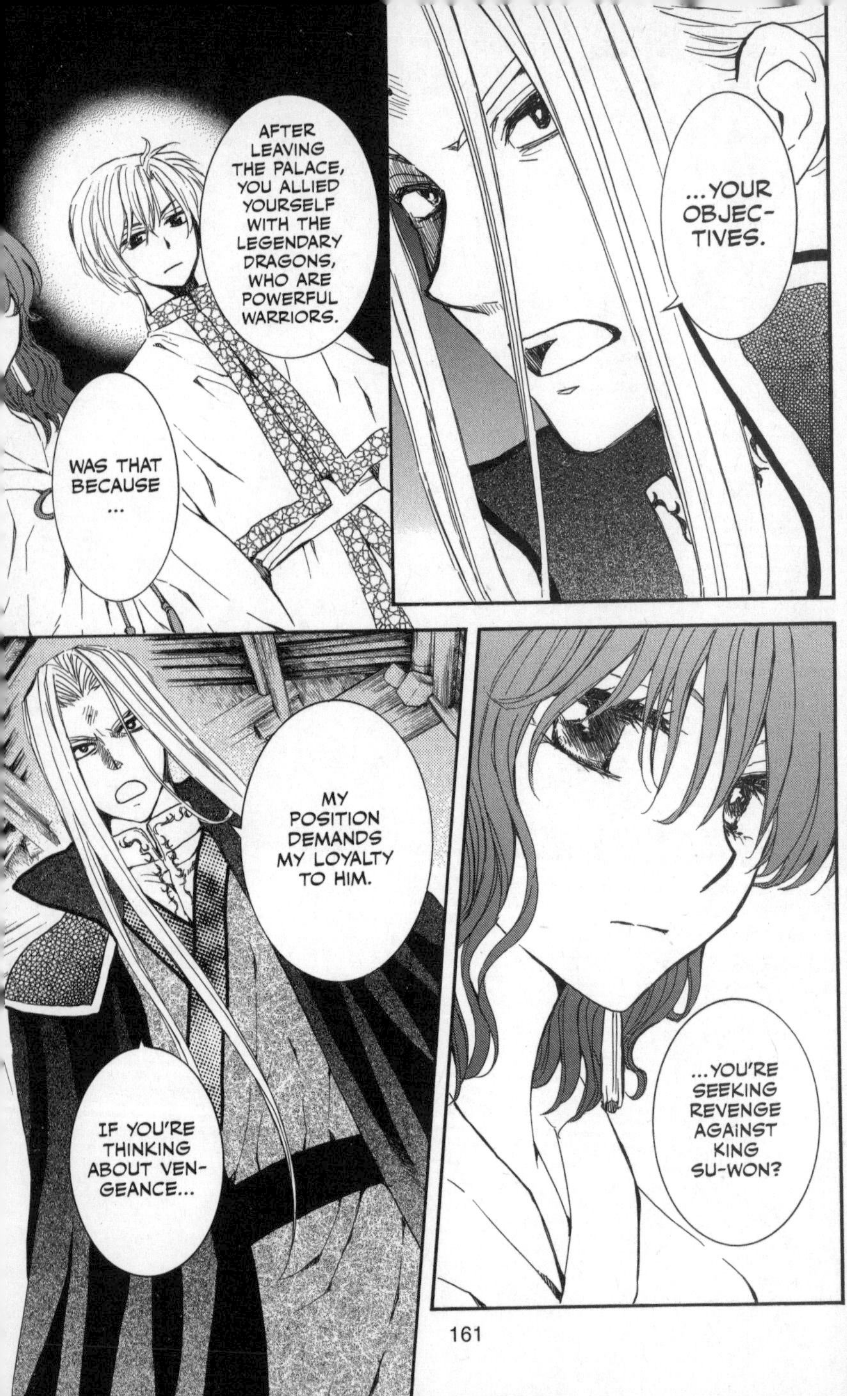
...YOUR OBJECTIVES.
AFTER LEAVING THE PALACE, YOU ALLIED YOURSELF WITH THE LEGENDARY DRAGONS, WHO ARE POWERFUL WARRIORS.
WAS THAT BECAUSE ...
...YOU'RE SEEKING REVENGE AGAINST KING SU-WON?
MY POSITION DEMANDS MY LOYALTY TO HIM.
IF YOU'RE THINKING ABOUT VENGEANCE...

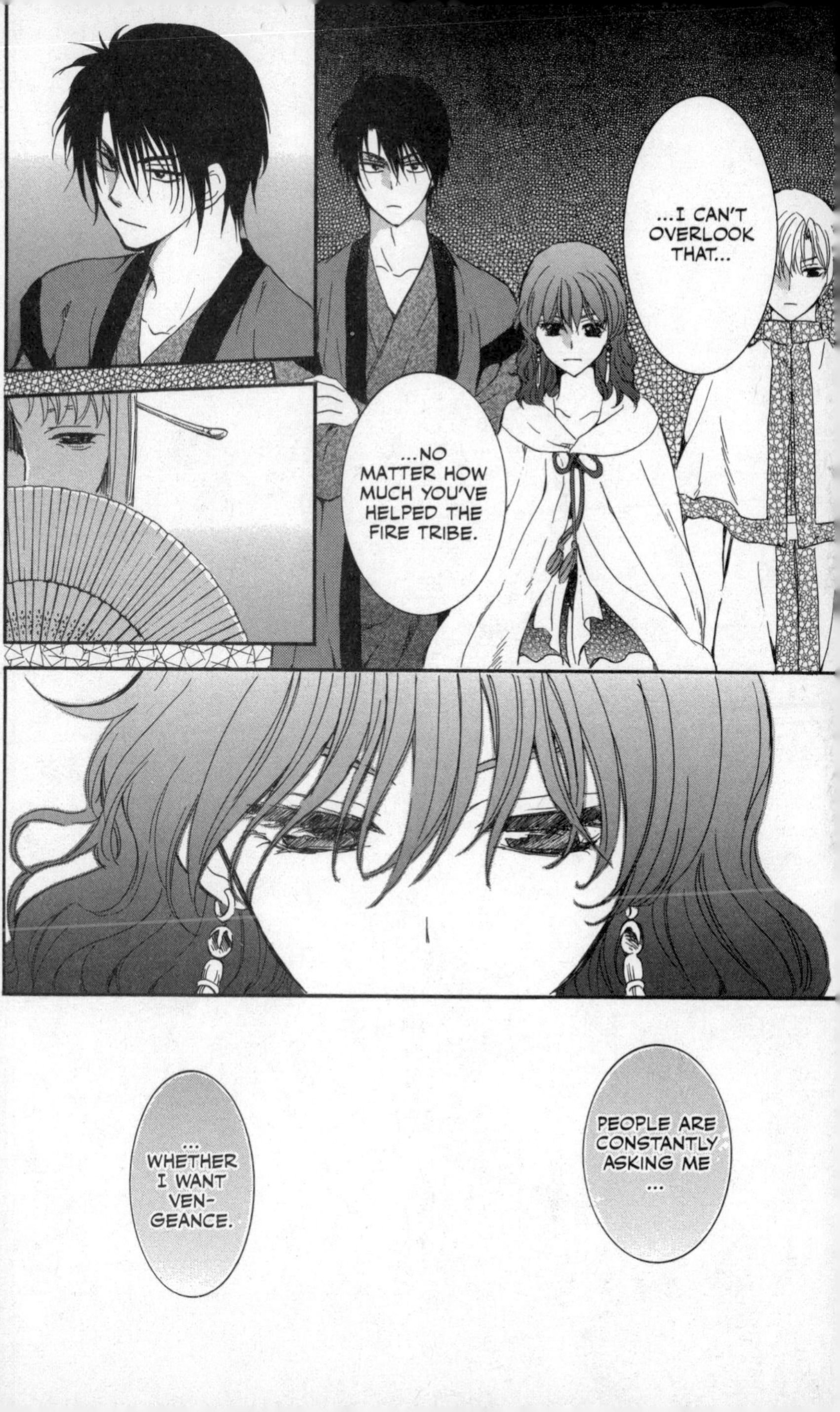
...I CAN'T OVERLOOK THAT...
...NO MATTER HOW MUCH YOU'VE HELPED THE FIRE TRIBE.
PEOPLE ARE CONSTANTLY ASKING ME ...
... WHETHER I WANT VEN-GEANCE.

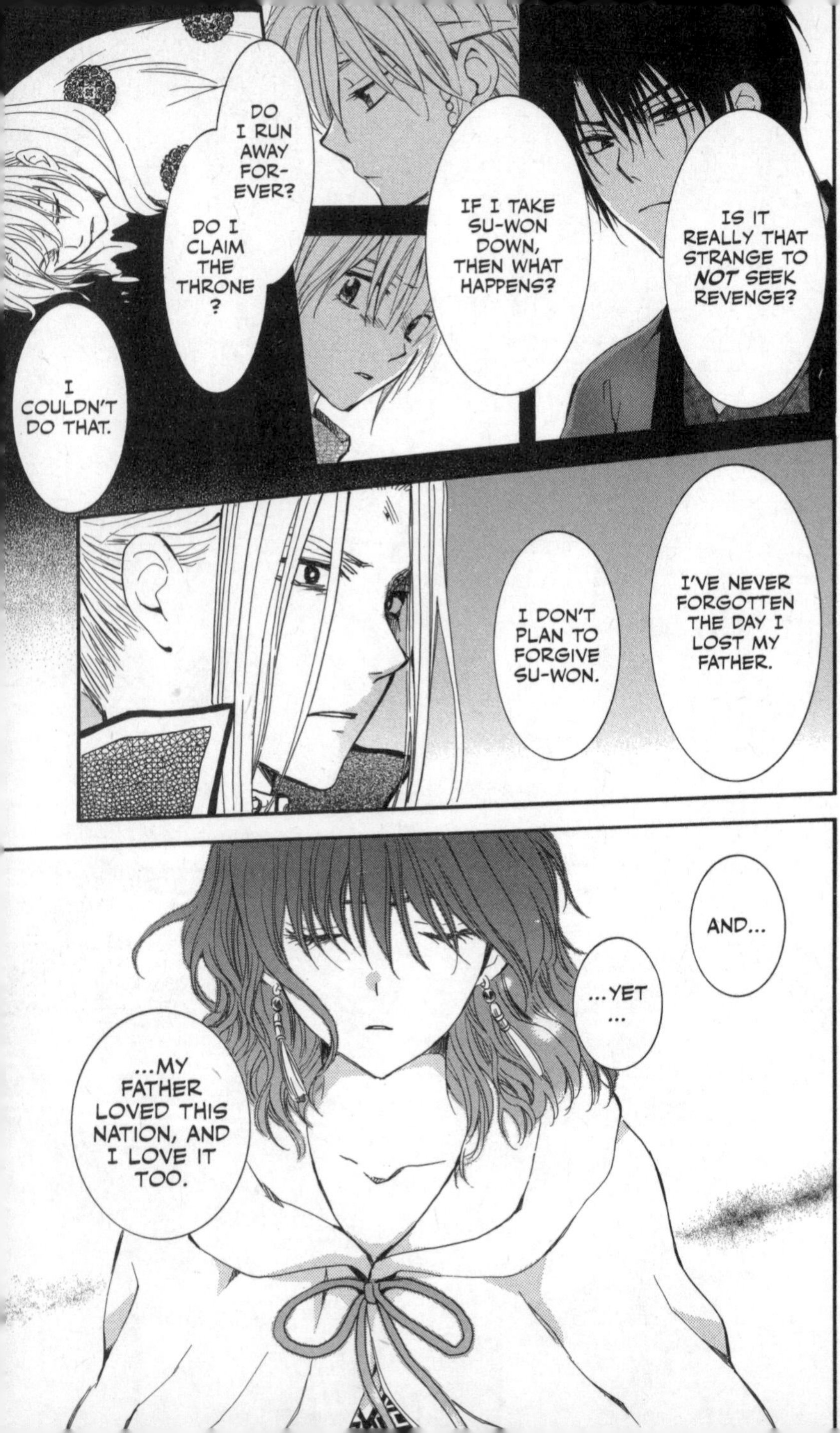
IS IT REALLY THAT STRANGE TO *NOT* SEEK REVENGE?
IF I TAKE SU-WON DOWN, THEN WHAT HAPPENS?
DO I RUN AWAY FOR-EVER?
DO I CLAIM THE THRONE?
I COULDN'T DO THAT.
I'VE NEVER FORGOTTEN THE DAY I LOST MY FATHER.
I DON'T PLAN TO FORGIVE SU-WON.
AND...
...YET ...
...MY FATHER LOVED THIS NATION, AND I LOVE IT TOO.

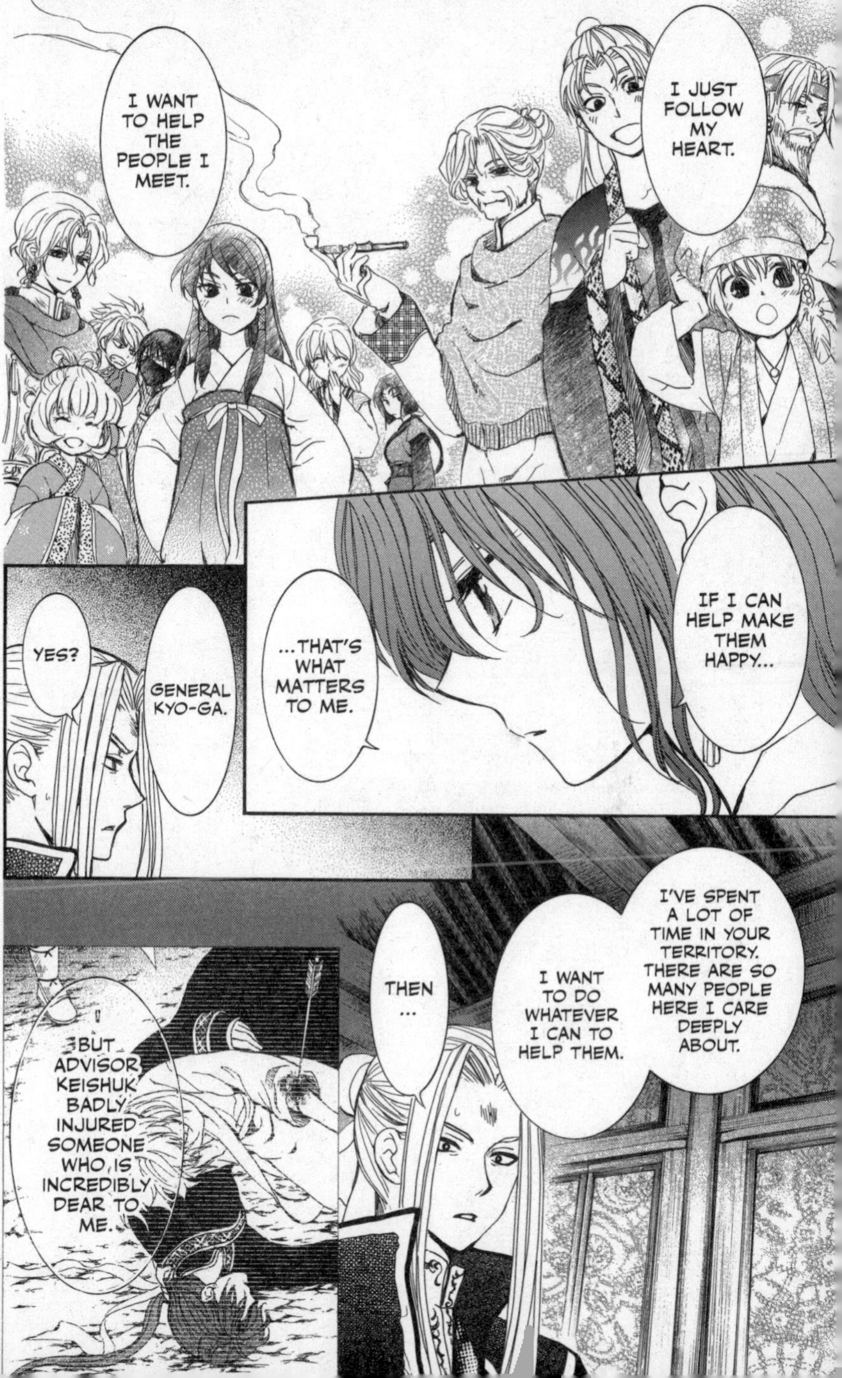
I JUST FOLLOW MY HEART.
I WANT TO HELP THE PEOPLE I MEET.
IF I CAN HELP MAKE THEM HAPPY...
...THAT'S WHAT MATTERS TO ME.
GENERAL KYO-GA.
YES?
I'VE SPENT A LOT OF TIME IN YOUR TERRITORY. THERE ARE SO MANY PEOPLE HERE I CARE DEEPLY ABOUT.
I WANT TO DO WHATEVER I CAN TO HELP THEM.
THEN...
!
BUT ADVISOR KEISHUK BADLY INJURED SOMEONE WHO IS INCREDIBLY DEAR TO ME.

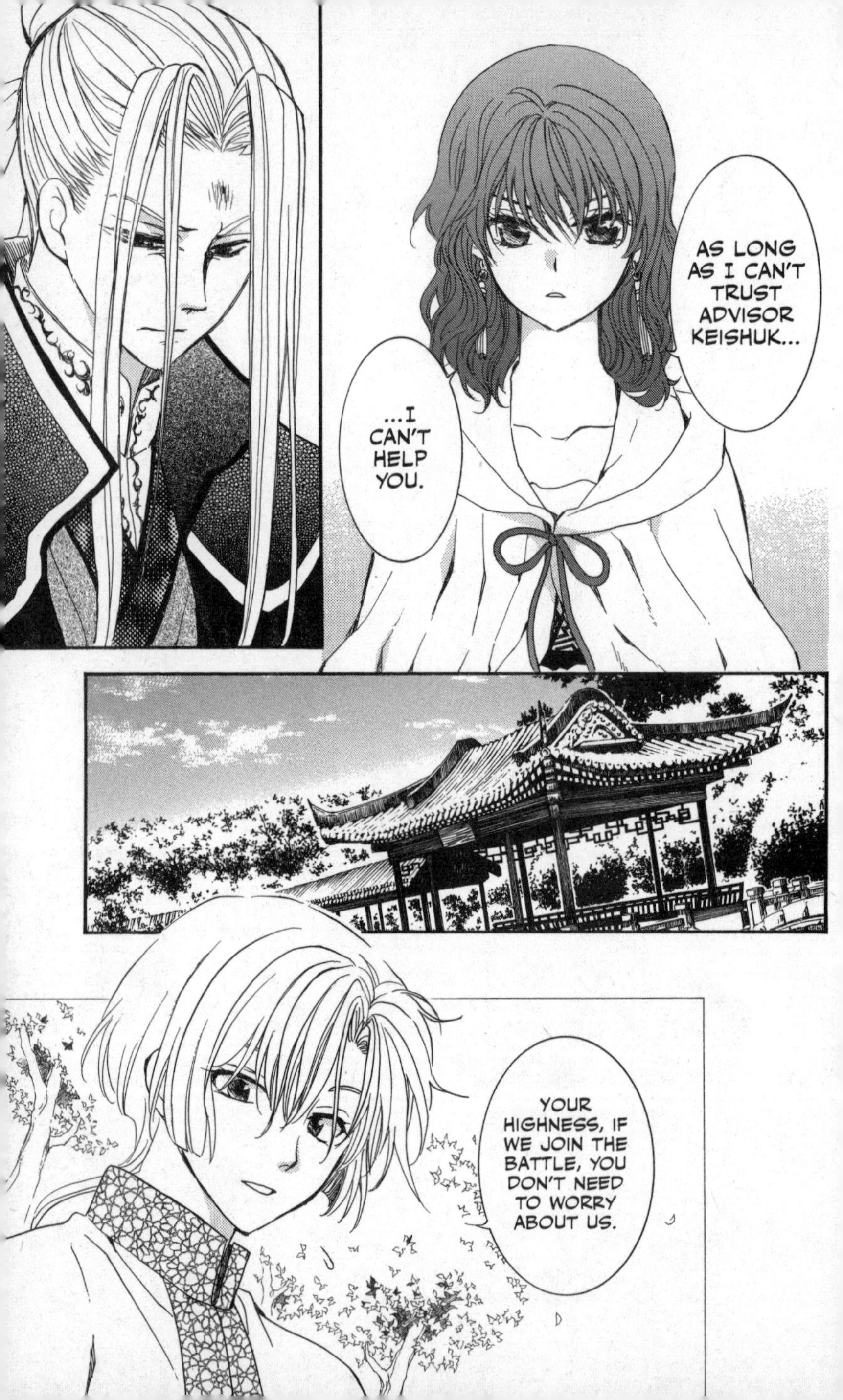
AS LONG AS I CAN'T TRUST ADVISOR KEISHUK...
...I CAN'T HELP YOU.
YOUR HIGHNESS, IF WE JOIN THE BATTLE, YOU DON'T NEED TO WORRY ABOUT US.

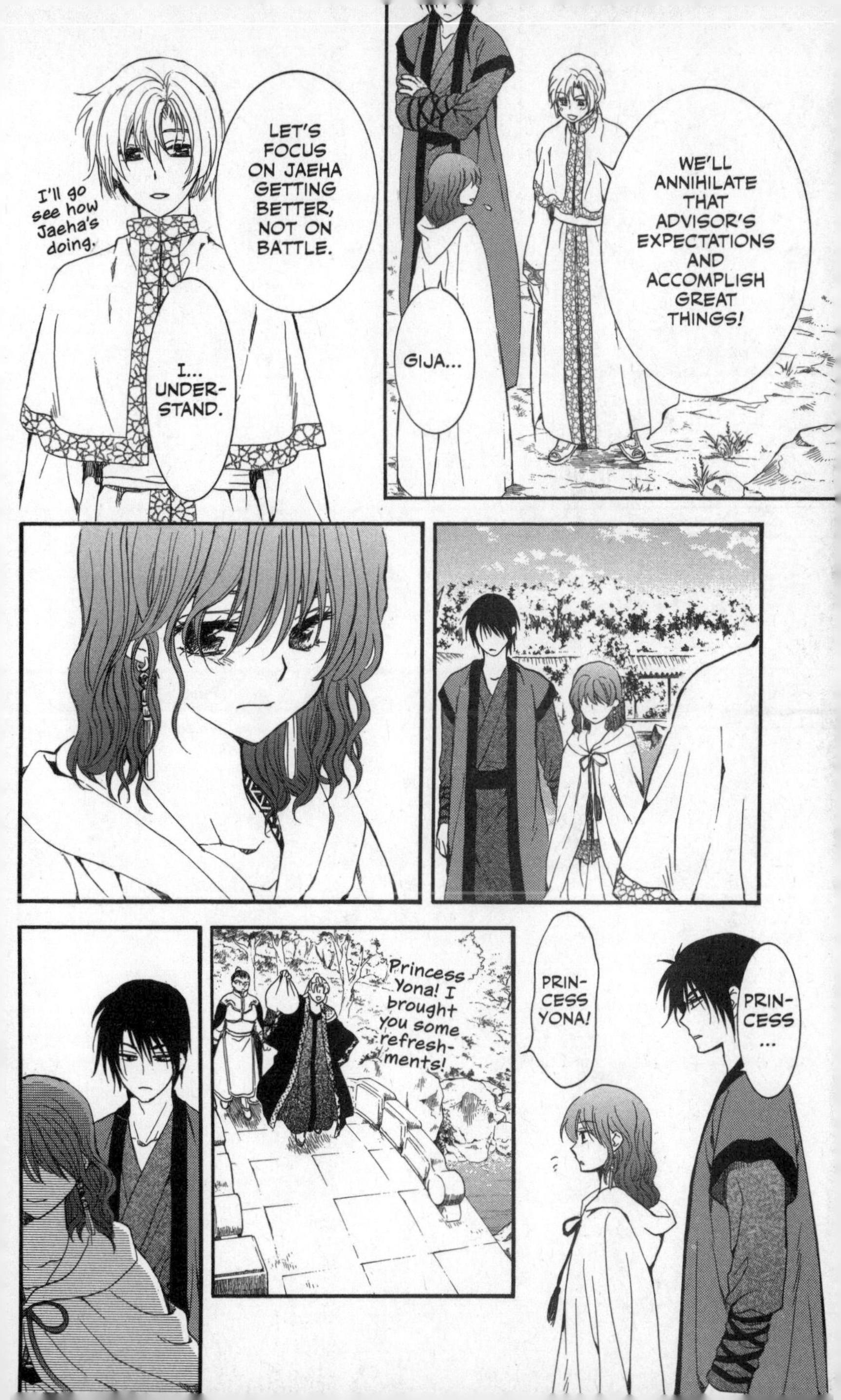
WE'LL ANNIHILATE THAT ADVISOR'S EXPECTATIONS AND ACCOMPLISH GREAT THINGS!
GIJA...
LET'S FOCUS ON JAEHA GETTING BETTER, NOT ON BATTLE.
I'll go see how Jaeha's doing.
I... UNDER-STAND.
PRIN-CESS...
PRIN-CESS YONA!
Princess Yona! I brought you some refresh-ments!

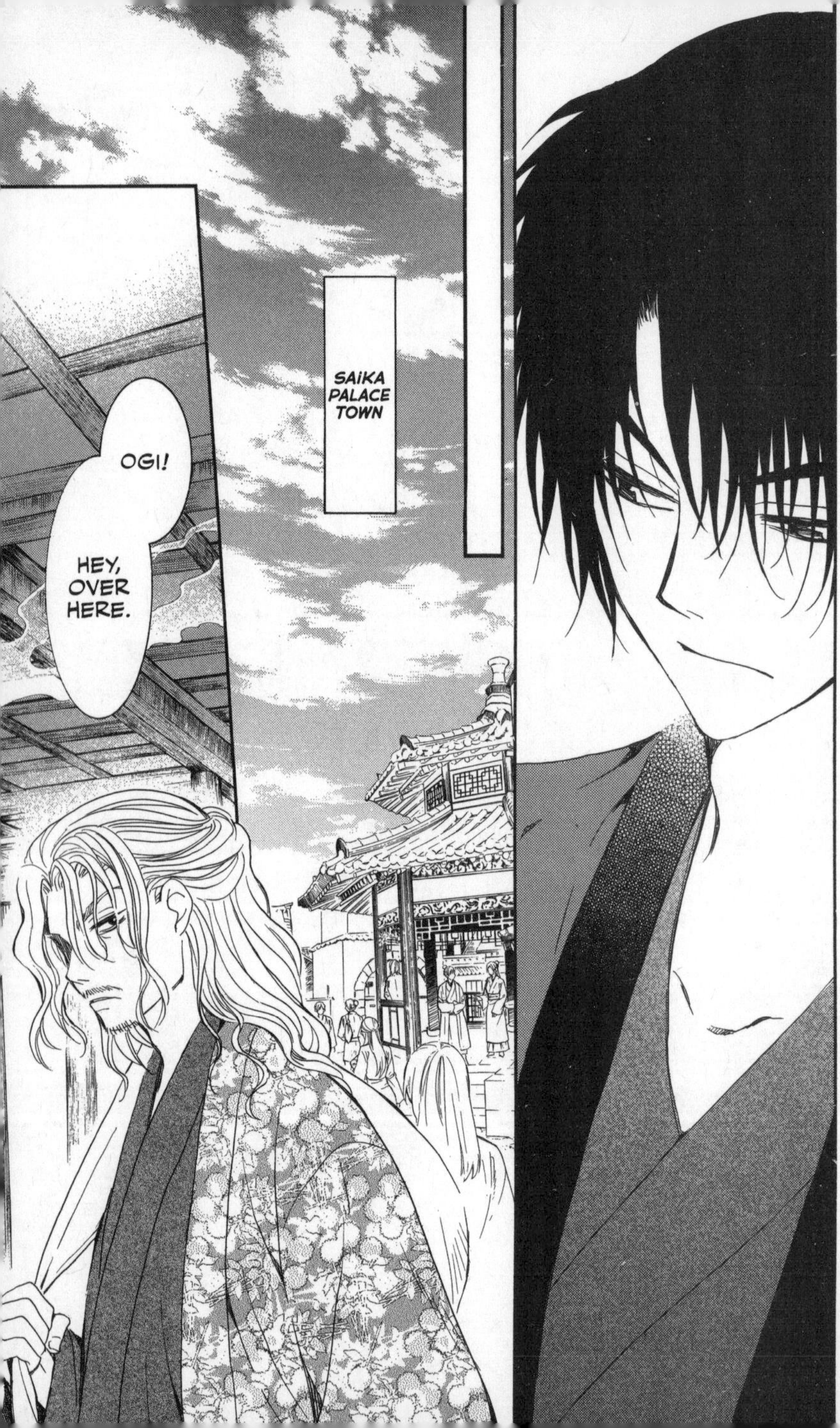
SAIKA PALACE TOWN
OGI!
HEY, OVER HERE.

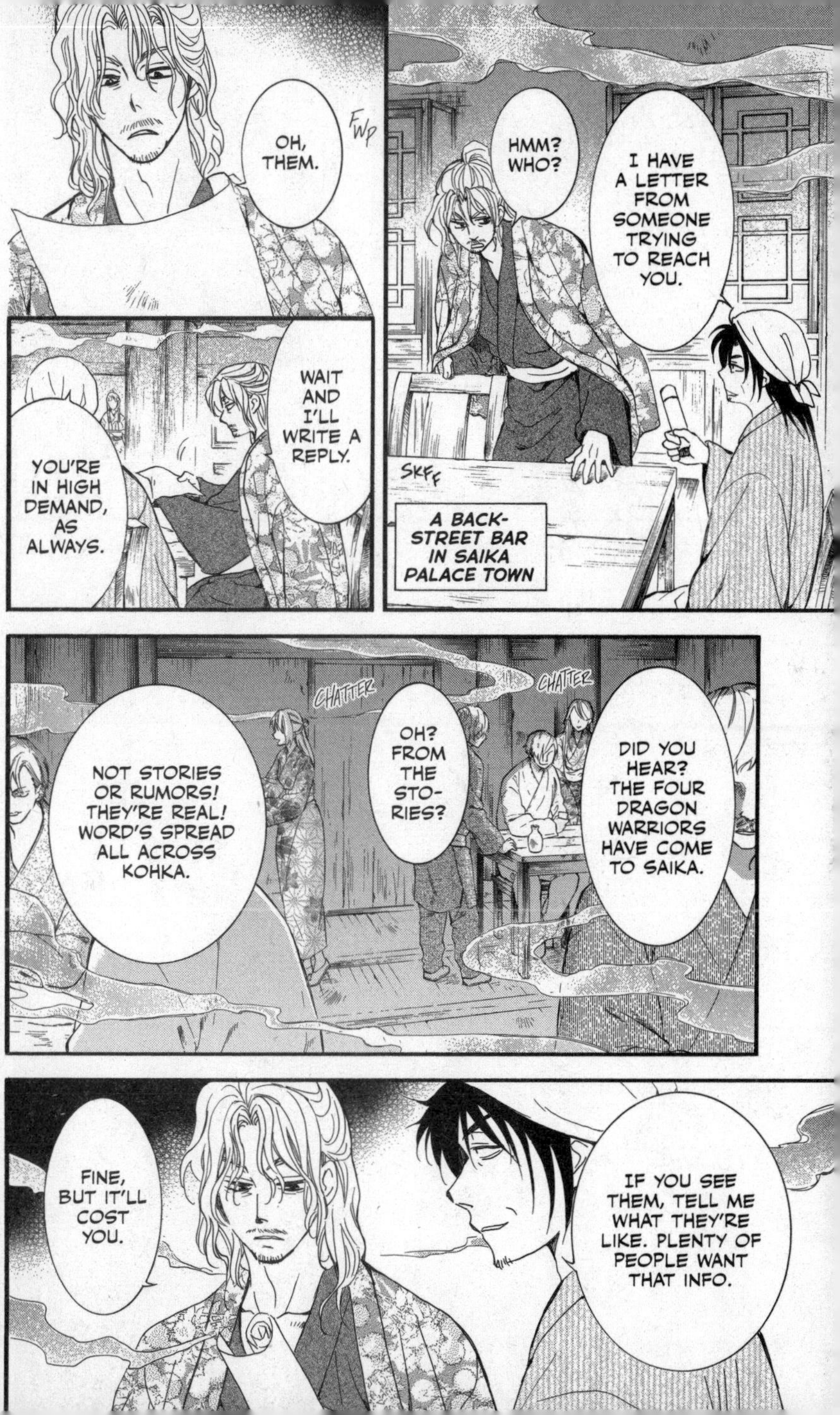

I HAVE A LETTER FROM SOMEONE TRYING TO REACH YOU.
HMM? WHO?
SKFF
A BACK-STREET BAR IN SAIKA PALACE TOWN
FWP
OH, THEM.
WAIT AND I'LL WRITE A REPLY.
YOU'RE IN HIGH DEMAND, AS ALWAYS.
CHATTER
DID YOU HEAR? THE FOUR DRAGON WARRIORS HAVE COME TO SAIKA.
CHATTER
OH? FROM THE STO-RIES?
NOT STORIES OR RUMORS! THEY'RE REAL! WORD'S SPREAD ALL ACROSS KOHKA.
IF YOU SEE THEM, TELL ME WHAT THEY'RE LIKE. PLENTY OF PEOPLE WANT THAT INFO.
FINE, BUT IT'LL COST YOU.

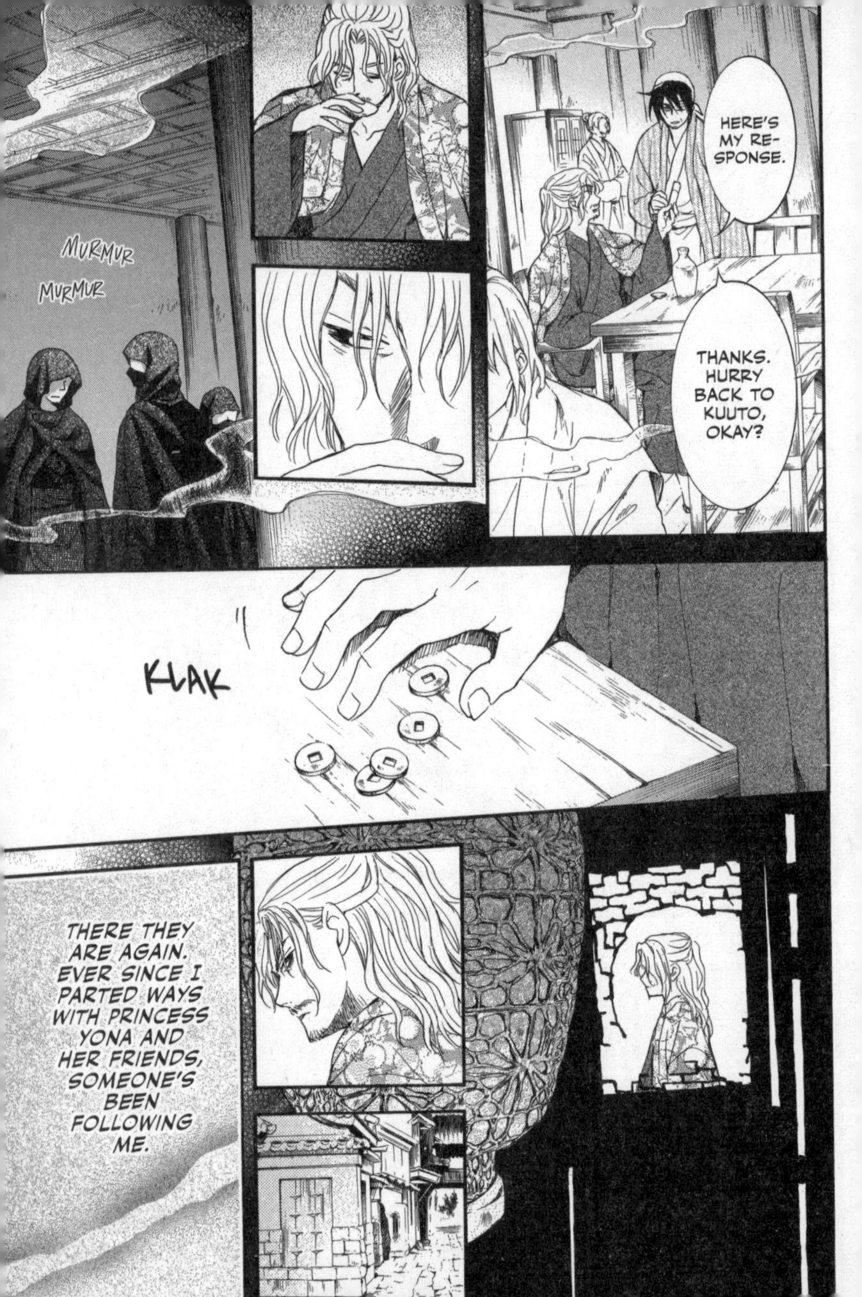
HERE'S MY RE-SPONSE.
THANKS. HURRY BACK TO KUUTO, OKAY?
MURMUR
MURMUR
KLAK
THERE THEY ARE AGAIN. EVER SINCE I PARTED WAYS WITH PRINCESS YONA AND HER FRIENDS, SOMEONE'S BEEN FOLLOWING ME.

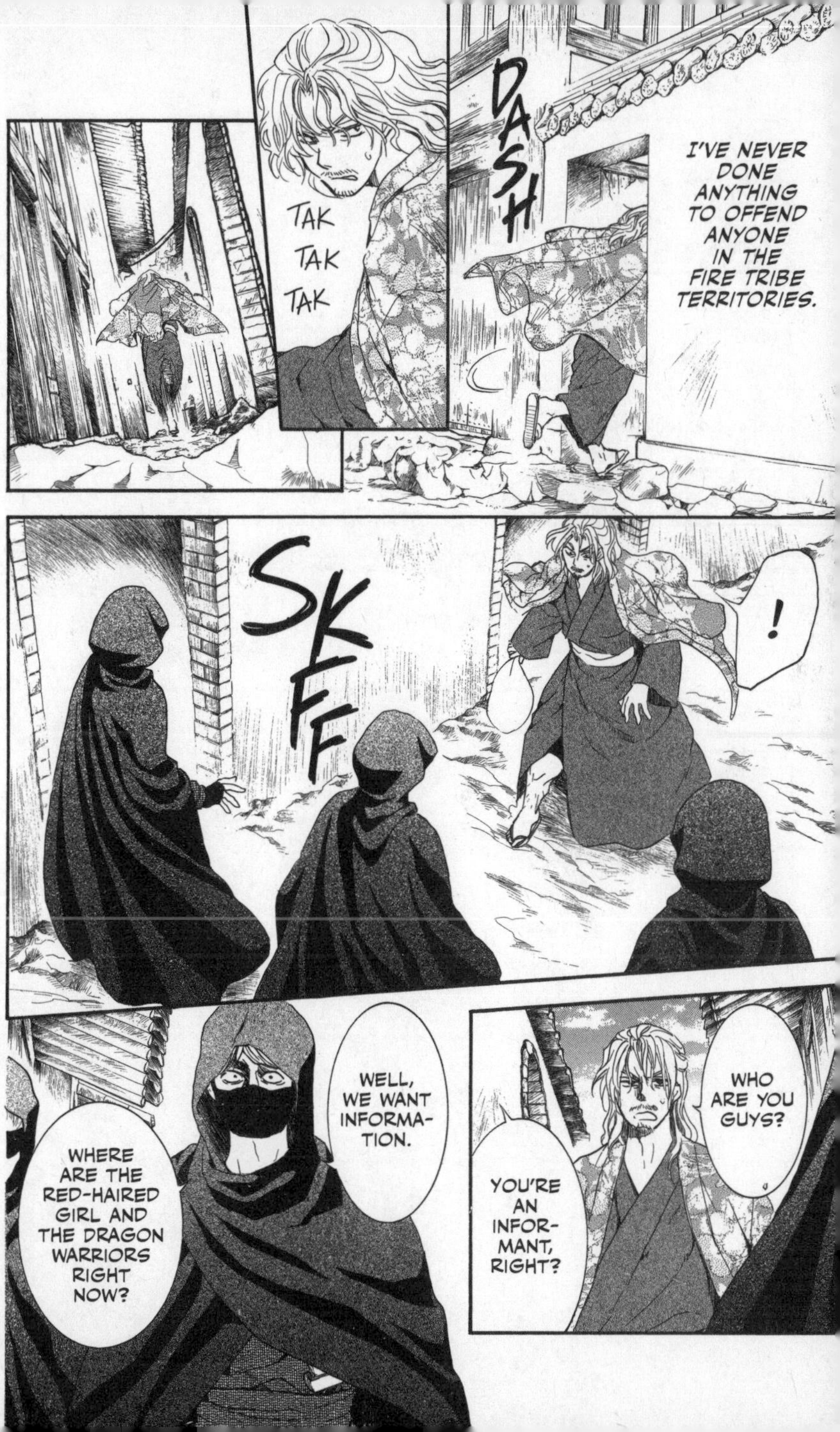
I'VE NEVER DONE ANYTHING TO OFFEND ANYONE IN THE FIRE TRIBE TERRITORIES.
DASH
TAK TAK TAK
!
SKFF
WHO ARE YOU GUYS?
YOU'RE AN INFORMANT, RIGHT?
WELL, WE WANT INFORMATION.
WHERE ARE THE RED-HAIRED GIRL AND THE DRAGON WARRIORS RIGHT NOW?

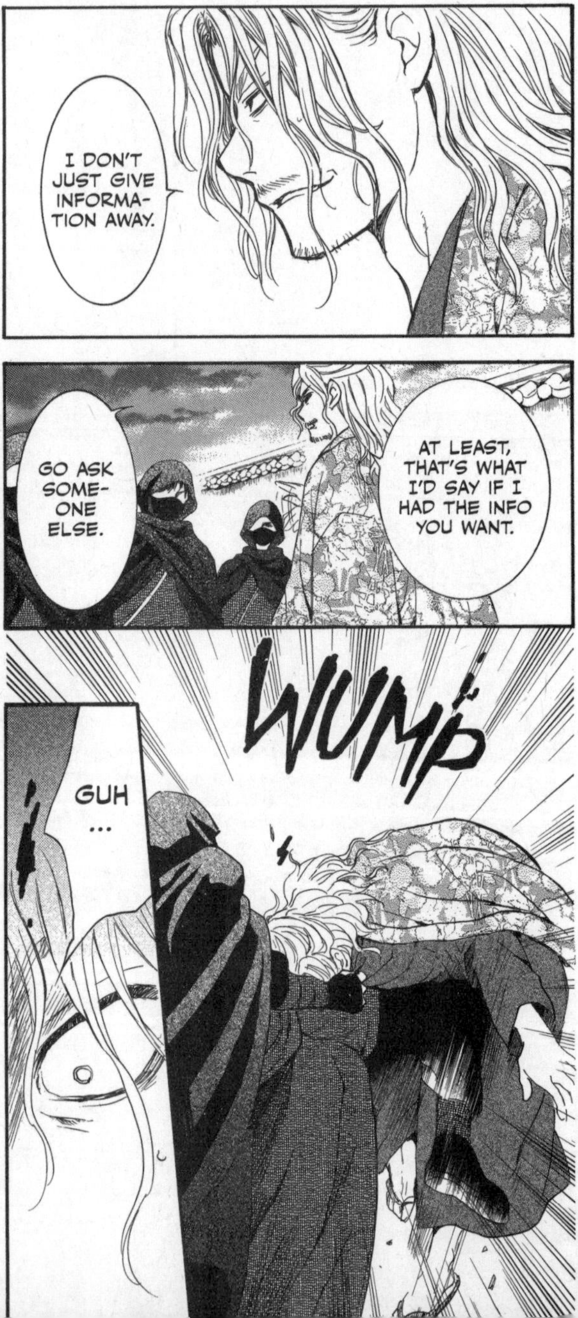
I DON'T JUST GIVE INFORMATION AWAY.
AT LEAST, THAT'S WHAT I'D SAY IF I HAD THE INFO YOU WANT.
GO ASK SOME-ONE ELSE.
WUMP
GUH ...

Hmm... This is as far as the story goes in volume 28. I wish I could have included chapter 164, but I hope you'll check out volume 29!

I didn't realize volume 30 was coming so soon. The time it takes to draw each chapter just flies by. After doing this for so long, my sense of time's passage isn't very good anymore.

It's going to take a bit more time to get through things before I get to the ending point of *Yona of the Dawn*. I hope you'll stick with me a while longer.

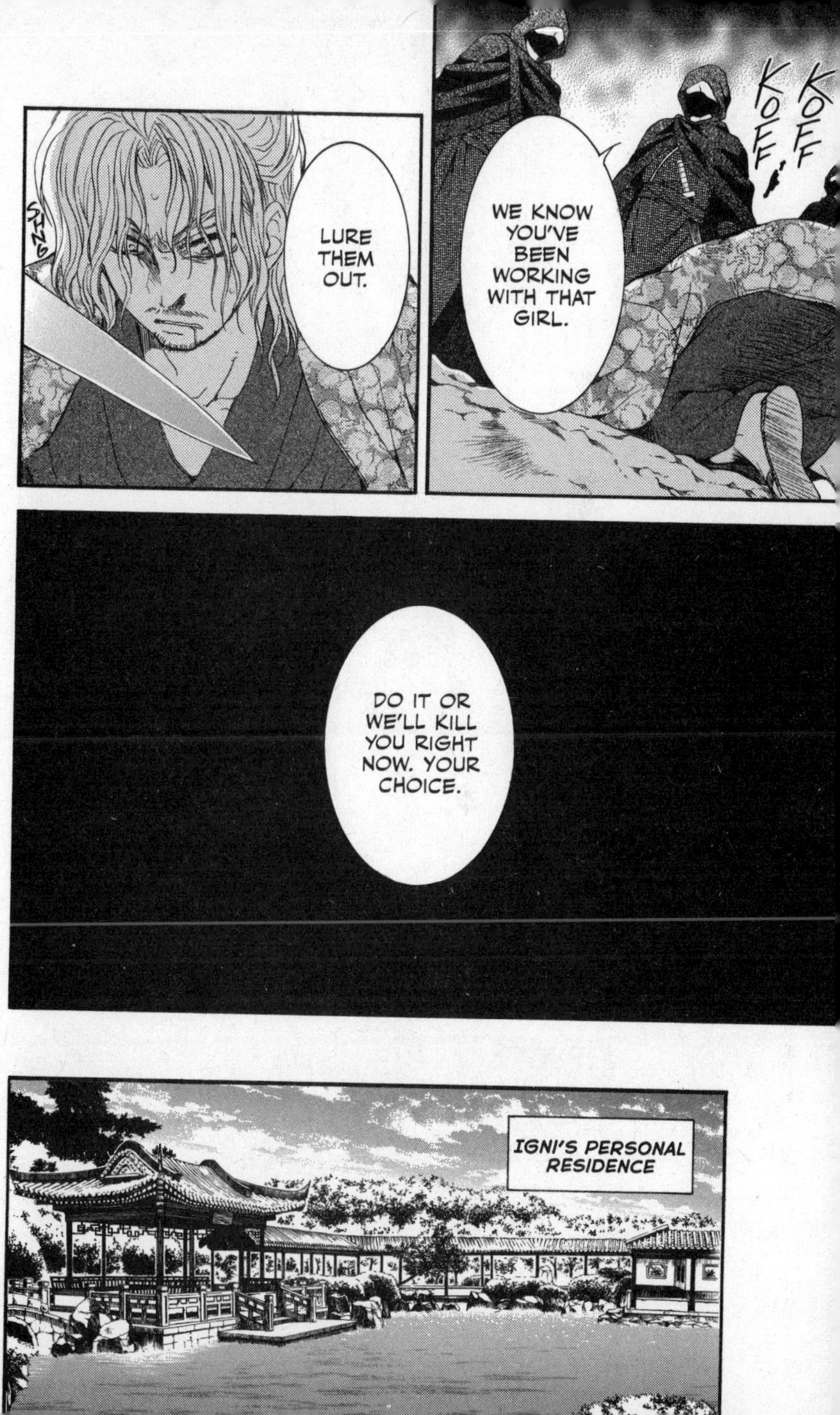
KOFF KOFF
WE KNOW YOU'VE BEEN WORKING WITH THAT GIRL.
SHNG
LURE THEM OUT.
DO IT OR WE'LL KILL YOU RIGHT NOW. YOUR CHOICE.
IGNI'S PERSONAL RESIDENCE

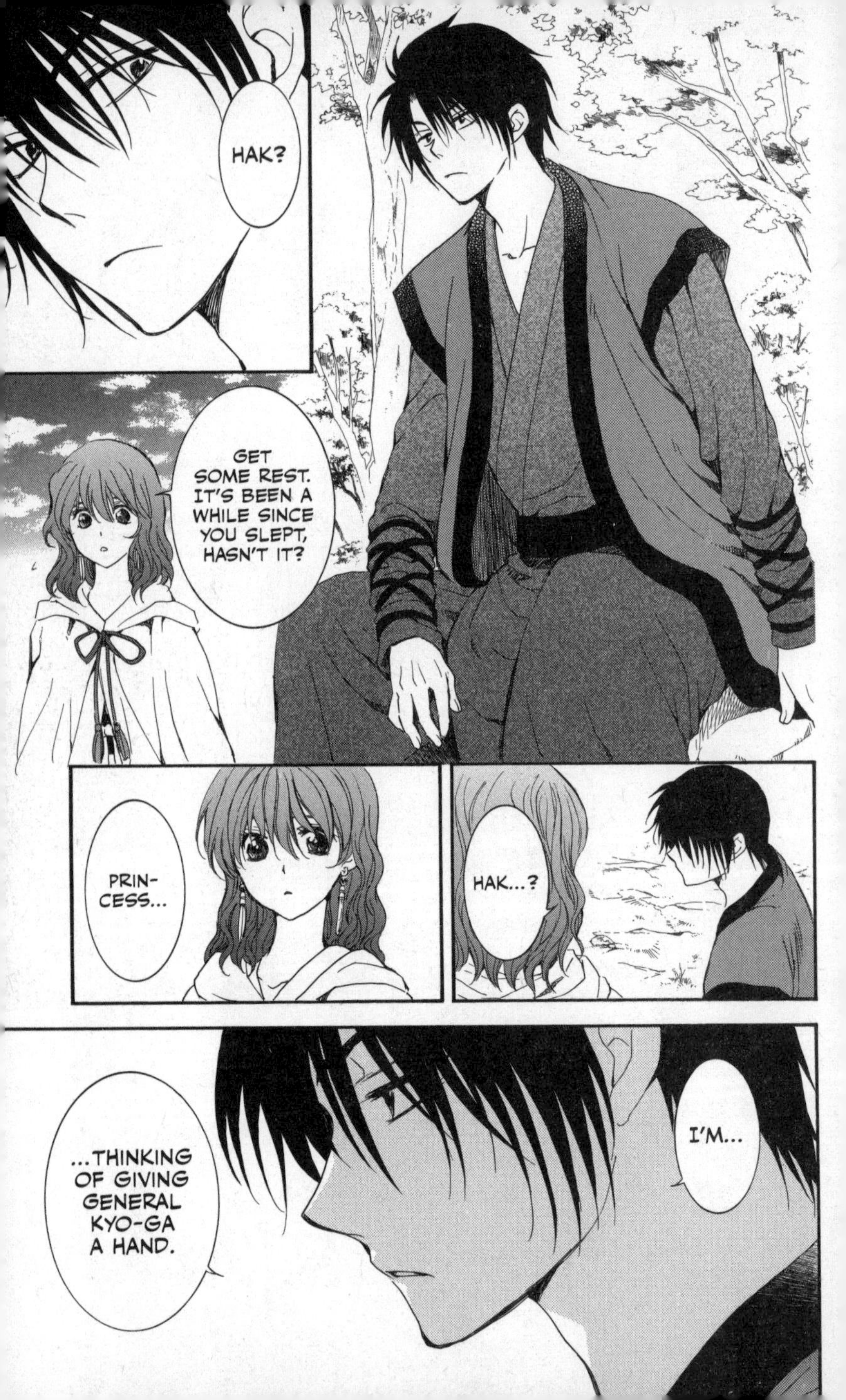
HAK?
GET SOME REST. IT'S BEEN A WHILE SINCE YOU SLEPT, HASN'T IT?
HAK...?
PRIN-CESS...
I'M...
...THINKING OF GIVING GENERAL KYO-GA A HAND.

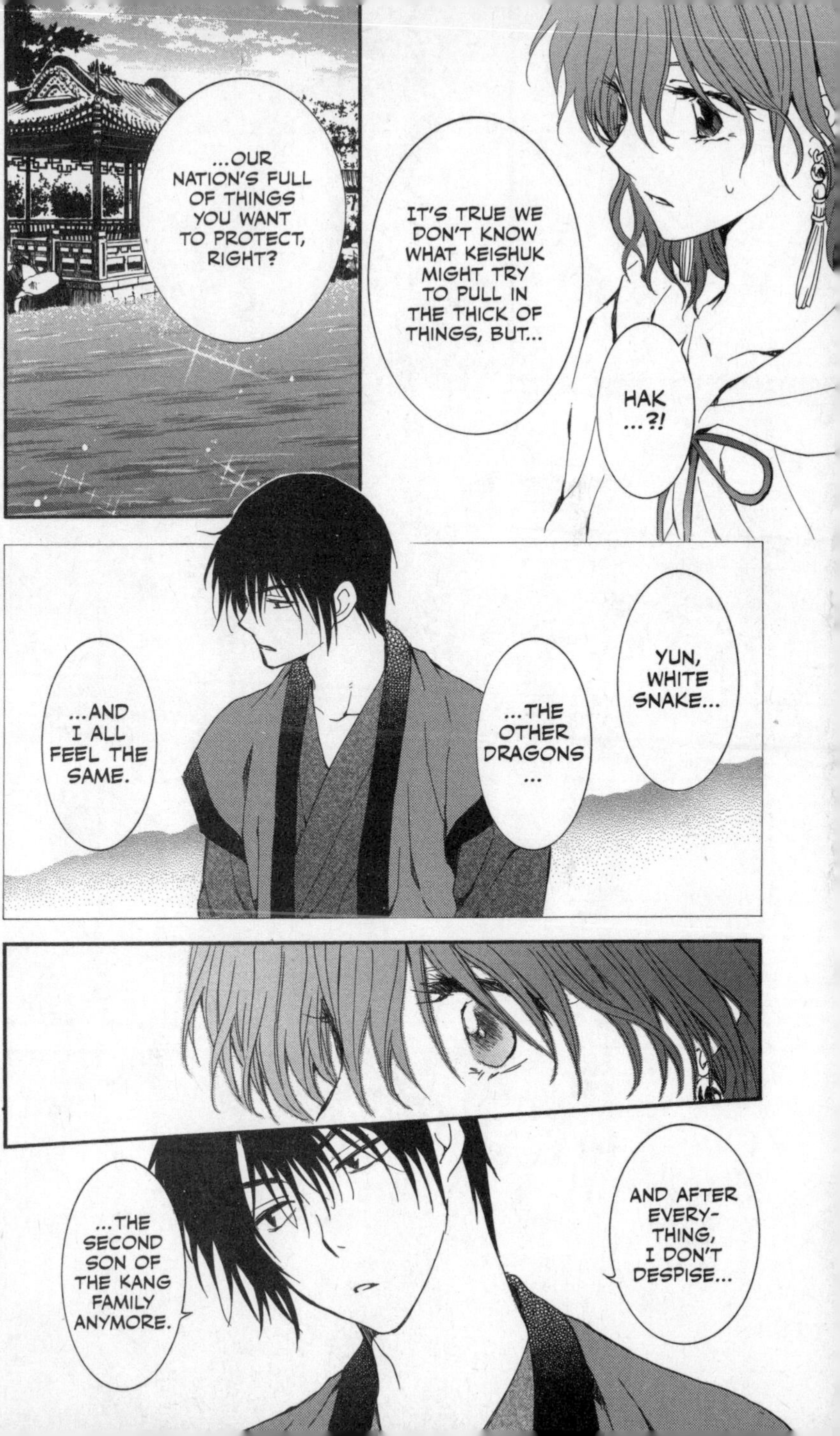
HAK ...?!
IT'S TRUE WE DON'T KNOW WHAT KEISHUK MIGHT TRY TO PULL IN THE THICK OF THINGS, BUT...
...OUR NATION'S FULL OF THINGS YOU WANT TO PROTECT, RIGHT?
YUN, WHITE SNAKE...
...THE OTHER DRAGONS ...
...AND I ALL FEEL THE SAME.
AND AFTER EVERY-THING, I DON'T DESPISE...
...THE SECOND SON OF THE KANG FAMILY ANYMORE.

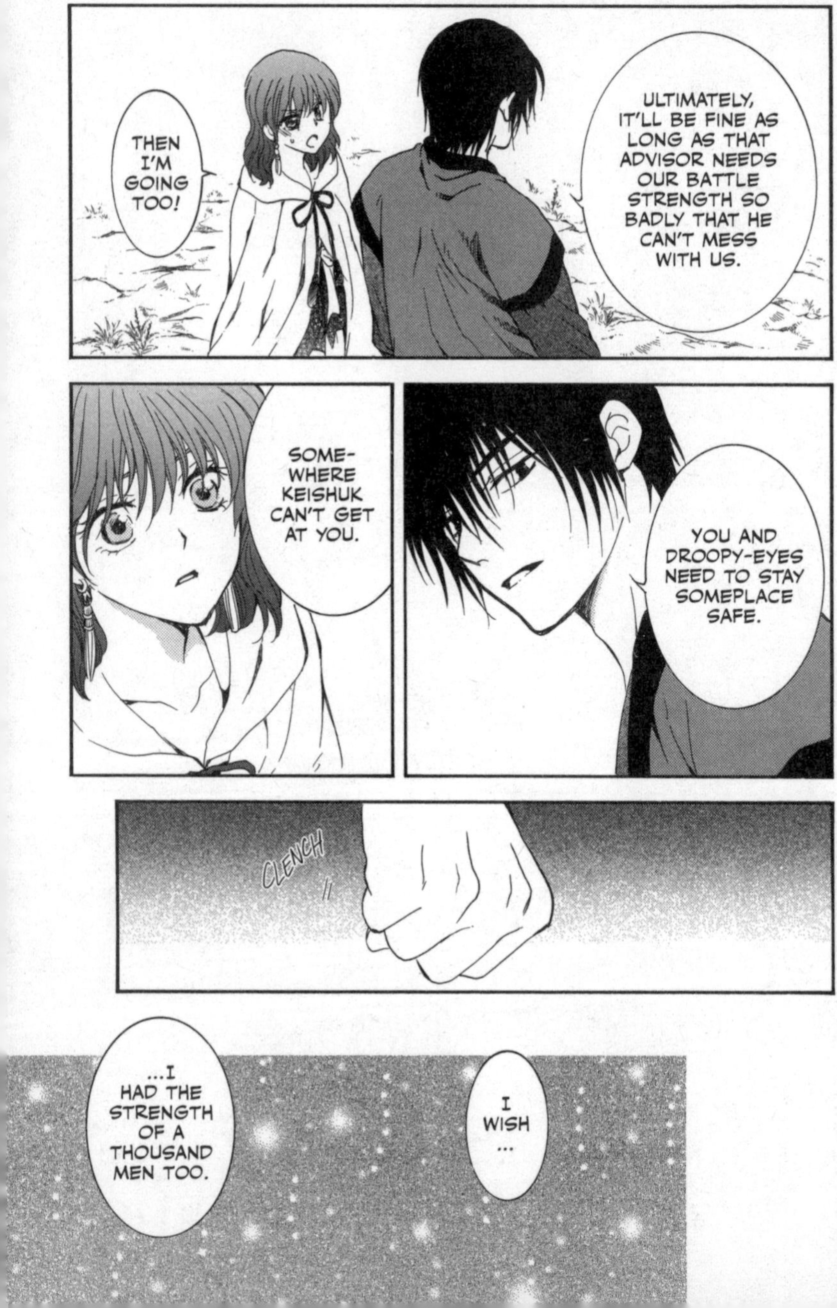
ULTIMATELY, IT'LL BE FINE AS LONG AS THAT ADVISOR NEEDS OUR BATTLE STRENGTH SO BADLY THAT HE CAN'T MESS WITH US.
THEN I'M GOING TOO!
YOU AND DROOPY-EYES NEED TO STAY SOMEPLACE SAFE.
SOME-WHERE KEISHUK CAN'T GET AT YOU.
CLENCH
I WISH...
...I HAD THE STRENGTH OF A THOUSAND MEN TOO.

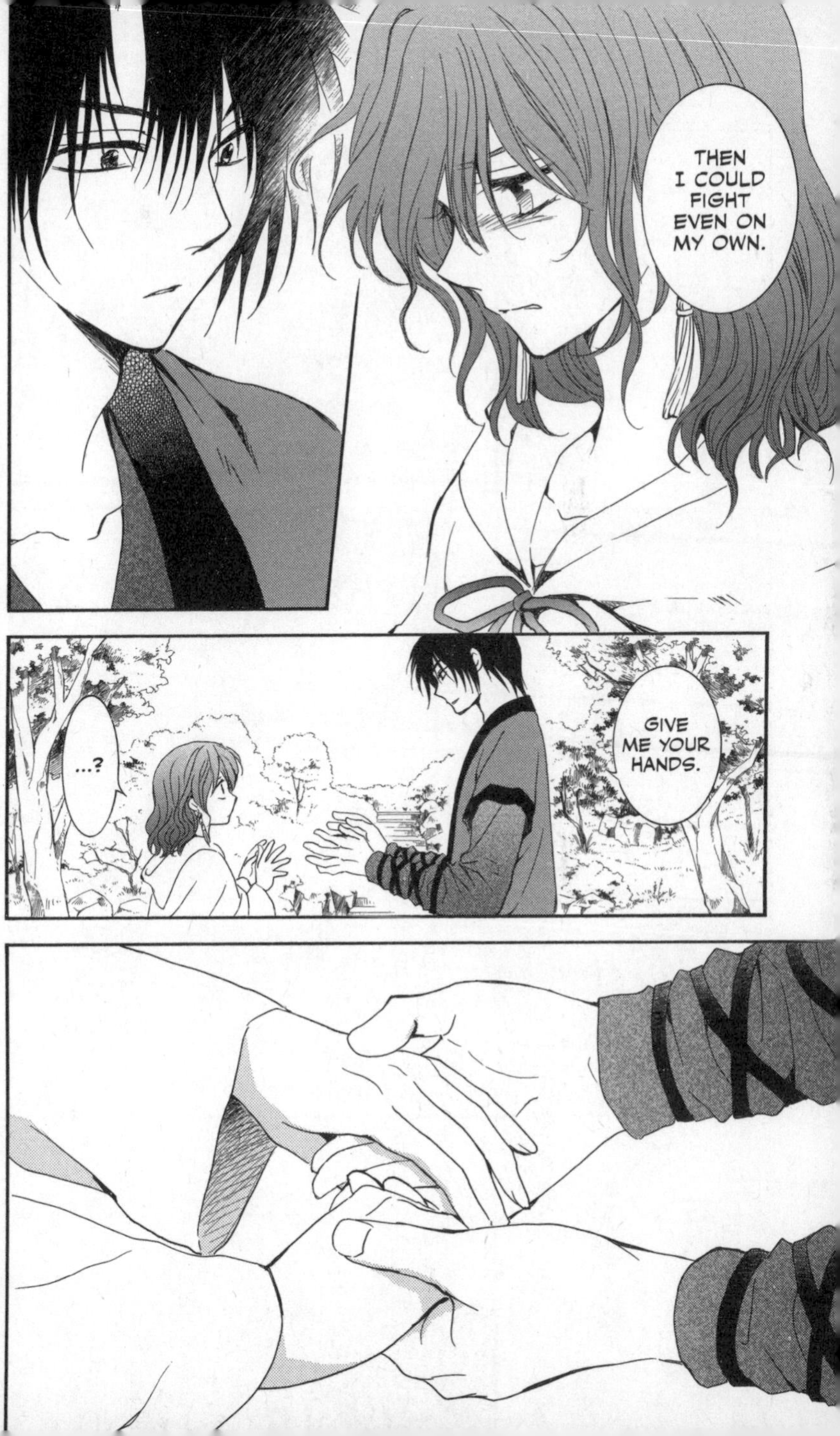
THEN I COULD FIGHT EVEN ON MY OWN.
GIVE ME YOUR HANDS.
...?

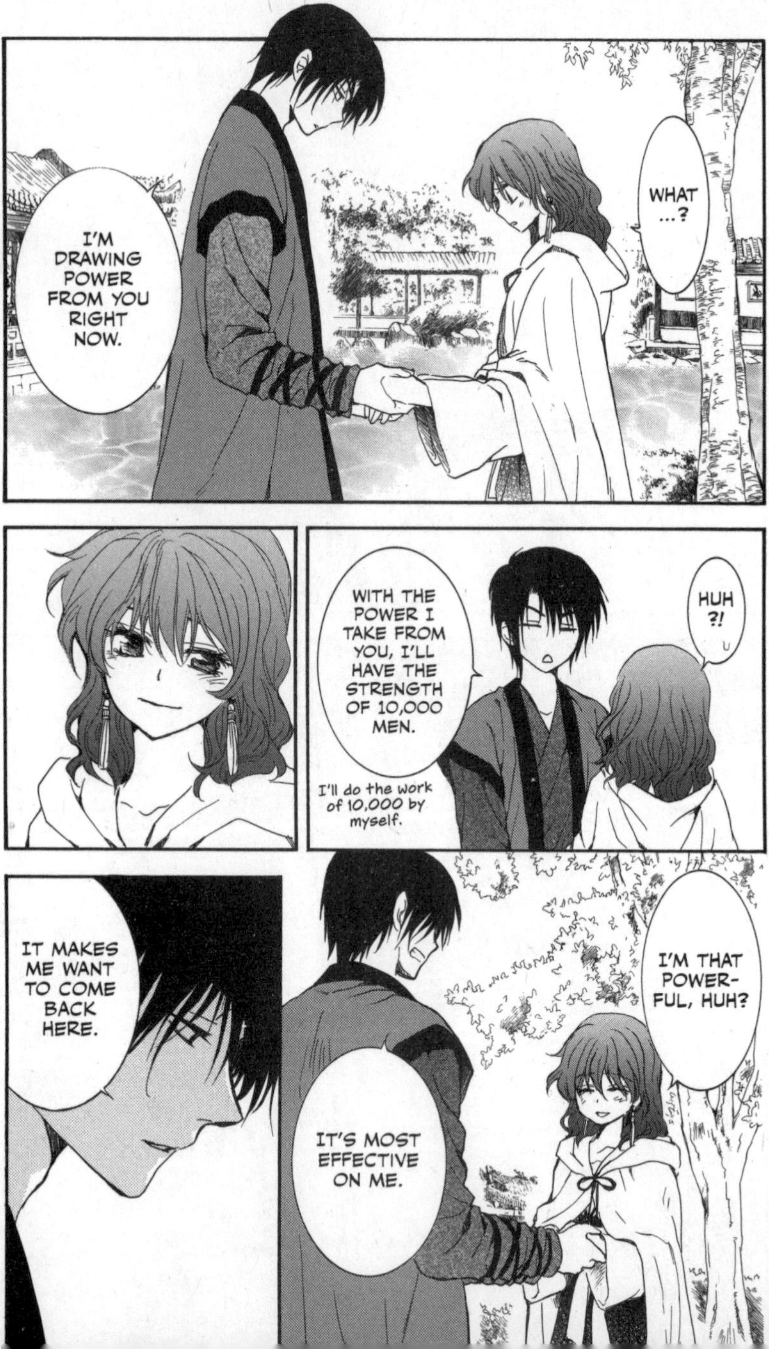
WHAT ...?
I'M DRAWING POWER FROM YOU RIGHT NOW.
HUH ?!
WITH THE POWER I TAKE FROM YOU, I'LL HAVE THE STRENGTH OF 10,000 MEN.
I'll do the work of 10,000 by myself.
I'M THAT POWER-FUL, HUH?
IT'S MOST EFFECTIVE ON ME.
IT MAKES ME WANT TO COME BACK HERE.

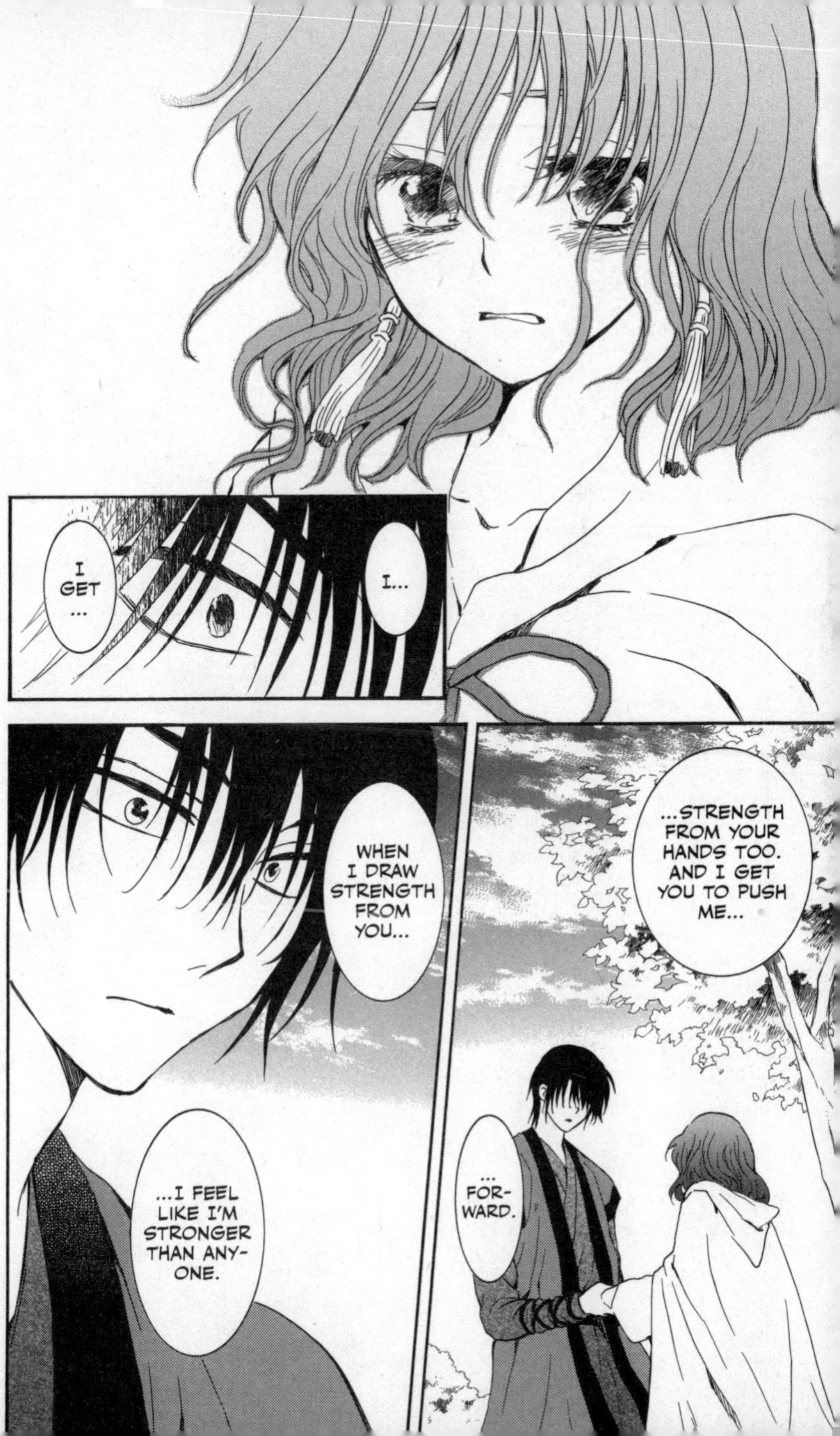
I...
I GET ...
...STRENGTH FROM YOUR HANDS TOO. AND I GET YOU TO PUSH ME...
... FOR-WARD.
WHEN I DRAW STRENGTH FROM YOU...
...I FEEL LIKE I'M STRONGER THAN ANY-ONE.

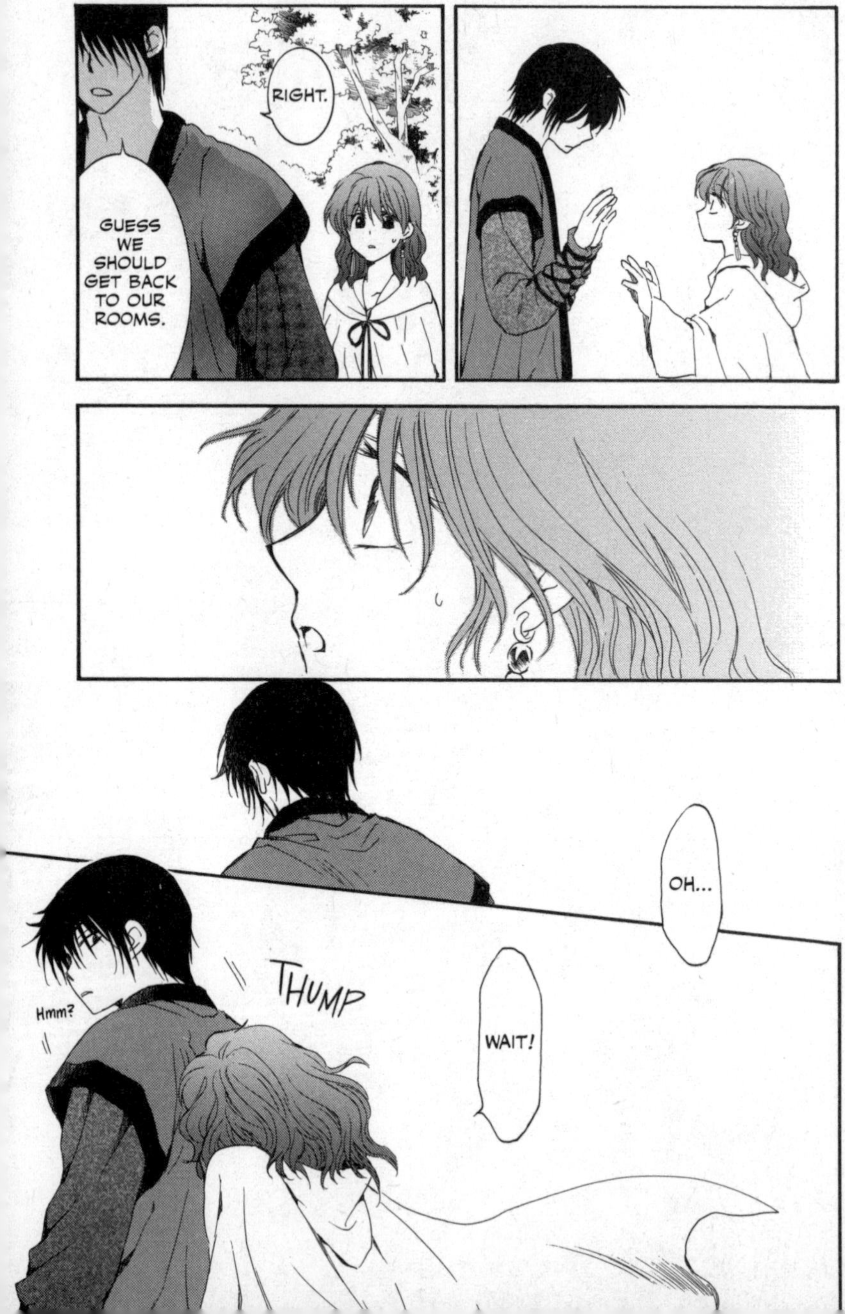
RIGHT.
GUESS WE SHOULD GET BACK TO OUR ROOMS.
OH...
WAIT!
THUMP
Hmm?

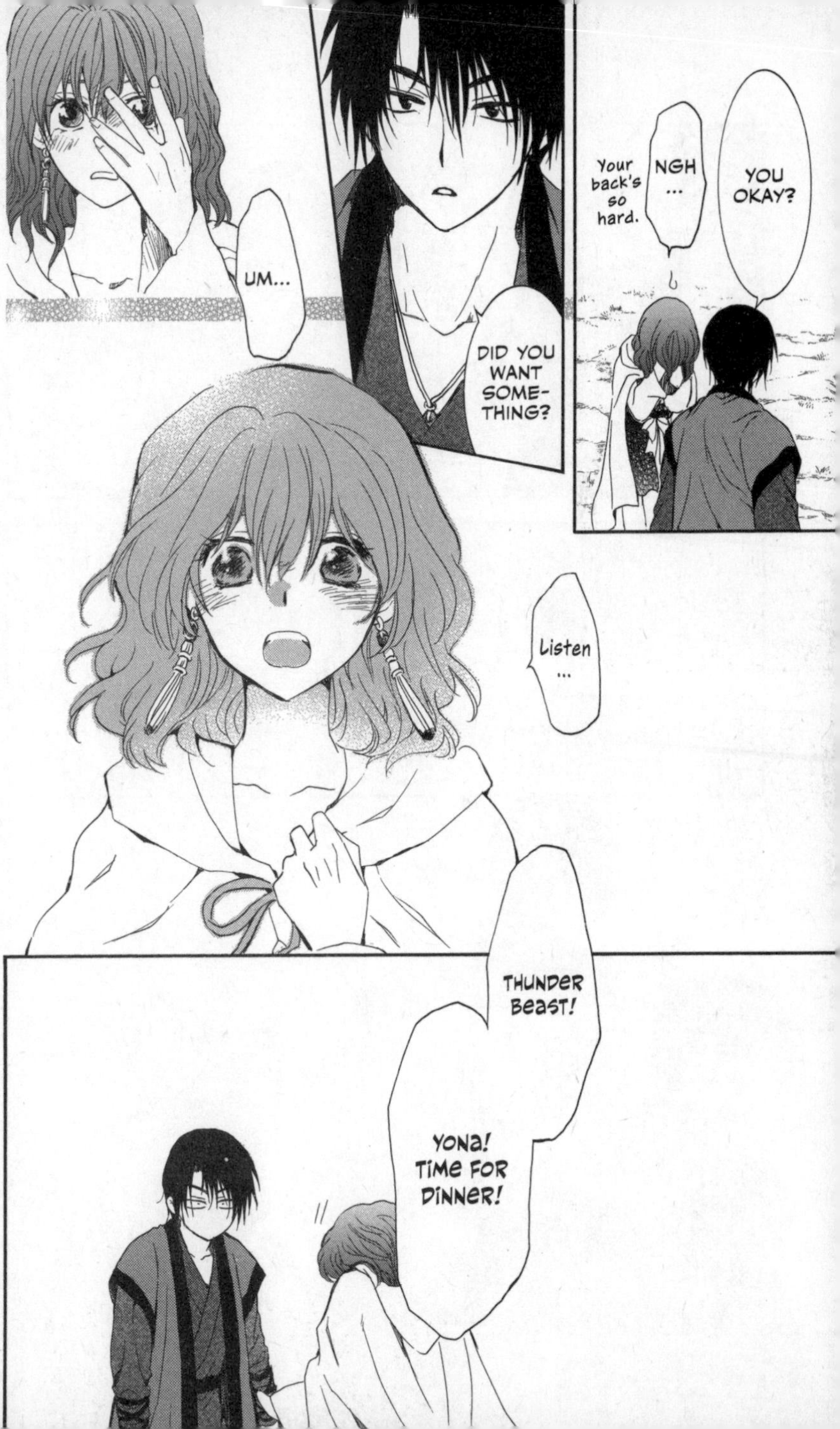
YOU OKAY?
NGH ...
Your back's so hard.
DID YOU WANT SOME-THING?
UM...
Listen ...
THUNDER BEAST!
YONA! TIME FOR DINNER!

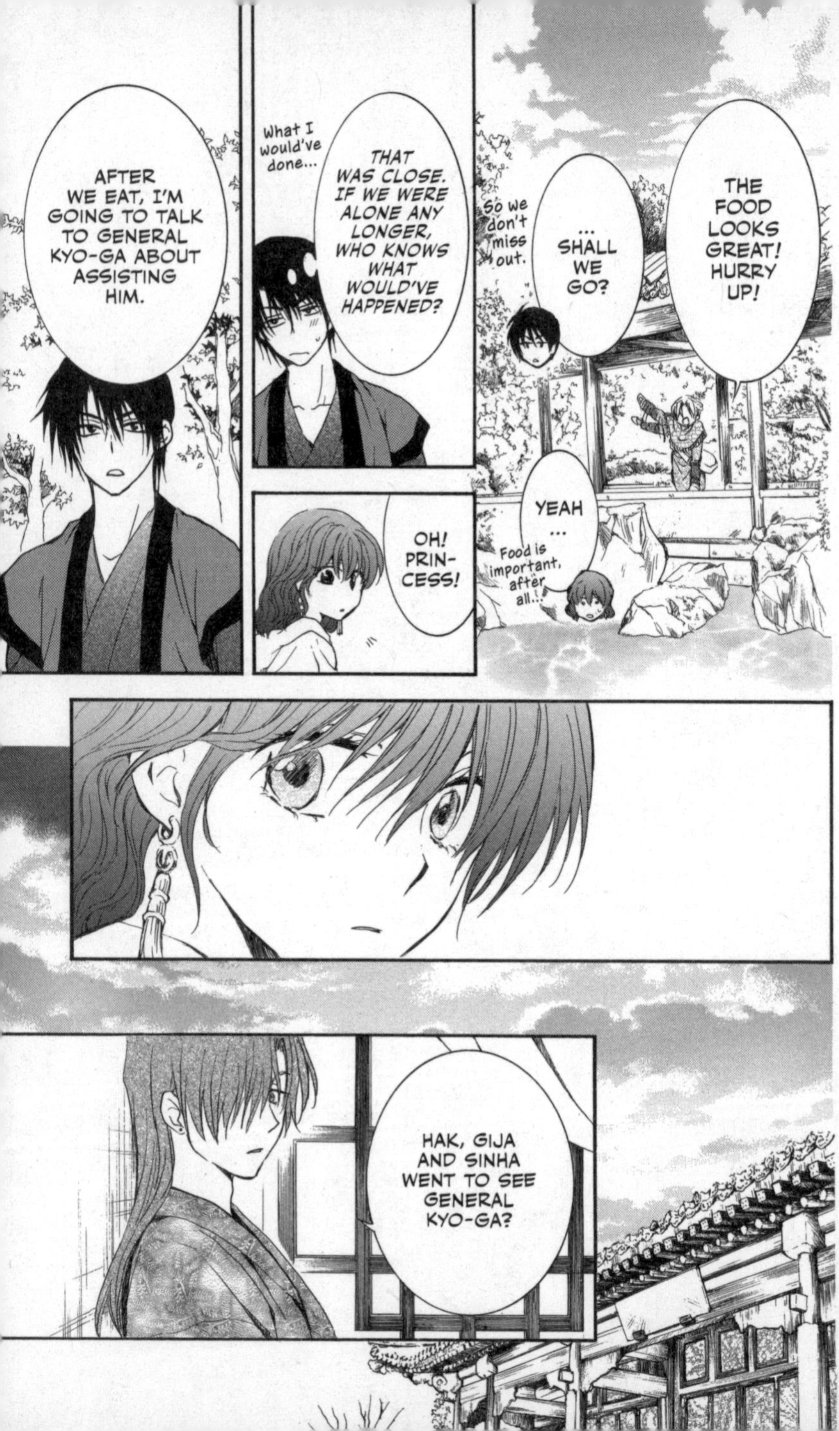
THE FOOD LOOKS GREAT! HURRY UP!
... SHALL WE GO?
So we don't miss out.
YEAH ...
Food is important, after all...
THAT WAS CLOSE. IF WE WERE ALONE ANY LONGER, WHO KNOWS WHAT WOULD'VE HAPPENED?
What I would've done...
OH! PRINCESS!
AFTER WE EAT, I'M GOING TO TALK TO GENERAL KYO-GA ABOUT ASSISTING HIM.
HAK, GIJA AND SINHA WENT TO SEE GENERAL KYO-GA?

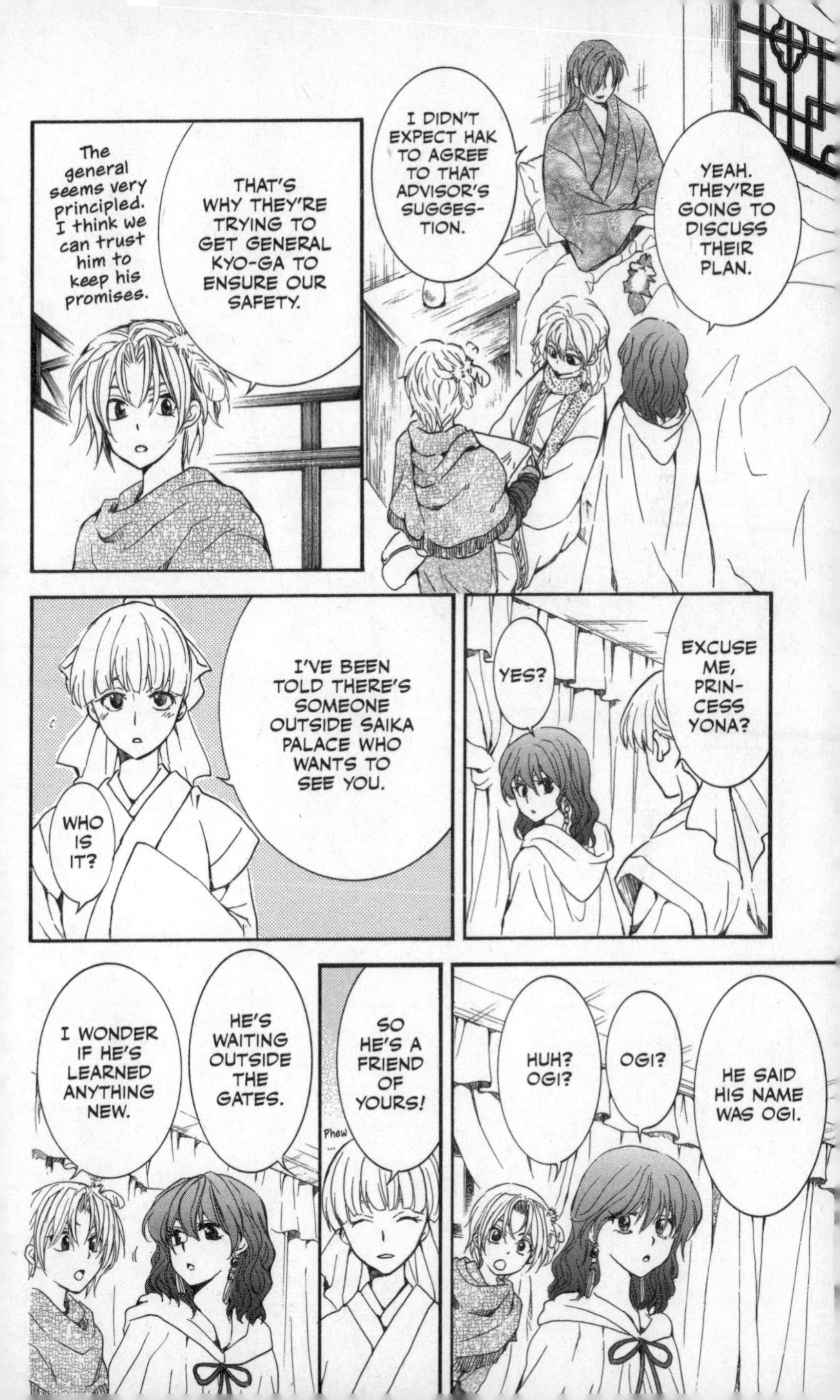
YEAH. THEY'RE GOING TO DISCUSS THEIR PLAN.
I DIDN'T EXPECT HAK TO AGREE TO THAT ADVISOR'S SUGGESTION.
THAT'S WHY THEY'RE TRYING TO GET GENERAL KYO-GA TO ENSURE OUR SAFETY.
The general seems very principled. I think we can trust him to keep his promises.
EXCUSE ME, PRINCESS YONA?
YES?
I'VE BEEN TOLD THERE'S SOMEONE OUTSIDE SAIKA PALACE WHO WANTS TO SEE YOU.
WHO IS IT?
HE SAID HIS NAME WAS OGI.
OGI?
HUH? OGI?
SO HE'S A FRIEND OF YOURS!
Phew...
HE'S WAITING OUTSIDE THE GATES.
I WONDER IF HE'S LEARNED ANYTHING NEW.

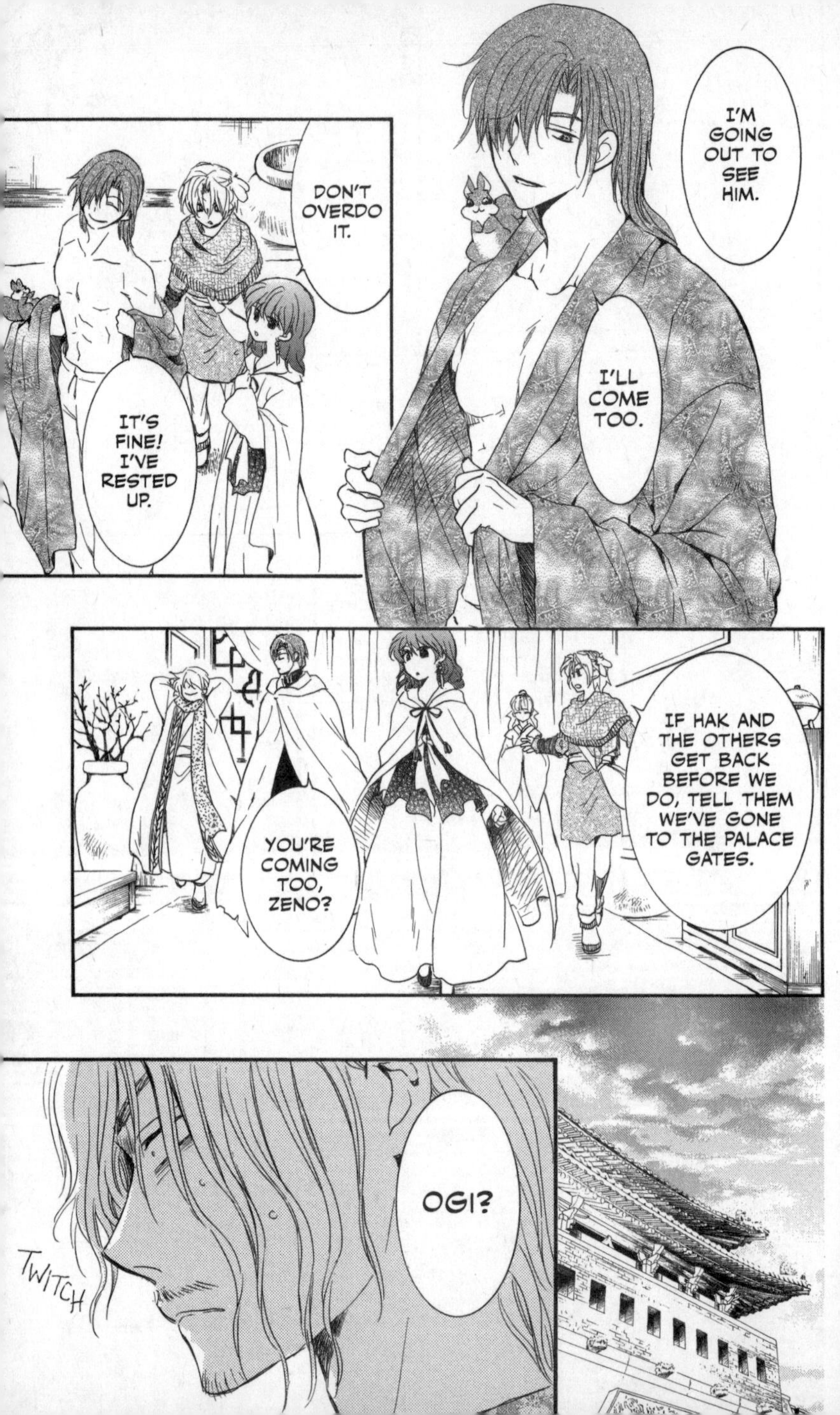
I'M GOING OUT TO SEE HIM.
I'LL COME TOO.
DON'T OVERDO IT.
IT'S FINE! I'VE RESTED UP.
IF HAK AND THE OTHERS GET BACK BEFORE WE DO, TELL THEM WE'VE GONE TO THE PALACE GATES.
YOU'RE COMING TOO, ZENO?
OGI?
TWITCH

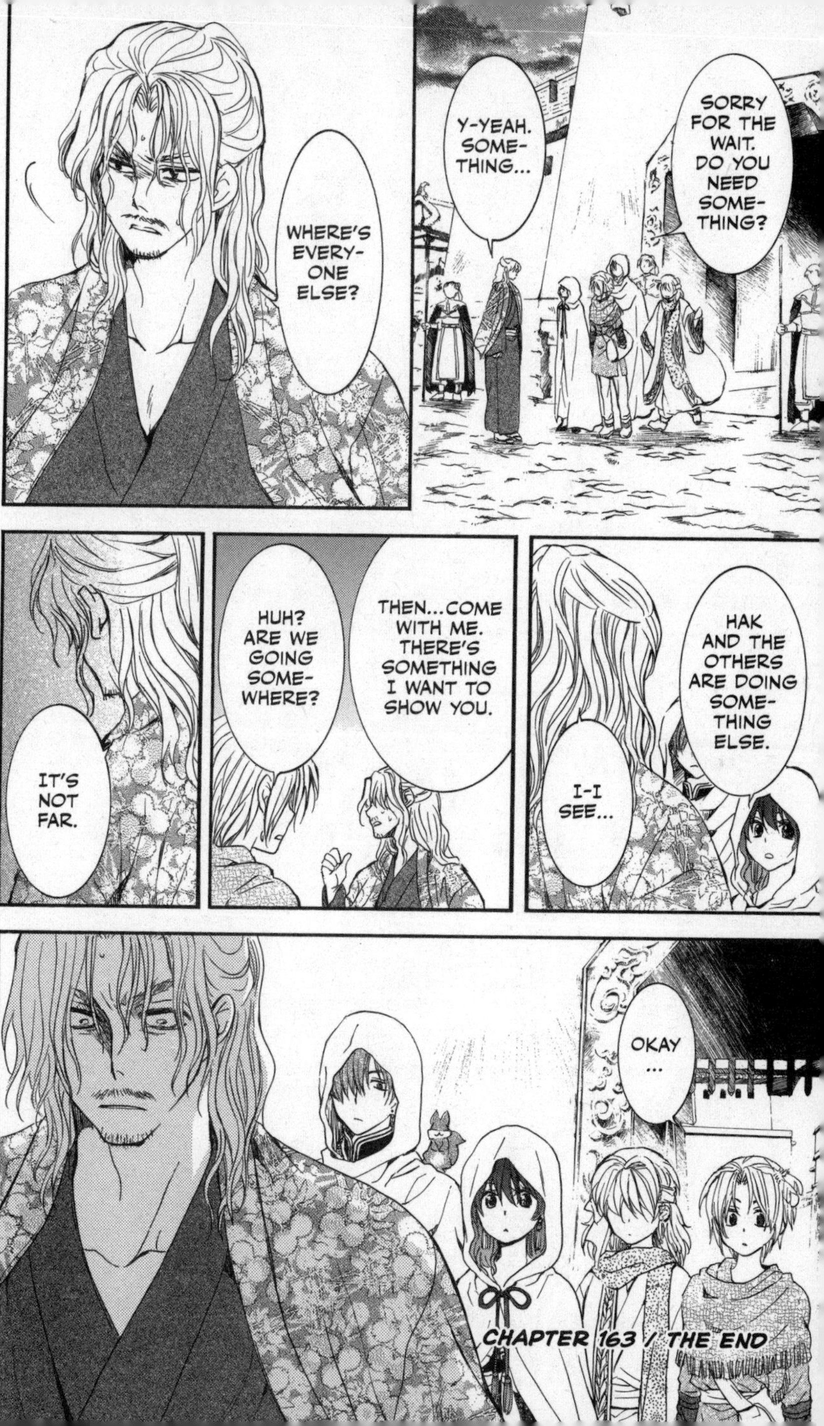
SORRY FOR THE WAIT. DO YOU NEED SOME-THING?
Y-YEAH. SOME-THING...
WHERE'S EVERY-ONE ELSE?
HAK AND THE OTHERS ARE DOING SOME-THING ELSE.
I-I SEE...
THEN...COME WITH ME. THERE'S SOMETHING I WANT TO SHOW YOU.
HUH? ARE WE GOING SOME-WHERE?
IT'S NOT FAR.
OKAY ...
CHAPTER 163 / THE END

True Stories

Little Jaeha on a Cup

The Issue: Yona of the Dawn Doesn't Have Many Couples

I think I was talking with my assistants about Keishuk...
KEISHUK DOESN'T SEEM LIKE HE LIKES WOMEN.
Assistant F
WHAT?! KEISHUK LIKES MEN?! (°Д°;)
Never said that
DRINK
Assistant M
In charge of hair glossing
I DO THE GLOSSING, SO I CAN TELL. I DON'T KNOW IF HE LIKES MEN, BUT HE'S EXTRA HARSH WITH WOMEN...
F's inking makes Keishuk look beautiful
Keishuk's hatred of women comes through in the gloss of his hair...
You don't know that. He might have a cute girlfriend at home! A real professional type.
...

Why don't you tell us, Keishuk?

Kyo-ga's Butt

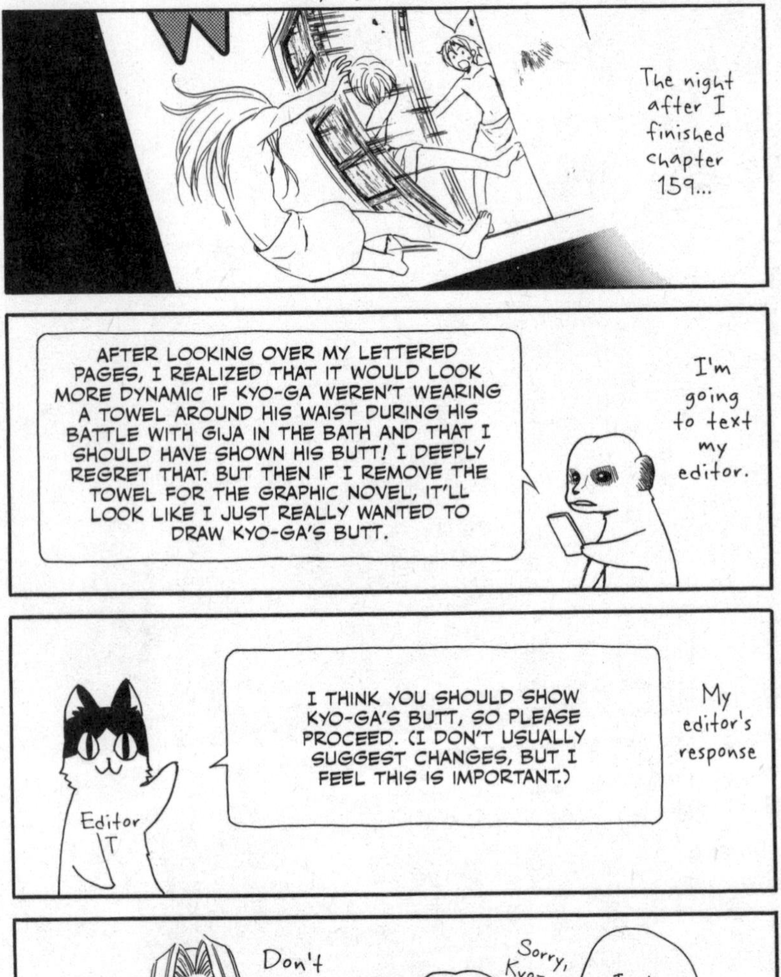

The night after I finished chapter 159...
I'm going to text my editor.
AFTER LOOKING OVER MY LETTERED PAGES, I REALIZED THAT IT WOULD LOOK MORE DYNAMIC IF KYO-GA WEREN'T WEARING A TOWEL AROUND HIS WAIST DURING HIS BATTLE WITH GIJA IN THE BATH AND THAT I SHOULD HAVE SHOWN HIS BUTT! I DEEPLY REGRET THAT. BUT THEN IF I REMOVE THE TOWEL FOR THE GRAPHIC NOVEL, IT'LL LOOK LIKE I JUST REALLY WANTED TO DRAW KYO-GA'S BUTT.
My editor's response
I THINK YOU SHOULD SHOW KYO-GA'S BUTT, SO PLEASE PROCEED. (I DON'T USUALLY SUGGEST CHANGES, BUT I FEEL THIS IS IMPORTANT.)
Editor T
In the end, time constraints kept me from drawing it.
Sorry, Kyo-ga.
Don't do that!!

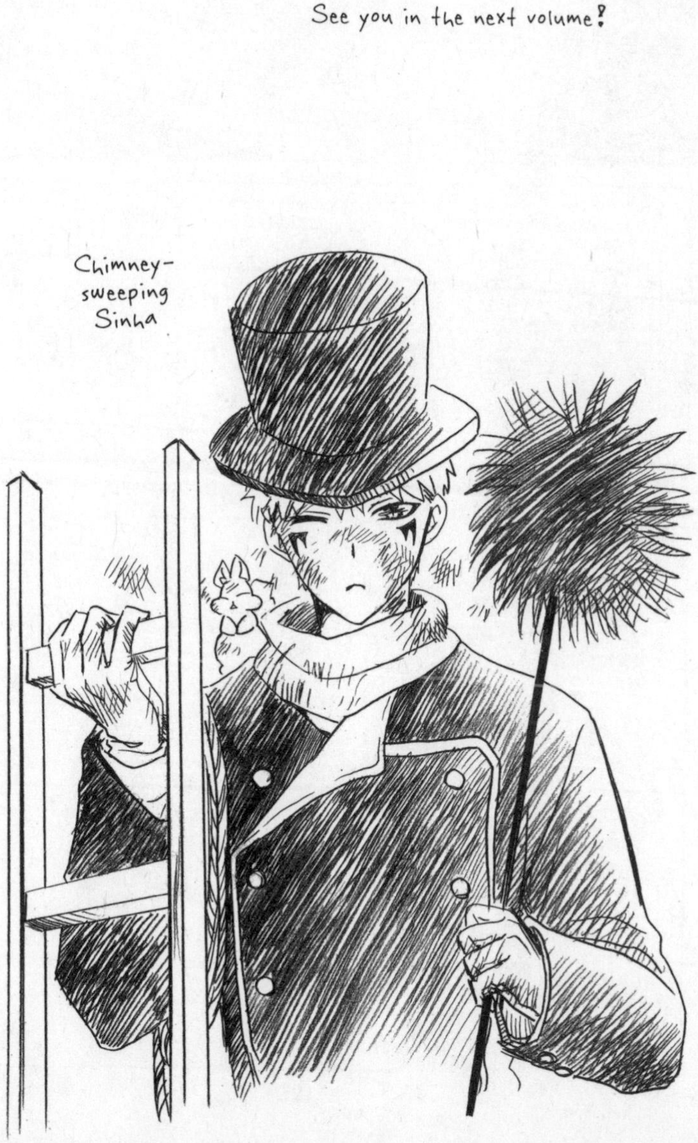
See you in the next volume!
Chimney-
sweeping
Sinha

The image on the cover is completely unrelated to volume 28's contents. It's the most girly picture I've drawn of Yona when she was a princess. I wanted to put Kyo-ga and Tae-jun on the cover, but I wasn't able to draw them well. (Sad.)

—Mizuho Kusanagi

Born on February 3 in Kumamoto Prefecture in Japan, Mizuho Kusanagi began her professional manga career with *Yoiko no Kokoroe* (The Rules of a Good Child) in 2003. Her other works include *NG Life*, which was serialized in *Hana to Yume* and *The Hana to Yume* magazines and published by Hakusensha in Japan. *Yona of the Dawn* was adapted into an anime in 2014.

YONA OF THE DAWN
VOL. 28
Shojo Beat Edition

STORY AND ART BY
MIZUHO KUSANAGI

English Adaptation/Ysabet Reinhardt MacFarlane
Translation/JN Productions
Touch-Up Art & Lettering/Lys Blakeslee
Design/Philana Chen
Editor/Amy Yu

Akatsuki no Yona by Mizuho Kusanagi
© Mizuho Kusanagi 2018
All rights reserved.
First published in Japan in 2018 by HAKUSENSHA, Inc., Tokyo.
English language translation rights arranged with
HAKUSENSHA, Inc., Tokyo.

Printed in the U.S.A.

Published by VIZ Media, LLC
P.O. Box 77010
San Francisco, CA 94107

10 9 8 7 6 5 4 3 2 1
First printing, February 2021

viz.com   shojobeat.com

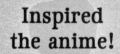

This is the last page.

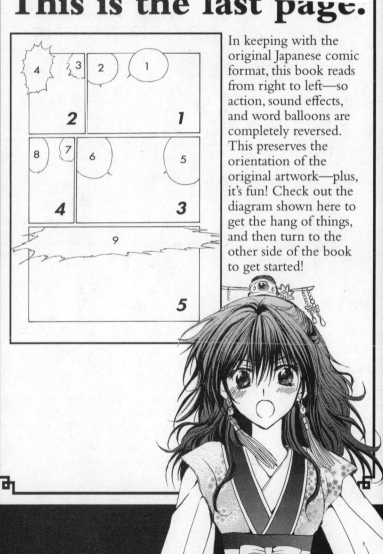

In keeping with the original Japanese comic format, this book reads from right to left—so action, sound effects, and word balloons are completely reversed. This preserves the orientation of the original artwork—plus, it's fun! Check out the diagram shown here to get the hang of things, and then turn to the other side of the book to get started!